"Mark Foreman and Lindsay Leonard accessible—as well as academically ri and defense of a Christian perspectiv standard bioethics textbook in Christian undergradueducation, g and professional schools including medicine, busintheology, and law."

—Francis J. Beckwith, PhD
Professor of Philohy and Church-State Studies,
Baylor University

"*Christianity and Modern Medicine* is representative n emerging body of articulate, careful, and courageous Christian treatment of ethiissues. Foreman and Leonard employ an interesting blend of ethical theories to offa defense of a distinctly evangelical approach to critical bioethical issues."

—J. P. Moreland, PhD
Professor of Philosophy,
Talbot Schc of Theology, Biola University

"*Christianity and Modern Medicine* is an excellentxtbook: well written, clearly argued, philosophically informed, and theologicallyonservative, it is an excellent choice for introducing students to this highly special d field."

—Michael S. Jones, PhD
Professor of Philosophy al Religion, Liberty University;
President, Virnia Philosophical Association

"This volume has so much going for it. It is up tolate and immensely readable, addressing the major issues of medical research and ractice. It provides the scientific and legal background for how we arrived at the pint we are today. Best of all, it provides powerful philosophical and theological tool for evaluating the issues and arguments, and defending a consistently biblical stanc."

—Craig Q. Hinkson, PhD
Professor of Philosophy, Liberty University

"Mark Foreman and Lindsay Leonard's bioethics text is highly readable and accessible to the typical undergraduate student. Students will enjoy the clear explanations and coverage of the important ethical theories as well as the in-depth coverage of pertinent court cases surrounding many of the most controversial areas of study in this field. Mark and Lindsay have astutely added several areas in bioethics that I need to cover in the usual bioethics class—a perfect addition for the classroom. I highly recommend this text for undergraduate and graduate courses in ethics, bioethics, and Christian ethics, as well as for professional schools focusing on medicine, law, and advanced nursing practitioners."

—Edward N. Martin, PhD
Professor of Philosophy and Interdisciplinary Studies,
Liberty University

"Mark Foreman and Lindsay Lerd have written a marvelous resource that provides significantly informed discussion hot button issues such as abortion, euthanasia, physician-assisted suicide, birtɒntrol, and others. If you are looking for a single resource with high quality contthat covers these issues, you have found it!"

—Michael Licona, PhD
Associate Professor of Theology,
Houston Baptist University

"Courageous, informed, and weasoned, this bioethics text is also distinguished by its additional portions on recental insights and perspectives. Highly recommended."

—Gary R. Habermas, PhD
Distinguished Research Professor,
Liberty University (Seminary PhD program)

"This significant work on biocics gives us a readable, well-informed, and carefully argued approach to a sject fraught with illogic, misunderstanding, and out-of-control passions. The ahors' knowledge of the pertinent facts, logic, and history serve the reader well ireveloping an intellectually satisfying and biblically informed view on crucial morassues facing us."

—Douglas Groothuis, PhD
Professor of Philosophy,
Denver Seminary

"Bioethics provides a revelator snapshot of deep worldview divides in our society today, as well as a nearly unpalleled opportunity for outreach and faithful witness. As a result, it is a topic alreadyf great importance and bound to become only more so in a culture increasingly berft of resources to take principled stances against abortion on demand, problematic tansgender policies, and embryonic stem cell research. More positively, a distinctivel Christian bioethic can effectively posit grounds for understanding human person as infinitely valuable, and ends in themselves, whose worth is neither a function oftheir abilities nor diminished by handicaps. It is with enthusiasm that I endorse this project and advocate its publication."

—David Baggett, PhD
Professor of Philosophy and Director of the Center for Moral Apologetics,
Houston Baptist University

Christianity and Modern Medicine

FOUNDATIONS FOR BIOETHICS

Mark Wesley Foreman
Lindsay C. Leonard

Christianity and Modern Medicine: Foundations for Bioethics

Published by Kregel Academic, an imprint of Kregel Publications, 2450 Oak Industrial Dr. NE, Grand Rapids, MI 49505-6020.

The section in chapter 10 titled "Embryonic Stem Cell Research" on pages 363–364 was first published as "Embryonic Stem Cell Research: Is there a limit to the medical imperative to end suffering and disease?" *Journal of the International Society of Christian Apologetics*, Vol 8 No. 1, Spring 2009, used with permission.

The Hebrew font, NewJerusalemU, and the Greek font, GraecaU, are available from www.linguistsoftware.com/lgku.htm, +1-425-775-1130.

ISBN 978-0-8254-4756-3

Printed in the United States of America

22 23 24 25 26 / 5 4 3 2 1

To all who face these issues daily, including but not limited to the medical community—may you continue to fight the battles worth fighting on behalf of your patients and be guided by your moral compass along the way.

To all the students who have given us the honor of being a part of their education—keep your feet on the ground and your eyes toward the stars.

Finally, thanks to our friends and families who have given us support, counsel, and wisdom during the writing of this book.

Contents

Preface 9

Chapter 1 Modern Medicine in a Moral Fog 13

Chapter 2 Principles of Bioethics 41

Chapter 3 The Second Civil War: Abortion 75

Chapter 4 From Cradle to Coffin: Infanticide 121

Chapter 5 A Good Death: Euthanasia 153

Chapter 6 Death with Dignity: Physician-Assisted Suicide. 181

Chapter 7 Eighteen Ways to Make a Baby: Procreational Ethics . . 215

Chapter 8 Made, Not Begotten: Genetic Ethics 251

Chapter 9 Principled Patient Treatment: Clinical Ethics 281

Chapter 10 For the Good of Mankind: Research Ethics and Human Experimentation 335

Preface

In an essay titled "Contemporary Christian Responsibility," the late Charles Colson threw down the challenge: "Christians must develop a well-reasoned Christian apologetic on all issues, and of course predominantly the issues of bioethics."[1] This book is an attempt to take up that challenge. Because it is an apologetic, it aspires to offer a reasonable defense of a Christian perspective on certain issues in bioethics. However, its spirit is not one of confrontational dogmatism, but of concerned dialogue. It defends, but is not defensive.

One can hardly read a newspaper or watch television these days without encountering controversial medical issues. Medical technology and new treatments are being developed, discovered, and promoted at a much faster rate than our ability to reflect on their social, legal, and theological implications. As a result many Christians are often unprepared to make the difficult choices that confront them today: Is abortion ever justifiable? If a loved one is suffering, can we take action that will relieve her suffering but will hasten her death? If a child is born severely impaired, can we allow it to die rather than face a life of suffering? Should doctors be allowed to help patients who wish to end their lives? If a couple desires a child but cannot have one on their own, should they seek a third-party donor of sperm/egg or have a surrogate carry their child through to birth? Are health-care workers ever allowed to lie to their patients if it's for their own good? Can health-care workers ever break confidentiality? Can we use genetic therapy to design children or otherwise enhance human beings? Should we seriously consider cloning human beings? The way we answer these questions is indicative of who we are, our relationship with God, and the kind of world we want for ourselves, our children, and future generations.

1. Charles W. Colson, "Contemporary Christian Responsibility," in *Genetic Ethics: Do the Ends Justify the Genes?*, eds. John F. Kilner, Rebecca D. Pentz, and Frank E. Young (Grand Rapids: Eerdmans, 1997), 226.

This book addresses these questions from a distinctly orthodox Christian perspective that takes Scripture and the historic position of the church seriously. We realize not everyone will agree with every point in it. For those who disagree with us, we welcome you. Our hope is that you will consider our arguments and that this book will be a catalyst for further discussion and reflection into these issues.

We have written this book as an introduction into these issues in bioethics. As such, it requires no prior knowledge on the part of the reader. We begin with a couple of chapters introducing the basics of bioethics, moral reasoning, ethical theories, legal reasoning and procedures, and the major principles that form the foundation in our exploration into issues in bioethics. Each of the following chapters explores the legal and moral implications of a specific issue in bioethics. We selected the particular issues covered in this book on the basis of their social and medical significance; these seem to be the perennial questions in bioethical discussions. There are many other topics we could have included and perhaps will in a revised edition. For the time being, there is certainly enough to consider here.

It should be noted that this book is a revised and updated treatment of an earlier book by Mark W. Foreman titled *Christianity and Bioethics: Confronting Clinical Issues* (originally published with College Press in 1999 and reprinted with Wipf and Stock in 2011). All the chapters have been updated and four new chapters have been added. In addition, Lindsay C. Leonard, a local lawyer with training in bioethics, was invited on to write the sections on the law and legislative activity on these issues.

This book would not have come about if it had not been for the support of a number of friends and colleagues. We both want to thank all of our bioethics students with whom we have had fruitful discussions and who have given us the pleasure of having a part in their education. I (Mark) want to thank my colleagues in the philosophy department at Liberty University who continue to challenge me in refining my arguments. I specifically want to express my deep appreciation to my mentors who have had a lasting impact on my thinking: James F. Childress, Gary Habermas, J. P. Moreland, Norman Geisler, Francis Beckwith, and David Baggett. You may recognize their voices in these pages. Finally, I would be nothing without the support of my wife, three daughters, and five grandchildren who make my life worth living.

I (Lindsay) would also like to acknowledge my legal colleagues and former professors. This book would not be possible without the training and guidance I have received from the legal community. I also want to specifically thank my parents for their unwavering support, specifically my father who has shown confidence in me with my contributions to this area of ethics. Finally, my husband and two children gave me patience and encouragement as I completed this work. They give me purpose and have brought me more fulfillment than I ever thought possible. *Soli Deo gloria.*

Mark W. Foreman, PhD
Lindsay C. Leonard, Esq.

1

Modern Medicine in a Moral Fog

The 249 passengers of KLM Flight #4805 were waiting in eager anticipation to continue to their final destination, Los Palmas Airport on Grand Canary Island. Los Palmas Airport had been closed due to a bomb threat, and so the Dutch flight was diverted to the smaller Los Rodeos Airport on neighboring Tenerife Island, one of the string of Canary Islands off the coast of Morocco. They waited for four hours until the Los Palmas Airport reopened. Now they were only forty minutes from completing their flight.

As the 747 jumbo jet pulled from the gate, Captain Veldhuyzen Van Zanten peered through the thick fog enveloping the small airport that early March evening and lurched the plane full of vacationing passengers forward to taxi into place. Because of the closing of the main airport, Los Rodeos was so overcrowded that planes had to taxi on the runway rather than the taxiway. Also on the runway that morning was Pan Am Flight #1736. Among its 394 passengers was a group of forty-one elderly tourists anxiously looking forward to a twelve-day Mediterranean cruise. Captain Victor Grubbs, the Pan Am pilot, also peered through the thick fog, as he followed the Dutch flight down the runway. At times visibility was zero, causing the Pan Am flight to taxi at barely six miles per hour instead of the usual twenty. However, both pilots were professionals with experience taking off and landing under challenging conditions. Captain Van Zanten was considered KLM's top pilot and was their chief flight instructor, with 13,000 hours of flight time under his belt.

When KLM 4805 reached the end of the runway, it performed a difficult 180-degree turn and waited for the tower's permission to take off. Pan Am 1736 was to have turned off the runway to a side taxiway, allow the Dutch flight to takeoff, and then continue down the runway for its own departure. The tower was waiting for Captain Grubbs's communication that they were cleared.

However, Captain Van Zanten did something that no one expected and, to this day, that no one can fully explain: he began his takeoff without permission from the tower. It must have been impossible for the Dutch pilot to see through the fog as he rolled down the runway at close to 180 miles per hour. Not until the last second could he have seen his error. There, directly in his path, was Pan Am 1736 desperately trying to maneuver out of the path of the oncoming jet. KLM 4805 tried to pull up, but there was simply not enough time. It struck the Pan Am jumbo jet, shearing off its familiar bubble top, and then slammed back into the ground and exploded into a ball of flame. In just a few seconds it was over. All 234 passengers and fourteen crew members on the KLM plane were killed. Three hundred twenty-six of the 378 passengers and nine of the sixteen crew members aboard Pan Am 4805 were killed. To this day, the total 583 deaths is the highest for any type of aviation disaster.

Because of tragedies like this, aviation has very strict guidelines and rules for activities in and around airports. The cardinal rule is that you depend on instructions from the control tower before landing and taking off. This especially holds when the pilot is visually impaired by fog. The control tower has a perspective that the pilot just doesn't have; they can see the whole picture and can keep all the different complexities of a busy airport working smoothly, reducing the chances for disastrous accidents like that at Tenerife on March 27, 1977.

We are living at a time when a moral fog has descended over Western culture. For many of us, it does not seem that long ago that most moral standards were clear. While there were some ambiguities here and there, most people had a pretty good idea what their moral obligations were. Today it seems as if every traditional moral rule is up for debate. Make a moral judgment about some action, and we are often told, "Well, it depends on the situation or the circumstances or the individual herself. After all, we cannot be judgmental. We need to be tolerant of the beliefs and practices of others."

It seems that no subject has been left untouched by this moral fog. One area where its presence has been especially influential is the practice of medicine. A whole new field has developed to act as kind of "control tower" helping to provide moral guidance in medicine and the life sciences: bioethics.[1]

The purpose of this book is to offer a Christian perspective on problems, questions, and issues in bioethics. This perspective itself encompasses a wide range of beliefs and practices, and not all Christians are going to agree with the positions this book will offer on these issues. Broadly, by the Christian perspective we mean the following: The triune God is the creator and sustainer of the universe. Humans are created in the image of God and as such are rational beings, which makes them morally conditioned.[2] However, this image is diminished by sin, and therefore humans are separated from fully experiencing God's love and justice. Jesus Christ is the incarnation of the second person of the Trinity, fully God and fully human, who lived on earth and taught how we are to relate to God and our fellow humans. His crucifixion, death, and resurrection were for the expiation of the sins of humankind, and through him eternal life is offered to all who believe in him. The Scriptures are the inspired revelation of God and are authoritative on matters of faith and moral practice. The church is the institution commissioned by Jesus to spread the gospel throughout the world by being the living revelation of the love of God in an effort to call all persons to a loving relationship with God. This call to fellowship and union with God and Christlikeness is the heart and

---

1. Several terms are used for the study we are about to pursue: Bioethics, Biomedical Ethics, and Medical Ethics. While there are some distinctions between the meanings of these terms, for our purposes I will use them interchangeably.
2. By "morally conditioned" I mean that humans are moral creatures able to understand and respond to the moral concepts of right and wrong. I am borrowing this term from Stanley J. Grenz, *The Moral Quest: Foundations of Christian Ethics* (Downers Grove, IL: InterVarsity Press, 1997), 212.

soul of Christian ethics and is what separates it from a purely secular ethic. This is the perspective from which this book plans on evaluating issues and problems in bioethics.

DEFINITION AND NEED FOR BIOETHICS

The term *bioethics* was first used in 1926 in an article by Fritz Jahr discussing the use of animals in research.[3] The term is derived from two Greek terms, *bio* which means "life" and denotes the life sciences and *ethos* which means "behavior" and denotes moral beliefs and behavior. We can define bioethics as *the analysis and study of ethical conflicts and problems which arise due to the interrelationship between the practice of the medical/biological sciences and the rights and values of human beings.* In other words, two good things have come into conflict: medical research and practice, and the rights and values of human beings. Bioethics attempts to arrive at principles and procedures to adjudicate this conflict. Bioethics deals in four basic areas where conflict often arises: (1) life and death issues, (2) clinical or health-care issues, (3) medical research, and (4) social health-care policy.

The need for a distinct field in bioethics came about as the result of two developments in the second half of the twentieth century, one in medicine and the other in the general culture. The first was the rapid growth in medical research and technology. Medical research accelerated during the 1940s, and it became common to use humans for medical experimentation. When the Nazi abuses in human experimentation became known, the need arose to develop ethical standards for researchers. Soon new technology was developed, allowing for kidney dialysis and transplants and raising concerns about the allocation of scarce medical resources. New technology also allowed doctors to prolong life with mechanical devices that can assist breathing and pumping blood. A person's life could now be extended or ended by choice. Problems occurred when choices came into conflict between individuals, families, and doctors. Technology was also developed to assist in the creation of new life in the form of artificial insemination, in vitro fertilization, and surrogacy. Questions of parentage and "ownership" of the unborn soon followed. Oral contraceptives allowed for more sexual freedom, and in those cases where the pill failed, newer forms of abortion became options to terminate pregnancies,

3. I. Rinčić and A. Muzur, *Fritz Jahr and the Birth of European Bioethics* (Zagreb: Pergamena, 2012), 141.

making the conflict of abortion one of the major social conflicts of the day. Modern research and technology is a double-edged sword, for it provides the great blessings and promises of better health alternatives while introducing more ambiguity and uncertainty into medical decision-making.

The second development was a significant cultural shift in morality that came in two forms. First, in 1955 the African American civil rights movement took hold as citizens became more cognizant of their rights. This led to other rights movements of the 1960s: women's rights, student rights, gay rights, and others. This movement also affected medical practice. Up until this time, codes of ethics were chiefly concerned with the duties and obligations of health-care workers. Now they shifted to the rights of patients. The American Hospital Association rewrote its code of ethics as the "Patient's Bill of Rights." Abortion became an issue concerning a woman's "reproductive rights" versus the unborn child's "right to life." Euthanasia and assisted suicide were framed as a patient's "right to die." Patients raised objections to treatment in hospitals and clinics, resulting in their having a greater voice in treatment plans and the handling of their information. Conflicts were inevitable with all of the competing groups claiming rights.

The other form of cultural change was the move from a stable view of morality to a flexible and relative conception of moral rules and practices. While it is difficult to pinpoint the beginning of this movement, it certainly gained steam during the turbulent 1960s as our culture was undergoing a practical revolution of ideas. One of the ideas to emerge was cultural pluralism. Before this period the general assumption of most persons was that we all agreed on a traditional core set of values and moral principles. Most people believed that honesty was the best policy, that you should treat your neighbor fairly and honestly, that stealing, marital infidelity, and cheating on taxes and homework were wrong. Patriotism was admired, and the majority of people had deeply held religious beliefs. With the introduction of pluralism, the idea of an agreed-upon traditional set of core values and morality gave way to relativism. Some adopted a moral subjectivism (also known as individual relativism), which held that moral rules change from person to person based on individual preferences, experiences, and desires. What may be right or wrong for you may not be so for me.

A more sophisticated version of relativism is conventionalism (also known as cultural relativism), which sees morality as a set of conventions adopted by a particular culture group due to its history and set of shared beliefs. Members of culture group A may practice a certain set of norms that are not recognized by culture group B. Whether a particular action is right or wrong depends on which culture group one is a member of. The result of both of these types of relativism is ultimately the same: Since there is no overarching moral standard by which to appeal, one must be a falliblist[4] concerning one's own view and be open to and tolerant of other views. Any idea of a "rich" or "thick" moral tradition must give way to a "light" or "thin" conception of morality that requires agreement only on the minimal common set of moral norms we need just to get along.[5] However, even with this thin set, conflicts often arise between individuals and cultures because there is no standard.

With the rise of medical technology, its attending ambiguity, a lack of moral stability, and the demands for one's rights, it is not surprising that modern medicine is in a moral fog. Bioethics developed as a field to help provide guidelines to steer through that fog. It started in the 1950s with a few articles written mostly by Roman Catholic theologians. However, soon philosophers and legal scholars became involved. In the 1970s the government formed bioethics commissions, books were written, and universities began to offer courses in bioethics. Today it is a recognized field of study offering graduate degrees and working positions. It is almost completely dominated from the secular perspective, but many Christians continue to provide perspectives on the conflicts in bioethics. That is what this volume intends to do.

MORAL JUSTIFICATION

To be able to discuss the issues in this book, we need to know a little about how ethics is done and ethical theory. The best place to start is with moral justification.

Everybody has beliefs about things. Our beliefs range from significant life-impacting ones like our belief in God to small unimportant ones like what they will serve for lunch today in the school cafeteria. A belief is justified when a person has good reasons to maintain that particular belief. For example, your belief in God might rest on reasons like his existence being the best explanation for the origin of the universe or because he has touched your life in some significant way. One's belief that they are serving pizza in the school cafeteria today might be based on the fact that they always serve it on this

4. Fallibilism maintains that one should be open to the idea that one's own view is wrong and that another view is right.
5. This is sometimes referred to as a political conception of morality and explains why almost all talk of moral obligations is done in the language of rights.

day of the week, that you saw them preparing it in the kitchen, or that other people told you they were serving pizza today. All of these are reasons for beliefs, and when we cite the reasons for a belief we are justifying that belief.

Not all reasons are necessarily good ones. They have to be related to the belief in a special way which we call an "inference." This means that the reasons "lead one" to a particular belief, or another way of putting it is that the belief "follows" from the reasons. For example, if I said that I believed they were serving pizza today because I am married and have three children, then that would not be a good reason since being married and having children have nothing to do with what they are serving for lunch in the school cafeteria. If one has good reasons for one's beliefs, then the belief is considered a justified one.[6]

A moral justification is the offering of good reasons for the moral beliefs we hold. Our moral beliefs are often formulated in a moral judgment. A moral judgment is a belief we have concerning the rightness or wrongness of a particular act. The kind of ethics in which we make moral judgments is called normative ethics. "Paul was wrong to steal money from the collection plate" is an example of a moral judgment. Every belief is subject to the rational challenge, which is simply the question, "Why do you believe that is true?" Our answer to that question will be our justification. So the question, "Why was it wrong for Paul to steal money from the collection plate?" might be answered by saying things like the following: "Because it doesn't belong to him" or "the church needs that money to meet its needs" or "that is not how Jesus would want us to live." All of these are reasons we might cite to support our judgment that Paul's stealing from the collection plate is wrong.

When we are asked to give a justification for our moral beliefs by citing the reasons, we call this a moral argument. We need to be careful because "argue" can mean a couple of things. Usually when we think of an argument, we mean an emotional fight between two persons that often ends up in hurt feelings. That is not what is meant here. An argument is another word for justification and is simply the citing of reasons for beliefs we regard to be true. All arguments have three parts: premises (the reasons), a conclusion (the belief we hold), and the relationship between the premises and conclusion

6. Just because a belief is justified does not necessarily mean it is true. I might be justified in believing my wife is at work (i.e., I have good reasons to believe it is true), yet it may still be false. She may have gone home sick without my knowing about it. Justification is one important step towards forming true beliefs, but it does not guarantee them with certainty.

(the inference). In morality we formulate moral arguments to arrive at our conclusion or belief which is a moral judgment.

As we present reasons for a particular moral judgment, it is common to appeal to higher levels of justification to support it. In other words, the rational challenge can be raised concerning our reason, and then the reason itself needs to be justified. As we continue to justify further reasons, we tend to become more general or abstract. We can point to at least four basic levels of justification: judgments, rules, principles, and theories.[7]

Suppose you know of a situation where a teacher, Professor Kim, tells a lie to one of his students, Wayne, concerning a class assignment that Wayne needs to do in order to pass the course.[8] You might formulate the following moral **judgment**: "It was wrong for Professor Kim to lie to Wayne concerning that assignment." Notice that the moral judgment is specific about a specific act against a specific person. There is an indefinite number of possible moral situations and therefore an indefinite number of moral judgments as well. Now suppose a friend asks you *why* that specific act was wrong. You would likely justify your judgment by appealing to a higher level to show why that action wrong. The next level up is generally the **moral rule** level. Moral rules are norms established concerning our moral conduct within a particular context. Different contexts have different rules. For example, in this context you might say, "It is wrong because teachers have a professional obligation to be honest with students concerning course requirements." Note that we are still fairly specific; we are speaking in terms of a distinct profession and its moral obligations, and yet we are not as specific as on the judgment level. Instead of speaking of a specific teacher in a specific situation, we are now speaking of all teachers in all situations similar to that of Professor Kim. While there may be a lengthy list of moral rules governing types of behaviors, there are not nearly as many rules as there are judgments. Moral rules can often be found in professional codes of ethics, and they vary from profession to profession. The moral rules for teachers may not be the same moral rules for lawyers or doctors.

However, suppose your friend continues to push the issue and now asks the rational challenge of why we have this moral rule in the teaching profession.

---

7. I am thankful to James Beauchamp and Tom Childress for their outline of this basic structure. See *Principles of Biomedical Ethics* (Oxford: Oxford University Press, 2013), 15.
8. While we might hope no professor would lie to a student, we will assume for our illustration that Professor Kim nurtures a grudge against Wayne, who has skipped a number of classes.

The next level you might appeal to would be the **moral principle** level. The difference between moral rules and moral principles might not be clear at first glance. The way I am using them here, rules are context specific while principles are general overriding moral guidelines that apply across a spectrum of different contexts. We often derive our moral rules from these overriding moral principles. While there may be some debate about moral rules and their application, principles seem to be more generally recognized by most rational persons. For example, you might justify the rule concerning a teacher's obligation to be honest with students as an application of the principle of respect for a person's autonomy or dignity. Respect for autonomy or dignity means recognizing that persons have the freedom to make choices concerning decisions and treating them in such a way as to allow them to freely make their choices. However, if they do not have accurate information, their ability to choose will be impeded. Therefore, to lie to someone disrespects their autonomy and dignity. When we get to this level, we are speaking on much more general terms than moral rules, and there are really only a handful of moral principles.

However, if challenged, what do we base our moral principles on? The takes us to the highest level in normative ethics, the level of **ethical theories**. An ethical theory is an entire system of moral justification coherently related to one overriding maxim that is established external to normative ethics itself. It is usually based on a particular worldview about the nature of goodness. For example, if one believes that goodness is a particular state of affairs, like being happy, then one's ethics will be based on what makes one happy. If one believes that goodness is found in the nature of God, then his or her theory will be based on what reflects God's nature. At this level we are extremely abstract, and we find very few actual ethical theories. What happens if we are challenged at this level? At this point we would need to step outside of the area of normative ethics and defend our entire worldview. Such a step is outside the scope of this book. However, as I stated earlier, this book is written from the Christian perspective or worldview. Therefore, our ethical theory will be a reflection of that worldview.

The illustration below shows the relationship between these four levels of moral justification. This is called a ladder of abstraction. Notice how, as one goes higher on the ladder, the level becomes more abstract. Moral judgments are very concrete, but moral theories are very abstract. Also notice that as one goes higher, there is a smaller area. This symbolizes that the particulars get fewer as they get abstract. There is an indefinite number of moral judgments but only a small number of ethical theories.

How far does one realistically need to go in justifying one's moral beliefs? In general, the level in which you cease to justify is that where agreement can be found or where one feels he or she has adequately supported his or her beliefs. For example, if you and your friend agree with the accepted professional ethics of teachers, then there is no need to justify one's moral beliefs further about the wrongness of Professor Kim's actions. However, if you or your friend have further questions, you need to explore the higher levels of moral justification, including your ethical theories. It is to those theories that we now turn.

ETHICAL THEORIES

I would propose there are at least three things involved in any moral event: a *person* performing an *act* that has certain desired *results*. In our example above, there is a person (Professor Kim) performing an act (lying to Wayne) that has a desired result (Wayne is deceived). The major ethical theories I want to examine ground themselves in one of these three aspects of a moral event. For some, the most important aspect of a moral action are the results. What makes an act morally good is that it achieves a **good** result. This view is called *consequentialism*. For others, certain acts are simply right or wrong regardless of the results. They might claim that telling the truth is right no matter what the results are and that morality is about doing what is **right**. What makes an act right is that one has fulfilled one's moral obligation or duty. This view, which concentrates on moral duties, is called *deontology*. Finally, there are those who say that the primary emphasis in ethics should not be on duties or results, but on what kind of person we are. The goal of morality is to become persons of high character or **virtuous**. If we become virtuous persons, right actions and good results will follow. This view is called *virtue ethics*. I wish to examine each of these three views in detail.[9]

Consequentialism

For the consequentialist, the primary emphasis in determining if an act is right or wrong is whether the consequences or results of the action are good. Take lying for example. For the consequentialist, lying is usually wrong

---

9. This list is not meant to be comprehensive, and many theories are not being mentioned here such as feminist ethics, communitarian ethics, an ethics of rights, an ethic of care, social contract theory, existentialistic ethics, and post-modern ethical theories. Some of these will be covered in other sections of this book. I believe these three views form the main views one finds today.

because it usually produces bad consequences, like mistrust between persons. Trust is necessary for relationships to succeed; therefore, trust is good. To lie usually betrays this goodness. Therefore, lying is usually wrong. However, if lying can produce a good result, then it would not be wrong. If I need to lie to save someone's life, that is a good result, and lying would not be wrong in that case. Therefore, lying is not always wrong; it depends on the consequences. The consequentialist might even believe that it is *usually* wrong, but not *absolutely* wrong. There are no absolute rights or wrongs for a consequentialist; at best all he can offer are general rules of thumb based on past experience with the usual results of our actions. If this sounds like "end justifies the means" thinking, that is exactly what it is. In fact, the consequentialist will tell you that the only thing that justifies the means is the end.

There are two major ethical theories that are consequentialistic. If you are talking about the ultimate consequences for me, that theory is called *egoism*. If you are talking about the consequences for everybody, that theory is called *utilitarianism*.

1. *Egoism.* Egoism itself can be broken into two types: psychological egoism and ethical egoism. Psychological egoism says that all our actions are ultimately done out of our own self-interest. It claims that we have no choice; we have to act ultimately for self. If we do a beneficial act for someone else, we are really doing it just to fulfill our own desires. They would point to such things like the good feelings we get when we do good things, or the reputation we have for doing something good as the real reasons we do good actions for others. We may think we are doing it for someone else, but we are just deceiving ourselves because we are really doing it for self. A completely altruistic act (one done totally for the welfare of another) is simply impossible according to this theory. An early proponent of psychological egoism was the British philosopher Thomas Hobbes (1588–1697).

While psychological egoism does seem to have some truth to it and many actions we do are to fulfill our own desires, there are some serious problems with it of which I will mention two. First, psychological egoism doesn't seem to recognize that there may be non-intentional byproducts to my actions that have nothing to do with how we assess them morally. We morally judge actions by intentions and motivations. For example, if you are driving in the rain and need to signal for a left turn with your hands (because your turn signal is broken), you may realize you are going to get your hand wet. However, your intention or aim is not to get your hand wet; it is to signal a turn. Getting your hand wet is an unintended byproduct of your action, even though it was foreseeable. No one would say that the intended reason you stuck your hand out the window was to get it wet. In the same way, though it is true that I may get personal satisfaction out of helping others, that satisfaction can merely be a byproduct of my intended action to help others. It certainly is possible that my intention was to help another and a byproduct was a sense of satisfaction. It is the intention whereby we assess the morality of the action, and, in this case, the intention was to help. Secondly, psychological egoism is not claiming that I normally act out of self-interest; it says it is impossible for me to act otherwise. That is a very big claim. However, no evidence is offered to support the claim that altruism is impossible. No matter how much a person claims his or her action was altruistic, the psychological egoist will merely assert that it was egoistically motivated. An assertion is not an argument. They really have no way to prove the theory at all; it is unfalsifiable, so it remains an unprovable assertion.

Ethical egoism differs from psychological egoism in that it claims that we *ought* to act in a manner that ultimately serves our best interest. This theory recognizes that it is possible to do an altruistic act, but in fact one never should. The use of the word "ultimate" is important here. It means that I may do actions from which others benefit, but ultimately I must do it because it serves my self-interest. Those who hold this view often say that this would produce the best kind of world—if everybody looks out for themselves all will benefit. This is the basis of a capitalistic economic system. As a businessman, I am looking out for my own profits, so I will build a better mousetrap than the next guy. Someone else will come along and, looking out for his profits, will try to build a better one yet. The result is that society benefits from an excellent mousetrap because of the competitive spirit a free market economy engenders. This was the classic argument of the economist and philosopher Adam Smith (1723–1790). One of the most well-known modern proponents of ethical egoism was Ayn Rand (1905–1982).

However, ethical egoism also has some serious problems. First, it is difficult to believe that all will benefit if we are looking out only for ourselves. What happens when our interests conflict? If my ethics is based solely on looking out for myself, no moral rules exist to keep me from doing cruel or unjust actions to others, or them to me. What's to stop me from sneaking over and burning down your mousetrap factory? As long as I don't get caught, I am not doing anything wrong. I am acting in my own self-interest. Second, if my primary justification for ethical egoism is that it is best for everyone, then I am not really arguing for egoism but for utilitarianism. Third, I have to hope that no one else becomes an egoist, for they might use it against me. Therefore, I can never share with someone that they should become an ethical egoist, for it could be self-defeating if they use it against me. I would not be doing that which was ultimately in my best interest. However, if I believe ethical egoism is the right view of accomplishing the good, but cannot promote it to others, then many recognize there is a problem with it as a rational ethical theory. A key aspect of an ethical theory is that it promotes the good, but with ethical egoism I cannot promote the theory that I believe promotes the good. Fourth, if ethical egoism is true, how are we to evaluate the death of Christ? We would have to say that either he did it ultimately for himself or he was morally wrong. Yet Scripture is clear many times that he "gave his life as a ransom for many" (Mark 10:45; see also John 3:16; 10:15; Eph. 5:25; 2 Cor. 5:19).[10] Finally, we often speak of good moral acts as praiseworthy. Yet there is something counterintuitive in praising someone for doing something that he ultimately just did for himself. Therefore, I believe both forms of egoism have enough problems that they should be abandoned as ethical theories.

2. *Utilitarianism.* Utilitarianism is the consequentialistic theory that says the morally right thing to do is that which provides the greatest happiness to the greatest number of people.[11] This is called the utility principle. Three philosophers are primarily responsible for developing this theory: Jeremy Bentham (1748–1832), John Stuart Mill (1806–1873), and Henry Sidgwick (1838–1900). Utilitarianism is one of the most well-known ethical theories in the history of ethics and is one of the most popular today. This is especially true in modern American society where we hold that the majority rules in decision-making. That is what utilitarianism says—whatever makes the majority happy is the right thing to do. Some utilitarians want to broaden "happy" to mean a number of things: fulfilled, contented, meaningful. Utilitarianism brings together three ideas. First, one should strive to create the greatest balance of good over evil. Utilitarians recognize that rarely is any single action totally good or totally evil, but usually a mixture of good and evil. For every good

10. It is true that one passage says that Christ endured the cross "for the joy set before him" (Heb. 12:2). However, this may just be a statement of a byproduct of his sacrificial act. It is difficult to think that Christ's intention in dying on the cross was to experience joy himself when so many passages point to his entire mission as one of saving mankind from their sins.
11. It should be noted that there are many different versions of utilitarianism, each of which replaces happiness for something else, such as preferences or desires. The view I am discussing here has come to be known as "classical utilitarianism."

thing you do, there are other good things you are not doing, and whenever a good thing is not done, we call that evil. Therefore, you should choose to do those actions that have a greater balance of good over evil. This is called proportionalism. Second, classical utilitarians identify good with happiness, that which everyone wants, and evil with pain, that which everyone avoids. Finally, they recognize that happiness should be spread as widely and as equally as possible, again with the recognition that rarely will everyone be happy. Some utilitarians apply the utility principle to each situation independent of other situations or general guidelines. "What will produce the greatest happiness to the greatest number in this specific situation itself?" This is called act utilitarianism. Other utilitarians believe that general rules can be formed that usually provide the greatest happiness for the greatest number of people and that these rules can guide one in each situation he encounters. These are called rule utilitarians.

Critics of utilitarianism cite several problems with the view. First, how can one measure the "amount" of happiness and compare it with some other "amount" of happiness that may be so different as to make them incommensurable? Jeremy Bentham actually attempted to measure happiness by creating a unit of happiness which he called a "hedon" and a calculus for measuring happiness. However, such ideas seem implausible. Who is happiest: a child who received the toy he really wanted for Christmas, a bride on her wedding day, or the elderly women who just found a liver is available for her transplant? There is just no way to comparatively measure happiness. Second, should happiness be the goal of morality? Isn't there more to life than just being happy? If I could offer you a pill that would make you happy, but would also make you severely mentally handicapped so that you could never accomplish anything in life but would be a vegetable, would you take it? Most persons recognize that happiness should not always be the ultimate goal of our lives. Third, under utilitarianism certain goods like persons and truthfulness end up having only extrinsic value with no intrinsic value. They have value only if they produce some social utility but have no value in and of themselves. Suppose that, in order to provide the greatest happiness for the greatest number, we would have to sacrifice an innocent person. The utilitarian would be forced to say that such a sacrifice would be appropriate. But then what is he saying about that person? In his view, the only value a person has is in providing social utility, happiness. Fourth, under this view the minority always suffer for the sake of the majority. Unfortunately in our society this often ends up being the same group of persons. Who is looking out for their desires?

Finally, both types of consequential theories hold that the primary emphasis in ethics should be on achieving good results, either for self or for all involved. But can we really know what the consequences of our actions will be? When we drop a pebble into a pond, we simply do not know where the ripples will travel or what they will touch. If we cannot know what the ultimate consequences of our actions will be, how can we use consequences as our primary guide for our ethical actions?

Deontology

Deontology is the view that looks at our actions and declares them right or wrong in themselves. For the deontologist lying is wrong and no consequences, even good ones, can ever make lying good. The deontologist thinks of morality in terms of duty or obligation. What makes an action morally right is that it fulfills a moral duty. I have some things I am morally obligated to do, like tell the truth, and some things I am obligated not to do, like lie.

While some deontologists believe in ethical absolutes, that one should always do one's moral duty, many deontologists recognize the possibility for ethical obligations to conflict. For example, it is possible that I might be faced with a moral dilemma in which I am obligated to perform two moral duties that are in conflict—if I do one I can't do the other. For example, lying to save a life. I am obligated to tell the truth, but I am also obligated to save life. How do I handle such a conflict? Many deontologists recognize that my duties are not absolute in the extreme sense but are *primae facie* duties. *Primae facie* means literally "at face value." *Primae facie* duties are moral obligations that hold in normal cases unless they conflict with stronger obligations, in which case they can be overridden by the stronger obligation. They are "absolute" in normal cases where there is no conflict. However, they are not absolute in the rare case where another more fundamental duty comes into conflict. This view has also been called qualified absolutism.

The major question for deontologists concerns the origin and foundation for moral duties. If one cannot appeal to consequences to determine the right thing to do, then where do our moral duties come from? Here lies a division within deontological thinkers between those who hold to a naturalistic foundation for moral duties and those who hold to a non-naturalistic foundation. By saying that a theory is naturalistic, philosophers mean that the grounding of the theory is in some natural property in this world. For example, the consequentialistic theories, egoism and utilitarianism, are naturalistic theories in that they ground the morality of our actions in a natural property:

self-interest or happiness respectively. On the contrary non-naturalistic moral theories ground moral actions in duties derived form an out-of-this-world source. The most common non-naturalistic theory is theism. I will discuss one naturalistic deontological theory and two theistic deontological theories.

1. *Classical divine command theory*. This ethical theory proposes that our ethical duties are grounded in the will of God. Since commands are by nature verbal, this means some form of verbal divine revelation is required to inform one of God's commands. This revelation is the authoritative basis for all ethical duties. Christians would point to the Bible as the authoritative basis of God's commands. Examples would be the Ten Commandments as well as the commandments of Jesus and the moral instructions scattered throughout the New Testament epistles. Some of these are explicit commands while others are models of how one should morally respond to a given situation. An important early proponent of this theory of ethics was William of Occam (c.1285–1389).

For many Christians this may seem like the correct ethical theory; however, it has some problems. Before commenting on the problems with this view, I want to make clear that I am not denying that the Bible is the authoritative Word of God, nor am I denying that it contains authoritative moral instruction. As a Christian myself I believe firmly that Scripture is the inspired and authoritative Word of God. However, I do believe there are some problems with basing one's ethical theory solely on the commands of God. First, one has to make a choice between different writings that claim to be the Word of God and yet are incompatible. Islam claims that the Qur'an is the Word of God. Yet the Qur'an and the Bible are incompatible in several areas. For example, the Bible teaches a man may marry only one woman at a time (Gen. 1:27; Matt. 19:4–6; 1 Tim. 3:2, 12). The Qur'an allows for a man to have up to four wives at a time (Surah 2:3). Since these messages are mutually incompatible, many would argue that the Qur'an and the Bible cannot both be the Word of God. Therefore, the divine command theorist will first have to justify why his choice of revelation is the depository of God's commands.

Second, what about those who do not have this divine revelation in their possession? What are they to base their ethical theory on if they do not have the commands of God? Some might point to natural revelation, but the classical divine command theory does not give you that option—commands are verbal instructions not accessible by looking at nature. Can we hold those who were not given the commands responsible for keeping them if they never had them? Would it be fair if I made my students responsible for an assignment that I had never told them about?

However, the most significant problem with classical divine command theory is that it reduces to *voluntarism*. Voluntarism is the view that morality is based on the will of God. In other words, what makes something good is that God simply wills it so. This is an ancient problem that even Plato addressed in his book *Euthyphro*. The problem is that if morality is just whatever God wills, then it is possible that God could have willed something we think of as evil, like child abuse, to have been good. Voluntarism sets up a dilemma. On one horn of the dilemma, God can decide whatever he wants about morality. But that seems to make morality purely arbitrary, like God is flipping a coin to decide what is right and wrong. The other horn of the dilemma is that if we say God cannot will something bad to be good, then he is not free and sovereign; there is a standard he has to answer to outside of himself that he is answerable to, the moral law. If God has to answer something outside of himself, then how can he be the "supreme" being? The dilemma of voluntarism has caused many philosophers to reject classical divine command theory as a viable moral theory.[12]

It is important at this point to note that newer versions of divine command morality have risen that avoid voluntarism and still retain the essence of grounding morality in God.[13] Some have pointed the way out of this mess is by abandoning the voluntarism of classical divine morality and opting for a view where morality is not based on the *will* of God, but on the *nature* or essence of God. The idea is that God is good himself and his commands reflect his goodness. This newer version would also affirm that God's commands can be discovered in other ways besides verbal revelation, such as mysticism and even reason, thus removing the other objections to classical divine command morality. One of the implications of this newer version is that God is not free to command just anything, but that he is restricted by his nature. While some Christians might be bothered by this, Scripture affirms God's limitations when it claims that God cannot lie (Num. 23:19, Titus 1:2; Heb. 6:18).

---

12. Unfortunately, it has also been a reason many atheists claim that morality is not dependent on God. However, as we shall see, classical divine command morality is not the only theory with a theistic foundation.
13. For more on this position see David Baggett and Jerry L. Walls, *Good God: Theistic Foundations for Morality* (New York: Oxford University Press, 2011).

2. *Natural law theory.* A second deontological theory is natural law theory. This theory has been around for many years and is traceable back to the Stoic philosophers of ancient Greece. Aspects of it can be found in Aristotle (383–321 BC), and it was given full expression in the writings of Thomas Aquinas (1225–1274).[14] Natural law theory holds that all men have an inherent capacity as part of their human nature to discover those actions that are right and those actions that are wrong. The key idea behind natural law theory is that every natural living kind has a nature and the purpose of all natural kinds is to function in accordance with that nature. This is the teleological view of creation: God designed creation to function a certain way. He provided rational laws in order for creation to function appropriately. The universe in general functions according to the laws of physics, chemistry, and biology. Non-human animals function according to the laws of instinct within their species. However, humans are made in the image of God with the ability to reason and reflect about those actions that promote human welfare and basic goods and those that diminish and devalue human welfare and basic goods.[15] The former actions are morally good while the latter are morally evil. Human beings then have the ability to discover, through reason and reflection, those moral laws which will lead them to live in accordance with their nature. The moral laws discovered through natural law are universal and eternal and can be known by all through reason and reflection (even if these moral agents do not recognize God as the ultimate ground for morality). They can also be used to judge individuals, societies, and human civil laws. Actions that are not in accord with the natural law are considered ethically impermissible. Finally, it is important to note that natural law does not discount the need for Scripture as some Christians have argued. Christian natural law theorists agree that natural law is not sufficient when it comes to man's relationship with God and that special divine revelation is needed for certain truths such as man's sinfulness and the need for God's grace in providing salvation. Natural law does not teach that man can earn merit standing before God apart from his grace.

Natural law has its critics who have raised some serious problems. First, with the advent of naturalistic Darwinian evolution, many seriously question

14. It is important to note that neither Aristotle nor Aquinas should be considered as primarily Natural Law theorists. While their ethical systems employ the natural law, they would base their theory more on the development of virtues and therefore are better characterized as virtue ethicists.
15. Basic human goods are those activities that universally promote human flourishing: life, knowledge, play, aesthetic experiences, friendship, family, religion, practical reason.

the teleological view of creation proposed by natural law. If naturalistic evolution is true, nothing in nature has a purpose. Everything is just chance and random selection. Therefore, there are no laws guiding creation, and man does not have a specific way he is supposed to function.[16] Second, some question the idea of man having a universal and unalterable nature which he shares with all men. Some would say there are no such things as "natures" at all, only particular things with similar features. This would mean that each thing is a law unto itself; there are no universal laws, no set way a thing is *supposed* to function. Others believe that while there is a human nature it changes between cultures or individuals. Finally, some argue that natural law is an attempt to create an *ought* from an *is*. Just because an action is good and promotes human welfare, does not necessarily imply that an individual has an obligation to perform it. Surgery is a good, but that does not imply we all have the obligation to become surgeons. Natural law might function for identifying moral goods but may not function for identifying moral duties.

How one answers these objections will depend on one's view of evolution, natures, and duties. If one rejects naturalistic evolution and accepts that a divine creator designed the world so that natural kinds are to function according to a certain manner, then some of these objections seem to lose their force. Sometimes arguing an "ought" from an "is" is possible. If the definition of a watch is that it is an object that accurately tells time, then we can say that because of what it "is" it "ought" to accurately tell time. If it does not, then we can justifiably say that it is not functioning properly. In the same manner, if a person is designed to live according to a particular nature and he does not, then he is not functioning properly. Natural law helps man to function properly.

3. *Kantian deontology*. A third type of deontology is Kantian deontology, which is perhaps the most well known of the deontological views. Many consider Immanuel Kant (1724–1804) the most influential modern philosopher. This is certainly true in the area of epistemology, or philosophy of knowledge.

---

16. Of course, if naturalistic evolution is true, then all ethical theories fail as there is no real value in the universe including moral value, just blind indifference. As naturalistic evolutionist Richard Dawkins says, "The universe we observe has no design, no purpose, no evil and no good, nothing but blind, pitiless indifference. DNA neither knows nor cares. DNA just is. And we dance to its music." Richard Dawkins, *River Out of Eden: A Darwinian View of Life* (London: Basic Books, 1995), 133.

However, he was also influential in developing a deontological ethic based on pure rational thought. Hence, this is a naturalistic form of deontology.[17]

Kant began by rejecting any sort of ethics based on consequences. If one depends solely on consequences, what will keep one from doing the wrong if it produces desirable consequences? He also rejected any ethics based on "natural inclinations." What Kant means by "natural inclinations" is actions we tend to perform due to emotions like love, compassion, pity, patriotism, and the like. For example, some might feed the poor because they have compassion for them. However, reasoned Kant, what would motivate us to feed the poor if we did not have such feelings? He believed one cannot base one's ethic on emotions because emotions fluctuate and are not stable. Only one motive counts for Kant: duty. He calls this "the good will," to do right for no other reason than because it is right. That is the only motive that matters. Kant is very strict as to what counts as a moral act and what does not. For Kant, if you do an act out of compassion or to achieve certain consequences, you may be acting *in accordance with* duty, but you are not acting *out of* duty and, therefore, you are not performing a moral act. This doesn't mean that if you feed the poor out of compassion you are doing something wrong, it simply means that it has no moral value.

According to Kant, how do we determine the right thing to do? Here he gives us one of the most famous statements in all philosophy, the categorical imperative. Kant formulated the categorical imperative several ways, but the one that is most well known is this: "Act according to that maxim by which you can, at the same time, will that it should be a universal law." In other words, if you want to know if an action is right or wrong, universalize it so that everybody must do it. What would happen? Take lying: what if everybody lied? "Well," we might say, "that would produce disastrous consequences." Is that what Kant means? No, because that would just make him a consequentialist and, as we saw, he rejects consequentialism. What Kant means is that it would be irrational because in universalizing lying, you defeat the very reason lying works. Lying works only because people assume you are being honest. But if everyone lied, no one would assume anyone was being honest including you. The very act of universalizing the lying defeats the goal of lying. So the act of

17. While Kant's method is naturalistic, that does not mean he does not see a string correlation between God and morality. Kant believed in order for morality to make sense, good has to win in the end. If evil wins in the end, then why bother doing good? Therefore, there must exist a guarantee that good will win. The only being that can guarantee that good will win in the end is God.

lying becomes self-defeating when we universalize it, and any action that is self-defeating is irrational. Kant thought this method of universalizing can help anyone determine if an act is right or wrong. In that sense he believed he had a truly rational ethic.

Kant has not been without his critics. First, many have been critical of Kant because he does not seem to allow for exceptions to our moral duties. He is an unbending absolutist in his view of morality. However, what happens if moral duties conflict? Kant does not seem to recognize this possibility and provides no way out of true moral dilemmas. It took another deontologist, W. D. Ross, to come up with the concept of *primae facie* duties we mentioned above. Second, there are some who have pointed out problems with Kant's method of universalization. Suppose we act according to the maxim, "Telemarketers should be exterminated." It does not seem to be self-defeating to universalize this maxim if one is not a telemarketer himself. There is no irrational contradiction as Kant claims. We can also do the opposite, universalize non-moral maxims such as "whenever one is in the shower, one should sing" without contradiction. However, this does not make singing in the shower morally obligatory just because it is universalizable without being self-defeating. Finally, Kant is criticized because of his absolute rejection of consequences and emotions and his strong insistence that the only acceptable motive for an act to be considered moral is duty. Can one simply ignore consequences the way Kant suggests? If my moral duty results in hundreds dying, should I simply ignore that? While consequences may not be an adequate basis for one's moral theory, one does not have to ignore them altogether. The same can be said for emotions. Most ethicists agree that there is something wrong with a person who does not feel compassion at the suffering of another human being and, out of that compassion, act to relieve that suffering. Yet for Kant such emotions have no moral value at all. The problem with "duty" is that it simply fails to inspire and motivate most persons to moral action.

We have looked at three deontological theories. While they are different in some respects, they all have at least one thing in common: they believe moral acts are intrinsically good. This intrinsic goodness may derive from different grounds. For the Classical Divine Command Deontologist, the intrinsic goodness of acts is grounded in the will of God. For the Natural Law Deontologist, the intrinsic goodness of acts is grounded in the nature of God of which our nature is a reflection. For the Kantian Deontologist, the intrinsic goodness of acts is grounded in the reason of man. We now move to a final theory that says the consequentialist and deontologist have totally misplaced the debate by emphasizing what we do instead of who we are.

Virtue Ethics

The theories we have concentrated on thus far have one thing in common: they have concentrated on the right thing to do in a given moral situation. For the consequentialist, the right thing to do is that which achieves the best consequences. For the deontologist, the right thing to do is that which fulfills our moral obligations. Virtue ethics is not concerned so much with what we do, but the kind of person we should be. It is the view that morality should be conceived as primarily concerned, not with acts or consequences, but with the cultivation of moral virtues or traits of *character*. The emphasis is placed on the character of the person as primary in evaluating and performing moral actions. A true moral act has its basis in a virtuous characteristic and the primary purpose of ethics is to develop virtuous persons. This view is among the oldest in the history of ethics, going all the way back to Plato (427–347 BC) and Aristotle (383–321 BC) as well as being adopted by many of the early church fathers, including Augustine (354–430) and Thomas Aquinas in the medieval period. It fell out of favor during the Enlightenment but has recently seen a tremendous resurgence.

What is a virtue? The word virtue comes from the Greek word *arete* meaning "excellence." Excellence always implied the idea of functioning well and appropriately on a regular basis: a knife cuts, a good knife cuts well all the time, its virtue is its sharpness. A horse's virtue is its speed. In the moral sense, a virtue is a trained behavioral disposition to live continually in a good and righteous manner, a manner of moral excellence.

By a "trained behavioral disposition" we mean something analogous to a habit. A habit is something we learn through practice and repetition. We get so accustomed to it that it is like second nature to us; we do not really have to think about it much to do it. Take driving a car: When you first learn to drive, you carefully pay attention to every detail of what you are doing. However, after years of driving, we often do not even think about what we are doing; we drive by habit. It becomes a part of us. Virtues are like that. We practice living a certain way until it becomes a part of our character. Virtuous persons are often described as men or women of integrity, courage, fairness, humility, diligence, and a host of other virtuous characteristics. Virtue is more than just doing good acts; these morally admirable traits have become a part of the person we are. It does not mean we are perfect, just consistent. If you knew a man of integrity and heard from someone that he wasn't honest in a particular situation, your first thought might be, "That doesn't sound like him. It is out of character for him to act that way." That is how virtues are supposed to work.

Virtue ethics holds that we are supposed to be developing continually into virtuous persons, aspiring every day to be better. We are not supposed to be struggling all our lives with the same vices or sins. We should overcome them and grow. We all need to acquire the virtues through training and practice. Suppose two students have an opportunity to cheat on an exam. John struggles with the temptation quite a while, and almost gives into it, but finally decides not to cheat. Meanwhile, Kelli does not even consider the option. She is aware of the opportunity, but never gives it a serious thought. While we would admire John for not giving in, virtue ethicists would claim that our goal is to become like Kelli. We should be growing morally to become people for whom vices are not a temptation. They also recognize that this is an ethic of aspiration, and therefore is more often the goal than the realization.

Another important characteristic of virtue ethics is how we learn the virtues. Rather than appealing to a list of rules, the virtues are learned by identifying and modeling virtuous persons. These can be important people of the past and present, such as Jesus, Socrates, Gandhi, or Mother Theresa, or someone intimately related to one such as a parent, relative, teacher, or a friend. Usually the virtuist will study the life of the person and get to know them as well as possible. They will approach moral situations by asking, "What would he or she do in this situation?" and attempt to emulate the person.

Another feature of virtue ethics is the manner in which it evaluates an action. Rather than thinking in terms of just right or wrong, virtue ethics tries to locate the mean between two vices. Take the use of anger in responding to an unjust situation. Too much anger results in uncontrolled wrath while too little results in a meek acquiescence. The mean between these is righteous indignation towards injustice. Virtue ethics has often been called an ethics of moderation, but it is better to think of it as an ethic of appropriateness.

There is no one set list of all the virtues, and many philosophers have listed many attributes as virtues. Handed down from the ancient Greeks were the four moral virtues: prudence (practical wisdom in living life), temperance (appropriateness in the use of the passions), fortitude (the courage needed to overcome obstacles as one grows), and justice (fairness and equity in dealings with others). To these were added the theological virtues that applied to one's relationship with God: faith, hope, and love. Combined, these become known as the seven cardinal virtues.

There is much to commend in virtue ethics. It provides the motivational component missing in the duty-based ethics of Kant and other deontologists. It recognizes that there is more to ethics than consequences because we all admire those who, like Mother Theresa, continually lived in a virtuous manner, even though they do not often see good results of their work. Also, unlike Kant, virtue ethics recognizes the importance of emotions in ethical reasoning and encourages compassion and love as motivations for moral actions. Virtue ethics also provides a foundation, a developed moral character, to support us when we encounter difficult moral decisions or dilemmas.

However, virtue ethics also has some problems. As nice as the virtues are, many have pointed out that they do not give us enough guidance in making practical decisions in specific ethical situations. Virtue ethics simply remains too abstract and is not practical enough. When I encounter a tough decision, it is often not enough to tell me to be a person of integrity. A second and related problem has to do with judging a person's actions as right and wrong. What if, in performing an evil action, a person displays one or more moral virtues? Suppose a father of a poor family breaks into a pharmacy to steal drugs for his ailing child. He is exhibiting great love and faithfulness in providing for his family but does that justify stealing? These are good virtues, so do they now make stealing virtuous? If not, then how do we judge the action as morally wrong if all we have are virtues? It seems some sort of rule theory is needed to supplement virtue theory in order for it to work.

A CHRISTIAN APPRAISAL OF THE ETHICAL THEORIES

How should we, as Christians, appraise these theories? We have seen that they all have problems. That is usually the case in most areas of philosophy. What we often have to opt for is the theory that has the best explanatory value. In other words, it explains things best with the least amount of problems. Which theory does that from the Christian perspective? It would have to be a theory that honors God and is reflective of his nature, plan, and desires.

I would like to suggest that rather than any one theory, a pluralism of theories best accomplishes that goal. We stated above that there are at least three things involved in a moral event: a *person* doing an *act* that has certain desired *results*. All three of these aspects are important, but not in the same way or at the same level. Therefore, though our ethical theory is pluralistic, it needs to be properly prioritized. It seems to me that the most important aspect is the person himself or herself, and therefore I believe virtue ethics should receive first priority in a Christian ethical theory. God is much more concerned with us than he is with our actions or our accomplishments. He did not create us just to do good works or accomplish good results. Nor did he send his Son to die on the cross for our works or accomplishments. He loves us, created us in his image, and wants us to fellowship with him. Therefore, it seems to me that God is primarily concerned with the kind of person we are, and that is what virtue ethics emphasizes.

This is what I observe in the New Testament. The emphasis is on who you are rather than your acts and accomplishments. Romans 12:2 says we are not to be conformed to this world, but we are to be transformed into a different kind of person. Paul picks up this theme again in Ephesians 4:24 when he admonishes us to "put on the new self, which is to be like God in true righteousness and holiness," a theme he repeats in Colossians 3. Also, we find in the New Testament an emphasis on modeling oneself after Jesus or Paul. Paul writes in 1 Corinthians 11:1, "Follow my example, as I follow Christ." Other passages emphasize the idea of modeling Christ (2 Thess. 3:7–9; 1 Pet. 2:21; Phil. 2:5).

However, none of this discounts the needs for action-guiding rules. As we saw in our discussion above, virtue ethics is inadequate by itself. We often need specific guidelines, and so action-guiding principles are necessary to supplement a virtue ethic. I believe the primary ethic is a virtue ethic, but second in priority would be a deontological ethic. Of the three we examined, I believe the natural law ethic has the best explanatory power. First, it grounds our moral norms in the nature of God while recognizing that Scripture both confirms and supplements the norms that are discoverable by reason. Second, in affirming a natural law ethic, we also acknowledge the universality of moral norms. We can apply our moral norms to all persons in relevant similar situations, for we all have the same basic human nature. Third, natural law is taught in Scripture. We are told that God has not left himselfwithout a witness to unbelievers (Acts 14:17), that God's power and nature have been clearly seen and understood through what has been seen so that those who practice godlessness are without excuse (Rom. 1:20), and that those who do not have the divine commands do by nature the things of the law because God has written the law on the hearts of all and their conscience bears witness to it (Rom. 2:14–15). So there is a place for a deontological natural law ethic in supporting the virtue ethic.

What about consequentialism? While I believe this is the weakest of all views, I would not rule out the place of consequences in our moral reasoning. They do have a consideration, though I would give them the lowest priority.

There are times when we need to consider the consequences of our actions and in living out our virtues. However, we need to exercise caution due to the uncertainty of the ultimate consequences of any action. I may be thinking that I am doing an act of kindness that results in an immediate good but may not be aware of the long range consequences that may not be good.

In putting this all together, I will borrow a term from the philosopher John Rawls, "reflective equilibrium."[18] The idea of reflective equilibrium is that as I approach a moral event, I need to continually reflect on three ideas: new information or insights the event may present, my moral judgments, and the three different aspects of my properly prioritized pluralistic ethical theory. My goal is to maintain a proper balance or state of equilibrium in my moral life: one where I am becoming more like Jesus every day. Sometimes this will mean an adjustment of my overall system to account for new information. I must be willing to reflect and change. That is what life is all about.

A LITTLE ABOUT THE LAW

A comprehensive understanding of bioethics cannot be done without addressing the legal limitations involved. In this book, each chapter will have a brief discussion on how the law has addressed the overall issue through cases and statutes. Fortunately, one does not need a background in legal training to understand the basics of how the law functions; a brief overview is all that is required.

As most of you know, the federal government is divided into three branches: executive, legislative, and judicial. The executive branch consists of the President of the United States, as well as those directly under him. The legislative branch is made up of Congress, meaning the Senate and the House of Representatives. Finally, the judicial branch is the Supreme Court, as well as lower federal courts. Individual state governments follow the same framework as the federal government. The executive branch includes the Governor, the legislative branch is the state legislature, which is comprised of the state Senate and state House of Representatives (or House of Delegates), and the judicial branch consists of the state Supreme Court and the lower state courts. At both the federal and state level, these three branches work together to provide a system of "checks and balances" so that no section has total control over the other two. For the purposes of this book, the focus will primarily be on the legislative and the judicial branches.

18. John Rawls, *A Theory of Justice* (Cambridge, MA: Harvard University Press, 1971), 20–21.

It is important to understand what controls and limits government intrusion into citizens' lives and endeavors. The guiding principle in the modern democratic state is that citizens are free to pursue private endeavors without the constraint of government unless those endeavors interfere with the lives and endeavors of other citizens. In America, these freedoms and restraints are guided and controlled by the United States Constitution. The Constitution not only creates the three-branch system of government; it also protects various liberties of American citizens. State constitutions have also been established to control what state governments can do. While each state constitution defines the rights and limitations of its citizens, these constitutions are subordinate to the United States Constitution. Thus, state laws cannot contradict federal laws.

Laws begin at the legislative level. At both the state and the federal level, bills are presented to either Congressional body, which is voted on by that body only. It then travels to the other body to be voted on. Once accepted, it is then sent to the President or Governor, who can either sign it into law or veto it. Vetoes can be overridden by another vote in Congress (two-thirds majority at the federal level). This is a very brief explanation of how laws are made, but the key takeaway is that only the legislative branch has the authority to make laws. The executive branch can suggest or propose laws, while the judicial branch only interprets existing laws. Courts do not make laws, but they can establish legal precedents (see below).

Lawsuits are filed when a party is challenging the application of an existing law. If the lawsuit alleges a violation of federal law, the case will begin in the federal court system. If the lawsuit alleges a violation of a state law, most of the time the case begins in the state court system. The only time state laws may be challenged in federal court is if the parties are located in different states and the amount being sought is greater than the minimum limit set by Congress (as of this writing, $75,000). Cases typically begin at the district trial court level, with a judge or jury rendering a decision. If appealed, the case moves to the appellate court, either the U.S. Court of Appeals or the specific state's Court of Appeals. In many cases, the appealing party must petition the appellate court to hear the matter, which the court can either grant or deny. Some cases are appealed as a matter of right, meaning the court is required to hear them. The appellate court utilizes a panel of judges to give majority rulings when rendering its decisions. It can affirm the lower court decision, reverse the lower court decision, or remand the case back to the lower court for further action or a new trial. At the state level, the final appeal goes to the state Supreme Court. A federal appeal can make its way to the highest court, the United States Supreme Court. These courts also use discretion in determining which cases will be heard.

A general rule of thumb is that the higher the court, the more binding the decision is on lower courts. In other words, higher courts create a precedent for future cases. This is known as the *principle of stare decisis*. Binding precedent is when a lower court must honor the findings of a higher court within its path (i.e., state district court through state supreme court). Persuasive precedent is when a court is guided by decisions made by lower courts or higher courts in other jurisdictions. These cases may be helpful when rendering decisions, but are not mandatory to consider. Of course, there are exceptions to this principle, but this is a simplified way of looking at case law for purposes of this book.

In this book, I utilize the Bluebook method for legal citations. Every case citation begins with the case name (e.g., "*Roe v. Wade*"), followed by the volume number ("410") of the report ("U.S." for United States Reports) and the page where the case starts ("113"), ending with the year the cases was decided ("1973"). So, this citation would read as *Roe v. Wade*, 410 U.S. 113 (1973). Statutes are cited in a similar manner. The citation begins with the name of the statute, if there is one, followed by the title number and the code, ending with the section number (using the abbreviation §). As an example, the law governing the reporting of child abuse is found in 42 U.S.C. §13031 (title 42 of the United States Code, section 13031). Again, this is a basic way of understanding common legal citations, but this will be sufficient as you proceed through this book.

While ethical standards are often consistent with legal standards, there will be times where the ethical considerations seemingly conflict with the law. It is possible for an action to be legal but not be moral, and one should not assume that one automatically justifies the other. These instances can create strong ethical and legal dilemmas, of which there is no simple solution. Such conflicts and dilemmas validate the need for principles to help steer more clearly through the moral fog. It is to those principles we now turn.

2

Principles of Bioethics

Karen Scullion, seventeen years old, has been admitted for surgery to evaluate a suspicious soft tissue mass for sarcoma. Radical resection of the tissue mass along with extensive skin grafting was performed. While Karen was in the recovery room, the physician informed her parents of the results of the surgery. They were understandably shaken. Both parents insisted that Karen not be told the results until she "gets stronger." The mother informed the physician that Karen's favorite aunt recently died of cancer. Karen became so upset that within a matter of months, she went from being near the top of her class at school to being in danger of failing several subjects. Her parents expressed the fear that, if Karen learns that she has cancer, she will suffer an even more serious breakdown. At first, the physician insisted that Karen must be told the truth, but after considerable pressure from the parents, he agreed to withhold the information from her.

A few days later when the physician was making rounds with Nurse Chan, Karen asked if the surgery went well. The physician assured her that everything was okay and said that she should just focus on her physiotherapy and concentrate on getting home.

Nurse Chan and the other nurses feel that Karen has a right to know the results of the surgery as soon as possible. They are further concerned that without such knowledge, she cannot give informed consent to the extensive post-surgery rehabilitation she requires. When Nurse Chan approached the physician about this, he responded that the parents probably do know their daughter best and said that he wants to wait until the parents "come around."[1]

1. Michael Yeo, *Concepts and Cases in Nursing Ethics*, 2nd ed. (Calgary: Broadview, 1996), 104.

There are a number of moral conflicts in the above case. First there is a conflict between what the nurses think should be done and what the physician has actually done. The nurses think Karen should be told of her condition while the physician thinks we should follow the lead of the parents and leave Karen in the dark. There is also a conflict of principles involved. There is the principle of veracity, or truth-telling, in conflict with the principle of non-maleficence, or not unnecessarily harming Karen. How do we go about resolving these conflicts? What principles should we appeal to? That is what this chapter is all about.[2]

HISTORICAL BACKGROUND

On July 12, 1974, the National Research Act, referred to as Public Law 93-348, was signed into law. The creation of this act was mainly in response to two recent events. The first was the publication of Henry Beecher's landmark article in the July 1966 edition of the *New England Journal of Medicine* titled "Ethics and Clinical Research."[3] Beecher cited a number of examples of ethically questionable research programs in which patients were often ignorant of the risks of procedures they were undergoing. The other event was the recent revelation of The Tuskegee Syphilis study, which was a forty-year ongoing study around the area of Tuskegee, Alabama, on the effects of syphilis with an African American population. The study had raised many ethically questionable practices.[4] The 1974 Research Act created the National Commission for the Protection of Human Subjects of Biomedical and Behavioral Research under the auspices of the Department of Health, Education, and Welfare. In February 1976, the commission met for a conference at the Smithsonian Institute's Belmont Conference Center in Elkhart, Maryland. During a breakout session of the conference, many the commissioners began a discussion regarding the overriding moral principles and ethics that should be considered concerning medical research involving human subjects. Over time, the commission arrived at three general principles: respect for persons, beneficence, and justice. These principles were

2. I am personally indebted to the training I have received under Dr. James F. Childress, PhD, the John Allen Hollingsworth Professor of Ethics at the University of Virginia. Much of the original ideas for this material comes from that training and from his book with Tom Beauchamp, *Principles of Biomedical Ethics* (Oxford: Oxford University Press, 2013).
3. Henry K. Beecher, "Ethics and Clinical Research," *New England Journal of Medicine* 274, no. 24 (1966): 1354–60.
4. We will discuss both these events in chapter 10, "Research Ethics."

connected to specific salient issues in research: respect for persons was linked with informed consent, beneficence with the assessment of risks and benefits, and justice with the selection of research subjects.

Around the same time, two philosophers, Tom Beauchamp (who would later become one of the principal authors of *The Belmont Report*)[5] and James Childress were working on their own book about biomedical ethics. They had identified the relevant principles that would form the framework for their approach to ethical reasoning on issues and problems in medical ethics. Coincidentally their list was strikingly similar to those the commissioners had arrived at: respect for autonomy, beneficence, justice, and a fourth principle, non-maleficence. The first edition of their book, *Principles of Biomedical Ethics,*[6] was published in 1978. The fact that these two works had been so similar, each being published around the same time, and Beauchamp being intimately connected to both has led many to assume a genetic relationship between the two: the *Belmont Report* having been written first and was a summary that is given a fuller treatment in the Beauchamp and Childress. However, while there are similarities, the two works are separate from each other and have no genetic relationship. In fact, there are several conceptual differences between the two, not the least being that the *Belmont Report* is strictly related to research ethics and incorporates only three principles while the Beauchamp and Childress book relates to other medical areas and issues outside of just research, and incorporates four principles.[7]

In 1978, there were few books dealing with the ethical norms, principles, and theories behind bioethics. The small number of books published in bioethics often just dealt with specific issues. So, it is not surprising that Beauchamp and Childress's book caught on and soon became the standard text in bioethics used in colleges and universities throughout the country. The "principlist approach," as it came to be called, became the dominant approach to reasoning in biomedical ethics. Soon, everyone was reciting the "Georgetown Mantra" of autonomy, non-maleficence, beneficence, and justice.

---

5. *The Belmont Report: Ethical Guidelines for the Protection of Human Subjects of Research* (Washington, DC: DHEW, 1978).
6. Tom L. Beauchamp and James F. Childress, *Principles of Biomedical Ethics* (New York: Oxford University Press, 1978).
7. Tom Beauchamp discusses the history of both *The Belmont Report* and the *Principles* book, as well as noting their similarities and differences, in his article, "The Origin, Goals, and Core Commitments of *The Belmont Report* and *Principles of Biomedical Ethics,*" in *The Story of Bioethics,* ed. Jennifer K. Walter and Eran P. Klein (Washington, DC: Georgetown University Press, 2003), 17–46.

Throughout the 1980s and 1990s, a number of other methods and approaches to ethical reflection have been proposed. While the principlist approach may not have the dominance it once had, it is still a significant force in the bioethics field. Beauchamp and Childress's book has gone through several editions and as of this writing is currently in its eighth edition. Beauchamp and Childress insist that, while the foundation for their four principles can be justified by a number of ethical theories, they present only a framework that expresses a common morality shared almost universally by all serious moral thinkers and a method for considering the common conflicts and problems encountered in biomedical ethics.

In this volume, I am going to make use of this basic framework as it is the approach I have been trained in and have found it to be useful and efficient in approaching the questions we will be dealing with. However, as useful as it is as a framework, it is inadequate as a foundation for ethical reflection. As this is a text giving a specifically Christian approach to bioethics, our foundation will come from the basic beliefs at the heart of the Christian worldview. This will be explicated throughout this chapter.

RESPECT FOR AUTONOMY

The term "autonomy" is derived from two Greek terms: *autos*, which means "self," and *nomos*, which means "rule." Thus, the term means "self-ruled." It was originally used in the ancient Greek city-states. Ancient Greece did not have a central federal government like we have in the United States, so each city ruled itself. Hence, they were autonomous. In our modern usage of the term, when we speak of an individual's autonomy, we are referring to their freedom to make choices for themselves apart from the controlling interferences of others. An autonomous choice implies two things: that others are not restricting our choices and that our choices are informed. Adequate and proper information is a necessary ingredient to make a free choice. If one has insufficient or incorrect information, the freedom to choose is limited. Therefore, the obligation to provide adequate and correct information is an important aspect in respecting another's autonomy. The opposite of autonomy is where one's actions or beliefs are either coerced or controlled by the interferences of others, or if they are uninformed.

There are three criteria for determining if an action is autonomous. First, it must be intentional. To say that an action is intentional is simply to say that it is aimed towards a specific goal. If I reach across the table to get a piece of bread and in the process spill the pitcher of milk, the getting of the bread was the intention of my act while the spilling of the milk was not intended; it was an accident. Some results from actions are neither intentional nor accidents but are just byproducts. For example, suppose I pull up to the drive-through ATM and need to access it by pressing certain numbers on a keypad. However, it is raining outside. I realize I will get my arm wet once I stick it out the window. However, my intention is not to get my arm wet, but to use the keypad. While we would not say I got my arm wet "accidently" like it was a mistake, we would also not say it was intentional as it was not my aim in sticking my arm out the window. It would just be called a consequential byproduct of my action, neither intentional nor accidental. Many of our actions have a number of consequences, most of which are just byproducts. All this discussion about intention is important as actions are often evaluated, morally and otherwise, based on intentions. One usually holds persons responsible for their intended actions and not the accidents or byproducts.

The second criterion for an act to be autonomous is the person must understand what he or she is doing. To understand what one is doing means that a belief has been formed about what one intends to accomplish, and one is justified in believing that the intended act will achieve the intended goal. If one lacks a basic understanding of the goal or has no justification for believing that a particular act will attain that goal, then it is suspicious to consider this to be an autonomous action. As stated previously, a lack of understanding information limits one's freedom.

The third criterion for an act to be considered as autonomous is that it must be freely chosen. The essence of autonomy is that one freely chooses one's actions. Freedom is a cherished value in modern democratic states and one does what one can to safeguard individual freedoms as much as possible. Therefore, actions that are coerced or manipulated encroach upon this cherished value and cannot be deemed autonomous.

However, there is a problem concerning these last two criteria. The question must be asked, how much understanding or freedom is necessary to say an act is truly an autonomous one? Does one have to have complete understanding in order to say an act is autonomous? If that is the case, hardly any of our actions could be autonomous. For, apart from God, who has complete understanding of anything? And what about freedom? Is anyone completely free? There are many things that restrict freedoms. Our nature as human beings, our historical condition, and decisions we have made in the past all restrict what we can choose to do now. None of us can sprout wings and fly to Canada and none of us can go back in time and stop the battle of the Alamo.

Ethicists and philosophers acknowledge that rarely is there complete knowledge and rarely is anyone completely free but find that these are not necessary to achieve the goal making an autonomous decision. The objective should be to obtain a substantial amount of understanding and freedom carefully reasoned in light of specific goals. So, one needs to know what the goals are in a specific situation to answer the question of how much understanding and freedom one should have. While this is a fairly general answer, one guideline is that one does not need to have any more understanding or freedom in making autonomous decisions in the medical context than in other contexts in life. For example, suppose you are taking your car in to the shop to have work done on it. The mechanic wants you to sign off on the work he is going to do. How much understanding do you need to say your decision is autonomous? Well, you certainly do not need to go to mechanic school or have read the entire Chilton Auto Repair manual for your specific model of car. However, I would say you are not making an autonomous if you do not know what he is talking about at all.[8] You should know some basics. What specifically is wrong with your car? What will the mechanic need to repair or replace to fix it? How much will it cost? Are there other alternatives? What will happen if you do not choose to have it fixed? Using these questions as a guide, a patient should have the same basic information in choosing a specific medical treatment plan.

Understanding what autonomy is leads to the next question of what it means to respect autonomy. It means at least two things: respecting the person as an autonomous agent and respecting the person's autonomous choices. To respect a person as an autonomous agent is first to recognize his autonomous capacities: the right to form beliefs, make choices, and act on choices and beliefs. As Christians, we recognize that God has given mankind this basic capacity to freely choose what to believe and act on those beliefs. One needs to respect the person for what he is, a person with the capacity to choose. Second, to respect a person as an autonomous agent is to treat him in a manner that allows him to express and exercise those choices. This involves

8. You might still agree to the work and assent to it. But *assent* is not the same as *consent*. Simply to agree to something is not an autonomous choice. See chapter 7 under "Informed Consent" for more discussion.

providing an environment that gives him as much freedom as possible to make the choices he desires and removing obstacles to his choice.

Respecting a person's autonomous choices involves more than recognition. It means at heart that *autonomous actions or choices are not to be subjected to controlling restraints by others.* This is the principle of respect for autonomy. Again, it flows from our understanding of God. He never coerces or restrains any person to choose to follow him but gives each man the freedom to choose his own way of life even if that way is contrary to what God would have him do. God does not always agree with what a person might choose to do, but he does not restrain him from making such a choice. One might not agree with an individual's choice, but respecting autonomy means the removal of any controlling restraints and allowing them to go the way they choose.

Respect for autonomy is a principle of non-interference. This means choosing not to interfere with a person's choice, which entails a *negative right.* Negative rights are rights that individuals have not to be unduly restricted in performing certain activities. Most of the Bill of Rights involve negative rights. The right to free speech, the right to worship, the right of a free press, and the right to assemble and protest are all negative rights: the government is not allowed to unduly restrict one's freedom to choose whether to participate in any of these activities. One might say that respecting autonomy is the basis for all negative rights.

There are many elements concerning respect for autonomy that need explanation. First, this principle, like all the principles we will promote, has *prima facie* standing. As was mentioned in chapter 1, the phrase *prima facie* literally means "at face value." This means that the principle is not an absolute but holds in normal cases unless it conflicts with a stronger obligation. This is significant, for while individual freedom is supported and promoted, there are limits to that freedom. One is not free to perform actions that would encroach, or that might reasonably threaten to encroach, on another's autonomy. One is not free to cause harm to another or place another at significant risk of harm without just cause. This is the reason there are laws that restrict some of these freedoms. One is not free to drive down the highway at whatever speed one chooses as it could cause a reasonable risk of harm to others, and such harm would certainly not respect another's autonomous choice not to be harmed or be placed at reasonable risk of harm. Therefore, there may be times when the state might infringe on someone's autonomous choice and restrict or restrain that choice.

This raises another element: the infringement of one's autonomy must be justified by a competing stronger moral principle. An important distinction needs to be made at this juncture. There is a difference between *violating* a moral principle and *infringing* on a moral principle. One violates a principle when one breaks the principle and has no reasonable justification for doing so. So if I pick up a woman's purse and just start rifling through it without her permission and no justification except that I am just being nosy, I have violated her right to privacy and her autonomy (as she has the freedom to choose who can look through her private things and who cannot). However, if I as an officer of the state believe she may be concealing drugs in her purse and produce evidence before a judge that justifies obtaining a warrant, then I can rifle through her purse without her permission. I would not be guilty of violating her privacy, but I am infringing on her right to privacy, yet I am justified in doing so. If infringement of one's autonomy is justified, it can only be done if a competing moral principle has come into play that is stronger in the situation. Taking the speeding example above, the state is justified in infringing on one's autonomous choice to drive at any speed because of a competing moral principle, the protection against harm or unreasonable risk of harm to other citizens.[9]

A third element is that the principle itself cannot determine when infringement is justified. One needs to examine the complete context of the particular situation to determine if one is justified at this time to infringe on autonomy or not. As stated above, all principles are *prima facie*. They all hold in normal situations. However, at times, these principles come into conflict with one another. None of them *always* trumps the other. The context of the situation plays a significant role in determining which principle should dominate in that situation. This is where much of the debate in biomedical ethics resides.

A fourth element of the principle of respect for autonomy is that it asserts both a right and a correlative obligation. The relationship between rights and obligations is not always easy to decipher. However, it is the case that sometimes if an individual has a right to something, then someone somewhere has an obligation concerning it. For example, the Bill of Rights stipulates that all citizens have the right to free speech. This right gives one the legal right to speak his mind and say what he wishes to say.[10] Such a right carries with

9. This is the principle of non-maleficence, which we will cover next.
10. Again, this is not without limits. If one's free speech might encroach on another's rights or freedom or if it might cause harm or significant risk of harm to another, the right to free speech can be infringed. This is where we get the well-known aphorism, "Freedom of speech does not give one the liberty to yell fire (without reason) in a crowded theater." The resulting panic would cause serious risk of harm to the other patrons.

it the correlative obligation of the State not to restrict one's speech unless it has a compelling justification to do so. It is debatable whether all rights have correlative obligations, but many seem to and one can often analyze a specific moral situation either from the side of obligations or from the side of rights.

A fifth element of the principle of respect for autonomy is the recognition that while is it is basically a negative principle, it often entails some positive obligations.[11] One can fulfill most negative principles just by doing nothing as they are principles of non-interference. However, respecting autonomy may require one to perform some positive action: to disclose appropriate information so the individual can make an autonomous choice, to ensure understanding on the part of the autonomous individual, and to establish an environment where voluntariness is promoted for the autonomous individual. These are positive actions that foster adequate and autonomous decision-making.

The sixth element of respect for autonomy is that for those in a fiduciary relationship, the obligation to respect autonomy is very strong. In ethics, a fiduciary relationship is one in which a weaker party places trust in a stronger party. While this can be any sort of weakness or strength, it usually entails a relationship where one party has more information than another party and the second party needs to trust the first party because they know more. The relationship between a physician and a patient is a prime example, as is the relationship between a teacher and a student. In both examples, the former party is in possession of greater knowledge than the second party. Therefore, the patient or student must trust and depend on the doctor or teacher to provide him with the necessary information needed to make an autonomous decision. Hence, the obligation on the doctor or teacher is very strong and all effort should be taken to maintain that trust and fulfill that obligation. For information is power and power can be a corrupting influence. Those who stand in fiduciary relationships must work hard to maintain respect for the autonomy of those who put their trust in them.

Finally, the principle of respect for autonomy does not apply to those who are substantially non-autonomous. Autonomy entails that one has the immediate capacity to act as a decision-maker.[12] This means one is capable of forming beliefs and judgments and is capable of communicating those beliefs and

---

11. A negative obligation is fulfilled by not doing something, and a positive obligation is fulfilled by doing something.
12. I discuss immediate and inherent capacities in the next chapter on abortion when we discuss personhood. For now, an immediate capacity is simply an ability that one can currently exercise.

judgments and acting on them. This would describe most adult individuals. However, there are some individuals who currently lack these abilities either due to lack of development or damage that inhibits accessing these abilities: infants, young children, those who are mentally handicapped, or those who are temporarily incapacitated, such as those who are inebriated, unconscious, or comatose. Such individuals are substantially non-autonomous and so decisions concerning their care often must be made by a proxy.[13] Often the principles of non-maleficence and beneficence will play a stronger role in such decision-making.

Before leaving the principle of respect for autonomy, it is important to take a moment and consider a sub-principle that is entailed by respect for autonomy, the principle of veracity. The term "veracity" is derived from the Latin term *veritas,* which means "truth." The principle of veracity is the obligation to communicate the truth and not to lie or deceive others. It is a basic principle of society and has its basis in the principle of respect for autonomy. As has been made clear, autonomy requires adequate and proper information. With the necessary information, one may not know all the options concerning one's choice and the freedom to choose is thereby restricted. Deception in the form of lying, pretense, or withholding necessary information is a form of control over another's choices and thus is a violation of the principle of respect for autonomy. The principle of veracity also derives from the often-assumed obligations of fidelity and promise-keeping people have with one another. On a consequential level, deception erodes trust, and relationships of trust are necessary for fruitful interaction and cooperation, especially within the health-care worker/patient relationship. Therefore, veracity is a *prima facie* principle whose foundation is found in the respect for autonomy.[14]

Does the Bible say anything in support of the principle of respect for autonomy? Not directly. However, the idea that human beings have free will and that free will should be respected and honored is a consistent biblical theme. Even when human beings choose to do evil, God still honors and respects their free choice though he certainly regrets it and desires that they choose to follow him. In the book of Deuteronomy, we read:

> Surely, this commandment that I am commanding you today is not too hard for you, nor is it too far away. . . . See, I have set before you today life and prosperity,

13. We will discuss this more under the topic of informed consent in chapter 7.
14. We will deal more with the issue of deception in chapter 7.

> death and adversity. If you obey the commandments of the Lord your God that I am commanding you today, by loving the Lord your God, walking in his ways, and observing his commandments, decrees, and ordinances, then you shall live and become numerous, and the Lord your God will bless you in the land that you are entering to possess. But if your heart turns away and you do not hear, but are led astray to bow down to other gods and serve them, I declare to you today that you shall perish. . . . I have set before you life and death, blessings and curses. Choose life so that you and your descendants may live. (Deut. 30:11–19)

If God honors and respects the freedom of human beings to choose, we should also.

THE PRINCIPLE OF NON-MALEFICENCE

My favorite Disney villain is Maleficent from 1959's *Sleeping Beauty*. I don't think Disney ever imagined a more evil and corrupt individual.[15] All she wanted to do was to cause harm to everyone around her. The King and Queen, Princess Aurora, Prince Phillip, and the three fairies, Flora, Fauna, and Merryweather, all suffered under her influence. Her desire to harm is understood given her name, for the term "maleficence" means "to cause harm, evil." The principle of non-maleficence is the obligation to avoid harming or injuring others either intentionally or through negligence. It is, by far, the most universally recognized moral principle and almost all serious moral thinkers agree that we have a duty not to unjustly harm others. Concerning medical treatment, it is expressed in the classic phrase *primum non nocere:* "above all, do no harm." Hippocrates of Cos (460–370 BC), considered the father of Western medicine, wrote seventy treatises and in one of the early ones, *Epidemics I*, he wrote one of the earliest ethical statements about medicine of which physicians "have two special objects in view with regard to disease, namely, to do good or to do no harm."[16]

Hippocrates's statement raises the question, which of the two is a stronger obligation, helping or not harming? Most ethicists agree that the stronger obligation is to not harm. One reason is that not harming is a negative obligation, like respect for autonomy. In general, one can fulfill this obligation by

15. I have in mind the Maleficent of the animated motion picture, who was truly evil, and not the more recent live action film, *Maleficent* (2014), who was just "misunderstood."
16. Hippocrates, *Epidemics* 1.2.4, trans. Francis Adams (London: Easton, 1849).

doing nothing. One must usually go out of one's way to intentionally cause harm. Also, the duty to do no harm is more universal in its application than the duty to help. Everyone should avoid harming others, but not everyone has an obligation to help.[17] Therefore, of the two obligations, not causing harm is the stronger obligation to keep.

There are three aspects in which this principle will come to play in the medical context. First is the general aspect, wherein everyone recognizes the overriding moral requirement that medical practitioners strive to serve the well-being of their patients and that this involves not harming them or placing them at risk in situations in which they could be harmed. The good of medicine is in its aims and goals which are to treat and cure disease and suffering, to make patients feel better and live more satisfying lives. Causing harm seems to be the exact opposite of everything medicine is about. This seems so obvious as to not even need to be stated. However, the problem is that health-care workers often find themselves in a conflict in which the only way to achieve the ultimate goal of good health is to cause a certain amount of harm. It would be incorrect to state that medical practitioners never cause harm. They do so on a regular basis. In order to save lives and restore health, they often have to remove organs, amputate limbs, inject harmful drugs in chemotherapy, bombard the body with radiation, and undertake a host of other activities necessary to fulfill their primary obligation of treatment.

When such procedures are necessary, there is a second aspect of the principle of non-maleficence to consider, the weighing aspect. Medical intervention often involves trade-offs of certain risks or harms for benefits. Therefore, one needs to go through a process of weighing specific risks or harms in light of the particular benefits one might achieve. Two kinds of assessments are necessary. A risk/benefits assessment evaluates the risk of harm compared to the possible benefit of a particular medical procedure. In performing a procedure, the physician may realize from training and experience that there might be byproduct results that are unfavorable. The likelihood, quality, and magnitude of these byproducts need to be appraised and a determination made whether to continue with the procedure. For example, if surgery is to be performed on someone's ear but there is a risk of a certain amount of deafness, the physician and patient will need to weigh the likelihood of the deafness, its magnitude, the quality of life should it occur in light of the likelihood and quality of the intended benefit the patient will experience from

17. We will discuss the obligation to help under the principle of beneficence.

the surgery. If it is determined the risk is too great, the patient may decide to forgo the procedure.

A harms/benefit assessment (also called a cost/benefit assessment) is necessary to assess the known harms compared to the possible benefit of a particular medical procedure. In many cases, physicians and patients are aware that in order to perform a particular procedure, certain unintended but foreknown harms will occur. If a patient has a severe case of endometriosis, it may warrant a hysterectomy in which she will lose her ability to have children. This is a known harm that might be necessary to avoid more serious harms, including death. Physicians and patients together must make the assessment to determine if the benefit of a known harm outweighs the harm itself. In one sense, almost all medical procedures are going to cause some harm or cost, even if just financial or minimal. In most cases, such as the discomfort of receiving an injection, we consider the cost/harm to be justified in light of the potential benefit. However, it is not uncommon for patients to reject a procedure that might be beneficial, but the cost or harm is considered too burdensome. For example, many advanced cancer patients might reject further chemotherapy or radiation treatments if the discomfort is deemed too great and the potential for benefit minimal.

It is important that both types of assessments be performed by trained and experienced professionals and the information should be as accurate and precise as possible so that patients can make an appropriate informed decision. While complete certainty is rarely attainable in making these assessments, all effort should be made to avoid allowing bias to affect one's results and undue pressure should not be placed on patients to make a specific decision.

A third aspect of the principle of non-maleficence is the specific aspect. This is the heart of the principle when it comes to medical treatment and we refer to is as maintaining standard due care. Standard due care is a moral and legal obligation to act in a careful and professionally reasonable manner in cases where one needs to impose risks on others. Due care involves at least three elements: the professional is trained in the specific procedure being applied in this situation, the professional has a demonstrable skill in performing the procedure, and the professional is acting in a diligent and careful manner when performing the procedure.

In general, standard due care is met when first, the goals sought are weighty enough to warrant the imposition of certain risks or harms on others. This means one's assessment has been properly performed. However, once the assessment is done and it is determined that the goals outweigh the risks or harms, then the second requirement of standard due care comes into play: due care is taken to keep these risks and harms at a minimum level. So, the first aspect is concerned with deciding to perform the procedure and the second is in the actual performance itself.

There have been cases in which this standard has not been met. While some cases were intended violations of maintaining standard due care, most cases were not intended. This is known as negligence, which is defined as the unintended failure to maintain standard due care by failing to guard against risks of harm to others. Negligence usually occurs due to a lack of one or more of the three elements mentioned above necessary for maintaining standard due care. The professional performing the procedure is either not trained, lacks the skill, or is not being diligent in their performance. Charges of negligence can lead to further charges of malpractice and may involve civil or even criminal proceedings.[18] It is important to note that one cannot charge a medical professional with negligence simply because a harm was done. If the assessment discovered a risk or harm and the patient was informed of the risk or harm and consented to the procedure, the patient cannot charge a professional who acted in accordance with the elements outlined above with negligence just because the harm came to fruition.

What does it mean to "harm" an individual? Broadly, harm can be defined as the obstructing, defeating, or hindering of the interests of one party by the invasive actions of another party. This would include the infringement or violation of any autonomous area. Harm goes beyond physical pain to include any occasion where one's interests are obstructed or hindered. Harms come in degrees of magnitude and may be physical or non-physical. Some harms can be minor, such as unintentionally causing offense, to serious, including taking life. The continuum is wide ranging. What determines a harm as minor or major is often dependent on the context and the perception of the individuals involved, though there are extremes where almost all serious moral thinkers find agreement. Harms can also be intentional or unintentional. Just because a harm was not intended does not mean it did not occur nor that one may not be culpable for it. If one accidentally backs into another car, a harm has occurred and the driver is culpable even though he did not intend it. While intention may play a significant role in tempering one's judgment of blame for

18. Malpractice is regarded as broader than negligence and can include intentional as well as non-intentional harm. Also, malpractice must result in an injury to a patient, whereas negligence can occur if no actual harm was done, but merely a genuine risk of harm was present.

a harm (we tend to be more sympathetic and understanding towards those whose actions cause unintended harms), it does not erase all responsibility for harm. This is the often the case in negligence.

An important distinction must be made between harm and hurt. While these terms are often used synonymously, many ethicists draw a distinction between them. Harm is the actual and real obstruction or defeating of an individual's interests; hurt is an awareness of harm, such as pain and suffering (whether physical or psychological). Under this distinction, it is possible to harm someone without hurting them. One can be harmed and never be aware of it. For example, a person may go behind an individual's back and say something that might obstruct some benefit for the person. If Marty is up for a promotion at work and Janet tells the boss some negative information about Marty so he does not get the promotion, Janet has harmed Marty as she has obstructed an interest Marty has to be promoted. Marty may never even know he was up for a promotion or that Janet destroyed his opportunity, but he was still harmed by Janet's action. So, while it is true that what you may not know may not hurt you, what you may not know can still harm you. The principle of non-maleficence is "do not harm," not "do not hurt." Awareness of harm has little to do with keeping the principle.

Finally, like all principles, the principle of non-maleficence has *prima facie* standing. Not all invasions of another's interests are wrong. At times, infringing on another's interests might be necessary. This was observed during the discussion of the weighing aspect of the principle. Sometimes, one must infringe on the principle in order to obtain a greater good, as in amputation to save a life. Whenever it is necessary to infringe on the principle, it must only be done so when another moral principle has greater weight, whether it be respect for autonomy, beneficence, or justice. Such times need to be considered in the context of a situation.

Raising the question of necessary harms in order to achieve good introduces us to a well-known tradition in ethics appealed to by many called the *principle of double effect*. The principle of double effect is the idea that there exists a morally relevant difference between the intended effects of a person's action and the non-intended, though possibly foreseen, effects of the action. Many actions have more than one effect. Some effects are beneficial, and some are harmful. Under double effect, the beneficial effect is direct and intended while the harmful effect is indirect and unintended, though perhaps a foreseen and unfortunate side effect. By "indirect," this means it is not intended as a means to an end nor as an end in itself, a very important point in applying this principle. Because there is a moral distinction between these effects, one is not held morally blameworthy of an unintended, even if foreseen, harmful effect.

A common example of double effect is the removal of an unborn child due to an ectopic pregnancy (a pregnancy where the child has attached itself outside of the uterus). One can foresee that removing the child will result in its death as it is not capable of living on its own outside of the special environment of the mother's body. However, if left to develop, the child will most certainly do significant damage to the mother, possibly even causing her death. Double effect is a way to allow the mother's life to be saved and not be held morally culpable for the death of the child. If the intention is to remove the child to save the mother's life, and this is the only way to save the mother's life, then double effect allows the action to take place and the physician would not be held morally culpable for the death of the child even if it is foreseen that removing the child will result in the child's death. The key points are that the *death* of the child was not intended, just its *removal,* and the death of the child is not the means by which we are saving the life of the mother, its *removal* is. If there was a way to remove the child and maintain its life, morally we would be obligated to do so. Currently, there is no way to maintain a child this early in the pregnancy when it is just a few weeks old. In the end it is better to save one life than to have two lives perish.

Double effect cannot be applied in just any situation where we want to achieve some good that might involve adverse effects. Some have tried to apply double effects to other situations such as giving a patient an overdose of morphine to end her suffering knowing that the overdose will also kill her. The problem here is that often the intention is the death of the patient as a means of ending her suffering. Even if death was not intended, the death of the patient is still how her suffering has been ended. Double effect cannot be appealed to as justification for such an action. For double effect to be applied as a means of justification the following criteria must be in place:

- The intended action itself must not be intrinsically wrong.
- The agent must intend only the good effect and not the bad effect (the bad effect may be foreseen and even tolerated, just not intended).
- The bad effect must not be a means to the end of bringing about the good effect.
- The good that results must outweigh the evil permitted.

Not everyone agrees that double effect draws a legitimate distinction between intended results or actions and results that are foreseen and unintended. Many think that proponents are just drawing semantics and that if one is aware of the bad results, one is therefore responsible for them. However, there is a long tradition within Christian ethics to hold that intention does often matter when it comes to moral culpability. If one is intending a good effect, and a bad side effect might result (assuming the other criteria hold, especially if the bad effect is not intended), then it seems double effect might be a legitimate means to resolve a difficult issue.

The principle of non-maleficence is so universally regarded as valid and justifiable that it seems almost absurd to question its biblical basis. Believers are often exhorted to avoid harming others. In his letter to the Romans, Paul urges, "Do not repay anyone evil for evil. Be careful to do what is right in the eyes of everyone. If it is possible, as far as it depends on you, live at peace with everyone" (Rom. 12:17). In his letter to the Ephesians, he encourages Christians to "Let all bitterness, wrath, anger, quarreling, and slander be put away from you, along with all hatred. And be kind to one another, compassionate, forgiving one another just as God has forgiven you in the Messiah" (Eph. 4:31–32). And in his letter to Titus, Paul exhorts followers of Jesus "to slander no one, to avoid fighting, and to be kind, always showing gentleness to all people" (Titus 3:2).

THE PRINCIPLE OF BENEFICENCE

The term "benevolence" derives from the Latin *bene,* which means "well," and *volence,* which means to "wish" or "desire." Thus, the term means "to desire the well-being of another" which is a good start for understanding the principle of beneficence: *The obligation to help others further their important and legitimate interests.* Beneficence is a positive obligation. In holding this principle, it is not just enough to ensure that one performs actions that do not harm others or place them at risk of harm, but there is also a further obligation to contribute positively to others' welfare. Because it is a positive principle, beneficence demands more than non-maleficence. It places an additional obligation on someone besides simply not doing something. To fulfill this obligation, one must affirmatively act in some way.

Unlike the first two principles, the principle of beneficence is more controversial and some question whether one actually has an obligation to help. The problem arises when one considers the scope of this obligation. Exactly how far does the obligation to help others extend? Certainly, it does not mean I am obligated to help everyone, for that does not even seem possible. It also seems unlikely to mean that I am to help everyone who I know needs help, for again that would entail all sorts of unreasonable scenarios. Am I really obligated to help every individual who approaches me for help? I would soon be drained of all my resources, unable to help even myself. Obviously, a line must be drawn. The question is where does one draw the line between the obligation to help and the ideal of helping.

To answer this question, it would be useful if a distinction is made between two types of obligations: general beneficence and specific beneficence. General beneficence is the obligation placed upon someone as a person to help other persons in general. This is often referred to as the obligation to help the stranger. Special beneficence is the obligation to help others due to a special relationship which grounds the obligation. Each of these will be addressed separately.

Does one have an obligation to help in general, i.e., the stranger? It is important to note that the question concerns the *obligation* to help. Most everyone agrees that it would be nice if one helped a stranger, but would it be wrong if one did not help? Would one be morally culpable of a wrongdoing? For example, a person whom you do not know approaches you on the street and asks for help. Are you *obligated* to help him? Some argue there is no obligation to help, though it may be an ideal. They reason, "Where do we draw the line if it's an obligation? Since we cannot reasonably draw a line it is best just to say there is no obligation to help the stranger." For most of us, this seems extreme. For Christians, it seems to defy what Jesus taught in the parable of the Good Samaritan (Luke 10:25–37). Jesus praised the Samaritan who showed mercy on a man in need saying we should "Go and do likewise" (Luke 10:37).

Most serious moral thinkers believe that there exists some form of general beneficence where one is obligated to help the stranger in need. However, one has to answer the question of where do we draw the line in which we step beyond the threshold of obligation and move into the morally ideal or supererogatory action.[19] Serious moral thinkers often suggest that a threshold for general obligations of beneficence is the interruption of one's life plans: a genuine threat or sacrifice to one's own life, liberty, or basic pursuits. Ethicist Michael Slote comments, "One has an obligation to prevent serious evil or harm when one can do so without seriously interfering with one's life plan's

19. See below for an explanation of supererogatory actions.

or style and without doing any wrongs of commission."[20] This is general, so Beauchamp and Childress offer some guidelines to help in determining if this threshold has been exceeded:[21]

> We propose that a person X has a *prima facie* obligation of beneficence, in the form of a duty . . . toward person Y if and only if each of the following conditions is satisfied (assuming X is aware of the relevant facts):
>
> 1. Y is at risk of significant loss of or damage to life, health, or some other basic interest.
> 2. X's action is necessary (singly or in concert with others) to prevent this loss or damage.
> 3. X's action (singly or in concert with others) will probably prevent this loss or damage.
> 4. X's action would not present significant risks, costs, or burdens to X.
> 5. The benefit that Y can be expected to gain outweighs any harms, costs, or burdens that X is likely to incur.[22]

Using such guidelines helps to delineate where one is obligated to help the stranger and where one is not obligated (though one might help anyway). If a stranger is canvassing the neighborhood in search of donations for the local school band to take a trip to London, one might donate, but one would not be obligated to do so. None of the conditions suggested above has been met. However, if one is driving down an empty road on vacation and is the first to come upon a serious car accident, then one would likely be obligated to help (assuming conditions 4 and 5 are met). The application of the conditions needs to be carefully assessed in specific situations to evaluate one's obligation.

Special beneficence is qualitatively different than general beneficence. It is the obligation to help others due to a special relationship that grounds the obligation. The obligation is not always explicit in the relationship, but a compelling case can be made for an implicit obligation based on the nature of the relationship. In general, there are three kinds of relationships that imply a certain amount of obligation to help: personal, contractual, and role-specific.

---

20. See Michael A. Slote, "The Morality of Wealth," in *World Hunger and Moral Obligation*, ed. W. Aiken and H. LaFollette (Englewood Cliffs, NJ: Prentice-Hall, 1977).
21. Beauchamp and Childress list these under the duty of rescuing another. I suggest they can be applied more broadly to a host of situations.
22. Tom L. Beauchamp and James F. Childress, *Principles of Biomedical Ethics*, 7th ed. (New York: Oxford University Press, 2013), 206–7.

Personal relationships are among the most intimate and most important relationships one has. These include family and friends. These can be analyzed further by noting that within these two groups, one can have closer and less close relationships that correlate with the obligation to help. Most would recognize that the strongest obligations are to one's children, especially when they are young and vulnerable. These are referred to as filial obligations. Parents are morally and legally obligated to care for children and see that their physical, psychological, and emotional needs are met. They are expected to keep them from danger and raise them in a way so that, as they become older, they can care for themselves. Next come other members of the family such as spouses, elderly parents, and siblings where it can be argued one has an implicit moral obligation to help if one can, based on a family bond, though not necessarily a legal obligation.[23] The next level of obligations would be friends who can be grouped by close friends, acquaintances, and colleagues. The less the commitment in the relationship, the less the obligation is to help.

Contractual obligations to help are based on explicit or implicit obligations grounded in a contractual relationship between two parties. An example is the teacher/student relationship. As a teacher, I am expected to be available to my students should they need help in understanding the material in my course. Such an obligation involves such things as communicating accurate information, helping to clarify information, and helping students to see the application of information to various areas within the subject the course is covering. Another example would be a health-care worker and the patients under her charge. She has an obligation to see to their medical care and physical needs while under her care. Such an obligation involves the duty to disclose relevant and necessary information, to help in fostering understanding of information, to safeguard the patient's privacy and confidentiality, and to provide the medicines and treatment agreed upon by physician and patient. These contractual obligations may be explicitly stated, but often they are implicit in the relationship. This can cause problems and conflicts and communication might be necessary to state the range and limits of such obligations so that all are on the same page.

23. In the famous case of *McFall v. Shimp*, Robert McFall attempted to legally compel his cousin David Shimp to donate bone marrow for a necessary transplant that could save McFall's life. The Pennsylvania district court ruled that you cannot legally compel someone to help, however the judge morally condemned Shimp's denial to help his cousin as "morally indefensible." 10 Pa. D. & C. 3d 90 (July 26, 1978).

Role-specific obligations are those in which the nature of certain roles places an obligation to provide help beyond the contractual relationship. Professionals like doctors, nurses, police officers, and firemen are examples of those who fall into this category. Because of the skill and training they have received they are obligated to render assistance even when they are not on duty or under a contract with a specific individual. Most of us have heard the phrase "Is there a doctor in the house?" This reflects the role-specific obligation we expect from doctors. If an individual is in an emergency situation in which his life or basic health is in imminent danger, a doctor is obligated to step in and help even if the person is not her patient or there is no contractual relationship. In the same way, if a police officer is aware of a crime or a citizen in need of help, he is obligated to provide assistance, protection, or prevention even if he is not on duty. This obligation is unique to certain roles in society. An accountant is not obligated to render aid to someone on the street panicking about meeting payroll next week. A philosopher is not obligated to help a stranger who is suffering from an existential crisis and desires to know the meaning of the universe. This does not mean he might not help, simply that he is not obligated to do so.

There is a final category of beneficence that warrants mentioning. Supererogatory actions are optional but morally praiseworthy actions performed for the benefit of others above and beyond the call of duty. Up to this point, this has been a discussion regarding the obligation to help those in need. Supererogatory actions are those which one is not obligated to perform but might do anyway. They are neither forbidden nor required and are undertaken for others beyond the obligatory. Often, these can be heroic and extraordinary actions, such as when someone might risk his life to help a stranger. According to the conditions outlined above, no one is obligated to run into a burning building to help a stranger.[24] This would be a supererogatory action. However, supererogatory actions do not need to be especially heroic or extraordinary. Any time one performs a beneficent action for another that one is not obligated to perform, it would be considered supererogatory.

Supererogatory actions are the hallmark of the Christian life and are the kinds of actions Christians should be known for. While it would be contradictory to say Christians are obligated to perform supererogatory actions (by nature they are not obligations), one could say that the Christian who only

24. Apart from a role-specific, contractual, or special obligation.

does what they are obligated to do and never goes above and beyond the call of duty is living a life that is far below what Jesus desires:

> But I say to you who hear, love your enemies, do good to those who hate you, bless those who curse you, pray for those who mistreat you. Whoever hits you on the cheek, offer him the other also; and whoever takes away your coat, do not withhold your shirt from him either. Give to everyone who asks of you, and whoever takes away what is yours, do not demand it back. Treat others the same way you want them to treat you. If you love those who love you, what credit is that to you? For even sinners love those who love them. If you do good to those who do good to you, what credit is that to you? For even sinners do the same. If you lend to those from whom you expect to receive, what credit is that to you? Even sinners lend to sinners in order to receive back the same amount. But love your enemies, and do good, and lend, expecting nothing in return; and your reward will be great, and you will be sons of the Most High; for He Himself is kind to ungrateful and evil men. (Luke 6:27–35 canvassing)

PRINCIPLE OF JUSTICE

The term "justice" is derived from the Latin *jus,* which means "right." The concept of justice is the maintenance of what is just (right) by the impartial judgment of conflicting claims and the assignment of merited rewards and punishments. The idea of justice involves three elements: fairness, just deserts, and entitlements. Fairness refers to equal treatment. Next to personal liberty, equal treatment is perhaps the most cherished ideal of the modern liberal democracy. The founding document of the United States, the Declaration of Independence, states "all men are created equal."[25] Taken literally, this is not true. Many persons are born in far better or worse situations than others. Many are born with superior natural gifts and talents than others. Some are born with genetic traits and physical handicaps that make life much more difficult. Some are born into wealthy families, in which they have all the resources they need to succeed in life, while others are born in poverty, making success in life extremely challenging. The point is that all men are *not* created equal. However, that phrase in the Declaration of Independence was not meant to be taken literally but was meant to express the ideal of equal treatment. All

25. The concept here is mankind, including women, though for many years, women were not given the same equal rights as men in many situations.

persons should be treated as fundamentally equal human beings when it comes to justice regardless of the accidents of birth and regardless of race, creed, color, or any other personal belief. That is why the definition of justice includes the idea of "impartial judgment." To be partial is to favor one party over another. A foundational element of justice is that no partiality be given to any person when it comes to questions of basic justice. The philosopher John Rawls once described justice as the "original position" where one is standing behind a veil of ignorance concerning ours and any other person's abilities and interests and making decisions of basic justice from that position.[26]

The second element of justice is just deserts, which is the obligation to recompense people what they fittingly deserve, both reward and punishment. When speaking of what persons deserve, it is referring to what they have earned by their actions. Certainly, the idea of employment immediately comes to mind. If an agreement is reached between two parties concerning a financial compensation based on hours worked or on the product produced, assuming the terms of the agreement are met, justice requires that the employee receives his just deserts, the agreed upon compensation. However, the concept of earning is broader than just employment. One can earn other benefits and punishments. For example, students earn grades for classes based on the quality of papers, quizzes, and exams. Criminals found guilty by the state earn fines and prison time based on the level of their crimes. A parent may agree to allow a child to attend an event if she does her chores around the house. In that case, she earned the privilege of attending the event. Deserts and punishments are justly administered when they are merited according to the agreed contract, whether explicit or implicit.

Unlike just deserts, entitlements are not earned. Entitlements are the obligation of giving a person her due in accordance with what she has a right to receive. A right is a justified claim that individuals or groups can make upon others or upon society. Whereas a just desert is based on fulfilling terms of an agreement, rights are based on one's status under the authority that grants the right. Rights can be divided into three types: legal, moral, and conventional. Legal rights are claims that are justified by legal principles or rules formulated by a legislative individual or legislative group and are usually found in documents produced by that person or group. The Constitution of the United

26. There is a lot more to Rawls's idea of the "original position" than I am referring to here, some of which I would not be in concert with, but his concept of the "veil of ignorance" is a good picture of fairness. See John Rawls, *A Theory of Justice* (Cambridge, MA: Harvard University Press, 1971), 118.

States is an example of the authority that grants rights to citizens. Moral rights are justified claims that are validated by moral principles and rules based on some moral theory such as utilitarianism or deontology.[27] Christians believe that God grants everyone certain moral rights such as the right to life and the right to be treated by others as an image of God-bearer. Conventional rights are claims justified by rules and principles adopted within certain conventional relationships. For example, in football, the team that wins the toss of the coin has the right to choose whether to kick or receive. An entitlement is something that one has a right to have regardless of what they done or earned. According to the U.S. Constitution, an individual has a right to a trial and to have counsel available to him even if he admits his guilt to the crime. One does not *earn* the right to a trial; one is *entitled* to it.

An injustice occurs when someone has been denied an entitlement, has not received their just deserts, or has been treated unfairly. In determining whether a moral injustice has occurred, there needs to be a basis or standard for doing so. This is called the *morally relevant property*. What property (characteristic, distinction, attribute) does one need to possess to say they are deserving of a reward, entitlement, or to be treated fairly? This will vary according to the particular situation or issue in which a determination of justice is playing a part. Some examples may help to understand this concept. My neighbor owns a yacht; I do not. Is that unfair? What is the morally relevant property? In this case it is money: he has more money than I have, so he can own the yacht and I cannot.[28] Lindsay received a higher grade on the test than Steven. Is that fair? What is the morally relevant property? It is understanding the material. Lindsay understands the material better than Steven, so it is perfectly fair that Lindsay gets the higher grade. Kelly's grandmother receives social security payments while Kelly does not. Is that fair? What is the morally relevant property? In this case, it is age. Kelly's grandmother is entitled to social security payments because she is over sixty-five while Kelly is not. In analyzing whether an injustice has occurred, a good starting point is to determine what the morally relevant property is and then to investigate to see if the justice has been distributed properly in accordance with that property.

This leads to a discussion of a particular area of justice known as distributive justice. Distributive justice aims to establish a connection between the properties

27. See chapter 1 for a discussion of these moral theories.
28. We will not, at this time, get into a discussion of whether it is fair for my neighbor to have more money than me, though that is also a question of justice.

of persons and the morally appropriate distribution of goods and services, or benefits and burdens, in society. This is an attempt to answer the question, "What morally relevant properties, if any, give one person or group of persons more of an entitlement to certain benefits or opportunities than others?" This question needs to be addressed for a couple of reasons. First, how does one determine which morally relevant property is the appropriate one? A story might help to see the significance of the question. One afternoon a few years ago, I was sitting in my office when a student came by to see me. She was upset over the grade she received on a recent exam. Her opening comment to me was "I think your tests are unfair." When I asked why she thought that, she said, "I studied for several hours for the last test and ended up with a D. But my roommate, who took the same test, studied for less than an hour and ended up with an A. That is not fair. I studied longer and worked harder than she did. She hardly did anything. I should get the higher grade." There were many things we needed to discuss, but part of her problem was a need to clarify the term "fair." This was a question of determining the morally relevant property for a fair grade.

I explained to her that she was using a quantitative concept of fairness. Under this concept, the quantity of time or effort one puts into a task was the morally relevant property. Those who expend more time and effort should get more than those who expend less time and effort. This is certainly a legitimate relevant property for fairness in some situations. We often pay wages on this basis: those who work more hours get paid more than those who work fewer hours. I explained, however, that this is not the only way to think of "fair." Another concept of fairness is the qualitative concept. Under this concept, it is the quality of understanding the material that is the morally relevant property. Those who have a good understanding of the material receive a higher reward than those who do not understand it as well. This is also a legitimate concept of fairness in some situations.

Which of these two concepts is appropriate in this situation? I explained to the student that the qualitative concept is appropriate for awarding grades. The primary purpose of education is to achieve a good understanding of content or to gain the ability to employ a skill. Students are awarded superior grades based on the quality of their understanding. While I commended her on the amount of time and effort she put into studying, time and effort alone are not enough to receive a high grade. We then went on to discuss ways she could better understand the material and achieve a higher grade on the next test. The point is that often, the question of justice is dependent upon identifying the correct morally relevant property in a given situation.

There is another reason needed to address the question of the appropriate morally relevant property in the distribution of goods and services. It involves the scarcity question. In many cases the resources available to us as a society are limited, and there is a competition for them. In 1961, Dr. Belding Scribner, inventor of the Scribner shunt, a device that makes regular kidney dialysis available, opened a clinic in Seattle, Washington. He had only six dialysis machines available and demand soon exceeded capacity. A system had to be put in place to decide who would have access to the machines and who would not, literally a life and death decision. He formed a committee to help decide who would justly have access. The first duty of the committee was to determine what morally relevant properties were going to determine an equitable, fair, and just distribution of the use of the dialysis machines. After consideration of age and general health, the committee went on to include considering such factors as sex, marital status, number of dependents, income, emotional stability, educational background, occupation, future potential, and references. In short, the committee relied heavily on the morally irrelevant properties of social worth and economic status, reflecting their own values and biases. The problem of scarce resources still plagues medicine today and principles are needed to provide just and fair guidance in making such decisions.

Aristotle is often appealed to as the philosopher who established the formal principle of distributive justice: "Equals must be treated equally and unequals must be treated unequally."[29] This means that, whatever the relevant moral property is, those who are equal with regards to it should be treated equally and those who are not should be treated as unequals. It would be unjust to treat an equal as an unequal or vice versa. For example, suppose I promise to award every student who gets a B or above on the next test with an ice cream cone. I would be acting unjustly if I refused an ice cream cone to any student with a B or above, but I would not be unjust by refusing one to the student with a C. That student did not have the morally relevant property. They might not care for my original agreement, but they cannot say I am acting unfairly. In the same sense, I would be unjust if I rewarded a student with an ice cream cone who did not have the morally relevant property. If a student got a D, but then I gave them an ice cream cone that would not be fair to those who worked hard to earn the ice cream cone. It might be kind, but it would not be just.

29. Aristotle, *Nichomachean Ethics* 5.3.

Of course, some might argue that the whole system of rewarding ice cream cones for grades is unfair. That raises an important flaw with Aristotle's formal principle of justice. While it is appropriate as a formal principle, it does not solve the practical problem of what the morally relevant property should be in each situation. To answer that problem, there must be material principles. These are referred to as "material" principles because they add material content to the formal principle. Material principles of justice specify relevant properties in specific situations under which fair distribution can be attained. The key issue is determining which of these properties are relevant to fairness and which are not. This must be decided contextually. There are a number of material principles, all of which are appropriate at one time or another. Here are several of the more common principles for distribution of goods and services:

- The principle of equality: An equal share is given to all. Under this principle there is no morally relevant property except to be a human being. This principle would apply to basic human goods like life, liberty, and basic pursuits and rights.
- The principle of need: The morally relevant property is need within the given situation; those who need more receive preference over those who need less. This would apply in certain welfare programs, scholarship programs, and, in the medical context, triage.
- The principle of effort: The morally relevant property is amount of effort they have put forward; those who have done more, measured by time or production, receive more. Compensations like hourly wages are fairly distributed under this principle.
- The principle of contribution: The morally relevant property is based on the contribution each has made within the given situation; those who contribute more toward the success of the project, receive more of the benefits. Whereas wages are based on effort, salaries are often based on contribution.
- The principle of merit: the morally relevant property is based on the quality of work done (as opposed to quantity); those whose quality is superior receive more than those whose quality is inferior. Grades in academia are usually fairly distributed on this basis.
- The principle of free-market exchange: The morally relevant property is based on ability to pay; those who have financial resources receive more than those who do not. This the most common method of distribution of goods and services in a capitalistic society.

In general, material principles are unjust when they attempt to make distinctions between classes of persons that are actually similar in relevant respects or fail to make distinctions between classes that are actually different in relevant respects. When Rosa Parks stepped on a bus in Montgomery, Alabama, one late evening in 1955 and was denied a seat due to the color of her skin, that was an incident of injustice because the supposed morally relevant property, her race, was an inappropriate basis for determining who gets to sit on a bus and who does not.

While there are a few theories of justice, two stand out in current culture: the egalitarian and the libertarian. While supporters of each of these often oppose each other, they both support ideals that most liberal democracies value: liberty and equality. Both these are basic values, but they often come into conflict with each other. In fact, many of the issues of justice can often be traced back to a conflict between liberty and equality. In order to have equality, one might have to surrender some of one's liberty. On the other hand, if the goal is individual liberty, then that often means goods and services will not be distributed equally.

Egalitarian theories of justice attempt to distribute goods and services as equally as possible across society. A completely egalitarian society would be one where every person would get an equal share of all goods and services. While such a society is an ideal it is probably not realistically attainable. Instead egalitarians attempt to distribute as equally as they can. Most offer a qualified egalitarian theory of distribution that recognizes basic goods but allow for inequalities in non-basic areas. For this theory, social equality is valued over individual liberty. Egalitarians reason that the fact that we are all humans in need should take priority over artificial differences of the class we are born into or natural talents and endowments we are born with. They reason most of the wealthy do not really deserve the goods they have. Many of the wealthiest either inherited their wealth, were born into advantaged families that provided the proper upbringing which gave them a jump up on the more disadvantaged, or they were born with natural gifts and abilities that gave them a head start above those less gifted. None of these were the result of any fair and equal opportunities for all and hence, it is unjust that they have more access to goods and services than the disadvantaged. Egalitarians' solution to the problem is through social engineering. Persons in a co-operative society should strive to make more equal the unequal situation of naturally disadvantaged members of society. This is basically done by taking from the rich and giving to the poor through social welfare programs to better equalize society. Concerning health care, many egalitarians believe that health care is a basic good and should be available to all. Hence, they advocate for some form of socialized health-care program.

Libertarian theories of justice are those in which distributive justice consists not in equal results, but rather in the unhindered and equal working of fair procedures. All receive the same opportunity because all have access to the same procedures, but not necessarily the same results. Libertarians emphasize individual liberty over social equality. Each individual is free to choose his own way in life and where and how to extend his effort in obtaining goods and services. Distributions of goods and services (like health care) are best left to the marketplace. Ability to pay is available to all since all have the liberty to make as much money as they desire. The reasoning is that any person can make of his life what he wants, and fair procedures should be open and available to all. Some will choose to work hard and will succeed where others will not, but each individual is free to choose. Of course, the contingencies of life may throw obstacles in the path towards success, but all are equally challenged by the contingencies of life. Libertarians believe that distribution of goods and services in a truly free market should not be a matter of social planning but instead should be exclusively a matter of individual choosing. Social intervention in the marketplace in the name of justice perverts true justice by placing unwarranted constraints on individual liberty. Government programs that take resources that one individual earned and give to another individual who did not earn it in the name of equality violate one's individual liberty to choose what to do with his own resources which would be unjust.

Of course, both these theories have their strengths and their weaknesses. Libertarians claim egalitarians are stealing their goods while egalitarians claim libertarians are greedy and socially irresponsible. A balance can be found in the Christian concept of God, who is just and yet loving and merciful. In the Psalms we read, "He loves righteousness and justice: The earth is full of the loving kindness of Jehovah" (Ps. 33:5). In Isaiah, we read similarly, "Therefore the Lord longs to be gracious to you, and therefore he waits on high to have compassion on you. For the Lord is a God of justice; How blessed are all those who long for Him" (Isa. 30:18). Both justice and mercy/love are part of the nature of God and, as Christians, we are to reflect both: "How blessed are those who keep justice, who practice righteousness at all times" (Ps. 106:3) needs to be conjoined with "Be merciful, just as your Father is merciful" (Luke 6:36). In striving toward balancing justice with mercy, we must recognize that we should never sacrifice one for the sake of the other. God shows his mercy to us in forgiving us our sins, but that does not mean he simply ignores our transgressions. The penalty for our sins was paid by the death of Christ. It is by his death that God's need for justice is met. In the same way, the church should and often does step in to meet the needs of the oppressed and the poor not by subverting distributive justice, but by paying the price itself through sacrificial giving that can meet the needs of those who are less fortunate. The greed that capitalism can foster can and should be tempered and balanced by a loving and giving body of Christ.

SPECIFICATION AND BALANCING

The value of these four principles is that they provide an effective framework for evaluating many of the issues and problems we will encounter in our study of biomedical ethics. However, there are two considerations to briefly undertake before these can be employed. First, a discussion must be had regarding the process of specifying the principles to attain more specific guidance to the issue at hand. Second, they must be balanced with each other when a conflict between them is apparent.

The four principles examined are too broad and abstract to be of use. Specification is the process of narrowing the scope of a principle to a specific incident or issue under consideration. In a well-known article on the specification of principles, Henry Richardson states that specification is accomplished by "spelling out where, when, why, how, by what means, to whom or by whom the action is to be done or avoided."[30] Back in the first chapter, we discussed moral justification and we introduced a scheme in which moral judgments are justified by appeals to moral rules and moral rules are justified by appeals to principles. This presents one means for specifying our moral principles, by embodying them in rules. Moral rules are guidelines established within different contexts or spheres of life. The rules for teachers will differ from the rules for nurses, lawyers, or carpenters. But they are united in that they are specifications of the same basic principles. So, the principle of respect for autonomy might be specified as a rule concerning confidentiality, veracity, or respect for privacy within the given context of a sphere of life. The rule then could be further specified to a specific person in a specific situation.

30. Henry S. Richardson, "Specifying Norms as a Way to Resolve Concrete Ethical Problems," *Philosophy and Public Affairs* 19 (1990): 289.

As we consider the different issues that will arise in bioethics, we will need to carefully ponder on how these four basic principles are specifically expressed on that issue.

A second consideration has to do with balancing the principles when they come into conflict. The issues encountered in biomedical ethics are rarely a conflict of good versus bad or right versus wrong, as is often assumed. It is almost always a case of two good things that have come into conflict in which we have to choose one over the other. These two goods can be expressed in terms of the principles we have been discussing. The issue in abortion is the conflict of the mother's right to privacy with the unborn's right to life. In principle terms, it is a conflict between respecting the mother's autonomy against the principle of non-maleficence regarding the unborn. In euthanasia, the case often involves mercifully ending a patient's suffering by taking the patient's life. Hence, we have a conflict between beneficence and non-maleficence.[31] How do we decide the proper balance between the principles and which principle should prevail when there is a conflict between two or more of them?

There is no general answer to this question. One needs to examine the specific context to determine how to balance the principles. One thing that helps is to remember that all the principles have *prima facie* standing. This means that they all hold in normal situations but may be overridden if they conflict with a stronger principle within a specific given situation. Beauchamp and Childress provide some appropriate guidelines that are worthy of consideration in weighing the principles.

1. Good reasons can be offered to act on the overriding norm rather than on the infringed norm.
2. The moral objective justifying the infringement has a realistic prospect of achievement.
3. No morally preferable alternative actions are available.
4. The lowest level of infringement, commensurate with achieving the primary goal of the action, has been selected.
5. All negative effects of the infringement have been minimized.
6. All affected parties have been treated impartially.[32]

31. Respect for autonomy may play a part as well if the patient has requested that his life be ended.
32. Beauchamp and Childress, *Principles of Biomedical Ethics*, 23.

While these are effective guidelines, they will need careful reflection as one works through them. One will need to consider and defend one's reasons for preferring one principle over another and the guidelines alone will not resolve all conflicts. But reflecting on them should provide one with a proper justification for adopting one plan of action over another.

A CHRISTIAN MANIFESTO ON BIOETHICS

Though we will take a principlist approach to bioethics in this text, principles do not exist in a vacuum. I have concluded that there is no such unqualified ethic. I believe the concept of a neutral "common morality" is a myth. All ethical principles come from some perspective. How we understand and apply ethical principles will depend on the background beliefs, metaphysical and epistemological as well as axiological, that we bring to moral reflection. In order for ethics to function, there has to be a shared conception of the good. As Christians, we have such a conception which we believe is divinely ordained. Therefore, it is useful before we look at actual principles and issues to call to mind the basic elements of our Christian worldview and to note how contrary that worldview is to the prevailing culture of our day.

God as Creator and Redeemer

As Christians, we recognize that we are not the ultimate source of being and value. We recognize that we are creatures created by God who alone gives life and alone can take it. We also recognize that this God redeemed man by becoming a man himself in the person of Jesus Christ and taking our sins upon himself paid the price for our redemption. Therefore, God is intimately involved in our life from beginning to end. One cannot resolve the complex issues in bioethics without taking these important foundations into account.

The Dignity of Humanity and the Sanctity of Human Life

As Christians, we acknowledge that a human is made in the image of God. While the meaning and specifics of this are open to debate among theologians, it is recognized that because we are made in God's image, humans have a dignity and special place in creation above all other created things. It is because we are made in God's image that we hold to the principle of nonmaleficence (do not harm) and the sanctity of human life. To unjustifiably harm or kill another human being is an affront to God himself. However, we also recognize that, while life is sacred, we are not always required in every instance to use any means to preserve any life. Our life is finite and mortal, and while we praise and value healers, eventually only God can be our savior.

Individuals in Community

As Christians, we recognize a need to balance our individual liberty with our communal responsibilities. We recognize that God has made us creatures with the freedom to choose our path in life. We recognize the need to respect every person's autonomous freedom to choose as God respects such freedom. However, autonomy needs to be balanced with responsibility. We are in a community in which we are responsible and because of which we are limited in our freedom. First, we are in community with God himself. We belong to him and are limited in what we may choose to that which is in accord with his divine nature and will. Second, we are in community with other believers. We are often called to carry their burdens and they are called to bear ours. Such burdens may limit our freedom. The point is that while there is a place for respecting individual autonomy, the language of individual rights is inadequate to describe the dignity of man. No man is truly an island unto himself.

Freedom and Finitude

As Christians, we also recognize that we are both finite and yet transcendent. As finite creatures, we recognize we are limited by our biological necessities and are historically conditioned. However, we are also free creatures able to transcend our limited bounds, to reflect on our situation and the world we are in. We are body and spirit. While I am not suggesting a dualism, I am suggesting a duality. I am not just my body or just my spirit. I am a unity of body and spirit. As spirit, I am able to distance myself from myself to examine and evaluate my life. I can also to some extent step into another person's story and see the world from their perspective. The danger is when we do not recognize the balance of our finitude and freedom. Our freedom is what drives us to know more and drives medical research and knowledge. In our desire to know and heal we may forget that as finite and limited creatures we cannot nor ought not to know or do everything we can. The medical imperative to cure and end disease and suffering is not without limits.

A Christian Understanding of Suffering

We live in a culture where the avoidance or removal of suffering has become almost a god itself and we will justify almost any action that removes suffering. However, a Christian philosophy of suffering must begin with the realization that we worship a suffering, crucified God. The cross should remind us that God understands our pain and that at times suffering may be necessary to defeat evil in the world. This is not to say that all suffering is good (though some may be), but it is to say that God can bring good out of suffering. It is also not to say that we should pursue or seek opportunities to suffer. However, we need to be balanced about it. We should try to care for those who suffer and end their pain while realizing that all suffering cannot be eliminated from human life or that the only good or appropriate human life is one that contains no suffering. We seek health, but not Health—our goal is to care for those who suffer (sometimes by just being fellow sufferers) but it is not to eliminate all suffering and disease. We cannot justify doing absolutely anything in the name of ending suffering. We should do what we can while recognizing that there is a limit to "what we can."

Medicine and Healing

As Christians, we recognize that medicine, medical practice, and medical research are a good and should be praised and pursued. We recognize that just as it dangerous to think we can do anything to end human suffering, it would be wrong to think we could do nothing. Again, balance needs to be achieved. It is not a demonstration of a lack of faith for one to seek medical help. While we acknowledge that God can heal miraculously or through prayer, we recognize that God often uses doctors and medicine as his instruments in treating our disease and suffering. All healing comes from God whether he does it immediately or through a mediator. We also recognize that, for reasons that may remain a mystery to us, God may choose not to heal. Doctors are not saviors. Finally, we must always be mindful that we are not citizens of this world but are merely travelers here. Ultimate healing takes place in another realm. We should never affirm a form of healing that betrays our ultimate citizenship. This may cause a tension in living in a culture that does not recognize this fundamental truth. But it is tension we must live with.

3 

The Second Civil War: Abortion

She could not believe it. Norma McCorvey was pregnant—again. She had only been dating this guy for four months. It was not her first pregnancy. Her first daughter was born during her earlier marriage. She was just sixteen when she dropped out of high school and within the year was married to twenty-four-year-old Woody McCorvey. When she told him she was pregnant, he smacked her across the room and claimed she must have been sleeping with someone else. She moved back in with her mother and worked in a bar until her daughter was born on May 25, 1965. Her mother took custody of the child, and Norma moved out. Her second pregnancy was just a year later; the father was a boyfriend she only refers to as "Joe." He wanted the baby and she did not. So when the baby was born, she gave it to him for adoption, not even knowing its sex. She never saw it again. And now here it was 1969, and she was pregnant again.

However, no one wanted this baby, least of all Norma. She wanted an abortion. But according to Texas state law at the time, abortion was only permissible to save the mother's life. Someone suggested that she tell the gynecologist that she had been raped. She tried that, but he didn't buy it. Fearful of an illegal abortion, poor, with a drug problem and alcohol addiction, Norma contacted attorney Henry McCluskey with the purpose of making adoption arrangements. McCluskey put her in touch with two young, ambitious lawyers: Sarah Weddington and Linda Coffee. They were looking for the perfect case to challenge the Texas law and all state laws outlawing abortions. By the time she met with them, she was eight months pregnant. They told her there was nothing they could do to get this baby aborted. They asked her at that first meeting, "Would you be willing to take your case all the way to the Supreme Court?" Norma didn't know anything about law, so she figured, "Yeah, let's go for it."

Norma gave birth to a boy in June of 1970 and immediately gave the child up for adoption. Meanwhile, Norma's lawyers, claiming that Norma had been gang raped, filed a class action suit in federal court charging that the State of Texas had infringed her civil rights, specifically her right for privacy. Arguing for the State of Texas was the Executive Assistant District Attorney, Henry Wade. To protect her privacy, Weddington and Coffee gave Norma the pseudonym Jane Roe. They won their suit against Texas. The federal court ruled that the Texas law was vague and unconstitutional. However, the state of Texas decided to appeal the federal court's ruling to the United States Supreme Court. The case was argued before the court twice, on December 13, 1971, and again on October 11, 1972. Finally, on January 22, 1973, the Supreme Court rendered its verdict on the case *Roe v. Wade* and, reminiscent of the shots fired on Fort Sumter, began the second Civil War.[1]

1. Details concerning Norma McCorvey's story were gathered primarily from Michelle Green, "The Woman Behind Roe v. Wade," *People*, May 22, 1989. It is interesting to note that in 1995 Norma announced that she had become a Christian and repudiated the court decision that she was responsible for. She worked with Operation Rescue for two years before beginning her own ministry in 1997, "Roe No More Ministry." Shortly before her death she claimed in a documentary, *AKA Jane Roe*, that her pro-life activities were just done for the money, claiming she was a pawn of the pro-life community. She passed away on February 18, 2017.

THE LEGAL SITUATION

Perhaps no other issue is as controversial or as divisive today as is the abortion issue. Just like the Civil War of the last century, it has pitted neighbor against neighbor and brother against brother. It has been the subject of editorials and sermons that rival those of the New England abolitionists and the antebellum Southern politicians. It has even been the cause of bloodshed, not just of the millions of unborn children, but of those who have performed abortions and of those who have protested their performance. Before we examine the arguments both for and against abortion, it is important for us to understand the legal road we have traveled that has brought us where we are today.

Laws involving abortion have only recently come into existence. Prior to the 1800s, abortion was primarily penalized if a woman obtained one against her husband's wishes. English Common Law[2] forbade abortion after *quickening*, or fetal movement. In 1821, the first legislation regarding abortion was passed in Connecticut, explicitly banning abortion after quickening. New York soon followed in 1828, making abortion pre-quickening a misdemeanor and a capital offense post-quickening. In addition, an exception was made to allow abortions necessary to preserve the mother's life. By the early 1900s, every state had abortion laws codified, each following a basic tenet: abortion at any stage in pregnancy was criminalized in some manner, whether pre- or post-quickening.

Abortion laws remained generally unchallenged until the 1960s. However, the United States began to take interest in the abortion issue in 1962 with the Finkbine baby case. Shirley Finkbine was an Arizona kindergarten teacher and mother of four when she became pregnant while taking the tranquilizer thalidomide. Thalidomide was known to cause extremely deformed children if taken by pregnant women. In fact, it was known as "monster former" and was illegal in the U.S., but not overseas where Finkbine had gotten her prescription. Finkbine originally requested an abortion claiming it was for "the health of the mother," a fact she would later deny. Not finding a state that would grant her an abortion, she eventually traveled to Europe where she aborted an extremely deformed baby. To warn others of the dangers of

2. English Common Law is unwritten law, based on custom and judicial precedent. While most laws are codified in statute, Common Law is still seen in the United States with regards to judicial decisions involving interpretation and application of laws.

thalidomide when pregnant, Finkbine went to the media, not realizing that this would bring focus to the abortion issue. The case received a lot of publicity and caused many to rethink their position on abortion. Soon, propositions began appearing on state ballots legalizing abortions. In 1967, Colorado became the first state to liberalize its abortion laws, decriminalizing abortions involving incest or rape, or in which pregnancy would lead to a permanent disability for the mother. It was soon followed by legislation in North Carolina and California, the latter of which was signed into law by then Governor Ronald Reagan. By 1970, New York, Alaska, Hawaii, and Washington all had loosened abortion restrictions.

Meanwhile, on the other side of the country, another important case was brewing that would have tremendous ramifications on the abortion issue. In Connecticut, a married couple was sold contraceptives by a health clinic. However, the sale of contraceptives was against Connecticut state law.[3] The 1879 law, which all agreed was outdated, had been challenged twice but had been dismissed due to technicalities. However, this time the law was challenged all the way to the United States Supreme Court. It was argued that the law violated a person's right to privacy. While there is not actual right to privacy in the Constitution, proponents argued that the right was part of the "penumbra" of the First, Third, Fourth, Fifth, and Ninth Amendments.[4] The court agreed and in 1965 ruled on *Griswold v. Connecticut*, establishing that a person indeed has a constitutionally guaranteed right to privacy. With the *Griswold* ruling and the pro-abortion movements on the state level, the stage was set for the landmark case involving abortion, *Roe v. Wade*. The beginning of this chapter outlines the facts of this case.

In *Roe v. Wade* (1973), the Supreme Court ruled (in a 7-2 decision) that the Texas law outlawing abortion was unconstitutional because it violated a

3. The Connecticut Comstock Law of 1879, banned not only the sale of contraceptives, but the use of contraceptives entirely, including between married persons (see *1879 General Statutes of Connecticut, § 6246*).

4. "Specific guarantees in the Bill of Rights have penumbras, formed by emanations from those guarantees that help give them life and substance. Various guarantees create zones of privacy. . . . The Third Amendment, in its prohibition against the quartering of soldiers 'in any house' in time of peace without the consent of the owner, is another facet of that privacy. The Fourth Amendment explicitly affirms the 'right of the people to be secure in their persons, houses, papers, and effects, against unreasonable searches and seizures.' The Fifth Amendment, in its Self-Incrimination Clause, enables the citizen to create a zone of privacy which government may not force him to surrender to his detriment. The Ninth Amendment provides: 'The enumeration in the Constitution, of certain rights, shall not be construed to deny or disparage others retained by the people.'" *Griswold v. Connecticut*, 381 U.S. 479, 484 (1965).

woman's right to privacy as had been determined in the *Griswold* decision. In striking down the Texas law, the Supreme Court struck down every other state law outlawing abortion. Pro-abortion[5] advocates are quick to point out that the court did place limits on abortion. However, as we will see, those limits can be and are often broadly interpreted. What exactly did the courts say? First, states could not restrict abortions during the first two trimesters (six months) of pregnancy except for normal procedural guidelines. **Viability** was the determining factor. In 1973, viability was between twenty-four and twenty-eight weeks, so they settled on a trimester system of dividing the pregnancy into three three-month (thirteen-week) periods.[6] This meant that a woman could have an abortion for any reason during the first six months. Second, in the last trimester, the state has a right, *but no obligation*, to restrict abortions to only those cases where the mother's health is in jeopardy. In other words, states don't have to restrict any abortions. However, if states do restrict abortions, they can only restrict them for the last three months of pregnancy and even at that time, they must allow them for the sake of the mother's health.[7] Finally, though not specifically addressed, implied in *Roe v. Wade* was that the father of the unborn and the parents of a minor have no say in this decision. The reason is that this was a privacy issue, and no one can interfere with a person's constitutional right to privacy.

On the same day the *Roe* ruling was announced, the court also made public its ruling on another abortion case, *Doe v. Bolton*. This has often been called *Roe*'s sister case. This case concerned a Georgia couple who attempted to get an abortion but did not meet the conditions of the then current Georgia law. The Georgia law allowed abortions only in cases where the woman's life was in danger, the pregnancy was the result of rape, or the fetus was seriously

---

5. Some may question my selection of terms, so a comment is in order I have decided to use the term "pro-abortion" instead of the more popular "pro-choice" because I believe it more accurately reflects their position on this debate. Despite the rhetoric, nobody is questioning any person's "right to choose." A person has a right to choose anything they want. I have a right to choose to steal if I want (and am willing to accept the consequences of that choice). The question is not my right to choose, but whether that choice is morally appropriate. I believe the debate centers around the moral appropriateness of abortion and have chosen the term "pro-abortion" because those who hold that view believe abortion is, at least sometimes, morally appropriate. I have retained the term pro-life because I believe that is the focus of those from that position. They believe abortion is morally inappropriate precisely because we are talking about killing a living person. The issue for them is the "life of a person." If it were not a living person, they would not have a problem with abortion. Therefore, their position is truly "pro-life."
6. *Roe v. Wade*, 410 U.S. 113, 160 (1973).
7. *Roe v. Wade*, 163–64.

defective.[8] The judgment would be left to a licensed physician and needed corroboration from two other physicians. The court ruled (again in a 7-2 decision) the Georgia law was unconstitutional because it violated a woman's right to privacy. Proabortion advocates again point out that in the *Doe* case, the court recognized that a woman's right to an abortion is not absolute and that the state has an interest in protective the health of a "potential of independent human existence."[9] However, the most important aspect of *Doe* was the broadening of the meaning of "health of the mother in jeopardy" (the restriction placed on abortions in the last trimester as per *Roe v. Wade*) to include "all factors—physical, emotional, psychological, familial, and the woman's age—related to the well-being of the patient."[10] This made abortion on demand legal for the entire nine months of pregnancy, a point made by the U.S. Senate Judiciary Committee: "Since there is nothing to stop an abortionist from certifying that a third-semester abortion is beneficial to the health of the mother—in this broad sense—the Supreme Court's decision has in fact made abortion on demand throughout the prenatal life of the child from conception to birth."[11]

The impact of *Roe* and *Doe* together made null and void every state's restriction of abortion and allowed abortion on demand for the entire nine months to any woman who requested it. It was not a moderate adjustment, as many pro-abortionists would claim. It was a complete upheaval of the then current legal thinking on abortion.

The next major Supreme Court decision concerning abortion came in 1976 with *Planned Parenthood of Missouri v. Danforth*. In this decision, the court ruled that sections of a Missouri law were unconstitutional in requiring, among other things, spousal consent for a woman getting an abortion and a "blanket parental consent" for a minor to get an abortion.[12] This case made explicit what was only implied in *Roe*. Next, in 1977, the Supreme Court reversed a lower district court ruling in Pennsylvania in the case of *Beal v. Doe* concerning Medicare payments for **nontherapeutic abortions**. **Therapeutic abortions** are those that are necessary for the health of the mother, while nontherapeutic abortions are those that are for convenience's sake, by far the

8. GA. Code. Ann. §26–1202(a) (1968).
9. *Doe v. Bolton*, 410 U.S. 179 (1973).
10. *Doe v. Bolton*, 410 U.S. 179 (1973).
11. U.S. Senate, Committee on the Judiciary, Report on Human Life Bill, S. 158, 1981, 5.
12. Mo. Laws 809 §3(3) and 3(4) (1974).

most common reason for abortions in this country.[13] The lower court ruled that nontherapeutic abortions should be paid for by the government-funded Medicare program. The Supreme Court reversed the lower court's ruling, finding that such payments were not required for nontherapeutic abortions.[14] It reasoned that a negative right of noninterference in a woman's private decision did not necessarily lead to a positive right of providing benefits to her.[15]

In 1983, the Court ruled on *City of Akron v. Akron Reproductive Health, Inc.* It would be the last of the major pro-abortion victories. The Court struck down a local city ordinance requiring (1) last trimester abortions to be performed in a hospital (as opposed to a clinic or doctor's office), (2) minors under the age of fifteen to have a parent's or court's permission for an abortion, (3) informed consent information designed to influence the woman's decision and irrelevant to the medical procedure (a "parade of horribles" to use one expression), (4) a twenty-four-hour waiting period to precede any abortion, and (5) humane disposal of fetal remains by the abortion provider.[16] The court recognized that such requirements were more to discourage a person from freely choosing a constitutionally guaranteed procedure, rather than justifiably regulating the procedure. Thus, the provisions were deemed unconstitutional.

In 1980, the election of Ronald Reagan as President of the United States signaled a turning point in our country. A more conservative element began to take over in legislative and judicial halls. By the time 1989 rolled around, the face of the Supreme Court had changed dramatically. It was this year that pro-life forces saw their first major victory. The case was *Webster v. Reproductive Health Services,* and the court ruled on it on July 3, 1989. Missouri had passed a statute in 1986 that enacted several restrictions on abortions.

---

13. William Robert Johnston, "Reasons Given for Having Abortions in the United States," 2016, http://www.johnstonsarchive.X/policy/abortion/abreasons.html.
14. *Beal v. Doe*, 432 U.S. 438, 447 (1977).
15. I may need to clarify the difference between a **negative right** and a **positive right**. A negative right is also called a "right of noninterference." In a sense, it is a right to be left alone. These are also called liberty rights. It means you have certain rights to do things and, because of those rights, others are not allowed to interfere with your doing those things. For example, the right to worship in the manner you choose means that others cannot interfere with how you worship. By far, most of our constitutional rights are negative rights. A positive right means that you have the right for something to be given to you. Rather than leaving you alone, others must actively provide something to you. As an example, our welfare system is based on the premise that everybody has basic rights to housing, food, etc. Therefore, the government has an obligation to provide these items to those who cannot afford them. Positive rights are more controversial than negative rights and are usually harder to justify.
16. *City of Akron v. Akron Center for Reproductive Health*, 462 U.S. 416 (1983).

The preamble of the statute read that the "life of each human being begins at conception."[17] Two of the restrictions were: (1) it outlawed abortions after twenty weeks and required physicians to test all women seeking abortions; and (2) it forbade the use of government funds, employees, and properties to be used in performing or counseling nontherapeutic abortions.[18] The statute was challenged in district court and was struck down. The Supreme Court reversed the district court's ruling and reinstituted the statute. In doing so, the Court rejected the earlier "trimester" model used in *Roe v. Wade*. The legislative barrier of the "first two trimesters" was now lifted.[19] Also, the court ruled that the statement in the preamble concerning when life begins was a statement of belief having no legal force and thus could remain.[20]

On June 25, 1990, two cases were ruled on that were strong pro-life triumphs. In *Hodgson v. Minnesota* and *Ohio v. Akron Center for Reproductive Health*, the Court affirmed state statutes requiring minors to obtain either parental notification or court-appointed guardian notification in order to receive an abortion.[21] Then on May 23, 1991, the Court ruled in *Rust v. Sullivan* that the federal government could withhold funds provided to healthcare organizations pursuant to Title X of the Public Health Services Act if such organizations "counsel or encourage abortion as a method of family planning."[22] The Reagan administration had issued this gag order, which was challenged in the Supreme Court. The Court ruled that the restriction was not unconstitutional because it did not affect a woman's right to an abortion under the Fifth Amendment, nor did it violate any First Amendment free speech guarantees because it only limited abortion-related speech for Title X recipients.[23] Therefore, the gag order could stand. (Bill Clinton's first act as President was the removal of this order.)

Things were looking positive for pro-life advocates and some were predicting that any day would see the overruling of *Roe v. Wade*. However, that day was not to come. In 1992, the Court made its ruling on *Planned Parenthood of Southeastern Pennsylvania v. Casey*. In many ways it was a victory for the pro-life movement. In a 5-4 ruling, the Court upheld four of the five sections

---

17. Mo. Revised Stat. §1.205.1(1) (1986).
18. Mo. Revised Stat. §1.205.2, §188.029, §188.205, and §188.210.
19. *Webster v. Reproductive Health Services*, 492 U.S. 490, 493–94 (1989).
20. *Webster v. Reproductive Health Services*, 491.
21. *Hodgson v. Minnesota*, 497 U.S. 417 (1990); *Ohio v. Akron Center for Reproductive Health*, 497 U.S. 502 (1990).
22. *Rust v. Sullivan*, 500 U.S. 173 (1991).
23. *Rust v. Sullivan*, 174–75.

of the Pennsylvania Abortion Control Act (1989), most notably including: (1) a requirement of minors to obtain consent of a parent or court-appointed guardian to receive an abortion, (2) a required twenty-four-hour waiting period between informed consent and the procedure, and (3) a requirement that the informed consent of the patient include information concerning fetal development, effects of abortion on both the patient and the fetus, and alternative solutions.[24] However, the Court struck down a portion of the law requiring women to notify husbands of their intent to obtain an abortion, reasoning that this placed an undue burden on the woman and invaded her right to privacy.[25]

When *Casey* was announced, neither side felt they had won any victories. However, the greatest blow to the pro-life movement was that the Court made it clear they had no intention of overturning *Roe v. Wade*. In the majority opinion authored by three of the more conservative judges—Justice O'Connor, Justice Souter, and Justice Kennedy—they wrote:

> But when the Court does act in this way, its decision requires an equally rare precedential force to counter the inevitable efforts to overturn it and to thwart its implementation. Some of those efforts may be mere unprincipled emotional reactions; others may proceed from principles worthy of profound respect. But whatever the premises of opposition may be, only the most convincing justification under accepted standards of precedent could suffice to demonstrate that a later decision overruling the first was anything but a surrender to political pressure and an unjustified repudiation of the principle on which the Court staked its authority in the first instance. So to overrule under fire in the absence of the most compelling reason to reexamine a watershed decision would subvert the Court's legitimacy beyond any serious question. . . . A decision to overrule Roe's essential holding under the existing circumstances would address error, if error there was, at the cost of both profound and unnecessary damage to the Court's legitimacy, and to the Nation's commitment to the rule of law. It is therefore imperative to adhere to the essence of Roe's original decision, and we do so today.[26]

The decision in *Casey* has afforded *Roe* greater protections from being challenged. Cases since then have focused primarily on methods and procedures

---

24. *Planned Parenthood of Southeastern Pennsylvania v. Casey*, 505 U.S. 833 (1992).
25. *Planned Parenthood of Southeastern Pennsylvania v. Casey*, 837.
26. *Planned Parenthood of Southeastern Pennsylvania v. Casey*, 867, 869.

involving abortion. In 2000, the Supreme Court heard *Stenberg v. Carhart*, a case challenging the constitutionality of a Nebraska state law banning partial-birth abortions. The Court ruled that the ban was unconstitutional because there were no exceptions for cases where the mother's health was in jeopardy, nor was there a clear distinction between partial-birth abortions and late-term abortions.[27] Partial-birth abortions had been interpreted by the medical community as referring to the use of the "dilation and extraction" method, or D&X, which involves partially extracting a living fetus and causing its death by dismemberment or maiming. The procedure is typically performed late in the second trimester, between twenty and twenty-four weeks. The wording in the Nebraska statute was ambiguous enough to ban an array of abortion methods beyond the commonly understood D&X limitation of a partial-birth abortion. The Court's holding affirmed that a treating physician should retain the discretion to determine the best abortion method to protect the mother's health.[28] The ruling in *Stenberg* effectively struck down all other state bans against partial-birth abortions if the same exceptions were not made.

On October 21, 2003, President George W. Bush signed into law the Federal Partial Birth Abortion Ban Act, banning the D&X procedure, but also containing an exception in cases where the mother's health was at risk.[29] Numerous lower courts attempted to strike down the law, citing *Stenberg* as precedent. But in 2007, the case of *Gonzales v. Carhart* made it to the Supreme Court, which upheld the federal ban in a 5-4 decision. The Court found that the case could be distinguished from *Stenberg* because the wording was less ambiguous in the federal law than it had been in the Nebraska state law.[30] Thus, while *Stenberg* was not overturned, *Gonzales* could fit within its parameters.

As of September 1, 2020, twenty-six states regulate the provision of an ultrasound before obtaining an abortion. Four of those states mandate that an ultrasound be performed on each woman seeking an abortion and the provider must show and describe the image (Louisiana, Tennessee, Texas, and Wisconsin). Eight states mandate the ultrasound, but only require the provider to offer the woman an opportunity to view the image.[31] Nine states require the woman be provided an opportunity to view the ultrasound image only if the

---

27. *Stenberg v. Carhart*, 530 U.S. 914, 915 (2000).
28. *Stenberg v. Carhart*, 916.
29. 18 U.S. Code §1531 (2003).
30. *Gonzales v. Carhart*, 500 U.S. 124 (2007).
31. Alabama, Arizona, Florida, Indiana, Iowa, Kansas, Mississippi, Ohio.

ultrasound is routinely performed as part of preparing for an abortion.[32] Six states only require a woman be offered the opportunity to have an ultrasound before obtaining an abortion.[33] In 2011, North Carolina passed the Women's Right to Know Act, which would have made it a requirement for doctors to not only perform an ultrasound prior to a woman obtaining an abortion, but also show the woman the sonogram and describe the fetus in detail, including location, dimensions, and gestational age estimate.[34] The law never went into effect due to an injunction imposed. The U.S. District Court for the Middle District of North Carolina struck down the law, which was upheld by the 4th Circuit of Appeals. The court reasoned that describing the ultrasound image is violative of a physician's First Amendment rights because it goes beyond giving informed consent by having the doctor explain the sonogram irrespective of the woman's needs or wants with regards to the information.[35] The U.S. Supreme Court declined to hear North Carolina's appeal in this case.

In recent years, many states (often Republican controlled) have attempted to place other restrictions on abortions to some degree. This includes laws requiring abortion clinics be located near hospitals with abortions only performed by doctors with admitting privileges. The Supreme Court ruled these laws unconstitutional as they place a "substantial obstacle in the path of women seeing a pre-viability abortion, [and] each constitutes an undue burden on abortion access, [and] each violates the federal Constitution."[36] In 2016, Indiana passed House Bill 1337, which banned abortions based on gender or disabilities such as Down Syndrome, making doctors liable if performed. It also required women be notified at least eighteen hours in advance of this non-discrimination clause. Finally, abortion clinics would be required to dispose of fetal remains in a manner consistent with a deceased person if the mother did not take ownership of the remains.[37] This law was met with sharp criticism from pro-abortion groups and was challenged in court. The lowers courts ruled that all three provisions were unconstitutional, violating the Fourteenth Amendment guarantee of a woman's right to privacy.

32. Arkansas, Georgia, Idaho, Michigan, Nebraska, Ohio, South Carolina, Utah, West Virginia.
33. Iowa, Missouri, North Dakota, South Dakota, Utah, Wyoming.
34. General Assembly of North Carolina, *Women's Right to Know Act*, Session Law 2011–405, House Bill 854 (July 28, 2011); N.C. Gen. Stat. Ann. §90–21.85 (2011).
35. *Stuart v. Camnitz*, 774 F.3d 238. 243 (4th Cir. 2014).
36. *Whole Women's Health v. Hellerstedt*, 136 S. Ct. 2292 (2016).
37. General Assembly of Indiana, *Sex Selective and Disability Abortion Ban*, House Bill 1337 (January 12, 2016).

In May 2019, the Supreme Court upheld the non-discrimination rulings while reversing the fetal remains disposal injunctions as these did not impact a woman's right to an abortion.[38]

For years since the *Casey* decision in 1992, the Supreme Court had not directly considered any case that challenges the fundamental ideas of *Roe v. Wade*. Pro-life advocates have concentrated on regulating abortion on the state level. In 2021, a new law in Texas took effect that allows private citizens to sue anyone who provides an abortion that is prohibited by law (that law being a ban on abortions after the physician detects a fetal heartbeat).[39] The United States Supreme Court refused to block the law due to procedural issues, but since the constitutionality itself was not challenged, the law could still be overturned in the future. The Supreme Court is due to hear another case in late 2021 challenging a Mississippi law that bans abortions after fifteen weeks, before viability, except for medical emergencies or fetal abnormalities.[40] The decision in this case could determine whether the Court will affirm *Roe* or overturn aspects of it. With the Supreme Court shifting since the Republican-led appointments of Chief Justice John Roberts, Justice Neil Gorsuch, Justice Brett Kavanagh, and Justice Amy Coney Barrett, it is anticipated that *Roe* will continue to receive more challenges, potentially resulting in an eventual reversal. However, even with the victories achieved in the pro-life movement, abortion on demand is still available in many parts of the country for any reason, including sex selection, birth control, pregnancy out of wedlock, and eugenic reasons (bone marrow transplants). According to the Guttmacher Institute, the most recent statistics[41] are: 862,320 abortions per year, which translates to about 2,362 abortions per day, or around 98 abortions every hour.

THE MORAL ARGUMENTS FOR AND AGAINST ABORTION

We turn now to moral arguments concerning abortion. It is important to note that we are looking at *moral* arguments, not necessarily *legal* arguments here. It is possible for something to be morally wrong and not legally wrong, and the opposite is true. Also, one has legal rights and, many argue, one also has

38. *Box v. Planned Parenthood of Indiana and Kentucky*, 139 S. Ct. 1780 (2019).
39. Texas S.B. 8, 87th Leg. (2021).
40. *Dobbs v. Jackson Women's Health Organization*, Docket No. 19-1392 (pending).
41. Guttmacher Institute, abortion statistics for 2017.

moral rights, and these may not always correlate. A prostitute in the state of Nevada may have a legal right to solicit business, but many would question whether she has a moral right to do so. It is important in going through these arguments to remember this distinction.

There are generally three positions taken on this issue. The pro-abortion position (also known as the pro-choice view) holds that it is always, or almost always, morally permissible for a woman to have an abortion. The opposite view is the pro-life view (also known as the anti-abortion view) which holds that it is always, or almost always, immoral for a woman to have an abortion. Finally, there is a moderate view which attempts to be somewhere in the middle. This view holds that abortion is usually not morally permissible, but under certain circumstances can regretfully be permitted. Oftentimes moderates will argue that the personhood of the fetus simply cannot be determined for certain. They will hold that it is more likely not a person early in the pregnancy and more likely a person later in the pregnancy. Therefore, earlier abortions are more justifiable ones than later ones. There are several different moderate views, depending on the circumstances one has in mind. The more conservative moderate view would allow abortions when the life of the mother is in danger. A bit less conservative are those who allow abortions for the danger to the mother's life and if the conception was the result of rape or incest. Finally, a liberal leaning moderate position would allow the preceding exceptions and would also include if the child suffers from extreme deformities, its life expectancy would be very short, or even more liberal, if it is not wanted. While these positions are clear in some respects, like most things they tend to blend into each other at the edges and it is not always easy to see slight differences. My plan is to look briefly at some of the main arguments for each of these positions and then to concentrate on what I believe to be the core issue, the personhood of the unborn.

Pro-Abortion Arguments

There are many different pro-abortion arguments. It is outside the scope of this volume to examine all the different possible pro-abortion arguments. I will instead concentrate on the main three types of pro-abortion arguments. Each type has many possible variables.

1. *The right to privacy argument.* This argument, also known as the bodily rights argument, states that everyone has an absolute right to privacy concerning what to do with their body. This moral argument is based on the principle of respect

for autonomy which includes a basic right to keep one's body and property private and personal. There is a point to this argument—most of us recognize that people do have a moral right to a private life. It would be morally wrong for me to walk into your house and start going through your things. It would be an invasion of privacy. The question is how "absolute" that right is.

Many would argue that the right to privacy can be infringed in certain situations, for example to protect the welfare of other persons. Most of us recognize that your right to privacy does not allow you to act in a manner that endangers the public welfare. You cannot drive down the road any way you choose at any speed you desire and claim right to privacy. You also cannot abuse your own children. If you were doing so, it would not be immoral for someone to step in and stop you from harming them, even though we recognize that the relationship between child and parent is normally a private affair. All our child abuse laws are based on such concepts.

Pro-life proponents argue that the same situation is true in a pregnancy. The fetus is not a part of the woman's body—it is her child. The fetus is a genetically distinct separate individual person with its own gender, blood type, and identity. It is not like an arm or organ that a person is said to possess. It is an individual attached to the mother, but not part of her body. When a zygote attaches itself to the wall of the uterus around the eighth day of pregnancy, the mother's body immediately recognizes this as a foreign entity and begins an immunological attack on the embryo which only survives by its own built-in defense system. The woman's body recognizes that this is not a part of her, even though it is dependent on her for its life.

One person who has argued for abortion based on right to privacy is Judith Jarvis Thomson. Her 1971 essay "A Defense of Abortion" is easily the most influential and widely read article on abortion.[42] In that essay she uses the illustration of a famous violinist who needs a kidney to live. It is determined that you are the only person who is a match. As a result, you are kidnapped and forcefully attached to this violinist so that he can share your kidneys. If you unplug yourself for him, you will kill him. Do you have an obligation to remain strapped to the violinist? After all, he is a person with a right to life who is depending on you to help him stay alive. If you do not, then, by analogy, neither does a woman have an obligation to keep a fetus "strapped" to her.

---

42. Judith Jarvis Thomson, "A Defense of Abortion," in *The Abortion Controversy: A Reader,* ed. Louis P. Pojman and Francis J. Beckwith (Boston: Jones and Bartlett, 1994), 131–46.

There are many problems with Thomson's analogy, but I will only mention three. First, there is a major difference between the relationship between you and the violinist and a mother and her child. I may or may not have an obligation to the violinist, but we recognize that parents have *primae facie* obligations to care for their children and children have *primae facie* claims on their parents to be cared for. All our child abuse and abandonment laws stem from this basic understanding of the family unit. If a parent had a three-year-old that needed serious medical attention but decided she didn't have any obligations to help the child, most persons would say there is something very defective in that parent's reasoning. Philosopher Stephen Schwartz comments, "The very thing that makes it plausible to say [as Thompson says] that the person in bed with the violinist has no duty to sustain him, namely that he is a stranger unnaturally hooked up to him, is precisely what is absent in the case of the mother and her child."[43]

Some have challenged the idea that the parent-child bond extends to the unborn child's dependence on the mother for its life. Thompson herself admitted that just because the unborn is biologically related to the mother, it does not follow that she has an obligation to carry it to term and allow it to live off of her unless she chooses to do so.[44] More recently, Bertha Alvarez Manninen challenges parental obligations toward children as defense against abortion. She writes:

> First, what is it *exactly* that grounds moral obligations between family members, in this case between parents and children? Second, assuming that there *are* certain moral obligations that exist amongst family members that don't exist among strangers, are those obligations *so strong* that they can entail that anything at all can be demanded of our family members? Are there limits of what we can expect them to do for us, and would compelled bodily intrusion surpass that limit?[45]

Manninen answers the first question by noting that the only bond that exists between parents and unborn children is a biological bond and that is insufficient to establish such a burdensome obligation. She writes, "However, what

43. Stephen Schwartz, *The Moral Question of Abortion* (Chicago: Loyola University Press, 1990), 118.
44. Thompson states that it is when the parents bring the born child home that they accrue obligations toward it, a rather arbitrary event to select when one has obligations toward one's own child.
45. B. A. Manninen and J. Mulder, *Civil Dialogue on Abortion* (New York: Routledge, 2018), 43, emphasis hers.

we have to ask here is whether biological bond alone grounds our moral obligations to our family, and between parents and children in particular. . . . What grounds our moral obligations to our family members seems much less about our biological connections and much more about our emotional connections and shared experiences."[46] There are a number of problems with Manninen's concept of filial obligations. First, as was noted above all of our child abuse and abandonment laws are based on the biological relationship between parents and their children. If a parent were to abandon their infant on the street because they didn't feel "emotionally connected" to that child they would be guilty of a crime. Second, there are many times that we may not *feel* connected to their children, but that has nothing to do with obligations toward them. We cannot base moral obligations on something as erratic and unreliable as "feelings." Of course the question of what grounds moral obligations towards family members is a question that expands beyond the scope of this discussion. Certainly one's overall worldview will play a large part in such a discussion. For Christians, we recognize that children are a gift from God, who sovereignly places their care in our hands. Our obligations towards them are ultimately grounded in our relationship to him. Natural law recognizes the natural value of family and prescribes obligations to preserve it. Throughout the history of humankind the natural bond between parent and child, the basis for our abuse and abandonment laws, has always been paramount in society. It is only recently that our excessive individualism and overemphasis on autonomy have questioned such obligations.

What is the limit of this obligation? As Menninen asked, "Are those obligations so *strong* that they can entail that anything at all can be demanded of our family members?" In support of limitations, many pro-choice advocates cite the landmark case of *McFall v. Shimp*.47

In 1978 thirty-nine-year-old Robert McFall was diagnosed with aplastic anemia and given a 20 percent chance of surviving another year. A bone marrow transplant was needed in order for him to survive, and the search began for a compatible donor. The most compatible donors are those genetically related; and so he went first to his siblings. When none of them proved compatible, he extended his search out to other relatives. David Shimp was McFall's cousin and agreed to the initial test where it was determined likely that he would be compatible. However, he refused a second, more

46. Manninen and Mulder, *Civil Dialogue on Abortion*, 43–44.
47. *McFall v. Shimp*, 10 Pa. D. & C. 3d 90 (July 26, 1978).

determinative test, at the urging of his wife and his fear that something could go wrong during the bone marrow donation. McFall then sued his cousin to force him to undergo the procedure to save his life. Judge Robert Flaherty ruled against McFall, stating that one cannot legally compel another individual, even a family member, to undergo an invasive medical procedure for another person even to save his or her life. It is contrary to every principle of our judicial system as it violates bodily integrity. McFall died a few months later. A number or pro-choice advocates have appealed to this case to support a woman's right to an abortion, even if the unborn is a person whose life is dependent upon gestating in the mother for nine months.

There are some problems applying *McFall v. Shimp* to the moral question of abortion. The first is that *McFall v. Shimp* is dealing with the legal question of compelling an individual to donate bodily material to another person. It is not dealing with moral obligations at all. Even Judge Flaherty stated in his ruling, "Morally, this decision rests with defendant, and, in the view of the court, the refusal of the defendant is morally indefensible."[48] While the case may speak to the issue of legal compulsion, it is not relevant to our discussion on the morality of abortion.

Second, one might ask, is a bone marrow donation procedure really analogous to a pregnancy? Pregnancy is a natural event that is designed to regenerate the human species. Women's bodies were designed to function in this manner. A healthy pregnancy is not an additional burden placed on a women; her body is designed for this, with all the natural organs (uterus, ovaries, fallopian tubes, cervix, vagina, etc.) as well as the resources and processes necessary to gestate a child built in. To argue that it is an additional burden is like arguing that passengers on a bus are adding an additional burden to the bus. But the bus was designed to transport passengers. A bone marrow transplant is an unnatural, man-made, emergency medical procedure designed for therapeutic purposes. It places an additional burden on a donor that was not naturally there. I am not claiming that only natural processes ought to be honored. But I am saying there is a significant difference to note between these two events.

Third, while there are aspects of *McFall v. Shimp* that may be analogous to abortion, there are a number of important differences between the two issues. One source comments:

48. *McFall v. Shimp*, 10 Pa. D. & C. 3d 90 (July 26, 1978).

> In order for a bodily rights argument to be analogous to abortion, the hypothetical [or, in the case of McFall, a real case] needs to include the following five elements:
>
> 1. If you refuse bodily donation, someone else will die.
> 2. You chose to risk making this person's life depend on you.
> 3. No one else can save this person.
> 4. Your bodily donation is temporary.
> 5. Your refusal means actively killing this person, not just neglecting to save him.[49]

McFall meets two of the criteria: Shimp refused to donate the bone marrow and McFall died; and a bone marrow donation is temporary for the donor as his/her bone marrow will be replenished by his body. However, the case fails to meet three of the criteria: Shimp had nothing to do with McFall contracting aplastic anemia making his life dependent on him, an unrelated person could have been a compatible match, and Shimp's refusal was not the cause of McFall's death.

Yet, as we have seen above, in the vast majority of abortions, the woman involved actively decided to participate in an activity that could reasonably lead to her pregnancy.[50] No one else can help keep the unborn alive during the pregnancy, fulfilling element two, and in obtaining the abortion the mother is participating in actively killing the child. She does not just want it removed, she wants it gone.

Further, in our discussion of beneficence in chapter 2 as well as immediately above, we noted that specific beneficence grounds moral obligations in relationships. We discussed that the strongest relationships are filial relationships, those between parents and children. It follows that our strongest obligations are filial as well, especially when it comes to very young children who are dependent for their life and sustenance on their parents or guardians. While one has obligations with other family members and friends, the distance in relationships incurs a correlative strength or weakness in obligation. The obligation to a cousin is still is strong, but it is not nearly the strength as filial obligations. In that way, the *McFall* case is disanalogous.

---

49. "McFall v Shimp and Thompson's Violinist Don't Justify the Vast Majority of Abortions," Secular Pro-Life Perspectives (blog), December 11, 2018, https://blog.secularprolife.org/2018/11/mcfall-v-shimp-and-thomsons-violinist.html.
50. We discuss the issue of pregnancies resulting from rape below.

Finally, we might address the legal issue of compelling others to help through bodily invasion. It is interesting to note that *Roe v. Wade* mandates that the state has an interest in preserving potential human life and ruled that states may limit abortion to only saving the life and health of the mother after viability has been achieved. The court made this ruling without acknowledging the personhood of the unborn.

In an article titled, "Coerced Donation of Body Tissues: Can We Live with McFall v. Shimp?" Fordham E. Huffman, JD, suggests a construct that might be seen as a middle ground between the "never can compel" factions of the debate and the "always can compel." His construct has four criteria which he first applies to the issue of coerced donation:

To obtain relief, the plaintiff must show satisfaction of four criteria:

> (1) that he is in imminent danger of dying from a disease that can be treated by transplantation of an organ, tissue, or fluid from another; (2) that he stands to experience substantial benefit from such a transplant with the defendant serving as donor; (3) that transplantation from the defendant is the exclusive mode of treatment that offers the prospect of substantial benefit to the plaintiff; and (4) that the organ, tissue, or fluid sought is expendable by the donor—given the quantity of tissue or fluid to be removed and its regenerative capacity—and that the removal of the organ, tissue, or fluid will not result in disfigurement.[51]

Huffman continues, "If the plaintiff satisfies these four criteria, the court moves to its greatest challenge under the construct—balancing the benefits shown as likely to accrue to the plaintiff against the risks to the defendant in acting as donor." [52] We often refer to this as a benefits-burdens assessment. The benefit to be achieved by the plaintiff must outweigh the burden placed upon the defendant in order for compulsory aid be required. "If the plaintiff is able to establish, by clear and convincing evidence, his satisfaction of all four criteria, and the court finds that the risks to the defendant/donor are greatly outweighed by the benefits to the plaintiff/patient, an order should issue."[53]

Huffman then moves to the question of abortion. Returning to *Roe*, he recognizes the state's interest in preserving potential life after viability fulfills the criteria of his construct. The unborn is in imminent danger of dying

51. Fordham E. Huffman, "Coerced Donation of Body Tissues: Can We Live with McFall v. Shimp?," *Ohio State Law Journal* 40, no. 2 (1979): 415–16.
52. Huffman, "Coerced Donation of Body Tissues," 419.
53. Huffman, "Coerced Donation of Body Tissues," 420–21.

if aborted, he/she experiences substantial benefit from being allowed to continue gestation, the mother is exclusive in her ability to maintain the life of the unborn while gestating, and in most cases the pregnancy is of a temporal nature as to not cause substantial harm to the mother. Huffman concludes, "While the fundamental nature of the pregnant woman's right never changes, the state may constitutionally compel her to forego the exercise of that right and to provide her body for the benefit of the fetus, which is itself without constitutional rights." Had the court ruled the unborn to be a person protected under the Fourteenth Amendment of the United States Constitution, it would likely have ruled that the state has a legitimate interest in preserving life of the unborn for the entire period of gestation.

A second problem with Thompson's analogy is that there is a difference between actively killing someone and passively allowing someone to die. We will discuss this distinction in more detail in the chapter on euthanasia; however, it is important to note that unplugging oneself from the violinist is analogous to removing someone who is dying from life supporting mechanisms. Soon the kidney disease that is affecting the violinist will take over and he will die. But he is dying from the disease, not from you not being attached to him. However, the child is being actively killed in an abortion procedure.

Third, many have suggested the Thomspon's argument is disanalogous with the vast number of abortions that occur. In her analogy you, the victim, have been forcibly attached to the violinist against your will. This analogy might be appropriate for women who have been raped and become pregnant against their will. But the vast number of pregnancies result from women who choose to be involved in sexual activities with the full knowledge that such activities could result in a pregnancies. With knowledge comes responsibility. Therefore the woman must take responsibility for the consequences of her actions, even if unintended. If a drunk individual is driving home one evening and kills another individual in an accident he is still held responsible even though he did not get in the car intending the death of another.

Some have found fault with this reasoning. If a women walks into a neighborhood knowing its dangers for violence late one night and is raped, surely she is not the one responsible for being raped. And we can all agree that it is the rapist who is responsible for the crime of rape. But one surely has to question the wisdom of walking into such a situation in full knowledge of the likelihood of being a victim of crime. She may not be responsible for the rape itself, but she bears some responsibility for placing herself in such a situation. When a couple become involved in a sexual relationship, they are aware that there is always the possibility that a pregnancy can result from the encounter and that they bear some of the responsibility for their actions.

In the end, I do not believe that Thompson's illustration works and that right to privacy does not give one the right to kill one's own children.

2. *The quality of life argument.* This argument basically holds that if a child is deformed or defective it should not be forced to suffer through "a life worse than death." This is argued on different levels: some argue based on the child's suffering itself, others on the burden that such a child might place on the family. The amount of suffering is also a variable in different forms of this argument. Some are referring to severe deformities, or situations where a child would only live for a very short period, while others would place any deformity into the argument such as mild retardation or Down Syndrome.

There are several problems with this kind of argument. First, if in fact the fetus is a person, then she has the same moral rights and we have the same obligations to her as to any other person. Most all agree that we certainly would not take the life of a deformed or defective child or adult purely because they are deformed.[54] No matter how badly we might feel for them, to do so would be the worst form of discrimination. This leads to the second problem with this argument. Any quality of life argument is going to depend heavily on subjective standards of what makes a life worth living. However, it is presumptuous to claim that certain lives just aren't worth living because they don't meet a certain standard. In fact, it is interesting to note that not one handicapped or disabled organization has come out in favor of abortion of those who are deformed or defective. If the pro-abortionists were right in using this argument one would expect to see large numbers of suicides of those who were suffering or disabled. While there have certainly been some it has not been at all what one would expect if the general feelings of the disabled were as the pro-abortionists imagine. Third, there is a logical problem with arguing that no life is better than a life of suffering. It is basically arguing that nothing is better than something. However, there is no logical way you can argue this because in order to compare two things, they both must exist and have properties to compare. "Nothing" does not exist and has no properties, so one cannot compare it to anything, even something bad, and say that it is better. Finally, even if this argument were to make sense, the majority of

54. I am speaking of a person who has not requested that we take such action. Concerning those who make such requests, see chapter 4.

abortions that take place don't fit into this category and therefore it cannot be used to justify abortion as a fundamental reproductive right.

3. *The non-person argument.* This argument says that the duty to do no harm applies only to persons. The unborn fetus, especially in the first and second trimester, has not attained the status of being a person. Therefore, the duty to do no harm does not apply to the fetus. Again, there is a good point behind this argument. Moral obligations are something that normally apply to persons. I do not have a moral obligation to my car, to my office, or to the computer I am writing on. If I were to take a hammer to the computer, I might regret it, but I have not wronged it. It seems that this argument, if right, may have a point. However, it is going to depend on what a person is and if we have good reason to believe that a fetus is one. Since we will examine that issue more closely below, we will leave this argument for now. I will give this argument the credit of hitting the nail on the head—*this* is the main issue in the abortion debate. If the fetus is a person, then whatever reason justifies our taking its life would be the same for any other adult person walking around. There are many other pro-abortion arguments: dangers of an illegal abortion, poverty, the child will be unwanted and unloved, etc. However, these have no force if the fetus is a person.

Even the moderate's position concerning rape and incest fails if the fetus is a person. Should the life of an innocent person be taken for an action he did not commit? Would we be free to take the life of an adult person, if he had been the result of rape or incest? While not denying the trauma and tragedy of such an incident as rape or incest, it is highly doubtful that killing the unborn will really resolve this issue or make it go away. The question of personhood is the single most important question in the abortion debate.

Pro-Life Arguments

Again, there are many different types of appeals and arguments from the pro-life camp. Even though I am arguing from the pro-life position, I must acknowledge that not all these arguments are good ones. For example, some pro-lifers have attempted to show that abortion is wrong by holding up pictures of aborted children and showing how much they "look" human or by showing how the fetus can feel pain at a certain stage. I believe these arguments are misguided and they give the wrong impression. The impression is given that if it looks human, or feels pain, then it is a human person. The problem is that the opposite impression, while not logically necessary, is also given: if it doesn't look human or feel pain, then it is not a human person. However, for those of us who believe the unborn it is a person from the moment of conception, what it looks like or what it feels is not the issue. I will comment more on this below.

There are many good arguments for the pro-life position. Don Marquis provides an argument that is based on an analysis of why killing is wrong.[55] He argues that what makes killing wrong is that it robs a person of the activities, experiences, and enjoyments that would have constituted one's future. These are intrinsic goods that are wrong to take away. Marquis's point is not that the fetus is necessarily a person, a question he believes can remain open for the present, but that it does have the future of a person and therefore to abort it is to rob it of that future.

Another argument is provided Harry J. Gensler who argues on the basis of consistency using a Golden Rule approach in a style reminiscent of Kant's categorical imperative.[56] He says that a consistent person will not have one moral position for others and an opposite position for himself. If people are going to be consistent, they must expect of themselves what they would expect of others. If I think it is normally wrong for someone to steal from me, then it is normally wrong for me to steal from someone else. Consistency demands that I hold both beliefs. Applying this to abortion, if I am consistent and think abortion is normally morally permissible, then I would have to consent to the idea of having been aborted myself in normal circumstances. Since most people would not consent to having been aborted, most people would have to agree that abortion is normally impermissible if they are going to be consistent.

There is much to commend both arguments, though I believe they have some problems as well. In general, I believe they don't go as far as they can. I believe the strongest pro-life argument is the personhood argument and it is that argument to which I now turn.

The Personhood Argument

The personhood argument holds that the fetus is a full human person from conception and therefore the duty to do no harm applies to the fetus regardless of quality of life. Patrick Lee summarizes the argument well in a syllogism:

55. Don Marquis, "Why Abortion Is Immoral," in Pojman and Beckwith, *Abortion Controversy,* 320–38.
56. Harry J. Gensler, "The Golden Rule Argument Against Abortion," (in Pojman and Beckwith, *Abortion Controversy,* 305–19.

> Intentionally killing an innocent person always is morally wrong.
>
> Abortion is the intentional killing of an innocent person.
>
> Therefore, abortion is always morally wrong.[57]

To understand this argument fully we need to analyze two issues: what is a person and when does one begin.

The Concept of Personhood

Francis Beckwith, in his excellent work *Defending Life: A Moral and Legal Case Against Abortion Choice,* writes,

> Metaphysics is an area of philosophy that deals with questions having to do with the ultimate grounding and nature of things in the world. It is concerned with such diverse topics as the mind/body problem, identity, God, the existence and nature of universals, the existence and nature of the soul, and so on. Thus the morality of abortion, if it is to be construed as contingent upon the nature of the unborn, is an issue whose resolution depends on which metaphysical view of the human being is correct.[58]

What is a person? In asking the question we need to begin by making some distinctions in terminology. For the present I want to separate the terms "human" and "person." "Human" can be an ambiguous term in that it can be used a couple of ways. One way we can use it is in the sense of a "human organism." This is a biological/genetic concept. By this term we are speaking of a member of the human species determined by their DNA and by a particular physical way of functioning. If one is asking when does the human organism begin the answer is fairly noncontroversial. Human organisms begin at conception when the haploid cell containing twenty-three chromosomes of each parent combine forming the diploid cell of the new human organism containing forty-six chromosomes. However, "human" can also be used to be speak of the entire "human being," which would be a combination of human organism and personhood. Because of this possible confusion, I

57. Patrick Lee, *Abortion and Unborn Human Life* (Washington, DC: Catholic University of America Press, 1996), 1.
58. Francis Beckwith, *Defending Life: A Moral and Legal Case Against Abortion Choice* (New York: Cambridge University Press, 2007), 44.

will be using the term "person" or "human person" in my discussion below. The term "person" is not a scientific concept; it is a philosophical concept. One cannot determine personhood purely through scientific investigation. Also, it is important to realize that is possible that not all persons are necessarily human and therefore one cannot equate the two as identical. God and angels would be non-human persons. It is possible that aliens from different worlds (if any exist) could be persons. A "human person" then is a species or type of the genus "person."

What are the necessary and sufficient conditions for something to be a person? What we are looking for are those properties or qualities that a thing must have to be a person—they are essential for it to be a person. What might these properties be? Several philosophers have attempted to list some of these. Joel Feinberg states the following: "It is because people are conscious, have a sense of their personal identities; have plans, goals, and projects; experience emotions; are liable to pains, anxieties, and frustrations; can reason and bargain, and so on—it is because of these attributes that people have . . . a personal well-being of a sort we cannot ascribe to unconscious or nonrational beings."[59] Philosopher Mary Ann Warren draws up a similar list:

1. Consciousness (of objects and events external and/or internal to the being), and the capacity to feel pain.
2. Reasoning (the *developed* capacity to solve new and relatively complex problems).
3. Self-motivated activity (activity which is relatively independent of either genetic or direct external control).
4. The capacity to communicate, by whatever means, messages of an indefinite variety of types, that is, not just with an indefinite number of possible contents, but on indefinitely many possible topics.
5. The presence of a self-concept and self-awareness, either individual or racial, or both.[60]

Warren herself does not claim this list is exhaustive. However, she claims that a person who has *none* of these five could not be rightfully called a person.

---

59. Joel Feinberg, "Abortion," in *Matters of Life and Death: New Introductory Essays in Moral Philosophy*, ed. Tom Reagan (New York: Random House, 1986), 256–93.
60. Mary Ann Warren, "On the Moral and Legal Status of Abortion," *The Monist* 57, no. 1 (1973): 43–61.

David Boonin argues that a fetus has rights only after it is capable of organized cortical brain activities that allows it to maintain dispositional desires. A dispositional desire is different than a present desire. We are conscious of our present desires, like my current desire to eat brownies. A dispositional desire is one that we have but are not conscious of at the present moment. My desire to keep my commitments and promises or to remain alive may not be on my mind while I am watching television, but I have such desires dispositionally. According to Boonin, while a comatose patient may still have dispositional desires, a fetus does not have as it does not have the ability to form either present or dispositional desires.[61]

Bertha Alvarez Manninen suggests that one becomes a person when one becomes a conscious sentient individual. Such a being has an interest in not experiencing pain and allows others to see that life from that being's point of view. Moving on from simple sentience, Manninen observe that to have interest means there must be a mental life present and advocates for the Embodied Mind Account of Personal Identity. Persons are those that have minds, and it is the birth of the mind that is the beginning of the person and not the beginning of the organism itself. Manninen places this somewhere between twenty-two and thirty-five weeks gestation.[62]

Other lists of the properties of personhood have been drawn up, but they contain similar properties: consciousness of the external world, self-consciousness, self-determination, rational capacities, emotional expressions, willful direction, and communicative/social abilities are almost universally found on most lists of properties essential to be a person.

However, the status of these properties is something that is very important in our understanding of what a person is. If you will note, the way they are listed above in terms of *presently functioning*. In other words, their position is that a person is one who functions in a certain way. This might be called a "functionalistic" definition of personhood.[63] According to Feinberg, Warren, Boonin, and Manninen a fetus is not a person because it is not presently functioning like one and cannot presently function as one. However, there is another way to think of these properties—not as presently functioning, but as having the potential or *capacity* to function in this manner.

---

61. David Boonin, *A Case for Abortion* (New York: Cambridge University Press, 2002), 74–85.
62. Manninen and Mulder, *Civil Dialogue on Abortion*, 28–32.
63. Christopher Kaczor refers to this as the "performance view" of personhood as the concept of person is one who presently performs is a certain manner. See his *The Ethics of Abortion: Women's Rights, Human Life and the Question of Justice* (London: Routledge, 2011), 93.

If we think about it, there are many times when these properties are not functioning in what we consider to be normal human persons, such as when you are in a deep sleep, in a coma, or under sedation. Certainly at these times you are not conscious of the outside world or yourself, have no ability to make decisions that would be characterized as self-determined, you are not reasoning, emotionally expressing yourself, or communicating with anyone. Yet we would certainly not say that you are not a person at that point. Someone cannot kill you while you are asleep and claim that they did not kill a person because you weren't presently functioning as one. Perhaps it is better to say that a person is one who has the *capacities for functioning* according to the above listed properties.

However, we cannot stop there. Someone might argue, "Okay, we obviously have the capacity to function that way, because we will soon wake up and begin to immediately function as a person. But the unborn does not have that ability. Therefore, it still cannot be considered a person." First, I am not sure what time has to do with it. The unborn, if allowed to live and naturally cared for, will someday function that way—it's just a matter of time. It is true that the capacity in a full-grown adult is more immediate, but time should not be the determining issue concerning personhood. Second, this immediate capacity to function as a person can only be present if something more basic is present.

There is something about a human person that gives him this immediate capacity to function as a person. It is something that seems to belong to him *by nature of what he is*—a human being. Some have simply called this our "human nature." Others refer to it as our essence or our soul. Stephen Schwartz calls it our "basic inherent capacity."[64]

We recognize that everything in the world is a certain kind of substance. What makes a particular substance to be the kind of substance it is, are the inherent powers and capacities to function as that kind of substance. An apple tree is what it is because it has the capacity to bear apples. A fish has the basic capacity to live and survive in water because that is the kind of thing it is. These apple bearing and fish-like capacities are inherent to what the substance is by nature of being that kind of substance. Persons have inherent capacities to function the way they do because that is the kind of substance they are. It is not the functioning that makes them persons, it is the fact that they are persons that allows them to function as persons. Personhood is ontologically prior to functioning. Cows will never function as persons, not because they

64. Schwartz, *Moral Question of Abortion*, 91.

do not have the immediate capacity to function, but because they don't have any kind of capacity by nature of the kind of thing they are. But humans are a kind of thing that has these capacities. We only have an *immediate* capacity to function as a person because we have a more basic *inherent* capacity to function as a person that is there by nature of what we are.

This brings out an important distinction—the distinction between *being* and *doing*. For a being to do something, it must exist. Existence must always precede action. In relation to personhood, a person must already exist in order to function as one. It is not the functioning that *makes* one a person, she already *is* a person—that is why she is functioning that way. It is the *being* a person that grants one the capacity to *function* as a person. This is an extremely important distinction and one that we shall return to many times in this book.

With this in mind, how might we define "human person?" Philosopher J. P. Moreland defines a person this way: "A genus that takes being human as a species constituted by a fairly standard set of highest order capacities for mental states and for forming a body (in the case of human personhood)."[65] By "constituted by a fairly standard set of highest order capacities," I take Moreland to be saying that these capacities are there by nature of the kind of being a human person is. What might we list as the "fairly standard set" of capacities? The actual list is not necessarily important. There are certain capacities that most would agree on. I would say, at least minimally, four capacities are essential for a being to be a person: the capacity for rational reflection, emotional expression, willful direction, and moral conditioning. Certainly these are debatable, but I believe they sum up the essence of what a person is. This is referred to as the substance view of personhood.[66]

However, there is one more issue we need to discuss. There will be those who might say, "There are some in the world who we would consider to be persons, but do not have these capacities. For example, severely retarded people do not have the capacity for rational reflection or willful direction. Or people in a coma." I believe humans in these unfortunate states are still persons and have these capacities, they are just unable to access them to function properly. Philosopher Stephen Schwartz describes these situations as "latent capacities." A latent capacity is one that is present, but is inaccessible due to permanent or

65. J. P. Moreland, personal correspondence, December 16, 1998.
66. Kaczor calles this the "endowment" view of personhood. See Kaczor, *Ethics of Abortion*, 98.

temporary damage, blockage, or underdevelopment. Schwartz writes, "Even a very severely abnormal or handicapped human being has the basic inherent capacity to function as a person, which is a sign that he is a person. The abnormality represents a *hindrance* to the actual working of this capacity, to its manifestation in actual functioning. It does not imply the *absence* of this capacity, as in a nonperson."[67] This is why we recognize that it is a tragedy when someone is impaired or disabled either physically or mentally. We recognize that it is not the normal way they should be by nature of what they are. A table cannot think, communicate with others, make plans, or perform actions. Yet we do not think that it is a tragedy that a table cannot do these things for tables are, by nature, not supposed to function this way. But human persons, by nature, are supposed to function in these ways. In admitting that something is wrong with a human in the present state of affairs, we are admitting that he is a kind of creature who by nature should be otherwise.

I believe we now have a pretty good idea of what a human person is. The question we wish to turn to now is when does one begin.

When Does Personhood Begin?

To begin with, it is important to realize what the question is asking and what it is not asking. The question is not "When does the human organism come into being?" Any medical scientist will tell you that the human organism is formed at the moment of conception. The zygote has its own genetic code and is considered a separate entity right from the start. What the question is asking is, when does it become a person? There are three general answers to this question: (1) we do not know, (2) at a decisive moment in the pregnancy, and (3) personhood gradually develops over the course of the entire pregnancy. I would like to look at these three possible answers in detail.

The agnostic theory. This theory says that no one can really know when personhood begins. It says the philosophers, scientists, theologians, and lawyers all disagree as to the beginning of personhood. No one has demonstrated anything with 100 percent certainty. Since no one can really know when personhood begins, they say, we should not entertain the question and the issue of personhood should not be a relevant one. Therefore, except for other possible ethical issues in a given situation (like informed consent, etc.), abortion is justifiable.

67. Schwartz, *Ethics of Abortion*, 97 (emphasis mine).

I believe there are as number of problems with this theory. First, there are a couple of logical problems with this view. In the first place, if it is true that "no one knows" when personhood begins, then what is to stop someone from killing a two-year-old because he believed that personhood did not occur until three? This is an example of a logical fallacy called the argument of the beard. It got its name by noting that, because we cannot pinpoint exactly when stubble ends and a beard begins, we can't say we know if something really is a beard or not. However, just because we may not be able to know the exact moment personhood might occur (a position I am not granting), does not mean we can't know anything at all. Most people certainly know a two-year-old is a person and would condemn anyone for murdering one. Therefore, personhood must go back farther than that. If we examine the properties that make a two-year-old a person, we may be able to understand if the fetus is one. There is a second logical problem with saying we "can't know" when personhood begins—it is making a knowledgeable claim about something it says no one can know. In other words, how does the agnostic know something about the beginning of personhood (that we do not know when it begins), if in fact nobody can know about the beginning of personhood? The claim is self-defeating.

Second, if we truly grant that we cannot know if the fetus is a person, that does not automatically lead one to justify abortion. In fact, it should lead to the opposite action. For, if we cannot or do not really know, then we must acknowledge the real possibility that in fact it *could* be a person. If it is possible that it could be a person, then the benefit of the doubt goes to that possibility. To act any other way would be considered negligent homicide. If I am out hunting with friends and we divide up and I hear a rustling in the bushes, if I take aim and fire without first determining if it is a deer or a friend, I am acting in a negligent manner. If I shoot, and it turns out to be a friend who dies because of my shooting him, then I am guilty of negligent homicide. Even if it is *not* my friend, I am still guilty of criminal negligence for it could have been he. The same could be laid at the feet of the agnostic.

A third problem with this view is that it is guilty of assuming that killing a human organism that is not a person is morally justifiable. Now, there are those who hold that such a separation cannot be. Assuming for the sake of argument that these two aspects can be separated, the assumption that killing a human organism is morally justifiable, just not killing a human person, has not been defended. It is certainly possible that a human organism may be the kind of thing that one just can't treat any way we want. After all, eagle eggs have laws that protect them, so why not human organisms? Many would argue that to torture an animal to death is morally wrong, and yet that is not a person. Some, like Don Marquis above, would argue that we should not kill human organisms because even if they are not currently persons, they have a future as human persons.

A fourth problem with this view is that by allowing abortion on demand, agnostics have for all practical purposes already decided when a human organism becomes a human person: sometime after birth. This is when the agnostic grants the person its rights not to be harmed or killed, and when we have duties toward it. However, there is no real difference in the actual being itself one hour before birth or one hour after it. Some agnostics will say that they feel certain that it is probably a person sometime earlier than birth, they are just not sure when that might be. However, just like with the event of birth, if pressed they will be forced to select an event in pregnancy at which they will draw the line. This leads to our next theory: decisive moment theories.

Decisive moment theories. The decisive moment theories say that there is a decisive moment in the pregnancy when the person comes into existence. There are eight possible decisive moments that are pointed to as possible events when the person could come into existence.

1. Conception. This has been the traditional view of the beginning of personhood and there are good reasons to hold this view. First, there is a radical break that occurs here that does not occur any other time in the pregnancy. In conception two things (sperm and egg) become one thing, a zygote. A whole new entity that did not previously exist comes into existence, and two other entities, sperm and egg, ceased to exist. Some might reply, "But the egg still exists, it has just been fertilized." This is missing the point. It is not a "fertilized egg," for the moment it became fertilized it ceased being an egg. Not only is this true on the conceptual level, but also on the biological level. Schwartz explains:

> The expression *fertilized egg* (or ovum) is also scientifically wrong. The new human being is no more the egg fertilized than he is the sperm fertilized, or modified. He is as little the one as the other, but a new being. The ovum is merely bigger than the sperm, hence the tendency to speak of it as a fertilized egg, but each contributes exactly one half to the genetic makeup of the new person. And in the process, each ceases to be.[68]

68. Schwartz, *Ethics of Abortion*, 70.

The fact that there is such a radical break at this point where a new being comes into existence provides, in the absence of defeaters, strong *primae facie* evidence that personhood begins here as well.

Second, this new being is a completely separate individual with its own genetic code, needing only food, water, shelter, and oxygen in order to develop, grow and continue its existence. It is not a "part" of the mother's body and nothing substantively new will ever be added to it that will change it in any dramatic way.

Third, metaphysically speaking, this new being is a particular kind of *being* with a nature and it is in the process of *becoming* in accordance with that nature. It is not a "becoming" who is striving toward "being." It is not a potential human person, but a human person; with potential limited only by its nature. It is *essentially* a human person, that is why it develops as a person instead of as something else. Personhood is there from the beginning; that is why it will develop as a person. Sunflower seeds develop as sunflowers, watermelon seeds develop as watermelons, human persons develop as persons. If personhood is not there from the beginning, at least in latent from, where did it come from? Any other theory is going to have to answer that question.

Fourth, this new being is the product of human parents. Whatever is the sexual product of members of a species is itself an individual member of that species. Since the species "human" includes, by nature, the quality of personhood, a member of that species will have that quality. In fact, a subcommittee of the Senate Judiciary Committee made this comment in its report after listening to witnesses testify concerning the 1981 Human Life Bill, "No witness [who testified before the subcommittee] raised any evidence to refute the biological fact that from the moment of conception there exists a distinct individual being who is alive and is of the human species. No witness challenged the scientific consensus that unborn children are 'human beings' in so far that the term is used to mean living beings of the human species."[69]

Fifth, the new person conceived has continuity through time. The same person that began at conception as a zygote will continue through birth, childhood, adolescence, and adulthood as the essentially same person. There is no other radical break. You did not come *from* a zygote, you *were* a zygote, just like you did not come from an adolescent, you were an adolescent. No stage of our development, inside or outside of the womb, imparts us with our

69. Report of Subcommittee on Separation of Powers to Committee on the Judiciary, Human Life Bill—S.158, 97th Congress, 1981. Cited in Beckwith, *Defending Life*, 43.

personhood. That is why it is proper to say, "When I was conceived . . ." The only place to draw the line is conception.

Sixth, personhood must begin at conception by process of elimination. No other event in the development of the fetus can account for when personhood begins. As we shall see, all other events suffer from a lack of explanatory power on this question.

2. *Implantation.* Implantation occurs six to eight days after conception. This occurs after the new zygote moves down through the fallopian tube where conception occurred and implants itself on the uterine wall. Some believe that personhood cannot occur before this event for a few reasons. Bernard Nathanson argues for this because this is when the time zygote establishes its presence by "transmitting signals" (hormones) and "interfacing" with the human community.[70] Communication with the outside world is essential for personhood. There are two problems with this view. First, there is a difference between *being* and *knowledge of being.* It is possible for something to exist and for us to have no knowledge of its existence. In fact, there probably exist many things in the universe of which no one is aware. That does not mean they do not exist. The essence of what a thing is does not depend on others' awareness of the thing's existence. Second, what about conceptions that occur *in vitro*? Any child conceived this way has "communicated its presence" before implantation.

Another reason some argue for implantation as recognition of personhood is that some products of conception are not human beings at all. Therefore, they reason, being conceived is not what makes you human, and one is wrong to argue that life begins at conception. What they are referring to are certain things like hydatidiform moles (a degenerated placenta), choriocarcinoma (conception cancer), or a blighted ovum (placenta lacking an embryonic plate). The problem with this argument is that it confuses necessary and sufficient conditions of being human. Just because human persons begin at conception does not imply that all things that begin at conception are human. This is the fallacy of illicit conversion. It is saying that **A**: "All human person are things that begin at conception" implies **B**: "All things that begin at conception are human persons." But since **B** is not true, proven by the examples given above, then **A** must not be true either. However, that is like

70. Bernard Nathanson and Richard N. Ostling, *Aborting America* (Garden City, NY: Doubleday), 216.

saying that "All apples are fruit" implies "All fruit are apples," which obviously does not follow.

Some argue that implantation must be where personhood begins because 30 percent of all conceptions die before implantation. "Yet," they argue, "we don't treat these as humans. We don't try to save them or give them funerals." However, it does not follow logically that the new being conceived is not fully human just because it is not treated as so. If we treated a fully-grown adult like this, it would not mean he is not a person. Unfortunately, in our history we have not always treated persons of different races as persons. In fact, in the Dred Scott decision (1857) an African American slave was declared only three-fifths a person. That did not mean he wasn't a full person.

The most formidable argument for implantation it the argument from segmentation or "twinning." This occurs before implantation. This argument says that a human person is essentially one absolute individual being. "Persons" cannot be split in two. Since the conceptus can be split in two, it must not be a person. There are a few replies to this objection. First, every being conceived is still a genetically unique individual, distinct from her/his parent. Just because twins came from one concept, it does not logically follow that the concept is not fully human and a member of the human species having, by nature, personhood. It just happens in the case of twins that the genetic code each possesses is identical to the other. This is also true after birth, but we wouldn't kill them then either. Second, there is no logical contradiction in having two persons existing in one physical concept. From conjoined twins, we know that two individuals can be joined together and share the same body parts, such as the heart or even the head, and yet we recognize that they are separate persons and always have been. The two newly conceived persons are joined in the same manner, just more closely. What we are arguing is that all human conceptions contain at least one person, but not necessarily only one. Finally, Patrick Lee comments:

> When a person is defined as a certain type of *individual*, the word means *logically* undivided as opposed to a universal or class, where the property or nature is divided among many. The division of the embryo shows only that he or she is *physically* divisible. . . . The fact is that all of us are *physically* divisible, but that does nothing to call into question our present individuality in the relevant sense.[71]

71. Lee, *Abortion and Unborn Human Life*, 91.

3. *Brain development.* About fifteen days after conception, the "primitive streak" appears that will develop into the brain and nervous system. By the twentieth day, the foundation for the brain and spinal cord is established and by the thirty-third day, the cerebral cortex is formed. Some argue that since a human being is considered dead at brain death, the person no longer exists in the body at this time, therefore it seems logical that when the brain begins to function, that is when personhood starts. They argue that you cannot have a person without a brain because there is no capacity for consciousness. There may be good reasons for arguing that with no brain, there is no capacity for those properties which we identified earlier as distinctive of what a person is. There is normally a strong relationship between brain states and the mental states necessary for a person to function. However, I do not think this argument works for a couple of reasons. First, the argument assumes a symmetry exists between brain-death and brain-life. If the "person" is gone at brain death, then he must not be there until the brain is alive. As much as this symmetry *seems* to exist, there is no *a priori* reason to assume it really exists. There is no evidence for it, it is just our tendency to be symmetrical. In fact, there is significant difference between "brain death" and "no brain yet." A dead person has lost the natural inherent capacity to live. The brain does not have the capacity to work because it has irreversibly ceased—it is dead. However, the unborn has not lost the natural inherent capacity to live. The capacity is there from conception and it is still living. Therefore, the absence of brain activity is not necessarily the same as the death of the brain.

Second, there is some ambiguity in the statement that the unborn has "No capacity for consciousness without a brain." If one is speaking of immediate capacity, then the statement is true. But the unborn does possess the essential structure for this capacity, so he does have the capacity in a latent form. Where would it come from if he did not already have it? There is nothing substantially added to the fetus after conception that would explain where the brain comes from. Again, because he cannot function like a person, it does not mean he is not one. One can argue that the brain has not fully developed in an infant, yet most would recognize that an infant is a person.

4. *The appearance of humanness.* Around eight to ten weeks the fetus begins to take on more and more of the appearance of being human. Facial features are apparent, hands and feet are almost fully formed, sex organs can be seen. There are those who argue that it is at this time that we begin to treat the unborn as a person. This argument is often subtly offered. Some will point to a

picture or drawing of a zygote and say, "How can you call *that* a person?" Pro-lifers will parade around pictures of aborted fetuses and proclaim, "See? You're killing little children!" Both these approaches to personhood are wrong. First, appearance is neither a sufficient nor a necessary condition to be a human person. One can have things appear as human persons that are not, such as manikins or robots like Data in the series *Star Trek: The Next Generation,* and one can be a human person without appearing as one: extremely deformed persons, badly burned victims, victims of massive amputations. Second, this objection assumes that personhood presupposes a certain form. However, our outward human form changes considerably throughout our life from childhood, through adolescence and adulthood, to our elderly years. If appearance depends on a certain form, then at what point are we a person? Finally, this is prejudice and bigotry. The poor treatment of African Americans in this country was, and unfortunately often still is, because they "look different."

5. *The attainment of sentience.* Somewhere between eight and thirteen weeks the unborn will begin to experience physical sensations such as pain. This is called sentience. Some argue that this is when the unborn should be treated as a person. This is based on the idea that a being that can feel pain has interests, and anything that has interests can be harmed. We have an obligation not to harm beings that can have interests, that is, persons.[72] Pro-lifers have also used this argument in films like *The Silent Scream* where they show a baby feeling pain. Like the above argument based on appearance, while these have dramatic value, the problem again is that sentience is neither a sufficient nor necessary criterion for personhood. First, this view confuses *harm* with *hurt* and the experience of harm with the reality of harm. Hurt implies an awareness of pain, harm is the obstruction or prevention of the legitimate interests of one party by the invasive actions of another party. You can harm someone without ever hurting them. For example, if you tell me something in confidence and I tell your boss so you don't get a promotion, I've harmed you even if you don't know and never know you were up for a promotion and didn't get it. Hurt occurs when one experiences harm, but harm does not need to be experienced to really exist. If the fetus already is a person, you are

72. There are those who argue that because animals are sentient beings, they should not be harmed (Peter Singer, *Animal Liberation* [New York: HarperCollins, 1975]). Some go further and claim that because they are sentient, animals have interests and therefore they have rights not to be harmed (Tom Reagan, *All That Dwell Therein* [Los Angeles: University of California Press, 1982]).

harming it by aborting it, whether it ever feels it or not. Second, if sentience is *the* criterion for personhood, then anytime we are not sentient, we are not persons. That would include being in a deep sleep, comatose, unconscious, or under general anesthesia. Yet most would acknowledge that you are still a person even in these states. In fact, the unity between two sentient states implies the underlying person still exists even though he or she is not sentient at the moment. When you wake up you are still the same person you were when you went to sleep. Therefore, there must be more to be a person then sentience.

6. *Quickening.* Quickening is an old term to describe the first time movement of the unborn is felt by the mother, usually between sixteen and seventeen weeks. This is an ancient theory before modern medicine. It was thought that this is when the soul entered the body and therefore marked the beginning of personhood. However, this is an example of a factual problem, not a moral problem. Those ancient and medieval scholars who condemned any abortion after quickening would surely do so today from conception. Again, knowing a person is there and a person being there are two different things that are unrelated. It is confusing epistemology with metaphysics.

7. *Viability.* Viability is the term used to describe when the baby can live outside of the womb. Today it is thought to be somewhere between twenty and twenty-four weeks, though this time frame is always getting pushed back further and further. The argument based on viability says that prior to this time the unborn is totally dependent on the special environment of the womb. The unborn then is not a completely independent human life and hence not fully human. This was the view suggested by the majority opinion in the *Roe v. Wade* case. However, there are problems with this argument. First, viability has nothing to do with transforming the nature of the fetus from non-person to person. It is more of a comment on our medical technology, than on personhood. Second, viability changes with medical progress. The time of viability cannot be determined precisely. What was not a person in 1973 at twenty-two weeks could be accepted as a person in the 1990s. This seems to be an arbitrary designator of what is a person. Third, each one of us can be non-viable in relation to the outside environment. For example, without a special means or apparatus on the moon, underwater, or at the North Pole, we would not be able to survive in the outside environment. It does not make us less of a person just because we are dependent upon some special means for our

survival. Finally, as Frank Beckwith points out, Justice Blackmun's argument in *Roe v. Wade* based on viability is circular.[73] Blackmun claims that the state only has an interest in protecting fetal life when it can live outside the womb. Why? Because prior to living outside the womb the fetus has no interests or rights. In other words, he is assuming (that the fetus has no rights) what he is trying to prove (that the fetus has no rights). However, he has provided no *independent* evidence for his conclusion that the fetus has no rights. It is like arguing that the Los Angeles Dodgers are the best team in baseball because no one is better.[74]

8. *Birth*. In general, forty weeks after conception a mother will give birth to a child. Some argue that since our society calculates the beginning of one's existence from birth (i.e. how old you are) and since it is only after birth that one is named and accepted into a family, then the child is not fully human until after birth. However, social customs and conventions have nothing to do with someone being a person. One is not less a person if unnamed, abandoned, or no one knows his or her birthday. A dog can be treated like a human (named, accepted into the family, celebrate its birthday) but that doesn't make it human. Also, there is no essential difference of an unborn child the day before birth and the day after birth. Its nature has not changed in any way. It is just a matter of location.

The decisive moment that has the best evidence going for it, and the most explanatory power, is conception. The other theories have too many problems and offer no explanation for the origin of personhood. Therefore, I believe that the person begins at conception. However, there is one other possibility that is popular today. It is to that position we now turn.

Gradualism. Gradualism is the view that says there is no one specific moment when personhood begins. Instead it is a gradual change that occurs over the entire pregnancy. In the beginning, at conception, there is no person and by the end, at birth; there is a person. There is no one decisive moment between conception and birth, personhood slowly develops as the fetus develops. Some, like Judith Jarvis Thomson have used the acorn as an example: it gradually develops into an oak tree.[75] It certainly is not an oak tree to begin with, but it is one at the end. Most gradualists would hold then, that the

73. Beckwith, *Defending Life*, 100–101.
74. I am fully aware that very few would attempt such an argument today, but I am hopeful that it can be made someday.
75. Thomson, "Defense of Abortion," 131.

unborn gain moral rights, including the right to life, as it develops. A zygote has fewer rights than a fetus who, in turn, has fewer rights than a newborn. Therefore, earlier abortions are more easily justified than later abortions.

There are two main reasons why gradualists hold this view. First, they argue that it is simply impossible to draw a line for when personhood begins. We just do not know where to do it. It is better to abandon all decisive moment theories than to go on pretending we can know something that is just impossible to know. Second, the unborn close to birth seems very much like the rest of us, whereas the zygote simply does not. Philippa Foot, for example, expresses this view well when she says, "As we go back in the life of the fetus we are more and more reluctant to say that this is a human being and must be treated as such."[76]

There are some serious problems with the gradualist position. First, at best the theory is a hypothesis. There is absolutely no evidence to support it. It may "seem" that a zygote is very different from a baby, and one may be "reluctant" to call a zygote a person, however this is hardly evidence to support the view. Any evidence that could be offered would need to be very strong because it would have to overcome some tremendous difficulties as we will see below. Therefore, it has a low degree of probability of being true.

Second, though there may be the gradual *development* of a person (physical, social, etc.), it is impossible to have the gradual process of *being* a person. There are only two possible concepts when it comes to existence: being and nothing. Things either exist or they do not. There is no such concept of something partially existing and partially not existing, or of something "becoming" into existence. What *exists* may develop, but there is no such thing as something that "develops into existence." Think of how you can trace your life back—teenage, adolescence, childhood, babyhood, fetus, embryo, zygote. *You* have developed, but you have always been you. The zygote was not you partly existing and you partly not existing. Development concerns functioning as a person, not being a person. Thomson's illustration supports this. An acorn has the basic inherent capacity to develop as an oak tree, that is why it develops as one. In the same manner the zygote has the basic inherent basic capacity to develop as a person, that is why it develops as one.

Third, if gradualism were true, the gradualist would have to hold to the awkward idea of beings like "half person/half non-person." At the beginning

76. Phillipa Foot, "The Problem of Abortion and the Doctrine of Double Effect," in *Moral Problems: A Collection of Philosophical Essays*, ed. James Rachels (New York: Harper and Row, 1971), 29.

there is no person and at the end there is a full person. Therefore, there must have been a half-way point where there was a half-person, but what kind of person is a "half-person?" A person is a simple undivided being.

Fourth, the gradualist ends up adopting an "assembly-line" picture of a person coming into being. For example, think of a car on an assembly line slowly coming into being as more parts are added to it. Gradualists apply this picture to the unborn in the womb. However, it is a false analogy. Cars are artifacts that are created by adding several parts together; they are the sum of their parts. Persons are "natural kinds" and are living organisms. They are not the "sum of parts" because personhood is a "simple" idea—it has no parts and is not able to be divided up into parts.

Finally, why does the gradualist stop at birth? Have we fully developed as persons at birth? Psychologists will tell you not even half-way psychologically. If you take gradualism to its logical conclusion, then the gradualist must affirm the absurd position that a baby is less a person than a two-year-old, and a two-year-old is less a person than a ten-year-old, and so on. Since the gradualist correlates the wrongness of killing a being with its development as a person, then it is less wrong to kill a two-year-old than a ten-year-old, and less to kill a ten-year-old than an adult. What the gradualist wants to do is limit this gradual development to pregnancy alone. However, that is inconsistent and contradictory. He says we cannot draw a line, but that is what he is doing. If gradualism is true, then you can't draw a line to end development any more then you can draw a line to when a person begins, inside or outside the mother.

SUMMARY

There is a point when personhood occurs—at the moment of conception. All other theories fail to provide an account for any other time personhood could come into existence, and the agnostic and gradualist run into problems of inconsistency and incoherence. There are three continuums that give evidence for personhood from conception to death: (1) The continuum of identity: because of our basic inherent capacity we keep the same identity through time. The same person who was conceived and was a zygote is the same "self" that will be an adult. (2) The continuum of essential structure: the essential structure for the basic inherent capacity to function as a person is present at the moment of conception and remains in various forms until death. Finally, (3) the continuum of capacities: the basic inherent capacity is the basis for all the other capacities needed in order to function as a person.

I have present capacities to function as a person: reason, moral reflection, etc. But these are all based on the basic capacity I have had from conception. There is no such thing as a "potential person" just "the potential to function as a person." We may not be able to achieve a satisfactory list of the properties of personhood. But whatever it is, it appears to be in humans from conception. At least the basic inherent capacity is.

I will conclude by noting what Christian philosopher Peter Kreeft has written.[77] He writes that either a fetus is a person or not and either we know it or not. Therefore, there are only four possibilities: (1) It is a not person and we know it. If this were true, then abortion would be permissible. But no one has been able to prove with any certainty that a fetus is not a person and the preponderance of evidence points to the opposite conclusion. (2) It is a person and we know it. If this is true, then abortion is murder. (3) It is a person and we do not know it. Then we are guilty of manslaughter. For we have enough evidence to acknowledge it at least could be a person (even the gradualist and agnostic admit that) and therefore should have taken care not to have killed it. (4) It is not a person and we do not know it. Then abortion is criminal negligence. For again, even if it is not a person, we have strong enough evidence to acknowledge it *could* be a person. Although we would not actually be killing a person under this option, we are acting in a criminally negligent manner. In short, abortion never comes off under any of these options as the right action to take and these are the only options.

SCRIPTURE AND ABORTION

What does Scripture say about abortion? It may surprise some to find that it does not say anything specific about abortion at all. Many pro-abortionists take this as tacit permission for abortion. However, it would be wrong to take that approach. If that was the correct method of handling Scripture, then one could argue that pedophilia is permissible because Scripture does not specifically address that issue. Instead, we might ask why Scripture does not address the issue. Part of it may stem from the fact that the very idea of abortion was contrary to the ancient Jewish view of having children. Children were seen as a blessing. In fact, for a woman to be barren was often interpreted as a curse

77. Peter Kreeft, "Human Personhood Begins at Conception," Castello Institute Medical Ethics Policy Monograph, 1995.

from God and something to be lamented about. Roland de Vaux, who wrote the classic *Ancient Israel: Social and Religious Institutions,* writes:

> In ancient Israel, to have many children was a coveted honor, and the wedding guests often expressed the wish that the couple would be blessed with a large family . . . Sterility, on the other hand, was considered a trial (Gn 16:2; 30:2, Is 1:5) or a chastisement from God (Gn 20:18) or a disgrace from which Sarah, Rachel, and Leach all tried to clear themselves by adopting the child which their maids bore to their husbands (Gn 16:2; 30:3, 9).[78]

Therefore, it should not be surprising that we find nothing in Scripture specifically addressing the abortion issue.

However, we do find scriptural comments on killing innocent persons. The most obvious place is the fifth commandment, "Thou shalt not murder" (Exod. 20:13). What is it about murder that makes it so wrong? Many answers have been raised. Murder robs society of someone of value to it or murder robs the murdered victim of a future are just two answers that have been proposed. However, the scriptural answer has nothing to do with society and, surprisingly, nothing to do with the murdered person. Murder is something you do to God. It is an affront on his image. We see this in Genesis 9:6: "Whosoever sheds the blood of man, by man shall his blood be shed; *for God made man in his own image.*" The fact that man is made in the image of God places him in a very unique status in comparison to all else that has been created. There are no other restrictions as to the killing of other animals in any general sense. However, because of this privileged position, man may not be killed by any other man—to do so is to desecrate the image of God. There has been much speculation of what this image actually is. I believe, without going into details, the image is found in man's personhood. This is what separates man from all other creatures. As persons we are image of God bearers and we are obligated to respect that image.

Does Scripture give us an idea of when personhood, i.e., image of God, occurs? Again, it does not make any specific comment. Any time Scripture talks about humans it always treats them as persons. There is no separation in Scripture between "human person" and "non-human person." However, perhaps we can approach the question differently. Christian philosopher Scott Rae suggests

---

78. Roland De Vaux, *Social Institutions,* vol. 1 of *Ancient Israel* (New York: McGraw Hill, 1965), 41.

that the best approach is "by equating the unborn child in the womb with a child or adult out of the womb."[79] He suggests the following argument:

1. God attributes the same characteristics to the unborn as to an adult [or child].
2. Therefore God considers the unborn a person.
3. Abortion is killing an innocent person.
4. Killing innocent persons violates the fifth commandment. (Exod. 20:13)[80]

What are some characteristics of persons that God attributes to the unborn? First, the same language is used for the unborn (Luke 1:41, 44) as is used for a child or baby who is already born (Luke 2:12, 16). Second, the same punishments are meted out for the injury or killing of the unborn (Exod. 21:22–25) as for killing or injury an adult (Lev. 24:19–20). Third, the unborn is considered sinful from the moment of conception (Ps. 51:5) as an adult is considered (Rom. 3:23). Fourth, God claims to have knowledge of the unborn in a personal way using personal pronouns (Jer. 1:5; Ps. 139:15–16) as he uses of other persons. Fifth, God calls the unborn to their vocation (Isa. 49:1) in the same way he calls other persons (Amos 7:14–15).

Along with the characteristics listed above, Scripture draws a continuity between conception and birth in personal terms. Genesis 4:1 tells us of the first birth: "Now the man had relations with his wife Eve, and she conceived and gave birth to Cain and she said, "I have gotten a manchild with *the help* of the LORD" (NASB). There is a continuity of personhood from the conception of Cain to the birth of Cain. Job 3:3 also draws the same continuity. Job is lamenting his situation and says, "Let the day perish on which I was born, and the night which said, 'A boy is conceived'" (NASB). Hebrew parallelism joins together the "I" who was born with the "boy" who was conceived. They are the same person.

Some pro-abortionists have pointed to Exodus 21:22–25 as implying that the fetus is not a full person:

> And if men struggle with each other and strike each a woman with child so that she has a miscarriage, yet there is no *further* injury, he shall surely be fined as the

79. Scott Rae, *Moral Choices: An Introduction to Ethics* (Grand Rapids: Zondervan, 1995), 122.
80. Rae, *Moral Choices*, 122–23.

> woman's husband may demand of him; and he shall pay as the judges *decide*. But if there is any further injury, then you shall appoint *as a penalty*, life for life, eye for eye, tooth for tooth, hand for hand, foot for foot, burn for burn, wound for wound, bruise for bruise. (NASB)

Some pro-abortionists point out that the penalty for causing a miscarriage is not the same penalty for taking a life and that therefore the value of the fetus is less than a person. The problem with this interpretation is based on an unfortunate translation of this text in versions such as the New American Standard Bible (normally a good version, but not here). The Hebrew word translated "miscarriage," *yahtzah*, in the above text literally means to "come forth" and is the standard term for giving birth. Since she was struck by one or more men, she gives birth prematurely. However, there is nothing in this passage that even implies it is a miscarriage. There is another Hebrew word for miscarriage, *shakol,* and that term is not in use here. Another problem with this translation is the insertion of the word "further" before "injury." In the NASB, whenever a word is in italics, it is to inform the reader that this is an interpretive insertion and not in the original. If one removes the word "further" and translates "miscarriage" to "gives birth" the original meaning becomes clear: If two men are fighting and they strike a pregnant woman so that she gives birth, but there is no injury, then they only must pay the husband a fine (to compensate for a premature birth). However, if there is injury then they must pay equal to the injury. And the penalty given here is exactly as that given in Leviticus 24 for injury to an adult: eye for an eye, tooth for a tooth, life for life. This passage supports the personhood of the unborn by stipulating the same penalty.

It seems clear from what we have seen that Scripture would support the personhood of the unborn. I am not necessarily presenting an open and shut case, but I do believe the evidence lies on the pro-life side.

CONCLUSION

In looking at the personhood argument and considering what Scripture seems to teach, I believe Christians have a good reason to believe that the unborn is a person from conception on. The final question is "Where do we go from here?" It seems to me there are two responses a Christian can take. One response is to withdraw into one's own community and let the non-Christian world go its own way. The other response is to be actively involved in the abortion issue. I call this second response activism and I believe it is the correct response. Christians should have a voice in the public square, sharing what they believe to be true. In fact, if they really believe it is true, I believe they have an obligation to share it with others. However, there are two kinds of activists: hard activists and soft activists. The hard activist will use any means to achieve his purpose. He will work both inside and outside the law if necessary. I personally believe this is the incorrect response. I especially deplore acts of violence against any other person in the name of "pro-life." In a democratic pluralistic society, we should, as much as we can, respect laws that are arrived at in fair and equitable manner. However, I would encourage soft activism. Soft activism is working within the laws and in respect of others by reasoning with individuals and encouraging legislative activity to change laws one believes are bad laws. The laws allowing abortion in this country certainly fall under the category of "bad laws." I believe we should actively and respectfully attempt to change those laws. We have good reasons to support our view, and we need to aggressively and respectfully share those reasons.

4

From Cradle to Coffin: Infanticide

Dan and Linda were eagerly awaiting the birth of their baby. They were a young couple who had only been married a short while when Linda became pregnant. Dan had worked hard expanding their small home in eastern Long Island and had built two extra rooms, one of which would be a nursery. They were like any of a number of lower-middle-class couples just starting out in life. They never dreamed the birth of this baby would thrust them into the national spotlight.

Keri-Lynn was born on the morning of October 11, 1983, at St. Charles Hospital on Long Island. She weighed six pounds and was twenty inches long. Immediately everyone could see that Keri-Lynn was badly impaired. On her back was a protruding bubble-shaped membrane with the spine exposed. This is called a *meningocele* and occurs when a gap does not close between two vertebrae in a developing fetus. This gap allows the *meninges,* a membrane that covers the spinal cord, to develop outside on the baby's back. Upon seeing the protrusion, the doctors knew that Keri-Lynn was born with *spina bifida cystica.* If left untreated, Keri-Lynn would likely die within a year or two. If treated, it would mean a lifetime of operations and severe physical handicaps.

Unfortunately, that was not Keri-Lynn's only problem. She also had a damaged kidney and microcephaly. Microcephaly means that Keri-Lynn was born with her head much smaller than normal, implying a minimal brain. This usually is a sign of mental retardation. Moreover, she had some of the usual disabilities that are found in *spina bifida* babies, including *hydrocephalus,* which is an abnormal accumulation of fluid on the brain. Keri-Lynn was immediately transferred to the neonatal intensive care unit (NICU) at the University Hospital of the State University of New York campus at Stony Brook, Long Island. Two physicians, a surgeon named Arjen Keuskamp and a pediatric neurologist named George Newman, became involved in Keri-Lynn's case. Controversy and disagreement started immediately. The issue was the problem of the hydrocephalus which needed to be drained immediately or Keri-Lynn would become even more severely retarded or even die. Keuskamp recommended immediate surgery and draining of the hydrocephalus to minimize retardation and get the child out of the immediate danger of death. Newman disagreed and upon examining Keri-Lynn consulted with Dan about midnight, fourteen hours after Keri-Lynn was born. Newman told Dan there were two options. They could perform the surgery that would save Keri-Lynn's life. But that would likely leave her paralyzed, retarded, and vulnerable to bladder and bowel infections for the rest of her life, and she probably would not live beyond her teenage years, if that long. Newman said, "She is not likely to achieve and meaningful interaction with her environment, nor ever achieve and interpersonal relationships, the very qualities which we consider human."[1] The other option would be to forgo the surgery and allow Keri-Lynn to die soon, sparing her from such a life.

Dan and Linda went through the agony of having to make a terrible choice. After talking together and then with others, they decided not to have the operation and allow Keri-Lynn to die. The baby went from being impaired to being imperiled. She received palliative care: food, water, and antibiotics. Everyone assumed she would die in just a couple of days. However, four days later Keri-Lynn was still alive. Kathleen Kerr, a reporter for *Newsday* magazine got wind of the story and interviewed the couple. It was important to Dan and Linda to express that their decision had been made from love for Keri-Lynn. Kerr's story broke on October 18, 1983, and with its publication came the winds of fury.

1. Quoted in Gregory Pence, *Classic Cases in Medical Ethics*, 2nd ed. (New York: McGraw-Hill, 1995), 181.

A HISTORY OF INFANTICIDE

The fact that having a baby is one of the greatest joys we can ever experience is what makes the tragedy of a congenital disease or other infant handicap so hard for most of us to accept. About 3.8 million babies were born in 2017 in this country[2] and a significant number of them are born severely impaired. Some of the conditions are: heart malformations (6,136), Down syndrome (6,037), spina bifida cystica (1,460), and anencephaly (859).[3] Until recently, infants born with these conditions often had little chance of survival beyond a few years or, in some cases, days. However, with the advances in medical knowledge and procedures many of these cases have much better chances of survival. In 1950 the infant mortality rate in the country was 29.2 per 1,000 births. By 2016 it had dropped to 5.9 per 1,000 births.[4] However, this new technology also raised some serious ethical questions: Who should make decisions about the care of these infants? Is it ever justified to cease or forgo treatment for impaired newborns? What would such nontreatment entail? Is active euthanasia ever justified in these situations?

Infanticide, the practice of allowing infants to die, or of killing infants, is not new. Throughout history many different cultures have practiced killing newborns for a variety of reasons: physical abnormalities, sex selection, economic considerations, and social considerations. Plato and Aristotle both advocated it in some situations. It was practiced later in Rome when children were simply abandoned in fields and left to die. Among the Bedouin tribes of Arabia, in China, and in much of India firstborn female infants were often killed so that the firstborn would be a son. However, the religious traditions of the three great Western religions—Islam, Judaism, and Christianity—strongly condemned most cases of infanticide and affected many of the cultures in which they arose. In modern times most civilized cultures do not practice infanticide in any but the rarest situations. However, in recent years infanticide has entered the medical community and now a new term has developed—neonaticide. It would be helpful to see how this has developed.

In 1972 the Johns Hopkins Hospital in Baltimore, Maryland, released a film called *Who Should Survive?* It told the story of an infant boy who had

2. National Vital Statistics System, Report 004, May 2018.
3. Updated National Birth Prevalence estimates for selected birth defects in the United States, 2004–2006. Center for Disease Control, December 2010.
4. Updated National Birth Prevalence estimates for selected birth defects in the United States, 2004–2006. Center for Disease Control, December 2010.

been born the previous year with Down syndrome. Down syndrome, named after Langdon Down who discovered it, is a chromosomal abnormality in which a person has forty-seven chromosomes instead of the normal forty-six. The extra chromosome is on chromosome 21, and therefore the disease is technically called Trisomy 21. Trisomy 21 is a genetic condition that almost always causes some form of mental retardation (either mild or severe), facial abnormality (which is why it used to be called *mongolism)*, and about a third of the cases are accompanied by cardiac or intestinal problems. Such was the case of a child born at Johns Hopkins.

The Down syndrome baby had a duodenal atresia, or bowel obstruction. Without surgery, the natural flow and digestion of food could not take place and the child would die. The surgery to correct such a problem was relatively routine and on any normal child would have taken place without question. However, both parents, one a nurse who worked with Down syndrome children and the other a lawyer, refused to consent to the surgery. Their reasons were never specifically stated, though the manner in which they spoke suggested they felt they couldn't, or just didn't want to, care for a Down syndrome child. The pediatric surgeons honored their wishes. The child was not fed intravenously and died of starvation and malnutrition fifteen days later. The film documenting the case was shown throughout the country. As a result, other doctors began to go public in the early 1970s. Duff and Campbell, two pediatricians at the Yale-New Haven Medical Center, admitted to accepting parents' decisions to forgo treatment of forty-three impaired infants who all died.[5]

The next significant event in the history of imperiled newborns occurred on May 5, 1981, when conjoined twins, Jeff and Scott, were born to Pamela and Robert Mueller in Danville, Illinois. They became known as the "Danville Twins." The twins were joined at the trunk and shared three legs. The Muellers decided they did not want any aggressive treatment and asked that the boys be allowed to die. However, Child Protection Services stepped in and obtained a court order for temporary custody of the children. The Muellers were charged with child neglect, but the charges were later dropped, and custody returned to them in September 1981 when pediatric surgeons testified that a separation would not be successful and the prognosis for survival was very poor. The twins were eventually separated and as a result Scott died but Jeff survived.

5. Pence, *Classic Cases,* 175–77.

THE LEGAL STATUS OF INFANTICIDE

It wasn't until the 1970s and 1980s when cases began to develop in the courts regarding life-saving treatment for children. Up to this point, courts had been focused on right-to-die cases; now the issue became right-to-live. Most of these cases remained in the lower courts. As of this writing, the United States Supreme Court has not heard a case involving imperiled newborns.

On February 9, 1974, a baby was born in Maine with a deformed left side. He had no left eye, practically no left ear, a malformed left hand, and some of the vertebrae in his spine had not fused. In addition, he had a trachea-esophageal fistula, which is a small gap located in the area between the windpipe and esophagus and could not be fed by mouth. This condition, the most imminently life-threatening one, could be corrected with a fairly standard surgery. However, the parents refused to consent to the surgery. Several physicians at the hospital brought a neglect case to the Maine Superior Court. Judge David Roberts began his ruling by stating, "The most basic right enjoyed by every human being is the right to life itself."[6] He found that regardless of the quality of life of the infant, if there was a medical need and a feasible treatment was available, it must be performed. This ruling made it so not only could a guardian not withhold consent for life-saving medical treatment, but also affirmed that children with disabilities have the same right to life as other children. The baby died before the operation could be performed.

The landmark cases for imperiled newborns, known collectively as the "Baby Doe Cases," occurred in the early 1980s. On April 9, 1982, a baby was born in Bloomington, Indiana, with Down syndrome and suffering from trachea-esophageal fistula. The obstetrician, Dr. Walter Owens, downplayed the chances of a successful operation and emphasized the tragedy of Down syndrome, saying these children are little more than "blobs" and the lifetime cost of treatment would be close to a million dollars.[7] The parents decided not to operate based on Dr. Owens's prognosis and the Down syndrome diagnosis.

The nurses at the hospital attempted to get a court order to operate and had an emergency meeting with county judge John Baker late one night at the hospital. No official record of the meeting was made. Dr. Owens again emphasized the poor condition of children with Down syndrome, saying that even a minimum quality of life was nonexistent. The infant's father, who by

6. *Maine Medical Center v. Houle* (Maine Superior Court, February 14, 1974).
7. Pence, *Classic Cases*, 175–77.

this time had been convinced by Dr. Owens, said he did not want the child treated. Judge Baker ruled that the parents had the right to make the decision about treatment for their children. The case was appealed to the Circuit Court and the Indiana State Supreme Court, both of which upheld Judge Baker's ruling. While attempting to appeal to the United States Supreme Court, the baby died, making the case moot.

The second case occurred in New York in 1983, where a baby girl was born in Stony Brook Hospital with *spina bifida* (a birth defect where the vertebrae in the back do not form properly around the spinal cord). While surgery could prolong her life, she would be paralyzed and suffer from severe brain damage. Her parents chose not to consent to any medical treatment. A private citizen from Vermont named Lawrence Washburn, who heard of the case through a confidential tip, filed suit in order to have to surgery performed. Because it was found that Washburn did not have standard, a guardian *ad litem* ("for the case") named William Weber was appointed. As guardian *ad litem*, Weber was authorized to make decisions for the baby. Originally Weber was sympathetic towards the baby's parents and was going to agree with their position, but he then read some comments in the baby's chart made by the pediatric neurologist. The neurologist, who had told the baby's parents that the child would be paralyzed, wrote that she would most likely be able to walk with braces after the surgery. Considering this information, Weber argued for the surgery to take place.

Meanwhile, the lawyer for the parents, Paul Gianelli, appealed to the Appellate Division of the New York Supreme Court. The Court overturned the appointment of Weber as the baby's guardian *ad litem*, finding that decisions involving medical treatment for children should be left up to the parents. On October 28, 1983, the court upheld the parents' right to decide, stating that the case should have never gone to court as there was no neglect present, and both Washburn and Weber should have never been involved.[8] Eventually, the baby's parents did consent to some medical procedures and the vertebrae corrected itself naturally. As of this writing, the baby, now a grown woman named Keri-Lynn, is still alive.

During these two cases, the Reagan administration directed the Department of Health and Human Services (HHS) to mandate that all hospitals that practiced this type of infanticide would lose all federal funding. This was based mostly on section 504 of the Rehabilitation Act of 1973, which forbade

8. *Weber v. Stony Brook Hospital*, 60. N.Y. 208 (New York Court of Appeals, 1983).

discrimination on the basis of a handicap.[9] The reasoning was that infants are citizens and it is a violation of their civil rights to end their life solely due to being handicapped. HHS established a set of guidelines requiring treatment of all newborns regardless of disabilities. These became known as the **Baby Doe Laws**.

The original laws went into effect in on March 21, 1993, before the second Baby Doe case was heard. Notices were sent to all hospitals concerning the laws, and large posters were hung around NICUs, informing all that it was against federal law to discriminate against the handicapped newborns. A hotline number was set up to report any abuses. Teams of investigators were established, nicknamed "Baby Doe Squads." Many pediatricians became concerned that anybody could call the hotline and report them for almost any sort of validation, whether justified or unjustified, making it impossible to work in such an oppressive environment. The American Association of Pediatrics (AAP) filed suit in federal district court almost immediately after the laws went into effect. On April 14, 1983, the court decided in favor of the AAP and put an end to the Baby Doe Laws. However, the suit was decided on a technicality and by February 12, 1984, new Baby Doe Laws were enacted. The second Baby Doe case was heard during this interim period.

Before the second Baby Doe case was decided, the federal government stepped in. On October 22, 1983, Stony Brook Hospital was notified by investigators to turn over the baby's medical records to see if she had been discriminated against. On October 25, the hospital announced its refusal to do so. Two days later, the HHS turned the case over to the Justice Department, which filed suit against the hospital. In late November, after the appeals court had made its finding, the federal court ruled that the hospital did not need to release the records. The judge, Leonard Wexler, found that the decision not to treat the baby was not discriminatory. The case was appealed to the Second Circuit Court of Appeals, which affirmed the lower court's decision.[10]

In a last desperate move, the Justice Department appealed to the United States Supreme Court. The case was argued on January 15, 1986, and a decision was rendered on June 9, 1986. The Court held that (1) the records did not need to be released, (2) no evidence was present that the baby was subjected to discriminatory treatment, (3) the hospital was not guilty of any discrimination because it was the father who was denying treatment, not the hospital,

9. Rehabilitation Act of 1973, 29 U.S.C. §794.
10. *United States v. University Hospital*, 729 F.2d 144 (Second Circuit Court of Appeals, 1984).

and (4) Section 504 of the Rehabilitative Act was never intended to be used as a mechanism for the federal government to step in and mandate treatment decisions between hospitals and patients.[11] With that decision, the Baby Doe Laws were dealt the final blow.

While defeated with regards to the Rehabilitation Act, the Reagan administration shifted its focus to a different legislative measure. In 1984, the Child Abuse Prevention and Treatment Act (CAPTA) was revised to incorporate the Baby Doe Rules. The Act reads as follows:

> The term "withholding of medically indicated treatment" means the failure to respond to the infant's life-threatening conditions by providing treatment (including appropriate nutrition, hydration, and medication) which, in the treating physician's (or physicians') reasonable medical judgment, will be most likely to be effective in ameliorating or correcting all such conditions, except that the term does not include the failure to provide treatment (other than appropriate nutrition, hydration, or medication) to an infant when, in the treating physician's (or physicians') reasonable medical judgment any of the following circumstances apply:
>
> > i) the infant is chronically and irreversibly comatose;
> > ii) the provision of such treatment would merely prolong dying, not be effective in ameliorating or correcting all the infant's life-threatening conditions, or otherwise be futile in terms of the survival of the infant; or
> > iii) the provision of such treatment would be virtually futile in terms of the survival of the infant and the treatment itself under such circumstances would be inhumane.[12]

These revisions to CAPTA were very similar to the original Baby Doe Laws that had been at issue with the Rehabilitative Act. These Rules are still in effect today, and cases challenging these are practically nonexistent. In fact, most medical bodies that had an issue with the prior Baby Doe Laws have since issued guidelines for treatment along similar lines.

Outside of the United States, in 2002 doctors at the University Medical Center Groningen in the Netherlands established the Groningen Protocol for dealing with infants who were born with severe disabilities and abnormalities.

---

11. *Bowen v. American Hospital Association*, 476 U.S. 610 (1986).
12. 45 CFR 1340.15 (last amended July 5, 1990).

The protocol states that the life of an infant under the age of one could be terminated if the following four conditions were present:

> The presence of hopeless and unbearable suffering.
> The consent of the parents to termination of life.
> Medical consultation having taken place.
> Careful execution of the termination.

The Groningen protocols have become the model throughout much of Europe for those arguing in favor of infanticide. They were the basis for the concept of after-birth abortions as argued by Alberto Giubilini and Francesca Minerva (see below).

MORAL ARGUMENTS CONCERNING INFANTICIDE AND IMPERILED NEWBORNS

There are two ethical questions we need to discuss concerning the nontreatment of imperiled newborns. First, who should decide in these cases? Second, on what basis should decisions to forgo treatment and allow infants to die be made? The first question will be addressed briefly, and we will spend more time addressing the second.

Who should decide about treatment in cases of severely impaired newborns? The first reply would obviously be the parents. After all, it is their child and they are the ones who are legally and morally responsible for its upbringing. Patricia Phillips writes:

> Since the family must live with the consequences of any decision made with regard to sustaining or withholding treatment, it is imperative that the decision ultimately is left to the parents. Neither physicians, hospital infant care review committees, nor the legal system should be permitted to usurp the fundamental right that abides in parents to make important decisions with regard to what is best for the children they have brought into existence.[13]

This was also the conclusion of the courts in both Baby Doe cases and of the physicians in the Johns Hopkins case as well.

13. Patricia Phillips, "Parents Alone Have the Right to Decide if Infant Euthanasia is Ethical," in *Euthanasia: Opposing Viewpoints,* ed. Carol Wekesser (San Diego: Greenhaven, 1995), 187.

Normally, most would agree that the medical treatment of a child is the parents' decision—it is both their right and their obligation. However, the real question is, "Is this an absolute right?" Many would argue that it is a *prima facie* right, and not an absolute right. In other words, in normal situations parents have a right and an obligation concerning decision-making for the medical treatment or nontreatment of their own children. However, that right can be overridden if it comes into conflict with a more fundamental right. In the case of severely impaired newborns, their health and life are more fundamental than the parents' right to choose for them. If the parents' choice severely endangers the health or life of a child, then that right can be overridden. In fact, physicians and the legal system may have a duty to override parents in such cases. Physicians have a duty to "do no harm" to their patients, and the state has a compelling interest in protecting the lives of its citizens.

We recognize such a *prima facie* right in our laws concerning parental care and abuse of children. Richards and Rathbun write in their book *Law and the Physician: A Practical Guide*, "All states have laws that allow children to be treated without the parents' or guardians' consent in special circumstances. These laws are designed to protect either the child or the public health of the community."[14] The kinds of circumstances that they list would be: emergency situations when parents are unavailable, children suspected of being abused or neglected, children with certain communicable diseases, children seeking help for alcohol or drug abuse, and parents who refuse lifesaving medical treatment for their child.

One common reason for the last of these is when parents refuse lifesaving treatment for children due to religious beliefs. For example, Jehovah's Witnesses will not accept blood transfusions for their children. While courts generally honor adult refusal of blood transfusions, they have been disinclined to do the same for children. In *Mitchell v. Davis* (1947) and in *Wallace v. Labrenz* (1952) courts ruled that children should be transfused against the wishes of the parents, reasoning that the parents may have the right to be martyrs themselves, but they cannot force that on their children. This has been the standard ruling in courts concerning parents who refuse treatment to children. Richards and Rathbun explain the normal procedures in such situations:

14. Edward P. Richards and Katharine C. Rathbun, *Law and the Physician: A Practical Guide* (Boston: Little, Brown & Co, 1993), 170.

> The child should be evaluated at once to determine if immediate care is needed. If it is, a judge should be contacted to arrange a temporary guardianship. The child welfare department should also be notified because *denying a child necessary medical care is neglect in most states.* . . . Although the court may decide to accede to the parents' religious beliefs, the *physician's duty is to advocate for the child* until the court rules that the child need not be treated.[15]

These situations demonstrate that a parent does not have an absolute right to determine a child's treatment, especially if the parent's decision puts the child's life in danger. Certainly, if a parent's right to decide based on religious preferences can be justifiably infringed, then it seems at least plausible that a right to decide based on a desire not to raise a Down syndrome child can also be justifiably overridden.

However, many will say, "The situations you raised above are normal healthy children who need emergency care. That is not the case with impaired newborns. There is a *significant difference* between them and the Jehovah's Witnesses cases. This difference is enough to allow parents to decide not to treat severely impaired newborns." What are such "differences"? This brings us to the second moral question: "What basis can be offered to argue that one is justified for forgoing treatment and allowing infants to die?"

In February 2012, an article appeared in the *Journal of Medical Ethics* titled "After-birth Abortion: Why Should the Baby Live?"[16] written by two Australian ethicists, Alberto Giubilini and Francesca Minerva. They argued that after-birth abortion, a new term for infanticide, was justified on the same grounds as any elective abortion. They offer two main reasons for this conclusion:

1. The moral status of an infant is equivalent to that of a fetus, that is, neither can be considered a "person" in a morally relevant sense.
2. It is not possible to damage a newborn by preventing her from developing the potentially to become a person in the morally relevant sense.[17]

Giubilini and Minerva go on to explain that an infant, while being a human being, is not a person in the morally relevant sense but is only a potential person. They conceive a person as "an individual who is capable of attributing

15. Richards and Rathbun, *Law,* 166.
16. A. Giubilini and F. Minerva, "After-birth Abortion: Why Should the Baby Live?," *Journal of Medical Ethics* 39 (2013): 261–63.
17. Giubilini and Minerva, "After-birth Abortion," 262.

to her own existence some (at least) basic value such that being deprived of existence represents a loss to her."[18] While they do not definitively state a specific time in the newborn's life when she is able to attribute value to her life, it seems clear that a newborn infant is not at the level of mental development to attribute anything. Hence while it has the potential to develop into a person, it is not one, this moment and therefore cannot be harmed. Harm can only be done to "a person who is at least in the condition to value the different situation she would have found herself in if she had not been harmed."[19]

While Giubilini and Minerva hold that after-birth abortions can apply to any infant in a manner similar to any elective abortion, they focus mostly on abortions (after and before birth) that are done for one of two main reasons: (1) abortions that are performed due to third party harms and (2) abortions performed due to extreme deformities that would reduce a newborn's chance of survival or would cause extreme lifelong hardships and "unbearable suffering." These two are not unrelated for the second certainly adds to the first. Interestingly, Giubilini and Minerva acknowledge that "people with Down's syndrome as well, as well as people affected by many other severe disabilities, are often reported to be happy."[20] However, they go on to say:

> Nonetheless, to bring up such children might be an unbearable burden on the family and on society as a whole, when the state economically provides for their care. On these grounds, the fact that a fetus has the potential to become a person who will have an (at least) acceptable life is no reason for prohibiting abortion. Therefore, we argue that, when circumstances occur after birth such that they would have justified abortion, what we call after-birth abortion should be permissible.

Giubilini and Minerva offer then three main reasons for justifying infanticide: (1) the infant is not a person, (2) the infant's quality of life has dropped below a certain threshold where ending her life is justified for merciful reasons, (3) harms and burdens to third parties, such as the mother or family, would be of such sever difficulty that it justifies ending the life of the infant. We will discuss each of these in turn.[21]

---

18. Giubilini and Minerva, "After-birth Abortion," 262.
19. Giubilini and Minerva, "After-birth Abortion," 262.
20. Giubilini and Minerva, "After-birth Abortion," 262.
21. I am grateful to my colleague and friend, Dr. J. P. Moreland, for his appraisal of these arguments. Much of the material I am presenting here is based on his analysis of these positions as found in his chapter "Infanticide" in J. P. Moreland and Norman L. Geisler, *The Life and Death Debate: Moral Issues of Our Time* (Westport, CT: Greenwood, 1990).

The Nonperson View

This argument says that the "difference" lies in the status of the infant. Moral rights, especially the right to life, are grounded in being a person, and infants are not persons. They are human beings, but they are not persons in the full sense of the term. One philosopher who holds this view is Michael Tooley. Whether or not one agrees with Tooley's concept of person, he at least is consistent in saying that there is no real difference between an infant and a fetus when it comes to moral rights. However, his point is that neither fetuses nor infants have any moral rights. Tooley holds that there is a condition that an organism must have in order to have a right to life. He writes, "An organism possesses a serious right to life only if it possesses the concept of a self as a continuing subject of experiences and other mental states, and believes that it is itself such a continuing entity."[22] Tooley calls this the *self-consciousness* requirement. Since infants do not have a self-concept or are not self-conscious there is no moral requirements to treat them.

Tristram Englehardt is another who argues that the infant is not really a person, though for a different reason. Children are not persons in the "strict" sense because they are not adults. Therefore, they have no moral rights. He writes:

> Adults belong to themselves in the sense that they are rational and free and therefore responsible for their actions. Adults are *sui juris*. Young children, though, are neither self-possessed nor responsible. While adults exist in and for themselves, as self-directed and self-conscious beings, young children, especially newborn infants, exist for their families and those who love them. They are not, nor can they in any sense be, responsible for themselves. If being a person is to be a responsible agent, a bearer of rights and duties, children are not persons in the strict sense."[23]

How might one respond to these arguments? First, there is a difference between *functioning* as a person and *being* a person. We referred to this argument in chapter 2 when some attempted to deny the personhood of the fetus. A functionalistic definition of personhood fails because there are many times

22. Michael Tooley, "Abortion and Infanticide," in *Classic Works in Medical Ethics*, ed. Gregory Pence (New York: McGraw-Hill, 1998), 206.
23. Tristram Englehardt, "Aiding the Death of Young Children: Ethical Issues," in *Last Rights: Assisted Suicide and Euthanasia Debated*, ed. Michael Uhlmann (Grand Rapids: Eerdmans, 1998), 390.

people do not function *as* persons, and yet we would still consider them to *be* persons. A person does not have a self-concept nor is self-conscious when she is sleeping or under and anesthetic. Neither is she "self-possessed" or "responsible." For example, if a person sleepwalks and breaks an item while sleepwalking, we do not hold him "responsible" for his actions, but this hardly means they were not a person at the time, though one could argue they may not have been functioning as one. It is possible to be a person and not function as one.

Second, the basic inherent capacity for functioning as a person is present from conception. In other words, the essence of personhood is present from conception, through birth, and throughout all of a human being's life. An infant has this basic capacity in a latent undeveloped form. If proper care is given to him, he will grow and develop as a person. In severely impaired infants this development might be suppressed due to neurological damage. However, that does not mean it is not there. The only time a human organism ceases to have personhood is when it has died. Personhood is there by nature of what kind of being it is.

Third, this view goes counter to some of our most basic intuitions. For example, Tooley suggests that it is possible for a normal adult animal to have more worth than a defective infant because some higher-level animals can have more of a self-concept than an infant. However, most people recognize that there is something inherent about humans that make them different from other animals. Christians would argue that it is because we are image-of-God bearers. Therefore, morality applies to us in a way different from other animals.[24] This also goes counter to the way we intuitively treat infants: as persons having value. Englehardt gives the impression that an infant's only value is being "possessed" by a family. However, persons aren't possessions. They have intrinsic value of their own.

Finally, if infants are not persons, then why kill only severely impaired newborns? Why not kill or experiment on any newborn before it has developed into a person? If they are not persons then, in fact, none of them have any moral rights. Both Tooley and Englehardt apply their arguments only to severely impaired newborns. However, if they were consistent, it would not be

24. I am not arguing that we have no moral obligations to animals. I believe that we do have certain obligations. For example, we cannot cruelly torture animals. Our obligation to our environment is the recognition that God has given it to us and we are to be proper caretakers of it and respect it as his creation. While Scripture allows the slaying of animals for food and clothing, they are never to be needlessly tortured.

morally wrong for any parent to kill or allow *any* child to die for *any* reason including economic reasons or sex selection.

Quality-of-Life Arguments

Some have argued that the "difference" between healthy and impaired children lies in the quality of life that an infant might have to face if he is allowed to live. The basic argument is that it is morally justifiable to withdraw or withhold treatment from a severely impaired infant if its present or future quality of life will drop below a certain threshold. Those who hold this view argue that life is a relative good, not an absolute good. It is good relative only to the quality of life it achieves. It is possible that one's quality of life could be worse than death itself. At that point withholding/withdrawing treatment could be justifiable. Quality of life can be based on a number of different criteria; however, two criteria will be noted.

Richard McCormick has argued that the standard should be "relational potential," or the ability to have meaningful relationships. For McCormick the question is, "Granted we can easily save the life, but what kind of a life are we saving?"[25] McCormick's view is that:

> Life is not a value to be preserved in and for itself. To maintain that would commit us to a form of medical vitalism that makes no human or Judeo-Christian sense. It is a value to be preserved precisely as a condition for other values, and therefore insofar as these other values remain attainable. Since these other values cluster around and are rooted in human relationships, it seems to follow that life is a value to be preserved only insofar as it contains some potentiality for human relationships.[26]

Therefore, McCormick would hold that any infant who lacks the potential for future relationships can be said to have no interests and therefore has a low enough quality of life that one can justifiably allow it to die.

Another criterion for quality of life can be found in a research project on care of imperiled newborns sponsored by the Hastings Center. Participants argued that withholding or withdrawing life-sustaining treatment from impaired infants should be determined primarily using a "best interest

25. Richard McCormick, "To Save or Let Die: The Dilemma of Modern Medicine," in *Biomedical Ethics*, 2nd ed., ed. Thomas A. Mappes and Jane S. Zembaty (New York: McGraw-Hill, 1986), 431.
26. McCormick, "To Save or Let Die," 431.

standard" for the infant. The best interest standard would be applied under three possible conditions: the infant is dying, treatment is medically contra-indicated, or continued life would be worse than death. Concerning this last condition, they state, "The third condition opens the door to quality of life considerations but requires that such conditions be viewed *from the infant's point of view*. That is, certain states of being, marked by severe and intractable pain and suffering, can be viewed as worse than death."[27] Therefore, in considerations of "best interests" for the severely impaired infant, he or she can be allowed to die.

One can make a number of responses to the quality of life argument. First, the criteria in determining "quality of life" are too vague and subjective, rendering this determination difficult to use as a moral basis for allowing an infant to die. John A. Robertson comments, "Comparisons of relative worth among persons, or between persons and other interests, raise moral and methodological issues that make any argument that relies on such comparisons extremely vulnerable."[28] There are several reasons why it is difficult to make these kinds of judgments. First, different people mean different things by a "low quality of life," and there is just no way a proxy can know what the "infant's view" would be. Second, the people who are making this judgment on the infant, usually the parents and physician, are themselves dealing with the impact of treatment on their *own* interests, and therefore it's unrealistic to expect them to make a disinterested objective assessment of what the infant's interests might be. Third, our view of quality of life changes throughout our life. Some restrictions we wouldn't accept at one time might not be so unacceptable at another time. Oftentimes a particular state of affairs we think we could never live with, turns out not to be as bad as we had thought. Fourth, we make quality of life already lived. But an impaired infant may never share such experiences and so that judgment might be completely different for her because she has no basis for comparison. For a person who has spent life with sight, blindness would be a terrible loss that may impact him deeply. People who have been born blind all their lives don't experience the loss in the same way. The same could be said of the loss of ambulatory abilities or of

---

27. Members of the Hastings Center Research Project on the Care of Impaired Newborns, "Standards of Judgment for Treatment of Impaired Newborns," in *Biomedical Ethics*, 4th ed., ed. Thomas A. Mappes and David Degrazia (New York: McGraw-Hill, 1996), 423, emphasis added.
28. John A. Robertson, "Involuntary Euthanasia of Defective Newborns," in Mappes and Degrazia, *Biomedical Ethics*, ed. 423.

being mentally retarded. This doesn't mean such disabilities aren't tragic in an objective sense, but it is to say that they are not experienced the same way by all and therefore a proxy quality-of-life judgment is very difficult to assess. In light of these considerations, we need to acknowledge that there is just too much subjectivity to weigh proxy quality-of-life judgments heavily.

A second problem with the quality-of-life argument is that it is logically impossible to demonstrate that death is better than life. We need to note what is being claimed here. Those offering this argument are not saying that eternal life or the after-life is better than *existence*. Now what precisely is "nonexistence"? It is simply nothing. That is why there is a logical problem. The problem is that when you compare two things, you are comparing their properties or characteristics. When you make a valuative claim, that thing "A" is better than thing "B," you are saying that the characteristics of one are in some way superior to the characteristics of the other. However, "nothing" does not have any characteristics. Therefore, there is no basis for comparison between something and nothing; you can't compare something to nothing because there is "nothing" to compare it to. One can logically never make the claim that something is better than nothing or that nothing is better than something. Therefore, to claim that a particular state of life, a "painful" state, is "worse than death" simply does not follow. It is incoherent.

Third, the quality-of-life argument involves a view of persons that is seriously flawed. Christian philosopher J. P. Moreland writes that this view "fails to treat persons as entities with intrinsic value simply as human beings, and it tends to reduce the value of human beings to their social utility or to a view of humans as bundles of pleasant mental and physical states or capacities."[29] The impression is given that the only times persons have value are when they can have certain states like "relationships" or "freedom from pain." If one loses one of these states, then his value as a person is in jeopardy. However, persons have inherent and intrinsic value by nature of what they are. We do not say the mentally retarded are less valuable than the highly intelligent just because the mentally retarded cannot experience relationships at the same level as the intelligent. To say so would be elitist thinking and the height of arrogance. One is reminded of the Ghost of Christmas Present chiding Scrooge, "It may be in the sight of Heaven, you are more worthless and less fit to live than millions like this poor man's child."

29. Moreland, "Infanticide," 52.

Fourth, "the presence of suffering is simply not enough by itself, to signal the presence of morally inappropriate situation."[30] No one denies that all should be done to relieve as much suffering as possible, both presently and in the future. But as we have said in previous chapters, relief of suffering is not a mandate justifying one to do *any* action in the name of relief of suffering. Suffering itself, while it is an evil, is not always morally bad. It is not enough to warrant the overriding of our accepted norms concerning treatment of the non-dying.

Fifth, quality-of-life judgments can simply be wrong. Robertson comments that "the margin of error in such predictions may be very great."[31] Even McCormick admits this; in fact, his admission and response is somewhat surprising:

> Because this guideline [relational capacity] is precisely that, mistakes will be made. Some infants will be judged in all sincerity to be devoid of any meaningful relational potential when that is actually not quite the case. This risk of error should not lead to abandonment of decisions; for that is to walk away from the human scene. Risk of error means only that we must proceed with great humility, caution, and tentativeness. Concretely, it means that if err we must at times, it is better to err on the side of life—and therefore tilt in that direction.[32]

What McCormick is saying about erring on the "side of life" is not that we should, in the face of doubt, allow severely impaired newborns to live, but that we should allow them to die because they cannot *really* live any kind of qualitative life. We can see examples of the mistakes that have been made. The parents of Keri-Lynn were told that she would be paralyzed, which would probably not go much beyond a few painful years, if that long. Yet she is not anywhere near the condition that was predicted. Dax Cowart, the fire-burned victim I mentioned in a previous chapter, wanted to end his life because he thought it would be completely meaningless. He had lost his sight, and the use of his hands and was badly disfigured. Today he is a successful lawyer, married, and generally happy. Many Down syndrome children live happy and meaningful lives for many years. Therefore, one needs to approach quality-of-life predictions with extreme caution.

---

30. Moreland, "Infanticide," 52.
31. Robertson, "Involuntary Euthanasia," 224.
32. McCormick, "To Save, or Let Die" 432.

Finally, the principle of justice demands that we protect the weakest in society. What a severely impaired child needs are those who are caring and looking out for her or his needs. There is a subtle form of discrimination under the guise of care in not treating impaired infants. As we saw in the Johns Hopkins and Baby Doe cases, if the child had been normal, the medical procedures they needed would have been performed without a second thought. However, because of their impaired condition, the parents could deny that care. That is discriminatory treatment and goes against our practice of equal protection under the law.

The Harms-to-Others Argument

Finally, some argue that the "difference" between healthy and severely impaired infants must take into account not only the suffering of the infant, but the suffering of others who are impacted by this tragic circumstance. The most obvious group of people are the parents and immediate family members. They will have to raise the child and care for it in its impaired condition. This will place a great emotional, psychological, and financial burden on the family. Tristram Englehardt Jr., notes the importance of "costs" to the family:

> The accent is on the absence of a positive duty to treat in the presence of severe inconvenience (costs) to the parents; treatment that is very costly is not obligatory. What is suggested here is a general notion that there is never a duty to engage in extraordinary treatment and that "extraordinary" can be defined in terms of costs. This argument concerns children (1) whose future quality of life is likely to be seriously compromised and (2) whose present treatment would be very costly. The issue is that of the circumstances under which parents would not be obliged to take on severe burdens on behalf of their children or those circumstances under which society would not be so obligated.[33]

Carson Strong argues even more firmly that "when a heavy burden would fall on the family with the survival of an impaired newborn, it is permissible to put the interests of the family above those of the infant."[34]

Not only will the family suffer, but others will suffer as well. Society will need to spend more resources on this child than the average person; therefore

---

33. Englehardt, "Aiding the Death," 392.
34. Carson Strong, "The Neonatologist's Duty to Patient and Parents," *Hastings Center Report* 14 (1984): 13.

the impaired infant is receiving more than his or her fair share, leaving less for others. Also, in some way the physicians and nurses suffer though not to the same degree as the family. There is a lot of strain in the NICU taking care of impaired newborns. Physicians may feel their skills are being misused in caring for an impaired newborn. Therefore, due to these harms to others, the nontreatment of the severely impaired newborn is justified.

The first problem with considering these kinds of harms is that this is based on a utilitarian type of calculation. In weighing the benefits and burdens, the costs to the parents and family or society are weighed as greater than the life of the child and therefore the child's life is sacrificed for the good of the family or society. However, as you might remember from our discussion in the first chapter, utilitarian calculations are very problematical. First, there is the incommensurability problem. The judgment that the benefits of family outweigh the infant's interests "requires a coherent way of measuring and comparing interpersonal utilities."[35] Yet there does not seem to be any way to accomplish this. Second, a common problem with utilitarian calculations is that people get treated as means to ends rather than ends themselves. The value of the infant is now placed in terms of costs or benefits for the family or society. The infant is not being treated as a person, itself, intrinsically valuable. Robertson writes, "If the life of one individual, however useless, may be sacrificed for the benefit of any person, however useful, or for the benefit of any number of persons, then we have acknowledged the principle that rational utility may justify any outcome . . . we reach the point where protection of life depends solely on social judgments of utility."[36]

Second, what criteria for judging between the family's/society's needs and the baby's life are offered? Not only is such comparison not possible due to incommensurability, but the criteria to use in making the comparison are highly debatable. How much burden on the family justifies not treating the infant? Financial costs of continued care? The cost of a mother having to give up a career to care for an impaired child? Major adjustments in home life? The problem is that a whole range of burdens is possible, and it would be very difficult to regulate which ones are enough to allow the infant to die and which are not. Because there are no clear objective criteria for balancing the burdens of treating the infant with the benefits of not treating the infant,

35. Robertson, "Involuntary Euthanasia," 225.
36. Robertson, "Involuntary Euthanasia," 225.

treatment cannot be justifiably withheld from newborns. One needs to have justifiable reasons to take an innocent life, but none are offered here.

Third, parents have a filial obligation to care for their children, and the fact that the children are impaired does not negate that obligation; in fact, that obligation is stronger because the need is greater. If the "harms to others" argument really worked the way proponents suggest, then why stop with impaired newborns? Why not argue that parents may do away with their children any time they become too much of a burden? Why does he have to be suffering? It is not the child's suffering that is the thrust of this argument; it is that he or she is a burden. Therefore, any time the child is a burden I should be allowed to dispose of it. Most recognize the lunacy of such a suggestion. Part of the basis of family morality is that parents have obligations to children which they cannot neglect purely because the child is now a burden. As we said in our abortion chapter, child abuse, neglect, and abandonment laws recognize this obligation. That is why Congress placed medical neglect under the Child Abuse Prevention and Treatment Act of 1973. It states, "The term 'medical neglect' includes, but is not limited to, the withholding of medically indicated treatment from a disabled infant with a life-threatening condition."[37]

None of this is to deny the devastating impact an impaired child can have on a family. The initial effect always carries feelings of guilt, grief, and loss of dignity to the parents. Adjustments must be made in the home which cause anxiety and tension among all family members. There is a significant drain on financial resources as they care for the infant. However, it is not a hopeless situation. Counseling is available to deal with the adjustments and initial feeling. Resources are often available to help in caring for the infant. For Christians, such an experience can be positive as one learns how to live sacrificially for another. This is not to downplay the real difficulty of such a situation, but, "Suffering there is, but seldom is it so overwhelming or so imminent that the only alternative is death of the child."[38]

PASSIVE EUTHANASIA AND THE IMPAIRED NEWBORN

Is there ever a time when nontreatment is justified for an impaired infant? The answer is yes—when the infant is dying. If the infant is not dying, then medical treatment should be given. Such a view has been called a "medical

37. Final Rule: 45 CFR 1340. U.S. Department of Health and Human Services (1985).
38. Robertson, "Involuntary Euthanasia," 227.

indications" or "medical feasibility" view. It has been held by a number of people, but perhaps the most well-known proponent was the Christian ethicist Paul Ramsey. Richard Sparks summarizes Ramsey's position well:

> If a patient, competent or otherwise, has entered the dying process, in which all curative efforts are futile or at best serve only minimally to forestall the *imminently* inevitable, then such medical procedures are optional, perhaps even contraindicated . . . In the cases of patients, competent or incompetent, who are not irreversibly dying, a medical indications policy asserts that any treatment that prognostically will be medically beneficial is automatically morally indicated.[39]

It is important for a moment to discuss the next chapter (chapter 5) of the distinction between passive and active euthanasia. In that chapter we make the distinction that active euthanasia involves both (1) the intention of death and (2) that the direct actions of the agent are the cause of death of the patient. Passive euthanasia occurs when (1) the intention is not the death of the patient, but relief of the burdens of treatment and (2) it is not the direct action of the agent that is the cause of death, but the particular debilitation. This distinction is somewhat blurred in the case of nontreatment of the impaired newborn. In this case, it is the withholding or withdrawing of treatment of the newborn that is the direct cause of death. While this might be interpreted as passive, in this case it is active because in normal cases such treatment would be beneficial without being excessively burdensome. Ramsey makes this point:

> When care is not even attempted in the case of defective non-dying infants, there is no morally significant distinction, between actions and abstention. Morally what in this case is not done is the same as doing. The benign neglect of defective infants—who are not dying, who cannot themselves refuse treatment, who are most in need of human help—is the same as directly dispatching them: involuntary euthanasia.[40]

Examples of the kinds of cases that might normally fit into the "dying" category would be extremely premature infants of which even strongly aggressive

39. Richard C. Sparks, *To Treat or Not to Treat: Bioethics and the Handicapped Newborn* (Mahwah, NJ: Paulist Press, 1988), 34, 37, emphasis his.
40. Paul Ramsey, *Ethics at the Edges of Life: Medical and Legal Intersections* (New Haven: Yale University Press, 1978), 195.

therapy would be futile, and possibly anencephalic infants (which will be discussed more below). In these cases, palliative and comfort care should be maintained, but aggressive life-saving care would not be warranted. Examples of the kinds of cases that would generally not be considered dying would be children born with Down syndrome, mentally retarded children, spina bifida children, or children born with physical, but not life-threatening, deformities. All judgments concerning the dying/non-dying status of the impaired infant are medical judgments, and it needs to be readily admitted that such cases are not always clear. However, once a judgment is medically determined, the infant's status of dying/non-dying becomes the determining factor concerning treatment, not quality of life, third party consideration, or personhood.

There are a number of reasons to support this view. First, it preserves the basic moral notion that all human persons have intrinsic worth and grounds that worth in being a member of a natural kind, humankind. It holds to the mandate not to kill innocent persons without just cause. The fact that the infant is deformed or impaired is not a justifiable cause for its death. Second, it avoids the vagueness and subjectivity of both the quality-of-life view and the nonperson view. We are no longer trying to decipher what the "best interests are from the infant's point of view." We are also rejecting the functionalistic concept of personhood. Third, it places the focus on the person and on the treatment instead of discriminating between the morally irrelevant properties of severely impaired infants and healthy infants. Ramsey comments, "This requires no comparison of patient-*persons* or of different stages or conditions of the same patient-person in order to determine his quality-of-life struggles or prospects. It requires simply a *comparison of treatments* to determine whether any are likely to be beneficial in any way other than prolonging dying."[41]

Finally, this view places the discussion of nontreatment within the broader area of euthanasia instead of specifically pinpointing infants. One can treat infants like adults in evaluating their treatment. We allow adults to die when we recognize that care is no longer of benefit and there is nothing more that can be done. There is no reason not to treat infants in the same way.

ANENCEPHALICS—A SPECIAL CASE?

In recent years several physicians and ethicists have attempted to argue that the anencephalic child is such a special case that it needs to be considered

41. Ramsey, *Ethics at the Edges of Life*, 178.

apart from the other forms of impairment we have discussed thus far. Merely the fact that this has been raised calls for a separate discussion.

What is anencephaly? The word literally means "no brain", however, that might communicate the wrong idea. Anencephaly results from a failure of the neural system. This closure normally occurs between the second and third week of pregnancy. The cerebral cortex or upper level of the brain is missing but the brain stem is always present. Infants born with anencephaly usually do not have a closed cranium and one can often investigate the head and see the missing Cephalus brain, which controls the involuntary operations of heart rate, lungs, blood pressure, salt and water balance, kidneys, and other organs and systems. However, the cerebral cortex contains the area where such operations as consciousness, memories, purposive action, emotional states, social abilities, and, some believe, sentience take place. Therefore, while the infant is definitely alive, it has no capacity, nor ever will have a capacity, for functioning as a person.

Anencephaly occurs in about one thousand pregnancies per year and is usually diagnosed during pregnancy. About 95 percent of these are aborted even though there is a possibility of misdiagnosis. Of those carried to term, about half are stillborn.[42] Those anencephalics who survive through birth rarely live for more than a week, often dying because of the exposure of the brain stem. However, some have been known to live longer due to special care. In fact, one source writes, "If the brain were sufficiently protected, life could be prolonged for years."[43] The question concerning anencephalics has to do with their status as persons and the medical status of their treatment. These questions arise due to several cases concerning anencephalics have occurred, specifically the following two cases.

In the Matter of Theresa Ann Campo Pearson

On March 21, 1992, Theresa Ann Campo Pearson was born in Florida to Laura Campo and Justin Pearson, an unmarried couple. Because Laura did not have medical insurance, she did not find out until the eighth month of pregnancy that her baby was anencephalic, which was deemed too late for an abortion. Laura claimed that had she known earlier, she would have aborted

42. Statistics from Pence, *Classic Cases,* 327.
43. Paul A. Byrne, Joseph C. Evers, and Richard G. Nilges, "Anencephaly—Organ Donation?" *Issues in Law and Medicine* 9, no. 1 (Summer 1993): 32.

the baby. However, hoping for some good to come from the tragic situation, Laura decided to carry the baby to term so its organs could be donated.

The idea of organ donation from anencephalics has been a topic of debate within the medical community for some time. There is a desperate need for organs for infants, and such organs need to come from other infants. The problem is that in the normal course of dying, the blood flow slows down as the heart gradually stops beating. Organs suffer from a lack of oxygen and begin to rapidly deteriorate, becoming unusable for transplantation. But, if the organs are excised from a breathing infant, then they would stand a much better chance for successful transplantation. After birth, anencephalics could be placed on a ventilator to ensure that the organs remain oxygenated. A determination could be made that the infant is brain dead and the organs could then be transplanted to other infants. At least one transplantation from an anencephalic had taken place previously in California. This was what Laura and Justin wanted for Theresa.

The problem was that Theresa was not born brain dead. Upon birth, Theresa was placed on a ventilator. After one week, the ventilator was removed and she was able to breathe on her own for a period, indicating that the brain stem was still functioning. Laura and Justin requested to have Theresa legally declared dead so that her organs could be removed for transplantation. However, the hospital refused, claiming that under Florida State Law, which uses the Harvard Criteria for whole brain death,[44] Theresa was not officially brain dead, and organs cannot be removed from a living human being. Laura and Justin petitioned the Circuit Court of Broward County for a declaratory judgment stating that Theresa was legally dead. The Circuit Court denied their request, citing that Theresa was not dead according to state law. The case was appealed, and the Appellate Court affirmed the lower court's ruling. The case was then appealed to the Florida Supreme Court.

Theresa died on March 30, 1992, before the case went before the Florida Supreme Court. However, the Court agreed to review the case anyway and on November 12, 1992, it rendered a unanimous opinion on the issue: "Is an anencephalic newborn considered 'dead' for purposes of organ donation solely by reason of its congenital deformity . . . as a matter of Florida common law the cardiopulmonary definition of death should be applied in

44. In 1968, Harvard Medical School defined whole brain death as when one has suffered irreversible cessation of the brain functions, including the brain stem. For more details, see Ad Hoc Committee of the Harvard Medical School, "A Definition of Irreversible Coma," *Journal of the American Medical Association* 205 (1968): 337–40.

cases involving anencephaly that survive without life support."[45] Under this definition of death, Theresa was alive as long as her heart and lungs spontaneously function, and therefore she could not be used for organ transplantation until these functions ceased.

In the Matter of Baby K

On October 13, 1992, Stephanie Keene, an anencephalic infant, was born in Fairfax Hospital in Falls Church, Virginia. As is normal with anencephalics, she was placed on a respirator. Stephanie had been prenatally diagnosed with anencephaly, but her mother, being a Christian, refused to have an abortion. The mother and father were unmarried and were referred throughout the case as Ms. H and Mr. K. Stephanie's father remained only distantly involved in the case.

Within days of Stephanie's birth, hospital physicians approached Ms. H and requested that a "Do Not Resuscitate" order, or **DNR**, be placed in Stephanie's file, allowing for disconnection of the ventilator and subsequent death of Stephanie. DNRs are standard procedures in hospitals when it is determined that resuscitative efforts would be futile and only prolong the dying process. The medical personnel explained that no treatment existed for Stephanie's condition, that she would never be able to function as a person, and that the ventilator was medically unnecessary. Ms. H declined to do a DNR order, stating she believed God could work a miracle. The hospital then referred to the hospital ethics committee to assist in overriding the mother's wishes. The committee met with Ms. H on October 22, 1992, and again attempted to convince her that such care was futile. Ms. H again refused to follow the recommendation.

The hospital attempted to circumvent legal action by transferring Stephanie to a nursing home during a period when she was not in need of ventilator support. Ms. H agreed to move Stephanie, but only on the condition that the hospital would take her back should she develop respiratory distress. Stephanie was transferred to the nursing home on November 30, 1992. Over the next several months, Stephanie needed to be returned to the hospital twice due to respiratory issues. After the second of these visits, when Stephanie was returned to the nursing home, the hospital decided to seek a court order allowing them to discontinue treatment of Stephanie. The case before Federal Judge Claude Hilton and became known as the "Baby K" case.

---

45. *In re Theresa Ann Campo Pearson*, 609 So. 2d 588, 595 (Florida Supreme Court, 1992).

On July 1, 1993, Judge Hilton ruled that the hospital had a duty to provide medical care to Stephanie.[46] He came to his decision using the Americans with Disabilities Act of 1990, the Rehabilitation Act of 1973, and the Emergency Medical Treatment and Active Labor Act (EMTALA).[47] The case was appealed and in December 1994, the Fourth Circuit Court of Appeals upheld Judge Hilton's ruling, finding that the EMTALA states that hospitals covered under the act must provide the appropriate level of stabilizing treatment to any individual, regardless of the condition requiring such treatment.[48] This ruling extended all of the provisions of the EMTALA to anencephalic infants.

During the trial, Laura Flint from Jacksonville, Florida, appeared on behalf of Ms. H. She had given birth to an anencephalic daughter who lived beyond the age of four years before dying. Mrs. Flint reported that her daughter was able to recognize voices, see colors, hold up her head, and push toys. She showed pictures of her daughter sitting in Santa's lap and in front of a birthday cake. She stated, "To me, it was worth it every day we had with her."[49] Stephanie herself lived until she was two and a half. She died on April 5, 1995, and her mother contended throughout her life that life was precious and only God could take her daughter.

Cases like those above have raised serious moral questions about the status of anencephalics. Since such children are born without even the capacity to function as persons, should they be considered persons or not? Should the standard for brain death be changed to include neocortical death? If anencephalics are considered persons, what kind of medical treatment should they receive?

Concerning the first of these questions, there are those who suggest that the anencephalic infant is not a person. Gregory Pence doesn't even argue the issue, but simply states, "Nevertheless, anencephaly is the most serious of all birth defects, because the baby essentially lacks the higher brain necessary for personhood."[50] While he does not comment on anencephalics specifically, Christian theologian Robert Rakestraw might take this view as it follows from his view on persistent vegetative state (PVS) patients. He holds that, "Neocortical destruction is both a necessary and sufficient condition for declaring an

46. *Matter of Baby K*, 832 F. Su1022 (United States District Court for Eastern District of Virginia, 1993).
47. Emergency Medical Treatment and Active Labor Act, 42 U.S.C. §1395dd (1986).
48. *In re Baby K*, 16 F.3d 590, 598 (Fourth Circuit Court of Appeals, 1994).
49. The story of Laura Flint's appearance is from Lori Sharn, "Baby K's Right to Life Rests in Court's Hand," *USA Today*, October 27, 1993, 11A.
50. Pence, *Classic Cases*, 327.

individual dead theologically."[51] Certainly if personal life ends with the destruction of the neocortex, it must not be there if the neocortex is never present. One group of physicians summarizes this position well:

> Valuable human life is intrinsically related to higher brain function, or at least the potential of developing it. Brainstem function and artificial life support could maintain the bodies of anencephalic infants but would not give them what most people consider to be meaningful life as human beings. Hence, it is morally right to differentiate between biologic human life and personal life. Anencephalic infants may be living human beings, but they lack personhood.[52]

While it is possible that personhood is never in fact present in the anencephalic, we should approach the status of the anencephalic with extreme caution. There are several reasons for holding this view. First, the anencephalic is still a living, breathing human being. Human beings by nature are persons due to the kind of beings they are. Unless there is overwhelming evidence, that nature should be presumed to be present.

Second, one should be careful about identifying personhood so strongly with any specific part of brain. While it seems that the absence of the neocortex means that certain capacities for functioning as a person may not be present, it does not rule out the possibility that the basic inherent capacity may be rooted more deeply in the entire neural system. The fact that an anencephalic may not be able to realize these capacities does not mean they are not present. Stephen Schwartz refers to these as "latent capacities," and his comment is worth repeating here: "Even a very severely abnormal or handicapped human being has the basic inherent capacity to function as a person, which is a sign that he is a person. The abnormality represents a *hindrance* to the actual

51. Robert. V. Rakestraw, "The Persistent Vegetative State and the Withdrawal of Nutrition and Hydration," in *Readings in Christian Ethics*, ed. David K. Clark and Robert V. Rakestraw (Grand Rapids: Baker, 1996), 128. In a personal correspondence with Dr. Rakestraw, he stated that he was "not willing to say that they [anencephalics] are not persons because their condition is not able to be diagnosed and monitored as precisely as PVS patients." He stated that he would not support and abortion of an anencephalic because the diagnosis is not without error. He goes on to say that "If the newborn was really life a PVS patient and this could be determined with certainty, the I see no need for artificial sustenance" (February 9, 1999).

52. Avraham Steinberg, Eliezer Katz, and Charles L. Sprung, "Use of Anencephalics as Organ Donors," *Critical Care Medicine* (November 1993): 1788. It is unclear whether this is the position of the authors themselves.

working of this capacity, to its manifestation in actual functioning. It does not imply the *absence* of this capacity, as in a non-person."[53]

Third, those who hold that anencephalics should be declared nonpersons in order to excise organs for donation often make a point that anencephalics do not feel pain. However, this is a highly questionable premise. Dr. Alan Shewmon, considered the world's greatest authority on anencephalics, states:

> It simply begs the question to state categorically that [anencephalic babies] lack conscious awareness because they lack cerebral hemispheres. Much less is there any logical or physiological basis for the claim of some that an anencephalic infant can neither feel, nor experience, pain "by definition." For practical purposes, one should presume, at the very least, that anencephalic babies are no less aware or capable of suffering than some laboratory animals with even smaller brains, which everyone seems to feel obliged to treat "humanely."[54]

In short, it is possible that anencephalics do feel pain, and if so, they should be granted at least minimum humane treatment.

Fourth, while rare, there have been cases of anencephalics who have lived longer than the few days usually predicted. Stephanie Keene lived two and a half years and the child of Laura Flint lived until four and exhibited some possible traits of personhood. There are other cases where anencephalics have lived for a year or longer. When one considers these cases and the above comment that if the brain were protected, they could go on for years, it should give one pause in automatically jumping to the conclusion that such infants are not persons or should be harvested for organs. Some have claimed that such cases are simply misdiagnoses, and true anencephalics by definition will not live that long. However, if that is true, it only makes the case stronger for not using such infants for donations—in case there is a misdiagnosis.

Fifth, if one changes the criterion for death from whole brain death to neocortical death, which would include anencephalics, many believe there is a danger of slipping down the slope to including many other areas where absence of a functioning person might lead to termination of life. Some say that anencephalics are sufficiently similar to other debilitations, such as PVS, hydrocephaly, atelencephaly, degenerative brain disorders, profound

53. Stephen Schwartz, *The Moral Question of Abortion* (Chicago: Loyola University Press, 1990), 97 (emphasis mine).
54. Quoted in Byrne, Evers, and Nilges, "Anencephaly—Organ Donation?," 32–33.

retardation and advanced Alzheimer's that a clear distinction may not be seen, such that these may also be grouped in with those considered neocortically dead. If personhood is lacking in the anencephalic, perhaps it is lacking in these disorders also. If one argues that we would only change the definition to include anencephalics, then one also must ask if it is worth creating a whole separate category and changing a basic definition for such a small number of beings. It is estimated that only about three hundred anencephalics per year can be potential organ donors.[55] The increase in supply of organs for transplantation would be minimal.

Enough evidence exists that warrants that the benefit of the doubt should be given to the anencephalic child concerning personhood. While it is possible that personhood is absent, enough evidence is not available to suggest this. The benefit of the doubt should always go toward maintaining life if there is ever a reasonable question.

However, now there is the question as to the anencephalic child's medical status. This is a question in which a medical judgment is necessary and such a judgment lies outside the scope of this book. In general, however, Gilbert Meilaender's assessment for the normal care for anencephalics is acceptable: "How would we ordinarily care for this baby at her birth? The case suggests a standard, and it seems to me the right one: she would receive 'no aggressive treatment in the neonatal nursery.' She is born dying, and proper care for her does not entail useless attempts to sustain her life."[56]

Usually this would mean that once born the anencephalic would be placed on a respirator. After a period in the medical judgment of physicians, it would be determined if he or she were brain dead. As long as the infant remained alive, ordinary care should be used to maintain her or his life. However, aggressive care should be avoided. Again there comes a time to recognize that there is nothing more that we can do.

CONCLUSION

We need to revisit a recurring theme in the two previous chapters of this book. It is the theme of "caring, but not killing." It is the recognition that God has placed limits on how much we can do. Those limits inform us when we

55. Steinberg, Katz, and Sprung, "Use of Anencephalics as Organ Donors," 1788.
56. Gilbert Meilander, "The Anencephalic Newborn as Organ Donor—Commentary," *Hastings Center Report* 16, no. 2 (1986): 23.

can do no more and when medical care must end. However, the same limits also inform us that we cannot kill infants through nontreatment and justifying it as a way of healing. Certainly many of those who desire to end the lives of their children are acting out of pure motives. Wanting to end suffering, avoid a life of misery, or, in the case of anencephalics, to cause some good to come from a tragic situation is understandable. Nevertheless some are acting from less honorable motives, such as not wanting to be hassled with the raising of an impaired child, though surely most persons are not feeling this way. But as good as those motives are, we cannot ever intend the death of another person. That is a role meant only for the Lord of life, and we must not usurp it.

No one can even pretend to be able to answer the question of why God allows some children to come into the world with the disabilities we have discussed in this chapter. But God does give us guidance for how we are to treat them. We see it modeled in the parable of the good Samaritan. There we observe a person who was severely beaten and in dire need of help. The Samaritan, whom our Lord praises, went out of his way to care. He was the good neighbor to this man. Surely if he can be such a neighbor to a perfect stranger, we can be so to our own children. The Christian ethicist Paul Ramsey said:

> Persons are not to be reducible for their potential. Patients are to be loved and cared for no matter who they are and no matter what their potential for higher values is, and certainly not on account of their responsiveness. Who they are, in Christian ethical perspective, is our neighbors. They do not become nearer neighbors because of any capacity they own, nor lesser neighbors because they lack some ability to prevail in their struggle for human achievement.[57]

57. Ramsey, *Ethics at the Edges of Life*, 185.

5 

A Good Death: Euthanasia

By all accounts she was a free-spirited girl. Certainly, her parents thought that. Her friends knew she played fast and loose, claiming she was involved with drugs, though her parents denied it. On April 11, 1975, twenty-one-year-old Karen Ann Quinlan moved out of her parents' house and rented a room with two male friends a few miles away. A few days later, April 14, she joined one of her roommates, Thomas French, and a group of others to celebrate a friend's birthday at Falconer's, a local bar in the small North Jersey community of Lake Lackawanna. French reports that they had been drinking before the party and he had seen Karen "popping pills" earlier in the day. After a few drinks at the bar—the actual number is uncertain—Karen became dizzy and appeared faint. Her friends decided to take her home and let her sleep it off. By the time they had gotten her home she had completely passed out.

After putting her into bed, French decided to check on her about fifteen minutes later. He discovered that she had stopped breathing. French performed mouth-to-mouth resuscitation while another roommate called the police. When the police arrived, one took over the resuscitation efforts while the other questioned the two roommates. In their panic they lied and said that Karen was just staying over while her parents were on vacation, and that they had simply found her having difficulty breathing. The police finally got her breathing again. Her color began to return, but she did not regain consciousness.

Karen was transported to nearby Newton Memorial Hospital and admitted around midnight into the intensive care unit. In examining her possessions, a bottle of Valium was discovered in her purse with some pills missing. Valium is a tranquilizer and, if mixed with alcohol or other drugs, it can be dangerous in slowing down the respiratory system causing anoxia, a loss of oxygen to the brain resulting in brain damage and often death. Karen had also been aggressively dieting, possibly even fasting, for several previous days. All of this may have contributed to Karen's condition, though the actual evidence of why she became initially unconscious is disputed.[1] Because of her difficulty breathing, Karen was placed on a small respirator for the first few days of her treatment. After nine days, her condition had not changed and she was transferred to the larger St. Clare's Hospital in Denville, New Jersey, which was staffed with neurologists who were not available at the smaller facility. Karen had difficulty with the smaller respirator and four days after admission was transferred to an MA-1 respirator, which uses an intertracheal tube. A nasal-gastro tube was put in place for feeding purposes and she was placed on antibiotics.

Karen Ann Quinlan never regained consciousness. She was in a special coma-like state referred to today as persistent vegetative state. Her brain wave was not totally flat, but it was damaged to the point that it was believed she was not receiving any input from her senses. She would move her head, her eyes would remain open, she would even moan and make other vocal noises. But her body soon began to take on the rigidity found in most neurologically damaged patients and her weight dropped to seventy to eighty pounds.

Her family was understandably upset at her condition and were aware that her prognosis was hopeless. They were especially bothered in light of the fact that Karen had earlier shared with them her desire never to be kept alive in this condition. After three and a half months, and consulting with their family priest, they decided that this needed to

1. There exists contradictory evidence of what the initial toxicology screen reported about Karen. The attending physician said there was a small amount of barbiturates in her system; a consulting neurologist said there was evidence of quinine, Valium, and Librium, but no evidence for morphine or barbiturates; and her parents claim that the early reports showed only normal "therapeutic" levels of aspirin and Valium in her system. From Gregory Pence, *Classic Cases in Medical Ethics* (New York: McGraw Hill, 1990).

end. Karen was dead for all intents and purposes. On July 31, 1975, they signed a release to have the respirator and naso-gastric tubes removed.

Dr. Robert Morse initially agreed, but later backed down for a couple of reasons. First, St. Clare's was a Catholic hospital, and Morse was a Catholic himself. In those days many in the Catholic church thought that any form of euthanasia was equivalent to killing. Second, Morse consulted the hospital attorney who advised him not to disconnect Karen. Another important case had just concluded in Massachusetts in which a Dr. Eidolon was found guilty of criminal negligence for an unjustified late-term abortion. The hospital lawyers thought the cases were too similar.

The Quinlans sought legal help from the local Legal Aid Society and found one in a young, idealistic lawyer, Paul Armstrong. Armstrong could have easily solved the case by simply asking the court to appoint Karen's father to be legal guardian. As legal guardian, Mr. Quinlan could have had Karen transferred to another hospital where they probably would have privately and discretely honored the family's wishes. However, Armstrong announced to the presiding judge, Robert Muir, that they were intending to remove Karen from the respirator and allow her to die. When Armstrong made that announcement, Judge Muir realized he could not appoint Mr. Quinlan as guardian. The legal guardian had to protect the interests of the patient. What Karen's interests had been were now open to dispute because the issue of whether removal of treatment and allowing Karen to die was justified had not yet been established. Therefore, Muir had no choice but to appoint a *guardian ad litem* (meaning "for the case"), a lawyer named Daniel Coburn, who would be an advocate for Karen. Armstrong was now forced to argue in court that Karen should be allowed to die. In making that announcement to the judge he set the stage for one of the most famous trials in the history of medical ethics: In the Matter of Karen Ann Quinlan.[2]

2. Details concerning Karen Ann Quinlan's story were gathered through various sources including Pence, *Classic Cases*, 9–11, and Merrill Sheils, "Who Was Karen Quinlan?" *Newsweek*, November 3, 1975, 60.

DEFINITIONS AND DISTINCTIONS

The word "euthanasia" is a combination of two Greek words: *eu* is the prefix for "good," and *thanatos* is the word for "death." Many today argue that for some people euthanasia can truly be a "good death" especially if they are suffering greatly, or their lives are being unnecessarily prolonged by modern technology. Part of the confusion surrounding this issue is that the term "euthanasia" can be used a couple of different ways. In a narrow sense euthanasia can be defined as the intentional ending of a person's life, out of motives of either mercy, beneficence, or respect for personal autonomy. This has also been called "mercy killing." Under this definition, the aim of euthanasia is the death of the person to whom it is being applied. However, there is a broader definition of euthanasia which defines it as any act of relieving a person of the burdens of excessive medical treatment which one knows, with a high degree of reasonable probability, will result in the person's death. This definition is broader because it can incorporate the narrower view but can also allow for actions in which the death of the patient is not necessarily intended. In the early years of the euthanasia issue, the broader definition was employed. However, in recent years the narrower definition seems to be the one most bioethicists mean. I will make a further distinction between different types of euthanasia below. For our present purposes, whenever I use the term euthanasia without qualification, I will be referring to the broader definition.

Another term we need to discuss is "death." A lot of controversy has been stirred up recently surrounding discussions of exactly when a person is considered to be dead. We first need to distinguish between definition of death and determination of death. Some will argue that it is the definition of death which needs to be reconsidered. However, I believe it is not the definition of death that is what is really being debated, but its determination. Death can be defined as the cessation of the essential characteristics and capacities that are necessary and sufficient conditions in order for a person to be alive. What are the "necessary and sufficient conditions" in order for a person to be alive? These can be discovered in examining the ways we have determined that someone is dead. Over time, four different concepts of determining death that have been used:

1. *Failure of heart and lungs*. Throughout most of history, the traditional determining factor for death has focused on the heart and lungs. When the breathing of air and the flow of blood have irreversibly stopped circulating,

death has occurred. These are easily observed and even today most individuals are declared dead when circulation and respiration have ceased. Before the development of modern life-extending technologies, these were considered necessary and sufficient conditions for declaring death. With the advent of these machines, cessation of heart and lungs is no longer as decisive as it once was in determining death.

2. *Separation of body and soul.* Aristotle believed that the animating principle of life was the soul. Christianity takes a similar view and therefore defines death as when the soul leaves the body. For Christians, the separation of soul and body is the necessary and sufficient condition for declaring someone dead. However, this is not observable, and the question remains as to when specifically this occurs in the dying process. This is a theological truth and theological truths are difficult to defend empirically.

3. *Whole brain death.* Whole brain death is the absence and complete irrecoverability of all spontaneous brain activity and all spontaneous respiratory functions. This determination emerged when technological advances were able to intervene in the natural processes of heart and lung failure. Death is considered to have occurred when the entire brain has died. This is usually obtainable with the use of an electroencephalogram (EEG), which reads brain-wave patterns. In 1968, an ad hoc committee at Harvard University established the first brain death standard. Called the *Harvard Criteria,* it stated that if brain wave patterns are nearly or completely flat when administered twice over a twenty-four-hour period, all brain activity has ceased and the person is dead. In 1981, The President's Commission for the Study of Ethical Problems in Medicine and Biomedical and Behavioral Research established the Uniform Determination of Death Act. The act says: "An individual who has sustained either (1) irreversible cessation of circulatory and respiratory functions, or (2) irreversible cessation of the entire brain, including the brain stem, is dead. A determination of death must be made in accordance with accepted medical standards."[3] The UDDA is the standard determination of death today, and no one has ever survived brain death. However, some question whether this criteria for death is too narrow. They argue that this may be sufficient criteria,

3. The President's Commission for the Study of Ethical Problems in Medicine and Biomedical and Behavioral Research, *Defining Death: Medical, Legal, and Ethical Issues in the Definition of Death* (Washington, DC: U.S. Government Printing Office, 1981), 159.

but question if it is necessary. Is it possible that death could be determined before the whole brain is dead?

4. *Neocortical death.* According to this criterion, a person is determined as dead when the outer layer of the brain covering the cerebrum, the neocortex, has irreversibly ceased to function. Because the neocortex appears to be the biological precondition of consciousness, the result is the irreversible loss of consciousness and self-awareness, what some believe to be the primary basis for personhood. This is sometimes called "cerebral death," "higher brain death," or "apallic syndrome." Those patients who are deemed PVS (in a persistent vegetative state), such as Karen Ann Quinlan, fit this description. There is much controversy over this determination of death. Though in 1986 the AMA recommended to accept neocortical death as an acceptable criterion for determining death, to date no state or federal government agency has accepted this standard. Thus, neocortical death is viewed as a necessary condition for determining death, but at this time is not considered a sufficient condition.

Along with defining euthanasia and defining and determining death, we need to make some important distinctions. Again, it is because people have failed to make these distinctions, that there has been some confusion around euthanasia.

1. *Active/passive distinction.* Of all the distinctions, this is the most important. Active euthanasia is the intentional and direct killing of another human life either out of motives of mercy, beneficence, or respect for personal autonomy. This is sometimes called mercy killing (our narrow definition above). This can be performed many ways: overdosing medication such as morphine, the use of violent means such as shooting or suffocating someone, or starving a patient to death. Passive euthanasia is the withholding or withdrawing of a life-sustaining treatment when certain justifiable conditions are met and the patient is left to die from the debilitation or disease.

This is a very important distinction. There are two differences between these two types of acts. First is the difference of intention. In active euthanasia the intention or aim is to end the person's life. Should the person not die after the action is performed, the act would be deemed a failure. However, in passive euthanasia the intention is to relieve the patient of burdensome and unnecessary treatment. Should the patient not die, the act would not be deemed a failure because the patient would still be relieved of such treatment.

Second, they are different in what is the direct cause of the patient's death. In active euthanasia the actions of the agent are what directly caused the patient's death: the agent killed him. In passive euthanasia it is not the action of the agent that is the direct cause of the patient's death—for example, the removal of life-sustaining equipment; it is the debilitation or disease.

This distinction is not always clear to see. One example might be to think of a healthy person on a respirator versus a sick person on the respirator. If you take a normal healthy person and put them on a respirator, and then remove the respirator, nothing will happen to them because their normal respiratory system will continue to function spontaneously. However, if you take someone with a respiratory ailment and put him on a respirator and then remove him, he will die. What causes death in the second person is not the removal of the respirator. For if removing a person from a respirator causes death, then both persons would have died. It is the debilitation that causes death, and this is passive euthanasia. These days the debate is often framed in different terms. "Euthanasia" is used more for active euthanasia, while passive euthanasia is often referred to as "allowing one to die." As we shall see, there are those who want to erase this distinction altogether.

2. *Withholding/withdrawing treatment.* Withholding treatment simply means that treatment on a patient is never begun. Withdrawing treatment is stopping treatment that has already begun. Some confuse this with active/passive euthanasia. Withholding seems passive and withdrawing seems active. This confusion was present in the New Jersey State Supreme Court case of Karen Ann Quinlan. However, they are not synonymous. There may be an emotional or psychological difference between these two actions. It may be psychologically more difficult to stop treatment than to never start it. However, there is no morally relevant difference between them.

3. *Voluntary/non-voluntary/involuntary distinction.* Voluntary euthanasia occurs when a competent, informed patient autonomously requests it. This can be either while they are conscious or through an advanced directive like a living will or durable power of attorney. Non-voluntary euthanasia occurs whenever a person is incapable of forming a judgment concerning euthanasia and has left no advanced directive. The decision would have to be made for him by a third party based on what the third party would deem is in the best interest of the patient. Involuntary euthanasia occurs when a person expresses a desire to live but is killed or allowed to die. Of these three, the

first and second *may* be justifiable under certain situations (see below). Involuntary euthanasia is never justified, even though there have been instances of it occurring. Herbert Hendlin reports of a case in the Netherlands (where euthanasia is tolerated) of a Catholic nun who specifically requested not to be euthanized as it was against her lifelong religious beliefs. The physician did so anyway, claiming that she really wanted it but "her religious convictions did not permit her to ask for death."[4] We will consider the Netherlands situation more fully in the next chapter.

4. *The ordinary/extraordinary means distinction.* This has been used to classify treatment. "Ordinary means" has been used to describe all medicines, treatments, and procedures that offer a reasonable hope of benefit without placing undue burdens on a patient (pain or other serious inconvenience). "Extraordinary means" has been used to describe those medicines, treatments, and procedures that are not ordinary because they involve excessive burdens on the patient and do not offer reasonable hope of benefit. In recent years these two terms have pretty much been abandoned. The problem was that they were just too vague and unspecific in a climate of constantly changing technology. "Reasonable hope" and "excessive burdens" change as technology changes. What was excessive years ago may be routine and ordinary today. Today bioethicists are more likely to think in terms of a benefits/burdens evaluation. Is the treatment providing enough of a benefit to offset the possible burdens? If the burdens outweigh the benefits, it is generally recommended that the treatment be withheld or withdrawn. It is important to note that such an evaluation cannot be made abstractly but must be determined within specific contexts and with specific persons. While there are some medical standards based on the overall experience of the medical community, there are no universal or absolute guidelines for all treatments.

THE LEGAL STATUS OF EUTHANASIA

There are two very important legal cases concerning euthanasia: Karen Ann Quinlan and Nancy Cruzan.

---

4. Herbert Hendlin, *Seduced by Death: Doctors, Patients and Assisted Suicide* (New York: W. W. Norton, 1998), 20.

Karen Ann Quinlan

The case of Karen Ann Quinlan was the first euthanasia case to come before the courts. Some mark this event as the beginning of bioethics. In April 1975, Karen Ann Quinlan suffered respiratory failure and permanent brain damage after consuming a mixture of alcohol and various medications to assist her with weight loss. The event left her in a persistent vegetative state. She was given nasogastric feeding and was placed on a ventilator to help her breathe. Nearly six months later, Quinlan's parents requested she be removed from the ventilator and efforts no longer be made to prolong her life. Hospital officials would not comply, arguing that such actions would constitute murder. A lawsuit was thus filed.

The first trial took place in the Superior Court of New Jersey in Morristown. Judge Muir presided, Paul Armstrong argued for the Quinlans, and Daniel Coburn was advocate for Karen. Armstrong attempted first to argue that Karen was brain-dead. Muir pointed out that the only standard for brain death was whole brain death, which was not the case for Karen. Armstrong then tried to argue on the basis of "right to die." However, Muir responded that there was no precedent for such a right and the Constitution made no mention of it. Finally, Armstrong argued a right to privacy as determined in the *Griswold* case (see chapter 3). Coburn and the hospital lawyers argued that she was not brain-dead, that there is always hope for recovery, that there is no legal precedent for allowing Karen to die, and that removing life-sustaining treatments was equivalent to killing her. On November 10, 1985, almost seven months after Karen's lapsing into a coma, Judge Muir made his ruling. He ruled that (1) Karen was not brain-dead; (2) Coburn was to remain the legal guardian of Karen; (3) any supposed prior directives or wishes expressed by Karen were unsubstantiated theoretical conversations and cannot be taken as final; (4) because Karen was incompetent and her wishes were not known, there was no violation of right to privacy; (5) there is no constitutional "right to die"; and (6) a decision to terminate a respirator was a medical decision and therefore the doctor's decision.[5]

The case was appealed to the New Jersey Supreme Court, bypassing all other appellate courts because of its precedent-setting implications. After several months of deliberation, the State Supreme Court ruled the following on March 31, 1976: (1) a patient's right to privacy was broad enough to encompass the right to decline medical treatment under certain circumstances;

5. *In Re Karen Ann Quinlan*, 348 A.2d 801 (Superior Court of New Jersey 1975).

(2) right to privacy extends to an incompetent adult, and the guardian and family are permitted to assert the patient's right to privacy and render their best judgment; (3) ensuing death would not be ruled homicide or suicide; (4) the lower court was correct by not admitting prior statements by Karen as they were remote and lacked weight; (5) the lower court was also correct in denying the removal of the ventilator, but was incorrect in denying guardianship to Karen's father; (6) life support may be terminated upon request of the family or guardian if physicians conclude there is not reasonable probability of return to a cognitive sapient state; and (7) hospitals should form ethics committees to decide these types of issues in the future.[6]

This decision by the New Jersey Supreme Court established the precedent for passive euthanasia that is in practice in every state today. No longer are patients forced to remain chained to artificial machines in hopeless situations. However, it did not end so quickly for Karen. Even after the court's decision, and the Quinlans' official request to remove the ventilator, the hospital refused to do so. Instead of disconnecting Karen, which would have almost certainly have caused her immediate death, the hospital officials slowly "weaned" her off the ventilator over a period of several weeks. Because of this process, Karen was able to breathe on her own. In May 1976, she was moved out of the hospital and into a nursing home. She remained there until she finally died—*a full ten years later* on June 13, 1986.

Nancy Cruzan

On the night of January 11, 1983, twenty-four-year-old Nancy Cruzan lost control of her car on a lonely stretch of Elm Road in Jasper County, Missouri. She was thrown thirty-five feet from the car and landed in a water-filled ditch. Paramedics found that her heart had stopped and she had not been breathing for at least fifteen minutes. They were able to resuscitate her heart and lungs, but due to the loss of oxygen, she was left in a persistent vegetative state. Unlike Karen Ann Quinlan, Nancy could breathe on her own without the use of a ventilator. However, because she could not voluntarily swallow, she was connected to a feeding tube inserted through her abdomen. After five years in the condition, Nancy's parents requested that the tube be removed and she be allowed to die. In the Quinlan case, the parents never requested the feeding tube be removed, only the ventilator. So, the issues of artificial feeding and nutrition had never been addressed by a court.

---

6. *In Re Karen Ann Quinlan*, 70 N.J. 10 (1976).

The hospital was reluctant to remove the feeding tube, so the Cruzans filed an appeal with the Jasper County Circuit Court. The Circuit Court granted their request on July 27, 1988, but the case was then appealed to the Supreme Court of Missouri. The court reversed the lower court's decision, ruling that the state has a compelling interest in preserving life, regardless of quality of life, unless clear and convincing evidence exists regarding the patient's wishes concerning life-sustaining treatments.[7] Unfortunately, Nancy had left no advanced directives, and testimony from her parents and friends recalling casual conversations in which Nancy indicated she would not want to be kept alive in this circumstance was deemed to be not clear and convincing evidence.

The Cruzans appealed to the United States Supreme Court, making it the first "right to die" case the Court would take up. The case was heard on December 6, 1989, and the Court rendered its decision on June 25, 1990. With a 5-4 ruling, the following was held: (1) the Missouri requirement for clear and convincing evidence was constitutional and states are allowed to determine their own standards of evidence; (2) a competent patient has the right to refuse medical treatment, even if refusal will knowingly cause death; (3) in cases involving incompetent patients, states are acting appropriately in requiring clear and convincing evidence of a patient's wishes, but such a standard is not federally mandated; and (4) the withholding or withdrawing of artificial nutrition and hydration is no different that removing other life-sustaining treatments.[8]

Since the Supreme Court ruled that Missouri's standards of evidence were constitutional, the Cruzans were not able to remove Nancy's feeding tube. However, many of Nancy's friends did not testify in the original trial because they were unaware of the case at the time. Just before the accident had occurred, Nancy had gotten a divorce. Most of her friends knew her by her married name, Nancy Davis. As they became aware of what happened, they appealed to the Missouri Supreme Court to have the case reopened. When the state did so, it heard sufficient testimony to ascertain that Nancy indeed would have wanted to be allowed to die, thus satisfying the "clear and convincing evidence" prong of the court's ruling. On December 14, 1990, her feeding tube was removed, and Nancy died twelve days later. Her grave marker states that she died January 11, 1983, and "At peace December 26, 1990."

---

7. *Cruzan v. Harmon*, 760 S.W.2nd 408 (Supreme Court of Missouri 1988).
8. *Cruzan v. Director, Missouri Dept. of Health*, 497 U.S. 261 (1990).

MORAL ARGUMENTS CONCERNING ACTIVE EUTHANASIA

While active euthanasia is, at this time, illegal, there are those who have argued for its legality. In general, four moral arguments have been raised for the legitimacy of active euthanasia.

1. *Respect for autonomy.* Some have offered that persons should have the right to self-determination concerning all aspects of their lives, including the manner and time of their death. This idea is enveloped in the rhetoric of the right-to-die movement: "I have a right to choose to do what I want with my life. After all, it is my life. If I choose to want to end it, that is my free choice. I am not hurting any other person." Margaret Battin argues for this point when she says that a physician respecting a patient's autonomy means, among other things, "providing the knowledge, equipment, and help to enable the patient to die, if that is his or her choice; this is the other part of the physician's obligation, not yet recognized by the medical profession or the law of the United States."[9]

There are several problems here. First, this view of autonomy is too strong. It is simply too individual and independent. Philosopher Gilbert Meilaender calls this "excessive individualism." We are social creatures, and one almost never acts in a manner that is completely and totally independent of others or that does not affect the community of which he or she is a part. Because we are social creatures, we have obligations to society. Even Cuban leader and atheist Fidel Castro recognized this. When one of the officials his government committed suicide, he said, "Every revolutionary knows that he does not have the right to deprive his cause of a life that *does not belong to him*, and that he can only sacrifice against an enemy."[10] While it is true that as free creatures we do have the right of self-determination, it is a relative right, not an absolute one. With our freedom comes responsibility to the community of which we are a part.

A second problem with the right-to-die argument is what many consider to be a coherency problem. Some question whether one can coherently have a natural right to die (the right to die being argued for must be a natural right, for a legal right to die has never been established). However, all natural rights

9. Margaret Pabst Battin, *The Least Worst Death: Essays in Bioethics on the End of Life* (New York: Oxford University Press, 1994), 113.
10. Cited in Michael Walzer, *Obligations* (New York: Simon & Schuster, 1970), 172.

presuppose our self-interested attachment to our own lives. In other words, natural rights are rooted in the right to life, or in our natural self-preservation. For one to argue that one has a right to die is to argue that one has the right to annihilate the very basis of all rights, including the right to die. Therefore, to propose such an annihilation would be ultimately self-defeating.[11]

A third problem with the right-to-die argument has to do with the relationship between rights and obligations. All rights impose obligations on others. The fact that you have a right means others have some obligation to you concerning that right. Most rights are negative rights or rights of noninterference, which means that someone does not have the right to interfere with your choice. Those arguing for active euthanasia initially *seem* to be arguing for this kind of a right. However, they are asking for more than just to be left alone to die. They are not arguing for suicide (which we will discuss in the next chapter). They are arguing for euthanasia, that is, for the right for others to kill them. This means they are arguing for a positive right which means that others, presumably physicians, will now have an obligation to kill patients. However, what of the physician's autonomy? What if he believes that killing others is wrong for religious or other reasons? If a patient has a *right* to euthanasia, then physicians now have an *obligation* placed on them to kill patients who request to die. Also, since the physician now has an obligation to kill, it can be argued that he now also has a right to kill. Derail Charles points out the implications of this problem: "Should such a right be granted, what is to prevent the right to kill from being followed by the duty to kill? Will the 'right to die' only serve as the precursor to the duty to die?"[12]

Another problem with the autonomy argument is that, in the context of euthanasia, it is always coupled with suffering. If one is suffering enough, then one has the right to end one's life. However, if the argument from autonomy is valid and can really stand on its own, then one would have to argue that any autonomous individual at any time has the right to die and, as we argued, has the right to ask others to help. However, such a view is almost never argued for. Very few people would agree that a twenty-two-year-old young woman who has just gone through a divorce, recently lost her job, and believes that her life is meaningless, has the right to die. Even most suicide advocates

11. This argument can be found in Leonard Kass, "Is There a Right to Die?" *Hastings Center Report* 23, no. 1 (1993): 36.
12. Derail Charles, "The Right to Die in the Light of Contemporary Rights Rhetoric," in *Bioethics and the Future of Medicine: A Christian Appraisal*, eds. John F. Kilner, Nigel de S. Cameron, and David L. Scheidermeyer (Grand Rapids: Eerdmans, 1995), 272.

would disagree that she has a right to die in this case. Yet if one agrees with the view of autonomy that is offered here, one must take this position to remain consistent.

Finally, as Christians we recognize that is not *your* life. It is a gift from God, given to us only on loan, which we live in stewardship to him. It simply is not ours to dispose of. Christian philosopher Gilbert Meilaender puts this best when writes:

> What should be clear though, is that Christians do not approach this issue by first thinking in terms of a "right to life" or a "right to die with dignity." That is to say, we do not start with the language of independence. Within the story of my life I have the relative freedom of a creature, but it is not simply "my" life to do with as I please. I am free to end it, of course, but not free to do so without risking something as important to my nature as freedom: namely, the sense of myself as one who always exists in relation to God.[13]

2. *The mercy argument*. Returning to Margaret Battin, we find the principle of medical mercy to be, in part, "Where possible one ought to relieve the pain and suffering of another person, when it does not contravene that person's wishes . . . [and] where it will not violate other moral obligations."[14] Battin holds, as do others, that at times this principle will require euthanasia. The most common illustration used to support this principle is our treatment of injured animals. Out of compassion, we often kill animals to put them out of their misery; surely we should show the same compassion to persons as well. Doctors have an obligation to end suffering, and mercifully bringing about death can be one way to fulfill this obligation.

There are a few responses to this argument. First, we need to separate pain and suffering. By pain I am referring primarily to a physical condition in a person, while suffering generally entails a broader concept involving a number of psychological factors as well as physical pain. As far as pain is concerned, much has been done in pain management. In the past two decades we have seen tremendous advancements in medications and palliative treatment for pain. Dr. Matthew E. Connolly reports that: "In the truly good centers of palliative care, such as St. Christopher's Hospice in London, they control cancer pain in 95 percent of the patients they see. In the 50 percent

13. Gilbert Meilaender, *Bioethics: A Primer for Christians* (Grand Rapids: Eerdmans, 1996), 60.
14. Battin, *Least Worst Death*, 101.

where less than ideal control is accomplished, it is usually because the patients were presented too late for everything to be done before death occurs."[15] He argues that much still needs to be done. The number one problem in pain management is education. One of the fears Dr. Connolly has is that, with the present acceptance of active euthanasia and physician assisted suicide, there will be less of an emphasis on the need for education and research in pain management. In the next chapter we will see this fear is justified in examining what is occurring in the Netherlands.

Suffering involves more than just physical pain. It involves psychological states that may or may not also involve physical pain. Many people fear loss of control, depression, anxiety, and loneliness more than they fear the physical suffering itself. Rather than confirming their worst fears by encouraging active euthanasia, we need to be meeting these needs through caring relationships. Dr. Martha Twaddle comments that, "A good patient-physician relationship is worth 10mg of morphine, as presence alone can ease the anguish of fear."[16] She recommends hospice care, a relatively new form of holistic medicine dealing specifically with those who are dying. Hospice rejects the active euthanasia model and adopts a model of dealing with the total pain and suffering of the patient. The goal is to accompany patients in the dying process, easing the journey with medications, explanation, and presence.

A second response to the mercy argument is that it communicates the wrong message about pain and suffering. Suffering is a natural part of the human experience. It is part of life, a means of growth, and it should not necessarily be avoided at *all costs*. I am not advocating that we should actively seek suffering or even rejoice in its presence. We should do all we can to relieve suffering, but we should not think we can do absolutely anything to relieve suffering. Just because one is suffering does not mean any action is now justified for the cause of the relief of suffering. Dr. Marsha Fowler writes that the answer in dealing with the suffering patient is not in mastering suffering with medicine, avoiding it through euthanasia, or even explaining it theologically: "Rather the answer is in facing the experience of suffering."[17] This is specifically why the analogy with an animal breaks down. It is not just that humans

15. Matthew E. Connolly, "The Management of Cancer Pain," in *Suicide: A Christian Response*, eds. Timothy J. Demy and Gary P. Stewart (Grand Rapids: Kregel, 1998), 94.
16. Martha L. Twaddle, "Hospice Care," in Kilner, Miller, and Pellegrino, *Dignity and Dying* (Grand Rapids: Eerdmans, 1996), 186.
17. Marsha D. M. Fowler, "Suffering," in Kilner, Miller, and Pellegrino, *Dignity and Dying*, 50.

have a value that animals do not share (which I believe is true and is why killing an animal is not the same as killing a person). But more importantly, humans are persons with the ability to rationally reflect upon the nature of their circumstances, who they are, and what kind of person they want to be. They can respond to suffering in a positive way that an animal cannot. H. Richard Niebuhr said it best: "It is in response to suffering that many and perhaps all [persons] . . . define themselves, take on character, develop their ethos."[18]

For Christians suffering has an even deeper meaning. Gilbert Meilaender states this deeper meaning well:

> We remember, after all, that Jesus goes to the cross in the name of obedience to his father. We need not glorify or seek suffering, but we must be struck by the fact that a human being who is a willing sufferer stands squarely in the center of Christian piety. Jesus bears his suffering not because it is desirable but because the Father allots it within the limits of his earthly life.[19]

While we need to care for those who are suffering, and not kill them, we must remember that we cannot always relieve it and even God will not always take it away. But God understands suffering; he has lived through it himself in the person of Jesus Christ. "God himself lives that problem and bears it. His way is steadfast love through suffering, and it is the mystery of God's own being and power that this truly proves to be the way to maximize care for all who suffer."[20]

3. *The biographical/biological distinction.* This argument and the one below come from philosopher James Rachels. They both have been very influential in the euthanasia debate. This argument draws a distinction between a human organism's biological life and a person's biographical life. A biologically living being has no moral status. All living beings fit into this category: animals, plants, and so on. Moral status is granted only to a human being with a biographical life. What makes up a biographical life? Rachels claims it is "the sum of one's aspirations, decisions, activities, projects, and human

---

18. H. Richard Niebuhr, *The Responsible Self* (New York: Harper and Row, 1963), 60.
19. Gilbert Meilaender, "Euthanasia and Christian Vision," in *On Moral Medicine: Theological Perspectives in Medical Ethics*, eds. Stephen Lammers and Allen Verhey (Grand Rapids: Eerdmans, 1987), 457.
20. Meilaender, *Bioethics*, 66.

relationships."[21] Some types of humans do not have biographical lives. Infants have not had one yet. Certain comatose humans no longer have one. These people do not have any real moral status at all. He also places certain persons in this category who are competent and functioning as human persons. He uses the famous case of Dax Cowart, a young man who was severely burned in a gas explosion and who continually requested to be allowed to die but was kept under treatment in a hospital for about two years against his will. Rachels argues that because Dax can no longer live the active kind of life way he used to live, that he has lost his "biographical life" and should be euthanized.

There are many responses we might have to Rachels's distinction between the biological and biographical.[22] First, any concept of biographical life has to presuppose the importance of a biological human life. A "biographical life" is what we have called in other parts of this book personhood. We have already seen that biological human organisms are by nature of what they are, persons. It is a thing's nature that determines what kind of thing it is (dog, tree, human person). It is the fact that you have a human nature that makes you a human being. Conversely, a biographical life is only possible because it is grounded in a human being that can biologically have that kind of life. Therefore, the biological life is morally just as important as the biographical life. Human beings have intrinsic value simply because they are human beings.

Second, even if we grant Rachels's distinction, he assumes that a biologically living thing has no moral status, only persons. However, a thing does not have to be a person to have moral status in the sense of how it is treated. There are many nonpersonal things we say have intrinsic value and therefore cannot be treated any way one wishes. For example, artwork has this kind of value. Many would argue that the Mona Lisa or Michelangelo's statue of David have value of themselves. It would be immoral for a person to destroy or disfigure them, not just because of their monetary or social value but because they have intrinsic value, being the created works of human beings. Also, we place a certain value on other sentient beings, saying it would be immoral to torture or treat them cruelly. A third example would be future generations. Many argue that we have an obligation to future generations to guarantee that they

21. James Rachels, *The End of Life* (New York: Oxford University Press, 1986), 5.
22. I am indebted to my friend and colleague Dr. J. P. Moreland for his analysis and critique of Rachels's arguments. I am borrowing much of my material from his book with Norman L. Geisler, *The Life and Death Debate: Moral Issues of Our Time* (Westport, CT: Greenwood, 1990).

have a safe and pleasant environment to live in. Yet these persons do not even exist. Therefore, it goes against our experience to argue that only persons have moral status. Human organisms may be in the same category of these things, and therefore you can't just treat them any way you wish.

Third, Rachels's conception of the biographical life is too broad and subjective. Rachels defines it merely as a person's "aspirations, decisions, activities, projects, and human relationships." This means a person is free to choose whatever goals, interests, and desires that are important to him with no standards at all. They then may claim that when the capacity to participate in these interests is no longer available, their biographical life is gone, and they should be allowed to die. An example of this kind of thinking is in the play, and later film, *Whose Life Is It Anyway?* The story is told of a sculptor who is involved in an auto accident and paralyzed from the neck down. He will no longer be able to do sculpting, which was his life. The playwright takes Rachels's position in saying that the sculptor should be allowed to die. However, just because a person is restricted from doing what they are interested in, does that mean it would be morally justifiable for them to be killed upon request? Isn't it possible that the sculptor could still have a meaningful life? The lives of victims of tragic accidents such as Christopher Reeve and Joni Eareckson Tada show that a meaningful life is possible even after the tragedy.

Fourth, if this distinction is valid then a person who has lost his biographical life is no longer a person and therefore loses all other moral rights as well. This means it might be possible to perform medical experiments on him or kill him in a violent and brutal fashion. Since we are no longer dealing with an object with moral rights, in the absence of other ethical factors, you are free to treat such a person any way you wish.

4. *The bare difference argument*. This argument, also from Rachels, is an attempt to erase the distinction between active and passive euthanasia by showing they both result in the same end. It states that the active/passive distinction is a distinction without a difference. There is no difference between intentionally killing someone and allowing someone to die—in the end they are both dead as the result of your actions or your failure to act. Therefore, the conclusion is that if passive euthanasia is sometimes justifiable, then active euthanasia is sometimes justifiable. Rachels has produced a well-known story to illustrate this argument. It is called "The Boy in the Bathtub" illustration and I have summarized it here:

> Two men, Smith and Jones, both stand to inherit millions upon the death of their six-year-old cousin. Smith plans to kill his cousin and sneaks into the bathroom while he is bathing. He holds his head under water until he drowns. Jones also plans to kill his cousin. He sneaks into the bathroom intending to drown him. However, before he gets to him, the boy slips and hits his head and he slinks into unconsciousness before going under water. Jones does nothing but just stands there and watches the boy drown ready to push him back under if necessary, but the boy never comes back up. Thus, Smith killed his cousin, but Jones merely allowed his cousin to die. However, we would hold that both these men are morally despicable. Therefore, there is no real difference between killing and allowing someone to die.[23]

Several philosophers have had problems with Rachels's illustration. Dr. James Childress comments that "Rachels's examples may not be as conclusive as he thinks. Smith's and Jones's vicious motives may obscure other features of the case which might be important in other settings . . . his case throws no light on our dilemmas in the use of biomedical technology. These dilemmas arise precisely because we do not know what constitutes 'doing good' for patients in all cases." Childress's point is that Rachels's illustration is about persons doing bad, but it does not necessarily apply to people trying to do good.

Dr. J. P. Moreland points out that the real problem with Rachels's illustration is that it presents an inadequate analysis of moral actions. Moral acts are more than just the movement of body parts. Moral acts must consider motive and intention as well as the means to an action. Of the three, intention is where the real essence of the moral act lies. "The Boy in the Bathtub" illustration differs only in means to an end (killing vs. allowing to die), but the motive and intention are the same (both Smith and Jones desire and intend to have their cousin die). While Smith may be legally charged with murder while Jones is not, we hold them both morally responsible. In active euthanasia the intention is the death of the patient. In passive euthanasia the intention is the relief of the patient from excessive burdens with the knowledge that this will most probably, though not necessarily, result in the patient's death.

I do not believe that any of the arguments in favor of active euthanasia are as strong as they first appear, and none of them justifies killing another

---

23. James Rachels, "Active and Passive Euthanasia," in Gregory Pence, *Classic Works in Medical Ethics* (New York: McGraw Hill, 1998), 24.

person. I would like to finish this section with the following quote by Gilbert Meilaender about Paul Ramsey, one of the truly great Christian ethicists:

> In a chapter written a quarter century ago that remains to this day a classic discussion of the issues, Paul Ramsey sought to articulate an ethic of "(only) caring for the dying." Such an ethic he suggested, would reject two opposite extremes: refusing to acknowledge death by continuing the struggle against it when that struggle is useless, or aiming to hasten the coming of death. Neither of these can count as *care* for one of our fellow human beings; each is a form of abandonment. We should always try to care for the dying person, but we should only care. To try to do more by seizing either extremes is always to give something other or less than care.[24]

PASSIVE EUTHANASIA

We have argued that active euthanasia is not justified because it is actively and intentionally taking another life. We have also argued that there is a distinction between active and passive euthanasia. The question I want to address now is: Is passive euthanasia ever justifiable? I believe the answer to that is a qualified yes. It may be justifiable in certain situations when certain conditions hold. What would the conditions be? Most ethicists recognize the following: (1) the patient is terminal, meaning that he/she is in the latter stages of the dying process; (2) death is imminent and/or treatment is futile; (3) treatment is excessively burdensome with little benefit; (4) death is not directly intended and the action taken is not the direct cause of death; (5) the patient has autonomously requested or agreed to the action. Two comments about these conditions are in order. First, they do not all have to hold, though most of them should be present. The "intention" aspect of the fourth condition is the most important aspect and must be present. The intention in passive euthanasia is always to relieve the patient of excessively burdensome treatment, not to cause the patient's death, even though this may be a foreseen consequence. Second, there is some debate about some of these conditions. Some believe that the fifth condition is not absolute if the patient has not left any directives. One can use a "best interest" standard in deciding to allow a patient to die if the other conditions are in place. In addition, some hold that death must

24. Meilaender, *Bioethics*, 62. The work by Ramsey that he is referring to is chapter 3 of Ramsey's classic *The Patient as Person* (New Haven, CT: Yale University Press, 1970).

be imminent under the second condition while others recognize that futility plays a role in this decision as well. Death was not imminent for Karen Ann Quinlan, but her condition was futile.

One of the more controversial discussions concerns the fourth condition. Some believe that so long as the intention is right, the action taken may be the direct cause of death. In other words, if you give a lethal dose of morphine to a patient with the intention of relieving suffering knowing that it will kill the patient, it is not considered active euthanasia because your intention was not to kill but to relieve suffering. Those who hold this position often say it is an application of the principle of double effect. Others say that this is an incorrect application of the principle, because the first condition of the principle says that the action one is doing must be "either good or at least morally neutral." However, giving a patient a lethal dose of medication is neither good nor morally neutral; it is evil itself. Therefore, double effect does not apply to this action.

The major argument in favor of passive euthanasia is that it is an admission that medical science can only do so much, and that one must recognize this and allow death to come at the proper time. This is not killing someone; it is a recognition that there is nothing more we can do to keep the person alive. As Paul Ramsey said, a time comes when we need to stop "struggling against death" by any means possible. Along with this argument, we can argue that because death is not intended and the action is not causing death, a mistaken diagnosis would not be failure. The person could get well, or at least survive, and this would not be deemed a tragedy. No such possibility exists with active euthanasia.

OTHER ISSUES REGARDING END-OF-LIFE CARE

Before leaving the topic of euthanasia, there are three other issues I wish to address.

1. *Foregoing nutrition and hydration.* As we saw in the Cruzan case, the Supreme Court deemed that removal of artificial nutrition and hydration should be treated like any other medical treatment. However, while that settles the legal question, there is still an ethical question to be addressed: Should the administering of artificially induced food and water be handled in the same way as other medical treatments in the consideration of passive euthanasia? In other words, can they be withdrawn from a terminally ill patient in much the same way as other medical intervention might be withdrawn?

There is some division among Christian philosophers on this issue. Dr. J. P. Moreland, Dr. Norman Geisler, and Dr. Gilbert Meilaender have all argued that, in most cases, nutrition and hydration should not be treated the same as other treatments and therefore should not be removed.[25] They cite the following as reasons: (1) Medical treatment is performed for therapeutic reasons to treat some disease. Food and water do not have as their purpose the treatment of disease—they are for the sustaining of life. (2) In passive euthanasia, it is the disease that is the direct cause of death, not the action taken by the health-care worker. If artificial hydration and nutrition are withdrawn, that direct action is what will result in the patient's death. This is active euthanasia. (3) In withdrawing or withholding extraordinary life-sustaining treatment (passive euthanasia), the focus is on the quality of the treatment. The purpose is to spare a person an unduly burdensome means of medical intervention. However, in withdrawing or withholding food and water (active euthanasia), the focus shifts from the quality of the treatment to the quality of patient's life itself. (4) There are three criteria in which withholding or withdrawing nutrition and hydration might be justified: if the person is going to die in a very short time whether or not he had nutrition and hydration; death is not intended nor directly caused by the forgoing of nutrition or hydration; the means of administering food and water was excessively burdensome and extraordinary.

Other Christian philosophers believe that in some cases, most often the PVS case, artificial nutrition and hydration may be justifiably removed. Dr. Scott Rae seems more open to this view. He writes, "If one admits that this is indeed genuine medical treatment, and if one allows some place for substituted judgment, then removal of nutrition and hydration can be ethically justified apart from any considerations of personhood."[26] However, he says that certain conditions must be met before removing artificial nutrition and hydration: (1) it is medically determined that the patient cannot absorb nutrients; (2) the burdens outweigh the benefits; (3) there is no reasonable hope for the patient to regain consciousness; (4) if the patient has left an advanced directive concerning her desires should she end up in this situation. Another Christian who argues for removal of food and water is Dr. Robert Rakestraw. We will look at his argument below.

---

25. See Moreland, *Life and Death Debate*, 78–80; for Dr. Geisler, see *Matters of Life and Death* (Grand Rapids: Baker, 1999), 142–43; for Dr. Meilaender, see his "On Removing Food and Water: Against the Stream," *Hastings Center Report* 14, no. 6 (December 1984): 11–13.
26. Scott Rae, *Moral Choices: An Introduction to Ethics* (Grand Rapids: Zondervan, 1995), 177.

2. *The status of the PVS patient.* Another area where there is disagreement even among Christians is the status of the PVS patient. To understand this disagreement, one needs to understand what persistent vegetative state means. A persistent vegetative state (PVS) is a condition of permanent unconsciousness in which the person is completely unaware of himself or his surroundings, though he may appear to be awake and go through regular sleep/wake cycles. It is usually the result of permanent neocortical impairment and is considered irreversible. PVS patients may exhibit many lower brain stem functions: they usually do not need life-sustaining treatment except for a feeding tube, breathe spontaneously, have a regular heartbeat, digest normally, experience grasp reflex, chew, yawn, and even groan and make other vocal sounds. However, it is well established that all capacity for consciousness, self-awareness, memory, personality, communication, and sentience are irreversibly lost. People can exist as long as thirty years in this condition. PVS is not the same as a coma, which is a sleeplike state that is potentially reversible; "locked-in" syndrome where the patient is conscious but is unable to communicate orally; or whole brain death.

Many persons believe that because the neocortex is the seat of the capacities for the functioning of personhood, and because the neocortex is irreversibly dead, that therefore the person is dead and all that is left alive is the human organism. Christian theologian Dr. Robert Rakestraw adopts this view. Rakestraw holds the view of personhood similar to the one we defended in the last chapter. As a person man is made in the image of God "with the actual ability or potential to be aware of oneself and to relate in some way to one's environment, to other human beings, and to God."[27] He holds that personhood is present from the moment of conception until these abilities or potentials cease. In the language we used in the last chapter, personhood ceases when the basic inherent capacity of personhood cease to be present. He writes:

> It appears, then, that neocortical destruction equals the end of personal life because the correctly diagnosed PVS individual is a body of organs and systems, artificially sustained without the personal human spirit that once enabled this body-soul unity to represent God on earth. Since the Bible on occasion uses the language of the human spirit's departure—as something different from a

27. Robert. V. Rakestraw, "The Persistent Vegetative State and the Withdrawal of Nutrition and Hydration," in *Readings in Christian Ethics,* eds. David K. Clark and Robert V. Rakestraw (Grand Rapids: Baker, 1996), 127.

> person's life-force or final breath—to signify death (Luke 23:46; Acts 7:59–60), we may use similar language in suggesting that the spirit of the PVS individual has already returned to God.[28]

It is important to understand Rakestraw's argument here. He is *not* claiming that the immediate capacities for personhood are merely not functioning: he is claiming that the basic inherent capacity is no longer present. Therefore, the person is gone. Rakestraw also believes that recent breakthroughs have been made that have made the determination of neocortical irreversibility virtually certain. Medical Scientists now have a test, called a positron emissions tomographic (PET) test, to distinguish between coma, "locked-in" syndrome, and complete neocortical death making misdiagnosis more improbable. Some argue that if we do not recognize neocortical death as the death of the person, then we will be forced to keep thousands of bodies alive for several years with no hope of functioning as persons. The longest case of PVS is thirty-seven years. Rakestraw would argue that we can remove artificial hydration and nutrition from PVS patients and allow them to die, since they are not persons.

Many Christian philosophers disagree with Rakestraw's conclusion concerning the status of the PVS patient. Dr. J. P. Moreland states, "If there is evidence that a holistic living organism is present, then the human soul is present."[29] He takes the PVS patient to be a full person. Dr. Scott Rae also disagrees with Rakestraw and others who hold to neocortical death as the death of the person. Dr. Rae refers to Rakestraw's position as a "functional view" as opposed to an "essential" view of personhood, and considers such a view as "dangerous."[30] While I agree that a functional view of personhood is dangerous, I believe that Dr. Rae has misunderstood the thrust of Rakestraw's position. He is not saying that the PVS patient is simply not *functioning* as a person, but that he has lost the *basic inherent capacity* to function as one. In other words, Rakestraw is claiming that what Dr. Moreland described in our last chapter as "a fairly standard set of highest order of capacities for mental states" that "constitute" personhood is no longer present. Whether one agrees with Rakestraw or not, it would be wrong to place him in the same functionalistic camp as Feinberg and Warren.

28. Rakestraw, "Persistent Vegetative State," 128.
29. J. P. Moreland, personal correspondence, December 16, 1998.
30. Rae, *Moral Choices*, 176.

Those who believe that PVS patients should not be disconnected from artificial nutrition and hydration usually cite three reasons: (1) These persons are not biologically dead. The heart and lungs are functioning normally and brain death has not occurred. They are still living human beings. (2) There are cases, though rare, of patients diagnosed PVS who have spontaneously recovered, some as long as six months. (3) Food and water are not extraordinary care but are ordinary care for these patients. At this point two things have been legally acknowledged: no state has accepted neocortical death as a legal standard for death, and artificial nutrition and hydration is a form of medical treatment and can, with the patients or surrogate's permission, be removed just like any other treatment.

3. *Advanced directives.* An advanced directive is a set of instructions from a competent, autonomous, informed person regarding decisions about future medical treatment if the person becomes incapable of making a decision at a future time. An advanced directive expresses the person's desires regarding medical treatments and can designate a surrogate decision-maker. Many states require all hospitals to inform patients concerning their rights to refuse treatment and concerning advanced directives upon admission. Advanced directives are an important safeguard in our age of modern life-saving technology.

There are two basic types of advanced directives. First, there are living wills. A living will is simply a document that expresses an individual's preferences for treatment. In many states you do not even need an attorney to create a living will, so long as there are at least two persons who can witness the will. It is important to note that even after signing will, a person still has the right to make health-care decisions so long as he is able. You are not locked into the will if you are still competent to state your desires. Also, living wills are often intentionally vague so that they can meet all kinds of situations.

The second form of advanced directive is the durable power of attorney. This is a person, designated in advance by the patient, to act as a proxy decision-maker at the time that the patient is no longer able to make decisions concerning his own welfare. This is more flexible then a living will and therefore is generally preferable. A person can be more sensitive to changing circumstances and can clarify the wishes of the patient. Despite the title, they do not have to be an attorney. They are usually a close family member.

While either of these forms of advanced directives are preferable to nothing, the best form of advanced directive is a combination of both. The living will can give your stated preferences and the person in the role of durable power of attorney can help interpret these to the specific situation and make sure they are carried out. I would advise all to have some form of advanced directive.

CONCLUSION

The Christian philosopher Gilbert Meilaender wrote in a well-known essay on euthanasia, "Life is a great good, but not the greatest good (which is fidelity to God)."[31] In that sentence he sums up the twofold response that we as Christians must have toward euthanasia.

One response is the recognition that life has an end called death. Death is not something we eagerly seek, but it is not something to be avoided at all costs. God has appointed the limits of our life and we must accept them. Meilaender writes, "Recognizing our life as a trust we will be moved not by an 'absolute will to live' but a will to live within these limits."[32] Part of the recognition of such limits is to allow persons to die when that time has come and not require that they be endlessly attached to tubes and machines.

The other response is, in recognizing that fidelity to God is the highest good, we need to be faithful to him in allowing him to impose the limits on this life, and not take it upon ourselves to do it. It is not our role to bring on death; that role belongs to God alone. "We are tempted to be 'like God' when we toy with the possibility of defining our love—and the meaning of humanity—apart from the appointed limits of human life."[33] One of the limits that God has placed upon us is that we are not to kill other human beings. Meilaender continues: "This vision of the world and of the meaning of life and death, has within Christendom given guidance to those reflecting on human suffering and dying. That moral guidance has amounted to the twofold proposition that, though we might properly cease to oppose death . . . we ought never aim at death as either our end or our means."[34]

Both of our responses, to allow life to end but never to hasten its ending, flow out of Christian love. Some may argue that active euthanasia is done from love. While one who euthanizes may indeed do so out of compassion, I would offer that Christian love would not lead one to hasten another's

31. Gilbert Meilaender, "Euthanasia and Christian Vision," *Thought: Fordham University Quarterly* 57, no. 4 (1982): 457.
32. Meilaender, "Euthanasia and Christian Vision," 456–57.
33. Meilaender, "Euthanasia and Christian Vision," 459.
34. Meilaender, "Euthanasia and Christian Vision," 457.

death. "Such action cannot be loving because it cannot be part of the meaning of commitment to the well-being of another human being within the appointed limits of earthly life . . . it is not the creaturely love which Christians praise, a love which can sometimes do no more than suffer as best we can with the sufferer."[35]

In short, there is a distinction between minimizing suffering and maximizing love. Those who advocate active euthanasia often confuse this distinction. We should try to minimize suffering within the limits we can, but we should never go outside of those limits. I will close with a final comment by Meilaender:

> In that Christian world, in which death and suffering are great evils but not the greatest evil, love can never include in its meaning hastening a fellow human being toward (the evil of) death, nor can it mean a refusal to acknowledge death when it comes (as an evil but not the greatest evil). We can only know what the imperative "maximize love" means if we understand it against the background assumptions which make intelligible for Christians words like "love" and "care." The Christian mind has certainly not recommended that we seek suffering or call it an unqualified good, but it is an evil which when endured faithfully, can be redemptive.[36]

35. Meilaender, "Euthanasia and Christian Vision," 457.
36. Meilaender, "Euthanasia and Christian Vision," 458.

6 

Death with Dignity: Physician-Assisted Suicide

Diane could not believe what she was hearing on the other end of the phone. She let out an expletive. "Don't tell me that," she said, followed by another expletive. She had been in for a checkup; she had a rash and had been feeling a little tired. The last word she ever expected to hear was "leukemia." But that was the word he said. After all she had been through in her life. After conquering vaginal cancer, getting control over her alcoholism and depression, and now—this.

Dr. Timothy Quill told her that he would run the blood count again, but he knew it would not change. It did not. He called her and had her come into the hospital for more tests, including a bone marrow biopsy. In the end, the tests confirmed what all hoped would not be true: Diane was suffering from acute myelomonocytic leukemia. Without treatment she had weeks, maybe a couple of months. With treatment, Diane had about a 25 percent chance of long-term survival. However, treatment would not be easy. It involved a series of chemotherapy treatments, followed by a bone marrow transplant. Because of her advanced stage the oncologist began to make plans for chemotherapy treatment to begin that afternoon. Diane became angry that he would presume that she wanted treatment. After agreeing to meet with Dr. Quill in two days, she went home.

Diane was a strong, independent, artistic woman. She was married and had a college-age son. They now sat in Dr. Quill's office two days later. Diane informed Dr. Quill that she had decided not to undergo the chemotherapy treatments, nor the bone marrow transplant. She had decided that the 25 percent chance was not high enough to go through the pain of treatment and loss of control that living in a hospital would force upon her in what were, most likely, her last days alive. Dr. Quill felt he could not disagree with her. Her family wished she would have chosen treatment but had resolved themselves to her decision.

Dr. Quill and Diane met several times over the following week, and he was half-expecting her to change her mind. He suggested that she consider hospice care when she grew closer to the time the disease would take over. However, Diane had a different idea. It was important for her to retain control and dignity and she was unsure she would be able to do so in a hospice care setting. She decided that, when the time came, she wanted to take her own life. Dr. Quill was reluctant to provide her with any support at first, thinking it was out of the realm of current medical practice. However, as he considered the possibility that she might do something violent, which would have terrible effects on the family, or that she might be unsuccessful and end up in a worse state, he informed her to contact the Hemlock Society. The Hemlock Society is an organization dedicated to helping those who want to painlessly end their lives.

Diane called back a week later requesting a prescription for barbiturates. Dr. Quill knew that overdosing barbiturates was a favorite suicide method of the Hemlock Society and he asked Diane to come into the office. Diane claimed that she had been experiencing insomnia, though Dr. Quill knew that she was only trying to protect him from possible legal impropriety. They spoke for a while and Dr. Quill became convinced that she was not acting out of depression or despondency. He wrote out a prescription for the pills and informed her of the correct dosage for insomnia as well as the amount needed to commit suicide. They agreed to continue meeting regularly and that she would see him before taking her life.

Over the next three months Diane went through good days and bad days. At one point it even looked like she was in remission. However, she suddenly began to decline very rapidly, and it looked like the end was coming soon. The days Diane feared most were upon her—days of pain and dependence that could only be comforted by heavy sedation. She knew the time had come. She had friends stop by to say goodbye. She met with Dr. Quill and assured him she knew what she was doing. They tearfully said goodbye.

Two days later her husband called and said Diane was dead. She had said goodbye to her husband and son and asked to be left alone for about an hour. When they returned to the room, she was lying on the couch with a shawl over herself. Dr. Quill came by and checked her and then called the medical examiner's office. When asked the cause of death, he said she had died of acute leukemia. He justified his lie by claiming that he did not want an ambulance crew to arrive too soon and try to revive her, or for the family to suffer through an autopsy investigation. He was also concerned for the legal ramifications on the family and himself. However, Dr. Quill was bothered that Diane had to die alone and that he had to keep the real cause of her death a secret. He wondered how many other doctors and families had been involved in similar cases. And so, Dr. Quill decided to take Diane's story and publish it in one of the most prestigious medical journals in the country, *The New England Journal of Medicine*. When that issue hit the stands in 1991, it opened up a whole new debate in medical ethics.[1]

1. The story is a summary of the story as it is told by Dr. Timothy Quill, "Death with Dignity: A Case of Individualized Decision Making," (1991) in *Last Rights: Assisted Suicide and Euthanasia Debated*, ed. Michael M. Uhlmann (Grand Rapids: Eerdmans, 1998).

IS SUICIDE EVER JUSTIFIED?

One's view of physician-assisted suicide (hereafter referred to as PAS) is obviously going to be affected by one's view of suicide itself. If one believes that suicide in general is unjustified, then it would be difficult to justify PAS. I am not saying that it follows necessarily, but it would be inconsistent for one to reject suicide in a normative sense, and yet support PAS. Therefore, it is necessary that we begin our study by answering the above question.

What is suicide? One can define it in one of two ways. In a broad sense, it is the intentional taking or forfeiting of one's own life. The problem with the broad definition of suicide is that it includes actions that most would not consider suicide in the traditional understanding of the term. For example, what of a person who knowingly and intentionally sacrifices his life for others, such as the soldier who throws himself on a grenade to save the life of his buddies? Few of us would call this a suicide. Or what of a Christian who refuses to recant of his faith, knowing that he will die if he does not agree to do so, yet intentionally accepts death to recanting? This too would not be counted as a suicide by most persons. I would also suggest that refusal of treatment is not necessarily a suicide. It is possible that a patient may refuse treatment, even knowing such a refusal may end up in their death, and yet he does not intend it. For example, Jehovah's Witnesses will usually refuse a blood transfusion due to religious beliefs and do so knowing that it may very well result in death. However, this does not mean that they are intending to die. In fact, most hope that other methods of treatment can be used to save their lives. In short, we recognize that the broad definition of suicide is not appropriate due to many situations that are not usually considered suicide.

It is important to remember that a moral action is more than just intentions and actions—there is also the issue of motive. Whereas my intention describes *what* I am aiming for, my motive is a description of *why* I am aiming for it. To illustrate the difference, suppose a wealthy man is drowning, and two men dive in with the intention of saving him. Even though they both have the same intention—to save the man—they may have totally different motives. One person may be the lifelong friend of this man and be saving him out of loyalty and love for their friendship. The other may be thinking that by saving this man he will get a financial reward. While we would admire both for doing the right thing, most of us would think lower of the man who did it for a *self-serving* motive over the one who did it for an *other-serving* motive.

While self-serving actions are not always wrong (after all, we do them all the time) it seems to most of us that there is nothing morally praiseworthy about them. We praise others when they put self aside for the sake of others.

I would like to suggest that what makes suicide different from other forms of intentional taking or forfeiting of one's life has to do with motive. A suicide is done for primarily self-serving motives as opposed to self-sacrifice which is primarily other regarding. Therefore, I define a suicide as *the intentional taking or forfeiting one's life primarily for self-serving motives.* Does this definition answer every possibility or distinction between suicide and other actions? Perhaps not, but I believe it is a good working definition, and may be as good as we can get.[2] Philosopher Tom Beauchamp writes that it is "difficult to capture precisely which intention is required for suicide, and what the right excluding conditions are. Suicide is an ill-order concept, and the linguistic intuitions of indigenous users of the language are inadequate to correct it."[3]

Having defined suicide, the above question of its justification can now be addressed. In the past, several persons have argued that suicide is a justifiable option in certain situations. Some of the main persons who argue in favor of justified suicide are Derek Humphry, the founder of the Hemlock Society; Dr. Jack Kevorkian; and Dr. Timothy Quill. They have offered several arguments to support that view. First, the principle of respect for autonomy requires that people be allowed to commit suicide if they freely choose to do so. People have a right to privacy and a right to choose what to do with their own bodies. They have a right to choose when and how to die. Some have argued that this right is just as fundamental as the right to life. Second, rational suicide is possible. It is possible for a person to make a reasoned decision to end their life. The following criteria are usually advanced for a suicide to be deemed rational: (1) the immediate ability to reason; (2) a realistic worldview; (3) adequate information concerning his condition and its prognosis; (4) the desire to avoid harm or hurt to himself and others; and (5) the suicide is in accordance with his fundamental interests. Third, while it is true that

---

2. For example, some might argue that a person who commits suicide so as to not be a financial burden to their family, is acting in an other-regarding motive. However, I agree with J. P. Moreland that this is not so much a regard for others themselves as it is a regard for others' nonpersonal states of affairs (i.e., their wealth). See J. P. Moreland with Norman L. Geisler, *The Life and Death Debate: Moral Issues of Our Time* (Westport, CT: Greenwood, 1991), 87.
3. Tom L. Beauchamp, "The Problem of Defining Suicide," in *Ethical Issues in Death and Dying,* 2nd ed., eds. Tom L. Beauchamp and Robert M. Veatch (Upper Saddle River, NJ: Prentice-Hall, 1996), 117.

human life has value, it is a relative value, not an absolute one. It is possible to encounter a threshold where life has lost almost all its value. Those suffering in extreme pain and discomfort with little chance of recovery of the normal functions of human living would be an example. To require that these people maintain their lives is to condemn them to a life of agony. It would be more merciful to allow them to end their suffering and die with dignity.

How might one respond to these arguments? We have already commented about the autonomy issue in the last chapter and much of what we said there will apply here. First, it is an excessively individualistic concept of autonomy that argues it is "my life" without considering that one is a member of a community and has responsibilities to that community. Second, as Christians, we recognize that it simply isn't *your* life to do with as you please. We have a stewardship of responsibility to God for the life he has given on loan to us. However, the one problem that comes out very strongly in the above arguments is that the first and second reasons counter each other. If it is my right to choose, then how can you place any conditions on it? The problem is that those who support suicide almost always support it under only certain conditions. For example, Derek Humphry writes, "We do not encourage any form of suicide for mental health or emotional reasons."[4] He then lists two justifying reasons for suicide: terminal illness in which suffering is present and a grave handicap that is intolerable for the individual. He also lists at least seven "parameters" for justified suicide. However, if the main argument for justifiable suicide is respect for autonomy, why do I need any conditions or "parameters"? More importantly, since it is totally an individual choice, who are *you* to tell me what those conditions are?

As far as the possibility of rational suicide itself, I believe one can reason to the conclusion that suicide is a proper course of action. However, while rational suicide is possible, it does not mean it actually occurs or that it is the morally right thing to do. A person can take a very rational approach to committing a crime, such as robbing a bank. They may have very self-interested goals that in light of their worldview, makes robbing a bank a reasonable action. The fact that it is rational is not an argument that it is morally justifiable. Also, some raise the question of how often persons really are free from the mental or emotional conditions in order to make an objective "rational" decision about their own death. Dr. Herbert Hendin is a psychiatrist and

---

4. Derek Humphry, "The Case for Rational Suicide," in Uhlmann, *Last Rights* (Grand Rapids: Eerdmans, 1998), 307.

recognized authority on suicide. He is concerned that many of the supposed "rational" suicides may have been patients who were not adequately diagnosed and treated for depression or mental illness, or properly counseled about fear of pain, loss of control, and other end-of-life concerns. He writes:

> Patients do not know what to expect and cannot foresee how their conditions will unfold as they decline toward death. Facing this ignorance, they fill the vacuum with their fantasies and fears. When these fears are dealt with by a caring and knowledgeable physician, the request for death usually disappears. . . . Unfortunately, depression itself is commonly underdiagnosed and often inadequately treated. Although most people who kill themselves are under medical care at the time of death, their physicians often fail to recognize the symptoms of depressive illness or, even if they do, fail to give adequate treatment.[5]

We also dealt with the mercy argument in the previous chapter. We saw that much has been done to alleviate pain in the area of medicines, technology, and hospice care. Suicide supporters will often just refer to the autonomy argument and say that many just do not want to go that route. We have already discussed the problems with such a view of autonomy. Also, we commented in the last chapter on communicating the wrong information about suffering. Lastly, the view that life only has a "relative" value and not "absolute" value is too subjective. Who becomes the determiner of life's value? Who decides where the "threshold" is? The only consistent answer is the individual himself. But then there is no regulation to suicide at all—it is totally up to the individual. The teenage girl who breaks up with a boyfriend and thinks life is no longer worth living has just as much of a "right to die" as the elderly person who has lost her husband and has no purpose in life. Humphry may assert that he would never encourage either of these situations, but such a strong view of autonomy insists that he must allow for them.

In opposition to the justifiable suicide view, is the traditional view of suicide. Traditionally throughout human history, suicide has been viewed as an immoral act usually performed out of desperation, depression, or mental illness. However, you find few actual arguments against suicide in older records. The reason is clear: arguments against suicide have only been recently advanced due to the fact that suicide has only recently been advocated as

---

5. Herbert Hendin, *Seduced by Death: Doctors, Patients, and Assisted Suicide* (New York: W. W. Norton, 1998), 34–36.

a justifiable act. No one bothered to argue against suicide because it was just assumed to be wrong. This is probably why there are no direct prohibitions against suicide in Scripture. There are five cases of suicide recorded in Scripture (Abimelech [Judg. 9:54]; Saul [1 Sam. 31:4]; Zimri [1 Kgs. 16:18]; Ahithophel [2 Sam. 17:23]; Judas [Matt. 27:5]), and all of them are in the context of God's judgment on shameful or sinful lives.

Those who argue for the traditional view usually offer the following arguments: (1) Suicide violates the fundamental principle of the sanctity of human life. All life has intrinsic value and one should never deliberately take or forfeit his own life without just cause. From a Christian point of view, life is a gift by God, and we are created in the image of God. To take a life, even one's own, is to desecrate that image. (2) Suicide is contrary to the natural law. Humans have a natural human tendency to preserve one's life. It is natural for humans to live and to engage in human activities. Suicide perverts and violates this natural tendency. (3) Suicide harms society. It is an injury to family and friends and deprives society of an individual's contribution to it. By justifying suicide, we condone its usage throughout all society. And (4) because reasons for suicide are subjective to each individual, there could be no objective way of regulating it.

WHAT IS PHYSICIAN-ASSISTED SUICIDE?

In answer to this question, we need to distinguish PAS from voluntary active euthanasia. They have much in common—so much that Tom Beauchamp places PAS as a subcategory of active euthanasia. They both involve the intentional death of a person, usually at his/her own request, and they both involve a third party. Also, many of the arguments and problems we discussed under euthanasia will be applicable here. There are three distinctions that are important enough to warrant a separate look at PAS apart from euthanasia. First, PAS is specifically suggesting that a physician be involved in a patient's death, so there is the question of this being the proper role of a physician. Active euthanasia can be performed by anyone on anyone. Second, in PAS the physician is not the one who is actually administering the death-causing substance to the patient; the patient is administering it to himself. The physician is assisting in the person's suicide; he is not himself killing the patient. The moral relevance of this distinction is debatable, but it is a distinction. Third, active euthanasia almost always involves patients who are in the end stages of the dying process and are currently suffering. Assisted suicide may occur much earlier than the end stages of dying and, in several cases, the person has not been dying at all. While there is often some overlap between PAS and active euthanasia, I believe these distinctions are enough to raise some important issues, though we shall see that many objections to active euthanasia will be also true of PAS. I would define PAS as the intentional assistance of a physician in helping a patient to end his life through the provision of information and/or means necessary for them to accomplish that goal.

There are a few different models of PAS. I will mention three.

The Maverick Model

This model is best represented by Dr. Jack Kevorkian. Kevorkian was a pathologist living in Michigan. Beginning in 1990, he began to offer his services to those who wish to commit suicide. His first suicide was Janet Adkins, a woman in the early stages of Alzheimer's disease. At the time, Michigan had no law against assisted suicide, and even after Kevorkian was admonished by the court not to repeat the incident he continued to do so. In fact, he made a point of flouting any law or court request. He helped more than 120 persons commit suicide in places ranging from their own homes to the back of his VW van. His normal method had been to attach them to a "suicide machine" that would first inject a saline solution, then a sedative to put the person under, and finally potassium chloride which killed them. Most of the time, Kevorkian himself did not perform the injection; the person committing the suicide pushed the button starting the machine. However, in a November 1998 broadcast of the news program *60 Minutes,* Kevorkian was seen injecting the patient himself, thereby moving from assisted suicide to active euthanasia. He was arrested, convicted, and then released in 2007.

Kevorkian came under criticism by both supporters and objectors of physician assisted suicide for several reasons. His methods were considered crude, assisting suicides in the back of a van and then dumping bodies off at hospitals. Many were bothered that he was not the personal physician of any of his "patients," but appeared on the scene just to help them die. In fact, he advocated a new medical discipline that he called "obitiatry"—a medical specialty for physicians who just want to practice "medicide"—the killing of patients. The fact that he was not the regular personal physician of his "patients" means that he often hardly knew the people he was helping to die, often having just brief conversations with them before agreeing to help them die. He was not a clinical physician at all, but a pathologist. Many of his assisted suicides have been called into question. Herbert Hendin writes: "In some of Kevorkian's cases the push for the patient's death came from relatives, in others no medical pathology was found on autopsy, and in virtually no case were any alternatives to assisted suicide adequately explored."[6] Hendin goes on to report a number of questionable cases where Kevorkian helped in suicides: people who, upon autopsy were found not to be really sick, though Kevorkian insisted they were; people in suspicious situations, like when a husband arrested just three weeks earlier on a spousal assault charge helped arrange his wife's suicide; people of whom it is reported had doubts but felt pressured to go through with the suicide. Kevorkian did little of psychiatric investigation of the patients to see if they were suffering from depression or other abnormalities. He employed a psychiatrist, Dr. George Reding, on occasion who briefly met with patients, and admitted to having apologized to them for having to subject them to a psychiatric examination. Reding himself admitted to practicing active euthanasia several times during his medical internship. Finally, Kevorkian seemed to have a minimalist criterion for helping patients. He helped not only those presently suffering but also people with "intense anxiety or psychic torture inflicted by self or others."[7] This virtually opens the door to anything Kevorkian wanted to put in these categories. Kevorkian's license to practice medicine was suspended and he has been shunned by much of the medical community. His response was, "The medical profession made a mistake when they ostracized me. I have no career anymore. This is the substitute."[8] For these reasons, most persons who argue for PAS are not arguing for the Maverick model.

The Anonymous Philanthropist Model

A controversial article appeared in the January 1988 issue of the *Journal of the American Medical Association* titled "It's Over, Debbie." It relates the story by an anonymous resident being called to the bedside of a twenty-year-old woman dying of ovarian cancer late one night. The physician had never met the woman and only knew her by her first name, Debbie. After spending some time attempting to comfort her, she made the ambiguous statement "Let's get this over with." With that, the resident gave her an injection and she died quickly afterward. This article was very controversial at the time and both the physician as well as *JAMA* were heavily criticized for publishing it. Most critics, among whom were many supporters of physician-assisted suicide, believed that the resident acted wrongly in that he had inadequate knowledge

6. Hendin, *Seduced by Death*, 43.
7. Jack Kevorkian, *Prescription: Medicide: The Goodness of Planned Death* (Buffalo, NY: Prometheus, 1991), 318.
8. Hendin, *Seduced by Death*, 43.

of the patient and the patient's illness to have taken action on such a vague request. This would also be considered more of a case of active euthanasia then assisted suicide. Most who are arguing for assisted suicide are not arguing for the anonymous philanthropist model.

The Caring Personal Physician Model

More often cited as a good example of physician-assisted suicide is the case of Diane we related in the beginning of this chapter. This case first appeared as an article in the March 7, 1991, issue of the *New England Journal of Medicine* by Dr. Timothy Quill titled "Death with Dignity: A Case of Individualized Decision Making." This example is the one often promoted as the type of physician-assisted suicide that should be legalized. The personal physician who knows the patient and the patient's illness is involved. He provides the method for the suicide but leaves the ultimate decision in the patient's hands. Advocates argue that the shame in this case is that the woman had to do it alone and the doctor was forced to lie about the real cause of death. They would change those aspects if it were legalized.

Since publishing his case, Dr. Quill has published many articles and books advocating the legalization of PAS. In many of these, he sets up a few safeguards to assure that abuses do not occur. His proposed criteria include:

1. The patient must, of his own free will and at his own initiative, clearly and repeatedly request to die rather than continue suffering.
2. The patient's judgment must not be distorted—expert psychiatric evaluation should be sought if the primary physician is inexperienced in diagnosing depression.
3. The patient must have a condition that is incurable and associated with severe, unrelenting, intolerable suffering.
4. The physician must ensure that the patient's suffering and the request are not the result of inadequate comfort care.
5. Physician-assisted suicide should be carried out only in the context of a meaningful doctor-patient relationship.
6. Consultation with another experienced physician is required.
7. Clear documentation to support each condition above is required.[9]

9. Timothy E. Quill, "Potential Criteria for Physician-Assisted Suicide," in Uhlmann, *Last Rights*, 330–32.

Many advocates of PAS are favorably impressed with Dr. Quill's criteria. Other criteria have been suggested as well. Perhaps one of the most convoluted set of criteria comes from the assisted suicide/voluntary euthanasia law for the Northern Territory of Australia which went into effect on July 1, 1996. It lists no fewer than twenty-two separate steps a patient must go through in order to obtain help from a physician in ending his or her own life. This law was overturned on March 25, 1997. It is models like these that are today being advocated as the type of PAS that should be legalized. Which brings us to the next issue.

THE LEGAL STATUS OF PHYSICIAN-ASSISTED SUICIDE

Until recently, the topics of assisted suicide and active euthanasia were largely confined to academic discussions and professional journals. However, events like the Kevorkian suicides, the publication of articles such as "It's Over, Debbie," and the case of Diane brought the topic more into the public square. Some states have codified bans on assisted suicide, while others have legalized assisted suicide. The legislation status of assisted suicide will be discussed further in this chapter.

Because of movements both to legalize and prohibit assisted suicide, some important cases being argued in court. A common theme in these cases is the argument that laws prohibiting assisted suicide violate the Due Process Clause of the Fourteenth Amendment of the United States Constitution. The Due Process Clause actually pertains to language in the Fifth Amendment, which reads that nobody shall be "deprived of life, liberty, or property, without due process of law."[10] The Fourteenth Amendment merely extended this principle to the individual states.

Case Law

People v. Kevorkian. In the early 1990s, a number of states began passing laws specifically outlawing assisted suicide. One of the most well-known of these was a law enacted in February 1993 in Michigan, Public Act 270. The law made it a felony to assist in a suicide, punishable by up to four years in prison.[11] This was a temporary ban in response to the assisted suicides performed by Dr. Jack Kevorkian, which was discussed previously in this chapter. After the act went into effect, Kevorkian assisted a terminally ill person to commit

10. U.S. Constitution, Amendment V.
11. Mich. ComLaws §752.1027 (Su1996).

suicide, a direct disobedience of the new law. Kevorkian was charged in the district court for having violated the statute, where he moved to dismiss the charges claiming the law was unconstitutional. His argument was that a person has a due process right to commit suicide, and the law places an undue burden on that right. The circuit court agreed and invalidated the statute. The case was appealed to the Michigan Court of Appeals, which upheld the ruling of the lower court.[12] The case was further appealed to the Michigan Supreme Court, which ruled in May 1994 that the assisted suicide law did not violate the Michigan Constitution and therefore was a valid law.[13] Kevorkian appealed the United States Supreme Court, but the Court refused to hear the case. Thus, the ruling made by the Michigan Supreme Court was considered binding. In November 1995, the temporary ban on assisted suicide expired, but because the Michigan Supreme Court had already found that assisted suicide was a felony, the governor signed a permanent ban on assisted suicide in September 1998.

The crux of the opinion made by the Michigan Supreme Court involved whether there is a fundamental right to commit suicide. Proponents of assisted suicide rely on the United States Supreme Court's findings in *Roe v. Wade* and *Planned Parenthood v. Casey*,[14] both of which concern a person's right to bodily autonomy. They argue that a person's right to suicide falls under the right to personal autonomy. They also argue that assisted suicide is no different from terminating life-sustaining treatments, which had already been deemed legal in numerous prior court cases. The Michigan Supreme Court disagreed, ruling that while terminating life-sustaining treatment deals with acts that artificially sustain life, suicide deals with acts that artificially shorten life.[15] It went further in stating that "whereas suicide involves an affirmative act to end life, the refusal or cessation of life-sustaining medical treatment simply permits life to run its course, unencumbered by contrived intervention."[16] The Court found that the right to commit suicide is not rooted in the country's history and culture, nor is it implicit in the concept of liberty.[17]

Dr. Jack Kevorkian went on trial four times for assisting suicides between May 1994 and June 1997. He was acquitted three of those times by juries who

12. *People v. Kevorkian*, No. 154740 (Michigan Court of Appeals, 1994).
13. *People v. Kevorkian*, 527 N.W.2d 714 (Michigan Supreme Court, 1994).
14. See *Roe v. Wade*, 410 U.S. 113, 160 (1973) and *Planned Parenthood v. Casey*, 505 U.S. 833 (1992).
15. *People v. Kevorkian*, 527 N.W.2d 714, 728.
16. *People v. Kevorkian*, 527 N.W.2d 714, 728.
17. *People v. Kevorkian*, 527 N.W.2d 733.

found he was not killing patients, but relieving them of suffering. His fourth trial ended in a mistrial after his lawyer claimed the prosecution tampered with evidence. However, Dr. Kevorkian was found guilty on March 26, 1999, of second-degree murder in relation to the November 1998 *60 Minutes* broadcast where Kevorkian administered a lethal injection to a patient (up until that point, patients had generally administered the injections themselves). He was sentenced to ten to twenty-five years in prison, but was paroled after eight years, with the understanding that he was not to participate in any assisted suicides. He was released in 2007 and died on June 3, 2011.

Washington v. Glucksberg and Quill v. Vacco

In 1997, two cases were heard by the United States Supreme Court involving physician-assisted suicide. Because the cases are closely intertwined and were decided at the same time, it is prudent to discuss them together.

The state of Washington had a law on the books stating that promoting a suicide by aiding or causing someone to commit suicide was a Class C felony, punishable by up to five years in prison.[18] In 1994, this law was challenged by a group of physicians (including Dr. Harold Glucksberg) and a nonprofit organization called Compassion in Dying, whose purpose was to help terminally ill persons to hasten their deaths. The organization challenged the constitutionality of the law, claiming that it violated the Due Process Clause of the Fourteenth Amendment of the United States Constitution. In May 1994, Judge Barbara Rothstein ruled in Federal District Court for the Western District of Washington that the U.S. Constitution guaranteed a right to assisted suicide and that the statute was unconstitutional. The case was appealed to the Ninth Circuit Court of Appeals, which reversed Judge Rothstein's decision. Judge John T. Noonan, highly regarded as one of the greatest legal minds in the nation, wrote the majority opinion. Noonan held that there is nothing in the Constitution, nor in judicial precedents, that supports the idea of a guaranteed "right to die."[19] In fact, he argues the legal judgments have ruled just the opposite. He writes, "A federal court should not invent a constitutional right unknown in the past and antithetical to the defense of human life that has been a chief responsibility of our constitutional government."

18. Wa. Code. Ann. § 9A.36.060(1) (1994).
19. *Compassion in Dying v. State of Washington*, 49 F.3d. 586 (Ninth Circuit Court of Appeals, March 1995).

A year later, the case was reheard *en banc* to an eleven-judge panel in the Ninth Circuit.[20] The panel of judges reversed the ruling made by Judge Noonan. Judge Stephen Rinehart wrote the majority opinion. He claims that the 1993 Casey decision affirms that "the heart of liberty is the right to define one's own concept of existence, of meaning, of the universe, and of the mystery of life."[21] He held that this liberty, found within the Fourteenth Amendment, encompassed a right to determine the time and manner of one's own death.[22] Rinehart also held that the distinction between killing and letting die was a distinction without a difference.[23] Therefore, he upheld the district court's original ruling that the Washington law was unconstitutional.[24] The case was appealed to the United States Supreme Court in 1997.

Around the same time, another ban against assisted suicide was passed, this time in the state of New York. In July 1994, a group of three physicians headed by Dr. Timothy Quill filed a complaint against the state of New York, charging that the state laws prohibiting assisted suicide were unconstitutional, basing their reasoning on the Equal Protection Clause of the Fourteenth Amendment. The district court rejected the challenge, so it was appealed to the Second Circuit Court of Appeals. The Court of Appeals released its opinion on April 2, 1996, only weeks after the final opinion in *Compassing in Dying v. Washington* was announced. Judge Miner wrote the majority opinion and rejected Judge Rinehart's view from *Compassion in Dying* that the U.S. Supreme Court's ruling in *Casey* supports a right to die. However, the New York laws were found unconstitutional as well, but on different grounds. Judge Miner found that the laws did not provide a rational basis for a distinction between terminally ill patients who chose to die by refusing treatment and those who chose to die through assisted suicide.[25] This allowed for an unlawful discrimination against competent persons in the final stages of life who wished to hasten their death. Thus, the New York laws did not violate the Due Process Clause but were struck down regardless for violating the Equal Protection Clause. In 1997, this case was also appealed to the United States Supreme Court.

---

20. *En banc* refers to a hearing where all the qualified judges take part, rather than a smaller panel. In this situation, Judge Noonan wrote the opinion for the smaller panel, while Judge Rinehart wrote the opinion for the entire panel.
21. *Compassion in Dying v. State of Washington*, 79 F.3d 790 (Ninth Circuit Court of Appeals, May 1996).
22. *Compassion in Dying v. State of Washington*, 801.
23. *Compassion in Dying v. State of Washington*, 816.
24. *Compassion in Dying v. State of Washington*, 838.
25. *Quill v. Vacco*, 80 F.3d 716 (Second Circuit Court of Appeals, April 1996).

On June 26, 1997, the Supreme Court issued its rulings for both *Washington v. Glucksberg* and *Quill v. Vacco*. In unanimous rulings, the court reversed both the Second Circuit and Ninth Circuit Courts of Appeals, finding that states have the authority to prohibit physician-assisted suicide. Concerning *Washington v. Glucksberg*, Chief Justice William Rehnquist stated that no precedent existed in American laws or customs that guaranteed a constitutional right to assisted suicide and, in a manner similar to Justice Noonan, stated that courts cannot create such a right from an abstract concept of personal autonomy.[26] Therefore, Washington's law does not violate due process as defined in the Constitution. In *Vacco v. Quill*, Rehnquist also delivered the opinion and noted that New York had a lengthy history of distinguishing between killing and allowing someone to die, which had been widely recognized and rationally grounded.[27] Thus, New York's laws were also upheld. Because neither state's law prohibiting assisted suicide was found unconstitutional, both laws were allowed to stand. Even though these rulings were unanimous, five of the justices acknowledged the possibility that future laws prohibiting assisted suicide might be found unconstitutional.

Gonzales v. Oregon

In 1994, Oregon passed the nation's first Death with Dignity Act, which legalized physician-assisted suicide with certain restrictions. Numerous attempts were made to repeal the law, one of the most notable occurring in 2001 when then United States Attorney General John Ashcroft issued a rule that any doctor prescribing life-ending medications would be violating the Controlled Substances Act[28] and the doctor's license would be suspended. Ashcroft argued that physician-assisted suicide was not a legitimate medical procedure. The state of Oregon, joined by a physician and a group of terminally ill patients, challenged to Attorney General's rule in the U.S. District Court for the District of Oregon. The court ruled in favor of Oregon, which was affirmed by the Ninth Circuit Court of Appeals.

The case was then appealed to the United States Supreme Court in 2006. In a 6–3 decision, the Court affirmed the lower court findings. It found that the rule enacted by Ashcroft exceeded the powers granted to the Attorney General under the Controlled Substances Act.[29] While the Attorney General is

---

26. *Washington v. Glucksberg*, 521 U.S. 702, 710 (1997).
27. *Vacco v. Quill*, 521 U.S. 793, 800 (1997).
28. Controlled Substances Act, 21 U.S.C. §§ 824(a)(4), 829(a) (1970).
29. *Gonzales v. Oregon*, 546 U.S. 243 (2006).

given authority to make rules, the federal government is still prohibited from "declaring illegitimate a medical standard for care and treatment of patients . . . specifically authorized under state law."[30] It is important to note that the majority did not explicitly state whether physician-assisted suicide is right or wrong. Instead, it limited its ruling on what it found the Controlled Substances Act addresses, namely the misuse or illicit use of drugs, not the regulation of the medical practice altogether, including assisted suicide. Justice Antonin Scalia addressed assisted suicide directed in his dissent, stating "[if] the term 'legitimate medical purpose' has any meaning, it surely excludes the prescription of drugs to produce death."[31]

Legislation

There have been no federal laws regarding assisted suicide, whether protecting or prohibiting the practice. Instead, the only laws have been enacted by the individual states. All states allow patients to refuse medical treatment, even life-saving treatment. However, only a handful of states allow assisted suicide, or "death with dignity."

In 1991, the state of Washington attempted to pass legislation allowing assisted suicide. Called Initiative 119, the Washington Death with Dignity Act proposed to permit doctors to lethally inject patients under certain circumstances. It was defeated by a majority vote when it reached the polls. The following year, California attempted to pass Proposition 161, or the California Death with Dignity Act. The legislation made it to the polls but was also defeated. It is believed that both the Washington and California proposals were defeated because they were too broad and had few safeguards built in. This was an approach that would soon change. It is because of these defeats that there was a change in tactics and instead of passing laws legalizing assisted suicide, supporters attempted to decriminalize assisted suicide (leading to the some of the cases discussed previously).

In 1994, the first Death with Dignity Act was passed in Oregon. Those behind this Act had learned the lesson from Washington and California, toning down the proposition quite a bit. There were more safeguards and criteria built into the law. The patient must make the request twice with at least fifteen days between the two requests. The rest of the burden is placed upon the physician, who must:

30. *Gonzales v. Oregon*, 257.
31. *Gonzales v. Oregon*, 263.

1. Make an initial determination of whether a patient has a terminal disease in which he has six months or less to live, is capable, and has made the request voluntarily.
2. Inform the patient of his/her medical diagnosis, prognosis, potential risks associated with taking the lethal medication, probable result of taking the lethal medication, any feasible alternatives including, but not limited to, comfort care, hospice care, and pain control.
3. Refer the patient to a consulting physician for medical confirmation of the disease and the time frame or life expectancy, and also for a determination that the patient is capable and acting voluntarily.
4. Refer the patient for counseling if appropriate (counseling is only required if depression or another medical condition causes impaired judgment).
5. Request that the patient notify the next of kin.
6. Inform the patient that he or she has the opportunity to rescind the request at any time and offer the patient an opportunity to rescind at the end of a required fifteen-day waiting period from the date of the initial request to the writing of the prescription.
7. Verify immediately prior to writing the prescription that the patient is making an informed decision.
8. Fulfill medical record documentation requests.
9. Ensure that all appropriate steps are carried out in accordance with this Act.[32]

After these conditions are met, physicians are then allowed, though not compelled, to write the prescription. It is up to the patient to physically take the lethal drugs. Physicians are not allowed to inject patients with drugs, nor are they allowed to prescribe injections for the patient to self-administer; the medicine prescribed must only be taken orally.

Immediately after the law's passage, right-to-life groups and the Catholic Church, led by Dr. Gary Lee, sued the State of Oregon. The law's validity was brought into question when the lawsuit charged that the law is discriminatory to the disabled and terminally ill, in essence arguing that they are less deserving of protection than others because their lives could be taken without

32. This summary of the conditions of the law is taken from Wesley J. Smith, *Forced Exit: The Slippery Slope from Assisted Suicide to Legalized Murder* (New York: Random House, 1997), 121–22. The law can also be found in its entirety in the Oregon Revised Statutes §127.800–995.

due process. On August 3, 1995, Federal District Judge Michael Hogan struck down the law on the basis that it was unconstitutional.[33] His decision was based on the Equal Protection Clause of the Fourteenth Amendment. Judge Hogan stated, "certain fundamental rights cannot be dispensed with by majority vote." However, Hogan's decision was overturned in 1997 by the Ninth Circuit Court of Appeals due to a technicality when one of the plaintiffs in the original suit was deemed to not have standing.[34] The case was appealed to the United States Supreme Court, which refused to hear it. In response, the Oregon State Legislature put the matter before the people again and introduced Measure 51, which would have repealed the Death with Dignity Act. However, Measure 51 was defeated by a wider majority than before.

In 2008, the state of Washington passed its own Death with Dignity Act, which mirrored the existing Oregon law. This was followed by Vermont in 2013, which allowed physicians to opt out of the law, but they must still inform patients of its availability to them if they qualify. Most recently in 2015, California has also legalized assisted suicide. As of this writing, these are the only four states that explicitly allow physician-assisted suicide by statute. One state, Montana, gives protection against criminal liability to physicians who act according to a patient's end-of-life wishes, including assisted suicide.[35] Thirty-eight states have laws prohibiting assisted suicide. Three states (Alabama, Massachusetts, and West Virginia) do not have specific laws outlawing assisted suicide, but it is criminalized under the state common laws against murder. Four states (Nevada, North Carolina, Utah, and Wyoming) have no laws or have abolished common-law language addressing assisted suicide.

In 2014, a twenty-nine-year-old woman named Brittany Maynard was diagnosed with terminal brain cancer. She chose to move from California to Oregon so she could take advantage of the state's Death with Dignity Law. As an advocate for assisted suicide, she became the face for the right-to-die debate. Various media outlets reported her story and a younger generation became exposed to the issue. Maynard ended her life on November 1, 2014. Following Maynard's visible campaign for assisted suicide, numerous states

---

33. *Lee v. State of Oregon*, 891 F. Su1421 (Ninth Circuit Court of Appeals, 1995).
34. *Standing* addresses whether a party to a case can demonstrate a sufficient connection to and harm from the challenged law. A party must have suffered or will imminently suffer harm, the injury must be causally connected to the law at issue, and a favorable court decision must be likely to redress the harm (Article III of the U. S. Constitution, Section 2). In this case, the plaintiff could not show actual harm, but only speculative harm (see *Lee v. State of Oregon*, 107 F.3d 1382 [Ninth Circuit Court of Appeals, 1997]).
35. Montana Code §50–9 (1991).

have introduced or are reconsidering right-to-die legislation. It remains to be seen if the trend toward legalizing assisted suicide will continue to grow.

MORAL ARGUMENTS FOR AND AGAINST PAS

Moral Arguments for PAS

The two main moral arguments for PAS and for its legalization are the mercy argument, that people who are suffering should be allowed to end their suffering, and the autonomy or self-determination argument, that a person should be able to determine his own time and manner of death. We have already discussed these arguments in the previous chapter and earlier in this chapter and I have little to add here that has not already been stated. However, since we are discussing legalizing assisted suicide I want to amplify on a comment I made in the last chapter about the relationship between these two arguments, for they are always conjoined together by those who argue in favor of legalizing assisted suicide. In strongly conjoining them, a major problem develops between these two arguments. Daniel Callahan comments, "Once the key premises of that argument are accepted, there will remain no logical way in the future to: (1) deny euthanasia to anyone who requests it for whatever reason, terminal illness or not; or to (2) deny it to the suffering *in*competent, even if they do not request it."[36]

The point is that there is no *a priori* reason why these two arguments should be linked together. Yet when they are separated, there are enormous problems for the pro-PAS view. Take autonomy for example. If an adult has a right to assisted suicide based on self-determination, then why do they have to be suffering? By requiring suffering, you have placed a limit on my self-determination. How does one justify this arbitrary limitation on autonomy? When we remove the suffering limitation, anyone can insist on assisted suicide for any desires or motivations.

On the other hand, consider the problem of the mercy argument. What about a person who is suffering but is presently or permanently incapacitated and not competent to make a decision concerning suicide? If the person is suffering, it seems unfair and merciless to say that they must continue to suffer simply because they are incompetent. Are they less entitled to relief from suffering than the competent? Again, Callahan comments:

---

36. Daniel Callahan, "Physician-Assisted Suicide Should Not Be Legal," in *Suicide: Opposing Viewpoints,* ed. Michael D. Biskup (San Diego: Greenhaven, 1992), 72 (emphasis mine).

> Each [argument] has its own logic. . . . But in the nature of the case that logic, it seems evident, offers little resistance to denying any competent person the right to be killed, sick or not; and little resistance to killing the incompetent, so long as there is good reason to believe they are suffering. There is no principled reason to reject that logic, and no reason to think it could long remain suppressed by the expedient of arbitrary legal stipulations.[37]

Here is a key point. If it is judged that the incompetent has a right to assisted suicide, and equal treatment demands we make such a judgment, then we must allow not only assisted suicide but also nonvoluntary active euthanasia, for the incompetent do not have the ability to request assistance in committing suicide. It will have to be done for them. Thus, while there is a legitimate distinction between assisted suicide and active euthanasia, to legally allow one, you must legally allow the other. Nicholas Dixon says: "Those who defend physician-assisted suicide often seek to distinguish it from active euthanasia, but in fact, the two acts face the same objections. Both can lead to abuse, both implicate the physician in the death of a patient, and both violate whatever objections there are to killing."[38] In light of this my arguments below will often be against both assisted suicide and active euthanasia.

Having dealt with the mercy and autonomy arguments previously, I want to look at two arguments that are unique to PAS (and to a certain extent, active euthanasia).

1. *The obligation of physicians.* One argument is based on the obligation that physicians owe their patients. According to this argument physicians have an obligation to help patients overcome pain and suffering and not to abandon them in their time of need. Since patients are autonomous concerning their right to choose to die, physicians should be allowed to respect their autonomy and to help patients accomplish their goal in the most painless way possible and to ensure its success. To says to a patient that they may commit suicide "one their own" without a physician's help is to abandon the patient.

This argument is based on the strong tradition in medical care that a physician cannot abandon a patient in need. This is referred to as "continuity of care." For example, the American Medical Association Council on Ethical

37. Callahan, "Physician-Assisted Suicide," 73.
38. Nicholas Dixon, "On the Difference between Physician-Assisted Suicide and Active Euthanasia," *Hastings Center Report* 28, no. 5 (1998): 25.

and Judicial Affairs Code of Ethics has a section titled "Fundamental Elements of the Patient-Physician Relationship." In that document they state that: "The physician may not discontinue treatment of a patient as long as further treatment is medically indicated, without giving the patient reasonable assistance and sufficient opportunity to make alternative arrangements for care."[39]

However, there are many problems with this argument. First, the duty of a physician to not abandon a patient is a *prima facie* duty, meaning it upholds in most cases, but not necessarily all cases. For example, suppose a physician has a patient in need of a bone marrow transplant and he has a found a compatible person to donate bone marrow, but the person refuses to participate. The physician's obligation to his patient does not allow him to force the person into donating against their will. In other words, one cannot justify doing anything one chooses based solely on the principle of loyalty to a patient. There may be situations when the duty to not abandon a patient may conflict with a more fundamental duty. Physicians also have a duty to do no harm and a duty not to kill. Many would argue that these duties of non-maleficence are more fundamental than to provide continuity of care, which is a duty of beneficence.

Second, if the argument above is true, then physicians in fact really have no moral, and perhaps no legal, choice in the matter. They must honor their patients' wishes to be assisted in a suicide. But what if the physician believes that suicide is wrong? What if they think it is possibly justifiable in some cases, but not this one? His moral obligation of not abandoning his patient will not allow him to refuse to help him. The patient's autonomy ends up trumping the physician's autonomy. However, some PAS advocates will reply, "No physician will be forced to help a patient if that physician chooses not to. He may recommend the patient to a physician who will help the patient commit suicide." However, on what grounds could a doctor deny such a request? If it is true that his duty to honor self-determination and to relieve suffering are central to his profession, can he really deny a patient his "right" simply because of his "personal conscience?" As Callahan says, "The moral situation is radically changed once our self-determination *requires* the participation and assistance of a doctor."[40]

---

39. AMACEJA, "Fundamental Elements of the Patient-Physician Relationship," in *Contemporary Issues in Bioethics*, 5th ed., eds. Tom L. Beauchamp and LeRoy Walters (Belmont, CA: Wadsworth, 1999), 40.
40. Callahan, "Physician-Assisted Suicide," 73 (emphasis mine).

Also, there are two problems with the PAS advocates' response. First, what if there are no other physicians who desire to assist in a suicide, or at least none within a reasonable proximity? This may place an "undue burden" on the patient, and it is possible the physician could be legally forced to honor the patient's wishes to carry out a treatment that has been deemed acceptable by law, but which the physician believes is wrong. Second, to pass the patient off to someone else is to ignore one of the main criteria of most advocates of PAS: physician-assisted suicide should be carried out only in the context of a meaningful doctor-patient relationship. Behind this idea is has always been the concept of a long-term relationship of the primary physician with the patient. However, what kind of meaningful relationship can be established by a physician and patient when that physician's only association with that patient is to help them die? This is more like the Maverick model of "obiatrist" than the Quill model "caring physician."

A third problem has to do with what kind of judgment the physician is making here. The fact that the patient is requesting a medicinal method of committing suicide may lead one to believe this is medical decision. However, this is not a medical decision; it is a moral decision. Daniel Callahan brings this out in a discussion about euthanasia, but applies also to assisted suicide:

> The doctor will not be able to use a medical standard. He or she will only be able to use a moral standard. Faced with a patient reporting great suffering, a doctor cannot, therefore justify euthanasia [or assisted suicide] on purely medical grounds (because suffering is unmeasurable and scientifically undiagnosable). To maintain professional and personal integrity, the doctor will have to justify it on his or her own moral grounds. The doctor must believe that a life of subjectively experienced intense suffering is not worth living. He must believe that himself if he is to be justified in taking the decisive and ultimate step of killing [or assisting in the killing of] the patient: it must be *his* moral reason to act, not the patients.[41]

Again, the problem is, what if the doctor holds the moral position that suicide is wrong? According to Callahan, he cannot justify assisting someone on purely medical reasons, but he must justify them based on his own moral reasons. If he does not hold these moral reasons, then the abandonment argument says he must ignore his own conscience and fulfill his obligation to his

41. Callahan, "Physician-Assisted Suicide," 73.

patient. This obligation is even stronger if PAS is legalized or becomes an accepted standard of medical practice.

A fourth problem that many point out is that it is contrary to the traditional role of the physician as a health provider to now be in the business of hastening or helping in the death of patients. This tradition goes all the way back to the Hippocratic Oath which states in part, "I will apply dietetic measures for the benefit of the sick according to my ability and judgment; I will keep them from harm and injustice. *I will neither give a deadly drug to anybody if asked for it, nor will I make a suggestion to this effect.*"[42] Others have restated this basic principle of medical practice. A group of physicians, in responding to the "Debbie" case related above, wrote:

> The resident violated one of the first and most hallowed canons of the medical ethic: doctors must not kill. Generations of physicians and commentators on medical ethics have underscored and held fast to the distinction between ceasing useless treatments (or allowing to die) and active willful taking of life; at least since the Oath of Hippocrates, Western medicine has regarded the killing of patients, even on request, as a profound violation of the deepest meaning of the medical vocation. As recently as 1986, the Judicial Council of the American Medical Association, in an opinion regarding treatment of dying patients, affirmed the principle that a physician "should not intentionally cause death." Neither legal tolerance nor the best bedside manner can ever make killing medically ethical.[43]

David Orentlicher, an attorney for the AMA, comments, "What the sick need and are entitled to seek from the efforts of physicians is health. Accordingly, physicians provide medical treatments to the sick to make them well, or as well as they can become. Treatment designed to bring on death, by definition, does not heal and is therefore fundamentally inconsistent with the physician's role in the patient-physician relationship."[44] Medical science simply cannot solve every problem. That is asking too much of it. The temptation to deal with one's frustration of not being able to solve every instance

42. Hippocratic Oath, 4th century, BC, in Beauchamp and Walters, *Contemporary Issues*, 39 (emphasis mine).
43. Willard Gaylin, Leon R. Kass, Edmund R. Pellegrino, and Mark Siegler, "Doctors Must Not Kill," in *Arguing Euthanasia: The Controversy over Mercy Killing, Assisted Suicide, and the Right to Die*, ed. Jonathan D. Moreno (New York: Simon and Schuster, 1995), 34.
44. David Orentlicher, "Physicians Cannot Ethically Assist in Suicide," in Biskup, *Suicide*, 61.

of suffering by ending life needs to be constantly checked. It is a Pandora's box that we dare not open. If it is not checked, then medicine "becomes subservient to an undue aspiration for control: when the quality of *life* cannot be maintained at the desired level, the *situation* can be brought back under control by killing the patient."[45]

A fifth problem in requiring physicians to take on this new role, else they be guilty of abandoning their patients, is that there is good reason to believe that it will eventually undermine the physician-patient relationship. This can be illustrated by the cartoon of a man in bed who says to his wife, "I'm not feeling too well today, honey." His wife asks him if he would like her to call a doctor, to which the man replies, "I'm not *that* sick!" Even if the physician does not bring up the suicide option, it will be difficult for him not to influence the patient concerning it. Allowing the patient to act autonomously is giving him freedom to choose without substantial outside influence. Orentlicher points out why this is a problem in assisted suicide:

> If the physician appears sympathetic to the patient's interest in suicide, it may convey the impression that the physician feels the assisted suicide is a desirable alternative. Such an impression may not be very comforting to the patient. Moreover, if the patient decides to reject suicide will the patient have the same degree of confidence in the physician's commitment to his or her care as previously? In short, assisted suicide might seriously undermine an essential element of the patient-physician relationship, the patient's trust that the physician is wholeheartedly devoted to caring for the patient's health.[46]

If the patient does not suggest assisted suicide, should the doctor bring it up as an option? As an aspect of informed consent, the physician is responsible to provide a list of all the viable options to a patient. If assisted suicide is legalized or becomes standard medical practice, the physician will be forced to offer it as an option. How would this affect a hopelessly ill patient? "He will not feel entirely free to resist a suggestion from the physician that suicide would be appropriate, particularly since it comes from the person whose medical judgment the patient relies on."[47]

45. Henk Jochemsen, "The Netherlands Experiment," in *Dignity and Dying: A Christian Appraisal*, eds. John F. Kilner, Arlene B. Miller, and Edmund D. Pelligrino (Grand Rapids: Eerdmans, 1996), 176.
46. Orentlicher, "Physicians Cannot Ethically Assist in Suicide," 59.
47. Orentlicher, "Physicians Cannot Ethically Assist in Suicide," 59–60, citing Yale Kamiser.

2. *The regulation argument.* One of the major arguments raised against the legalization of PAS is that abuses are possible. People might be coerced into committing suicide, or it might be extended to include those not terminally ill. PAS advocates argue that while abuses are possible, criteria can be established that are effective protections against abuses by doctors and institutions. A number of regulatory standards have been suggested including those above by Dr. Timothy Quill, the State of Oregon standards, and the "Model State" standards provided by a group of Boston lawyers. Most of the regulatory standards have the same basic criteria: patient is competent in requesting it and repeats his request over time, severe pain or suffering with no other acceptable option in dealing with it, consultation with other doctors including a psychiatrist, good doctor-patient relationship, and so on.

There are several problems with the concept of regulating PAS. Daniel Callahan and Margot White have written an excellent work dealing with many of these titled "The Legalization of Physician-Assisted Suicide: Creating a Potemkin Village."[48] I will refer to some of the problems they raise. Some of these are general problems with the whole concept of regulation, while others are specific problems with criteria. First, those who argue for legislating PAS often say that assisted suicide is currently going on now in secret and that we need to legalize it so that it can be brought out in the public and properly controlled. The problem with this is that it admits that statutes probably will not help. If the present statutes outlawing PAS are ineffective in keeping people from abusing the law, what makes advocates think that regulation will be any more effective? If physicians do not take the law seriously now, what makes advocates think they will take it seriously later? They offer no evidence or studies to support the idea that regulation would really change any present practices. The majority of Kevorkian's suicides did not meet most of the regulatory criteria suggest by any of the advocates. Do they think that if it had become legal, Kevorkian would have stopped his suicides? He said that the criteria suggested are too limiting. That gives us a hint of what he would have done if PAS became legal—he would probably would have continued what he was still doing. Probably so would most physicians who are currently breaking the law. There is no reason to believe regulating PAS would significantly help in any way.

Second, even with all the regulation in effect the problem mentioned above of the power physicians have over patients, intentional or not, would

48. Potemkin villages were fake villages erected in Russia in order to hide the slums from the Empress as she rode through the country.

render many regulations moot. While advocates argue that the final decision is with the patient, the physician can have an incredible influence over the patient. Callahan and White argue:

> As for the power of doctors, their general prestige as professionals whose training and experience are widely thought to enable them to understand matters of life and death better than the rest of us, and their capacity to give or withhold lethal drugs, already establish the power differential between them and their patients. . . . [T]he desire to medicalize PAS already bespeaks the power and legitimation conferred by medical approval of it.[49]

I am not implying that most physicians will abruptly and willingly force patients to accept suicide, though I think some might. But the majority who have accepted suicide as a legitimate way of dealing with a person can, even quite unknowingly, subtly pressure patients into committing the act. Herbert Hendin analyzes two examples of assisted suicide that advocates use to promote the right way it is to be done, and shows how the physicians pressured the patient, even while they were claiming several times the it was their decision.[50]

In a videotaped case promoting PAS, a dying patient named Louise has requested suicide. Throughout the tape, the doctor, named Mero, and a member of Compassion for Dying (CFD) are concerned that Louise might lose judgment before she goes through with the act. They are seen subtly pressuring her to commit suicide before it gets "too late." When Dr. Mero must leave town for a while, he says, "You don't need to wait for me." At another point Mero and the CFD member discuss how they can be more direct with Louise without actually telling her to hurry up (after all, it has to be her idea). They say things to her and hope she will "read between the lines." While the doctor is out of town, Louise says she wants to wait until he is back before doing things. However, she is told, "Your doctor feels that if you don't do it this weekend, you may not be able to." At one point, Louise blurts out, "I'm not afraid. *I just feel like everyone is ganging up on me*. I just want some time." Her mother then expresses concern that she will change her mind. Hendin, a trained psychiatric expert on suicide, tells us that, "Louise has expressed two conflicting wishes—to live and to die—and found support only for the latter. . . . Everyone—Mero, the friend, the mother,

49. Daniel Callahan and Margot White, "The Legalization of Physician-Assisted Suicide: Creating a Potemkin Village," in Uhlmann, *Last Rights*, 580.
50. Herbert Hendin, "Selling Death and Dignity," *Hastings Center Report* 25, no. 3 (1995): 19–23.

and the reporter—all became part of a network pressuring Louise to stick to her decision and to do so in a timely manner. The death was virtually clocked by their anxiety that she might want to live."[51] And this is an example of the way advocates think it should be!

A third problem with regulation is the issue of patient confidentiality. Medical decisions are made between a patient and physician in the privacy of the physician's office and with an agreement of confidentiality between them. If this practice is maintained, how is it going to be possible to monitor physicians to make sure they are remaining within the guidelines of the regulations? Callahan and White state, "We submit that maintaining the privacy of the physician-patient relationship and the confidentiality of these deliberations is *fundamentally incompatible* with meaningful oversight and adherence to any statutory regulations."[52] Again, the fact that PAS is occurring today in secret demonstrates that it will continue in secret any time it is not in keeping with the regulations.

As far as specific regulations, the concept of suffering presented in most of them is too vague and would eventually have to include those who are not terminally ill. Also, the regulations either do not deal with the incompetent or those not physically able to commit suicide, or they must advocate active euthanasia (nonvoluntary for those who are incompetent) for them. Another problem with the suggested regulations has to do with the involvement of consulting physicians. The consulting physicians would have to be physicians who are already in favor of PAS in principle. Certainly, physicians who are not in favor will not be involved in consulting on a PAS case. That would mean the thinking of the consulting physicians would be biased in favor of PAS and therefore they might not be objective in judging a case. Callahan and White comment that often the regulations are set up more to facilitate PAS than to regulate it.

However, the best way to evaluate the success of regulatory assisted suicide or euthanasia is to look at one that has been in place for a while, the Netherlands. Before 1973, euthanasia was illegal and unacceptable in the Netherlands. In that year, a doctor was arrested and put on trial for killing her terminally ill mother with morphine. The court gave her a suspended sentence with one week in jail. This set a precedent and courts quickly began to establish some guidelines on how to judge these kinds of cases. Euthanasia and assisted suicide were, and are, still illegal in the Netherlands and punishable by fine

51. Hendin, "Selling Death and Dignity," 21–22.
52. Callahan and White, "Legalization of Physician-Assisted Suicide," 581.

and imprisonment. However, physicians were immune from prosecution if they followed the courts' basic guidelines. The basis for the immunity lies within the Dutch courts' concept of *force majeure*. *Force majeure*, French for "superior force," is a legal term for an event or effect that cannot be reasonably anticipated or controlled. Hendin explains, "Euthanasia is thus permitted when a doctor faces an unresolvable conflict between the law, which makes euthanasia illegal, and his responsibility to help a patient whose irremediable suffering makes euthanasia necessary."[53] In 1984, the Royal Dutch Medical Association proposed a basic set of guidelines that standardized what the courts had been doing. The RDMA guidelines stipulate that euthanasia is excused if it is (1) voluntarily requested by a competent adult; (2) the request is based on full information; (3) the patient is in a situation of intolerable and hopeless suffering; (4) there are no acceptable alternatives to euthanasia; and (5) the physician has consulted another physician before performing euthanasia. Doctors were required to keep records of euthanasia cases and to report cases of euthanasia to the Dutch authorities. In 1994 the RDMA guidelines were made into government regulations by the Dutch Supreme Court.

How successful is the Dutch euthanasia program? In January 1990, the Dutch government appointed a commission to investigate the practice of euthanasia. It was headed up by Professor Jan Remmelink, attorney general for the Dutch Supreme Court. More than four hundred physicians were interviewed and granted anonymity and immunity from prosecution. The study was published in Dutch in 1991 and in English the following year. Its results were disturbing to many.

The Remmelink study found that 49,000 deaths in the Netherlands in 1990 involved a medical decision at the end of life.[54] Most of these deaths involved either the withholding or discontinuing of life support (passive euthanasia) or the alleviation of pain and symptoms through medication that might hasten death (i.e., a lethal dose was given with the intention to alleviate pain). However, 2,300 deaths were cases of active euthanasia (about 2 percent of all deaths in the Netherlands that year), and about four hundred were assisted suicides. Most disturbing was the fact that just a little less than half of those euthanized, 1,040 of the 2,300, were actively killed *without the patient's knowledge or consent*. Fourteen percent of these 1,040 were fully

53. Hendin, *Seduced by Death*, 64.
54. *Medical Decisions about the End of Life*, The Hague, September 19, 1991. All the following statistics come from the above report.

competent, 72 percent had never given any indication that they would want their lives terminated, and in 8 percent of the cases doctors performed involuntary euthanasia despite the fact that they believed alternative options were still possible. Forty-five percent of these nonvoluntary or involuntary euthanasia cases were performed without the consent or knowledge of the family. More than 50 percent of doctors admitted to practicing euthanasia. Only 60 percent kept a written record of their cases and only 29 percent filled out death certificates honestly, meaning that 71 percent of doctors did not report their involvement in euthanasia, as required by stated guidelines. All these facts were infractions of the regulations then in place.

In addition to these 2,700 active euthanasia and PAS cases, the Remmelink report showed that 8,100 patients died as a result of doctors deliberately giving them overdoses of pain medication, not for the primary purposes of controlling pain but to hasten the patient's death. In 61 percent of these cases (4,941 patients) the intentional overdose was given *without the patient's consent*. In one report given to a 1990 bioethics conference in Maastricht, Holland, a physician from the Netherlands Cancer Institute told of approximately thirty cases a year where doctors ended patient's lives by first *intentionally* placing patients in a coma by means of morphine injections and then killing them. The physician said these were not considered euthanasia because they were not voluntary and to have discussed it with patients first would have been "rude" since they all knew they had incurable diseases.

Since the Remmelink report a landmark case occurred that extended euthanasia even more. The case concerned Dr. Boudewijn Chabot and a patient whom he calls Netty Boomsma. In July 1991, Dr. Chabot received a call from the Dutch Voluntary Euthanasia Society who referred him to a woman living in Assen who had lost both of her sons, one a few years earlier committed suicide and the other more recently died of cancer. Netty, who had left an abusive husband about three years earlier, was depressed and had no one left in her life to care for. She did not believe there was any reason to live and desired to commit suicide. She specifically told Chabot that she did not want bereavement therapy. Chabot met with a few experts and showed them his notes of Netty's case. Though most approved of the suicide, two of them advised him not to go through with the it. One of these was the chair of the department of psychiatry at Erasmus University who believed that Netty needed therapy for her depression. Chabot asked only one of the experts to actually see Netty and that expert declined thinking it was not necessary. On September 27, Chabot met with Netty for the final time. He gave her some capsules and she went upstairs, swallowed them, and died soon after. After Chabot reported that case, he was told he would have to appear in court. Netty was not terminal, she was not even dying, and she was not suffering in any physical sense. In other words, it was a case of euthanasia that did not fall under the regulations. However, in April 1993 the court acquitted him and following two appeals including the Dutch Supreme Court he was exonerated. The court stated that mental suffering was grounds for suicide, though Chabot was chided for not having had a psychiatric consultant see her. This case is important because it establishes the precedence "that a patient a physician claims is not suffering from either psychiatric or physical illness can receive assisted suicide simply because he or she is unhappy."[55]

Two sad consequences come out of the Dutch euthanasia program. First, as Dr. Hendin testifies, rarely is adequate attention given to the mental state of patients who request suicide or euthanasia. Often times psychiatrists are not called in at all to evaluate patients, or if they are called in they only meet briefly with the patient and do not perform a full psychiatric evaluation or test to see if the patient is suffering from clinical depression. In studying the cases, Dr. Hendin is certain that the majority of them could have been helped with the right kind of therapy. However, because euthanasia and assisted suicide are readily available it is just simply easier to immediately give into the patient's desire and claim it was respect for self-determination, rather than help the patient through the difficult process of therapy.[56] The other sad consequence is that, according to a study of the British Medical Association, the state of palliative and hospice care in Holland is very poor.[57] Where euthanasia is an accepted medical solution to patients' pain and suffering, there is little incentive to develop programs that provide modern effective pain control for patients. As of the mid-1990s, there were only two hospice programs in operation in the Netherlands.

I believe sufficient evidence from the Netherlands exists to call into question the whole idea of regulating assisted suicide as an assurance that abuses will not take place. Once we go down that avenue, there is no telling where we will end. The question is, if regulations have not stopped abuses from occurring in the Netherlands, what makes us think that we can stop them from occurring here?

---

55. Hendin, *Seduced by Death*, 84
56. Hendin, *Seduced by Death*, 155–62.
57. *Euthanasia: Report of the Working Party to Review the British Medical Association's Guidance on Euthanasia*, British Medical Association, May 5, 1988, 49.

Moral Arguments against PAS

Along with my criticisms of the moral arguments in favor of PAS, I wish to offer some arguments against it. First, it is fundamentally wrong to take human life without just cause. If a physician facilitates the taking of human life, then he is an accomplice to murder. Scripture is very clear about this. Exodus 20:13 gives the commandment not to kill; Jesus confirms this in Matthew 5:21; 19:18; Mark 10:19; and Luke 18:20. This command is based on the idea that man is made in the image of God and to kill man is to desecrate that image (Gen. 9:6). Those who are suffering toward the ends of their lives are still image-of-God-bearers. At no time does Scripture ever hint that these commandments are not in force even though many times people are suffering in Scripture. As mentioned earlier, though suicide is not specifically condemned, it is never condoned, can be considered self-murder, and in those places where people did commit suicide usually has a negative cloud hanging over it.

Second, there is too much vagueness in the area of preemptive decisions concerning suicide. Preemptive suicide is that which is undertaken not out of current suffering, but in anticipation of a predictably long, drawn out decline in an illness. This is different from surcease suicide, that which is done as an escape from current suffering. In several of Kevorkian's assisted suicide cases the patients either were not terminal at all (Janet Adkins, Kevorkian's first suicide, was in the very early stages of Alzheimer's Disease with a prognosis of several years of alertness still ahead of her) or death was still quite far off. The vague question is, how early should a person be allowed to be assisted in a suicide? One could push this to the absurd and argue that since we are all terminal, and more than likely will suffer from forms of deterioration throughout our life, any of us could request assisted suicide now. To attach a time requirement of, for example, six months is simply to be arbitrary.

Third, in the cases of surcease suicides, recent techniques of pain management and the advent of hospice care has made it possible to treat virtually all pain and to relieve virtually all suffering. The dying process can be a valuable and positive experience of intimacy and spiritual growth. Rare instances of complete sedation can be used where pain cannot be controlled. While this is not the ideal situation, it is better than the taking of life and all its ramifications.

Fourth, the concept of "death with dignity" is misunderstood by assisted-suicide advocates. To die with dignity is not so much an issue of the manner of your death (either immediately or drawn out) or the state you are in when you die (conscious or unconscious), but how you face death when it comes. It is recognition that death is a normal end to life and an acceptance of it as such. If anything, suicide has traditionally been seen not as death with dignity, but as a way to escape what life presents to you. A true death with dignity would respect life, see it as God's gift, and fight to keep it.

Finally, we cannot always answer the question of why God allows certain things to happen. But we have an obligation to live in faithfulness to him because this is not our life, it is his. Christian ethicist Stanley Hauerwas makes this point:

> The language of gift does not presuppose we have a "natural desire to live," but rather that our living is an obligation. It is an obligation that we at once owe our creator and one another. For our creaturely status is but a reminder that our existence is not secured by our own power, but rather requires the constant care of, and trust in, others. Our willingness to live in the face of suffering, pain, and sheer boredom of life is morally a service to one another as it is a sign that life can be endured and moreover our living can be done with joy and exuberance. Our obligation to sustain our lives even when they are threatened with, or require living with, a horrible disease is our way of being faithful to the trust that has sustained us in health and now in illness. We take on a responsibility as sick people. That responsibility is simply to keep on living, as it is our way of gesturing to those who care for us that we can be trusted and trust them even in our illness.[58]

58. Stanley Hauerwas, *Suffering Presence: Theological Reflections on Medicine, the Mentally Handicapped, and the Church* (Notre Dame, IN: University of Notre Dame Press, 1986), 106.

7

Eighteen Ways to Make a Baby: Procreational Ethics

William Stern, forty, a biochemist from Tenafly, New Jersey, and his wife Elizabeth, forty-one, a pediatrician, had been married for ten years without having children. They decided to wait until Elizabeth had finished her internship in pediatrics. During that time, she developed some eye problems and it was discovered that she probably had multiple sclerosis. She learned that pregnancy could exacerbate the MS and there was a real chance of her becoming temporarily or even permanently paralyzed. Rather than take a chance, the Sterns sought alternative means to have a child. Having seen an advertisement, they contacted the Infertility Center of New York, which suggested they use a surrogate to fulfill Elizabeth's role of providing a gamete and uterus for their child.

Surrogacy parenting was still very new at this time, having become recently an option incorporating the artificial method of insemination. Sperm would be obtained from William through self-stimulation and would be inserted into a syringe attached to a lengthy catheter. The catheter would be inserted through the cervical canal into the uterus of a surrogate woman during the optimal time of ovulation. Once conception occurred, the surrogate would carry the child the full term of the pregnancy and, upon delivery, would surrender it to the Sterns, who would take full legal custody. While the child would not be genetically related to Elizabeth, it would be genetically related to William.

Mary Elizabeth Whitehead, twenty-nine, a former dancer from Brick, New Jersey, had also seen an advertisement from the Infertility

Center seeking women who were interested in being surrogates. She contacted the clinic offering her services as a surrogate parent. Mary, the mother of two children from her husband Richard, was originally motivated out of a desire to help her infertile sister, who turned her down. The clinic brought the two parties together In January 1985 and, after meeting Mary, the Sterns thought she would be the perfect person to bear their child. The entered into a contract in February 1985 in which William Stern agreed to pay all of Mary's medical bills and compensate her $10,000, for which she agreed to be artificially inseminated with William's sperm and, upon delivery, surrender it to the Sterns, terminating all parental rights. Mary went through several attempts at artificial insemination before finally conceiving in June 1985.

Mary gave birth to a baby girl on March 27, 1986, and immediately had second thoughts about giving the child away. Two days after the birth of the child, whom the Sterns named Melissa, Mary confessed that she did not think she could go through with giving the child up. Nevertheless, on March 30, she relinquished the child to the Sterns. She called a few hours later saying she did not know if she could live anymore and then called again the following morning and reported how she woke up screaming in the middle of the night. She asked the Sterns for permission to keep the baby for just one week and afterward she would disappear from their lives for good. The Sterns reluctantly agreed. However, Mary changed her mind and on April 12 informed the couple that she had no intention of returning Sara, the name she had given the child. The Sterns obtained a court order seeking enforcement of the contract and appeared at Mary's door on May 5 to get Melissa. While being delayed, Mary passed Melissa through a bedroom window to her husband, with whom she escaped and fled to her parents' home in Florida. The Sterns obtained another court order and Melissa was forcibly removed from Mary at her parents' home and brought back to New Jersey, where the Sterns were awarded temporary custody until a trial could ensue to settle the question of enforcing the contract.

The trial began in the Bergen County Superior Court in February 1987 and lasted thirty-two days. It was followed vigorously in the national media, as it was the first time a surrogacy issue had been challenged in the courts. The Sterns argued that a legal contract had been formed in which the terms were clear and agreed upon by both parties. Mary Whitehead argued that the contract was against public policy and that surrogacy was tantamount to baby selling. In addition to the arguments presented by the parties, Judge Harvey Sorkow also needed to determine custody in terms of what was in the best interest of the child. On March 31, 1987, he rendered his decision that the contract should be upheld and that Mary must relinquish all parental rights. Full custody was awarded to the Sterns and Elizabeth could adopt Melissa the same day.

Mary's attorney appealed the judgment to the New Jersey State Supreme Court, who agreed to hear the case. On February 3, 1988, the seven-member higher court unanimously reversed the decision of the lower court and awarded Mary her parental rights. In doing so the court stated that commercial surrogacy, in which compensation is awarded to surrogates, violates state laws against the selling of persons. Mary may have won the battle, but in the end, she did not win the war. While the adoption of Melissa by Elizabeth was voided by their decision, the New Jersey State Supreme Court let stand the primary custody order of the lower court for the Sterns to raise the child, as it was in the child's best interests. Mary was given visitation rights. When Melissa turned 18, she ceased all visitation with Mary and signed papers permitting Elizabeth Stern to formally adopt her.

The desire to procreate and raise children is one of the strongest and most natural desires a human can experience. Until the last century, procreation was part of the normal process of life. It was assumed the most adults would marry and raise a family as part of the ongoing process of regeneration of society. While there was a certain amount of limited control over the process, such as abstention at appropriate times, the proliferation of life usually occurred through the natural process of sexual activity. On occasions, some couples were not able to have children due to infertility issues and they would either adopt children or forgo raising a family.

All of that changed in the second half of the twentieth century. On June 23, 1960, the FDA approved the commercial sale of Enovid, the first oral contraceptive. While mechanical means of contraceptives had been in use for at least a century, the oral contraceptive made birth control as easy and taking an aspirin. Not only did this place more control in the hands of married couples as to when to have children, but an increase in sexuality activity outside of marriage arose and a new sexual revolution sprung forth with more openness about sexual promiscuity, nudity, pornography, and homosexuality. On January 22, 1973, the United States Supreme Court announced its decision in *Roe v. Wade* and *Doe v. Bolton,* striking down most state laws restricting abortion, thus creating another legal form of birth control. In other words, if the pill did not succeed, one could still eliminate pregnancy. Then, on July 25, 1978, Louise Brown, the first child conceived *in vitro*, was born. People were now able to have control over the process of conception and this paved the way for other alternatives to have children, including the surrogacy case mentioned above. According to the PBS television series *NOVA*, in an episode titled "18 Ways to Make a Baby,"[1] there are at least eighteen ways to make a baby:

- Natural sex
- Artificial insemination—of mother with father's sperm
- Artificial insemination—of mother with donor sperm
- Artificial insemination—with egg and sperm donors, using surrogate mother
- *In vitro* fertilization (IVF)—using egg and sperm of parents

---

1. "18 Ways to Make a Baby," *NOVA*, Episode #2811, broadcast October 9, 2001, produced by Sarah Holt.

- IVF—with Intra-Cytoplasmic Sperm Injection (ICSI)
- IVF—with frozen embryos
- IVF—with Preimplantation Genetic Diagnosis (PGD)
- IVF—with egg donor
- IVF—with sperm donor
- IVF—with egg and sperm donor
- IVF—with surrogate using parents' egg and sperm
- IVF—with surrogate and egg donor
- IVF—with surrogate and sperm donor
- IVF—with surrogate using her egg, sperm from baby's father
- IVF—with surrogate using egg and sperm donors
- Cytoplasmic transfer
- Nuclear transfer and cloning

As the technology and the ability to have more control over the procreative process has evolved, a significant number of ethical issues and problems have arisen. In this chapter, a number of these issues will be examined. This discussion will be divided into three parts: technology to prevent procreation, technology to assist procreation, and technology to enhance procreation.

PRELIMINARIES ON PROCREATION

The language used to describe the process of conceiving and giving birth to children reveals a lot more about the attitude toward regeneration than one might realize. The Hebrews used the term *yalad* (יָלַד), which is translated as "to bear, bring forth, or to beget," and communicated the transmission of life from father to child. The Greeks used the term *genesis* (γένεσις), or "to come into being," emphasizing the springing forth of new life coming from human parents. For centuries, the English-speaking world used the word "procreation," emphasizing the partnership between man and Creator in bringing forth new life. In modern times, we have substituted the term "reproduction," a manufacturing term, for procreation. While not wanting to read too much into the common usage of this metaphor for having children, it is interesting to note with Gilbert Meilaender, "The shift from 'procreation' to 'reproduction' is in part a manifestation of human freedom to master and reshape our world. But especially when that mastery extends to the body, the place where we come to know a person, we should be alert to both creative and destructive possibilities in the exercise of our freedom."[2] While the use of the term "reproduction" is not wrong, in this chapter the term "procreation" will be used when speaking of having children. There are enough distractions to turn people from the reminder that this is an activity shared with God. Hopefully using that term will keep the focus on that truth as we muddle our way through the fog of modern technologies.

The other preliminary to address is the moral question of any technological involvement in procreation. Some have serious objections to technological involvement in an area as intimate and sacred as the conceiving and birthing of children. One common objection is that becoming involved in birth control or assisted procreation is playing God (if a couple cannot have children, then that is God's will). The problem with the "playing God" objection is that this can be said of any medical intervention. Should we deny that people seek medical help for all medical problems? Throughout the history of the church, Christians have affirmed that medicine and medical progress are good and that the ability of humans to understand and treat disease and disabilities is a gift from God. All healing comes from him, whether it occurs directly or through using medicine and doctors as his instruments. Medical intervention to assist or prohibit procreation is just another form of using medical knowledge to help others.[3]

A second objection is that procreative technology is not natural and is interfering with the natural process of biological procreation. This objection carries with it the presumption that what is natural is right and that one should never disturb the natural order. But for many, this is patently false. First, it is highly questionable to equate the natural with the right and good. There are many things that are natural, but one would not say are good. Floods, tornadoes, and earthquakes are all natural, but they are not necessarily good and can cause much suffering. The claim that one should never disturb the natural order seems clearly false as this occurs on a daily basis. Devices have been created to help those overcome natural obstacles on a regular basis, whether it be transportation, communication, or medicine. Many diseases are "natural" in the sense that they follow a natural order of the laws of biology, chemistry, and physics. Yet almost all medical treatments are attempts to interfere with the natural progression of a disease to cure and end suffering. Birth control is one of the means a person uses to overcome the obstacle of having children

2. Gilbert Meliaender, *Bioethics: A Primer for Christians*, 3rd ed. (Grand Rapids: Eerdmans, 2013), 11.
3. This statement is not without qualification. All medical intervention needs to be done within the limits of God's design. See the Christian manifesto in chapter 2.

at an untimely interval in his or her life. Furthermore, disabilities that cause infertility fall under the same category as any infirmity that medicine attempts to treat.

A third objection states that, while medicine is a necessary good when it attempts to treat disease and debilitations, it should not be used when the good attempting to be treated is not necessary. The argument is often stated, "Infertility is not a life-threatening situation. Therefore, using medical intervention is not necessary." Like the previous objection, this argument is based on a highly questionable assumption: medical intervention should only be employed when the situation is dire, and health and life are in serious danger. While it is true that medicine helps to treat life-threatening diseases, it also is valuable for correcting disabilities and defects that may not be dire but would make life more satisfying and fulfilling. When individuals are born with abnormalities and disabilities that make life challenging, medicine can certainly be employed to correct or treat them. It seems ludicrous to say to a child born with cleft palate, "Well, you can live with that," when a relatively standard surgical procedure would fix it. Infertility can certainly fall into the same category.

A final objection is the slippery slope objection. Many worry that in allowing some form of medical intervention in treating infertility, a Pandora's box will be opened to all sorts of unethical and morally problematic scenarios. They fear that it will be difficult to draw the line between therapy and enhancement and that infertility treatment could lead to eugenics programs like those that occurred in the early part of the twentieth century. This is a very real concern.[4] We must be diligent to be aware of where we are heading whenever we advocate the use of new technology. However, the need for diligence does not mean every new technology that comes along should be rejected. There is always a danger in medical progress of well-meaning researchers employing technology in morally problematic matters. However, this does not mean medicine should not progress. It just means one should be careful. In the pages that follow, some of the concerns regarding many methods of birth control and infertility treatment that require caution and, in some cases, nonparticipation, will be explored. But one must also be careful not to throw the baby out with the bathwater.

While I do not believe any of the above objections warrants a complete rejection of any form of procreative technology, I do think we need approach

4. I discuss some of these concerns at the end of this chapter and in chapter 6.

the issue with a serious degree of caution. These desires concerning the creation of new life and to have a part in raising children creates very strong passions and it is easy to allow those passions to control sound thinking about the moral duties one has with regards to procreation. Therefore, some wise general moral safeguards are helpful in guiding this thinking as the issues that follow are considered.

First, one must remember that, in general, medical technology is a good and is God's gift to human beings to counter the effects of sin in the world. At heart, medicine is the use of God's gift of knowledge, reason, and wisdom applied to the biological science for the purpose of treating and healing diseases and disabilities. Used appropriately, medicine is a moral good and medical researchers and health-care providers are dedicated to doing good. Of course, like any good, medicine can be abused or misguided. The desire to control and have power over nature has been a constant temptation since Satan tempted Eve with the promise, "You will be like God." Medical professionals need to be diligent in not giving in to the temptation to do more than is morally allowable.

Second, one must remember that procreation was designed by God to occur within the context of a stable, heterosexual, permanent, monogamous marriage. The state of marriage in the twenty-first century is often far from the ideal that God mandated in Scripture. Our modern culture has reinforced the idea that marriage is purely about fulfilling one's desires and felt needs. But God's picture of marriage and raising a family is about much more than that. The family unit is meant to be a reflection of God's light in a darkened world. When children are born, that light is replicated throughout the world. Procreative technology should be applied in that context and with that ideal in mind.

Third, as has been argued elsewhere in this text, it is important to remember that the unborn is a person from the moment of conception and should be treated as such throughout the procreative process. Once an embryo is created, whether through the natural process of human sexual interaction or through technological means such as artificial insemination or *in vitro* fertilization, it should be treated as having the full moral status of any person and should be thought of as the child of his or her parents. One should only do to it what one would do to one's own child. This flies in the face of much of what our culture believes concerning the status of the embryo and will be a source of tension and conflict, but it is tension we must learn to live with.

Fourth, for those who cannot have children of their own, adoption is a morally legitimate form of rescuing and raising children and may be preferable to some modern technological means of conceiving. There are many children born in situations where the birth parents cannot or do not wish to raise the child. These children are in need of loving parents and adoption is a blessed means of rescuing a child in need. It should be seriously considered before one begins to deliberate about using procreative technologies, some of which can be very morally problematic. It is true that the child will not be biologically related to the parents; however unlike those who devalue the organic relationship, I do think it is an important link. If couples cannot have children genetically related to themselves, this raises an opportunity to minister to other children who face the opposite end of the same tragedy, specifically not having parents genetically related to them. Adoption is a gift one can offer to those in need.

Finally, one should always remember that children should be viewed as a gift from God. This gift should be viewed not as something to fulfill one's desire and needs, but as an opportunity and responsibility to raise a child in a loving environment. Giving birth and raising children should be about them and not about us. This means one's motivations need to be carefully and reflectively considered. Has one made an idol of having children? Is this being done for the child or for oneself? Often what drives couples into using morally questionable technologies is because of the yearning to have a child to satisfy their own needs or to save or satisfy the marriage. There is nothing wrong with the desire to have children, which is perfectly natural and normal. But one needs to be careful that the desire does not become an obsession.

TECHNOLOGY TO PREVENT PROCREATION

As we begin our overview of methods of birth control, we need to again clarify some terminology. The term "birth control" is normally used to describe all sorts of mechanical and chemical devices that will successfully inhibit one from becoming pregnant and giving birth. However, this term can be misleading. What most people mean by "birth control" is better termed as "conception control" or "contraception." Many couples want to avoid conceiving a child and hence wish to employ methods to assure that conception will not occur. Birth control is actually broader than contraception and may include the use of abortifacients. The term "abortifacient" comes from two Latin terms: *abortus* which means "miscarriage," and *faciens* which means "making." An abortifacient has the purpose of causing a miscarriage in which an embryo would be eliminated. Some forms of "birth control" are not designed to prohibit conception but are designed to eliminate the "product of conception," the embryo, from implanting in the uterus or otherwise terminating the pregnancy. In this sense, abortion is a form of birth control as are interuterine devices (IUDs), the RU-486 pill, and the "morning-after pill" (discussed below). Abortifacients are morally problematic for those who believe that persons begin at conception. For the purposes of this chapter, the term "conception control" will be used as a general term for any mechanical or chemical device whose primary purpose is to prohibit conception from taking place.

Another term that needs to be discussed is "pregnancy." Traditionally, pregnancy has referred to the period from when a mother conceives until she delivers a child. Recently there has been a subtle shift in terminology. Pregnancy now often refers to the period after implantation of the embryo in the uterine wall until delivery. This shift in meaning allows many abortifacients to appear as contraceptives. Those devices that aim to prevent "pregnancy" by thinning the lining of the uterine wall and thereby restraining the embryo from implanting are promoted as not being abortifacients, because to have an abortion is to "terminate a pregnancy." However, for those who believe persons begin at conception, the embryo is being intentionally destroyed by not allowing it to implant and thus, this is an abortion.

There are some who believe that any form of conception control should be morally prohibited, the most well-known of these being Roman Catholics. In 1968, Pope Paul IV issued his encyclical *Humanae Vitae* (Human Life), in which he reaffirmed the traditional Roman Catholic teachings concerning contraception.[5] It begins, "The transmission of human life is a most serious role in which married people collaborate freely and responsibly with God the Creator. It has always been a source of great joy to them, even though it sometimes entails many difficulties and hardships."[6] The church recognized that a number of new medical devices and procedures had produced questions in the minds of the faithful, so this document was written to address those concerns. In section 14, the encyclical states the Church's official position:

> Therefore We base Our words on the first principles of a human and Christian doctrine of marriage when We are obliged once more to declare that the direct interruption of the generative process already begun and, above all, all direct

---

5. An encyclical is the pronunciation by the supreme head of the Roman Catholic Church and is accepted as the official teaching of the Church.
6. *Humanae Vitae* (1968), sec. 1.

> abortion, even for therapeutic reasons, are to be absolutely excluded as lawful means of regulating the number of children. Equally to be condemned, as the magisterium of the Church has affirmed on many occasions, is direct sterilization, whether of the man or of the woman, whether permanent or temporary. Similarly excluded is any action which either before, at the moment of, or after sexual intercourse, is specifically intended to prevent procreation—whether as an end or as a means.[7]

There are a number of reasons the Roman Catholic Church lists for this position regarding contraception. Natural law asserts that the primary and final cause of sexuality is procreation. While human sexuality also provides pleasure and expresses human intimacy and love, these are secondary byproducts to its primary function. To divorce sexual intercourse from its primary purpose is to violate the natural law: "The Church, nevertheless, in urging men to the observance of the precepts of the natural law, which it interprets by its constant doctrine, teaches that each and every marital act must of necessity retain its intrinsic relationship to the procreation of human life."[8]

Some Catholics appeal to Scripture to reinforce the Church's position. The story of Onan spilling his seed on the ground rather than inseminating his brother's wife (Gen. 38:8–10) as God commanded him to do and his subsequent punishment of Onan are appealed to as the scriptural condemnation of a form of contraception known as *coitus interruptus*.[9] They also point out that the illegitimacy of contraception has been the historic position of the church from apostolic times through modern times and that even Protestant denominations disallowed contraception until 1930, when the Lambeth Conference of the Anglican Church first allowed for contraception in some cases. Soon almost all Protestant churches, bowing to modern pressures, were relaxing their policies concerning contraception.

The Roman Catholic Church does not teach that all forms of delaying children are morally wrong. The delaying of children that observes the natural biological cycle of women is allowable in at least some circumstances: "If

7. *Humanae Vitae* (1968), sec. 14.
8. *Humanae Vitae* (1968), sec. 11.
9. While many Protestant theologians argue that Onan's punishment was for not obeying God in fulfilling a specific command and should not be generalized as a command against contraception, Catholic defenders point out that Deuteronomy 25:7–10 clearly states that the penalty for not fulfilling a brother's duty to his widowed sister-in-law was public humiliation. They argue something much more severe is happening in Genesis 38 and that contraception is the likely candidate.

therefore, there are well-grounded reasons for spacing births, arising from the physical or psychological condition of husband or wife, or from external circumstances, the Church teaches that married people may then take advantage of the natural cycles immanent in the reproductive system and engage in marital intercourse only during those times that are infertile, thus controlling birth in a way which does not in the least offend the moral principles which We have just explained."[10]

The strength of these arguments is evaluated differently by Christians. Many question whether the Onan story should be taken as universal condemnation of all forms and incidences of contraception. That may be reading more into the story than it is meant to convey. As far as the natural law argument, there is something to be said for recognizing that the primary purpose of human sexuality is procreation and that one should never completely abandon this purpose in the marital act. Some Christians use this argument to hold that it would be wrong for any married Christian couple who can have children to decide to never have children, especially if that decision is driven by selfish ambitions of career or convenience.

It also would be a major argument against homosexuality, in which the sexual act is a complete abandonment of this primary purpose. However, while we can affirm that a complete abandonment of procreation would be morally inappropriate, it seems an illegitimate bifurcation to argue that the only other option is that every sexual act needs to be open to procreation. A middle option might be to affirm that a temporary reprieve from procreation is justifiable in the context of a marital relationship. Many couples delay children early in marriage to allow for a time to become emotionally and financially stable. The plan is to have children, but with a temporary delay. Thus, we can affirm the basic natural law argument without affirming the extreme position taken by the Roman Catholic Church.

When my wife and I were newlyweds, we attended a seminar overviewing methods of birth control sponsored by a local clinic. We watched a film titled *Hope Is Not a Method.* That is a good title for this section of the chapter. If one is going to take conception control seriously, one needs to decide which form is the most preferable. One cannot just hope that pregnancy will not occur. There are two general forms of contraception: natural and artificial. Natural forms of contraception are those that do not introduce any man-made devices or interferences into preventing conception. These include temporary

10. *Humanae Vitae*, sec. 16.

abstention, *coitus interruptus*, the rhythm method, and natural family planning. Temporary abstention occurs when a couple agrees to abstain from sexual intercourse for a time in order to prevent the possibility of pregnancy. This method is incorporated in the rhythm method or natural family planning but can also stand on its own where a couple may abstain for a longer period of time than those methods require. Abstention is the only foolproof method of conception control where one is guaranteed to not become pregnant. All other methods have some risk of failure built within them. There is no moral problem with temporary abstention, though Scripture implies that it should be temporary and only at times for prayer and fasting: "Stop depriving one another, except by agreement for a time, so that you may devote yourselves to prayer, and come together again so that Satan will not tempt you because of your lack of self-control. But this I say by way of concession, not of command" (1 Cor. 7:5–6).

Coitus interruptus, also known as the "withdrawal method," is a Latin phrase that literally means to interrupt sexual intercourse immediately before the man ejaculates and for him to remove his penis from the woman's vagina in order to avoid releasing sperm into the woman. Apart from the Roman Catholic position and their interpretation of the Onan story, there is no moral problem with this method. However, there are some serious questions concerning the success rate of such a method. Not only does this method require strong self-discipline on the part of the man and trust on the part of the woman, but one must be careful about premature ejaculation. Some have also suggested that sperm may be located in the fluid released prior to ejaculation (called Cowper's fluid). Control and consistency are necessary for this method to be successful.

The rhythm method is a traditional method of timing one's engagements in sexual intercourse with a woman's ovulation/menstruation cycle. It is most successful with women whose cycle is stable and regular. Those with irregular cycles had best avoid this method. Once the cycle is known, a woman uses a calendar to pinpoint the time of the month she is most fertile and the time she is least fertile. This usually correlates with her period of ovulation and her time of menstruating. Sexual intercourse is temporarily suspended immediately before, during, and immediately after her ovulation and engaged outside of that time. There are no moral issues with using the rhythm method and it has been used for a long time not only as a form of contraception but as a method to increase one's chances to becoming pregnant.

Closely related to the rhythm method is natural family planning (NFP). While both methods schedule sexual intercourse around a woman's ovulation/

menstruation cycle, NFP uses symptothermal technology in determining when a woman is fertile rather than just depending on a calendar as in the rhythm method. This technology is often referred to as fertility awareness-based technology. It looks for three signs of fertility: the woman's basal body temperature, her cervical mucus, and her cervical position. Like the rhythm method, there are no moral problems with using NFP as a form of contraception. In fact, its accuracy is considered much greater than the rhythm method and it is becoming the standard of families who wish to use a more natural means of birth control as opposed to artificial methods, especially among Roman Catholics.

Artificial means of contraception are those methods that introduce man-made devices and procedures for the purposes of preventing conception. They can be divided into mechanical devices, chemical devices, pharmaceutical devices, and surgical procedures. Mechanical devices would include the use of condoms and diaphragms, which are used to physically impede the ability of sperm to travel past the cervix to conceive an ovum. With the exception of the Roman Catholic position, there is no moral problem with the use of these devices.[11] Often, these devices may be coupled with the use of a chemical spermicide designed to eliminate sperm though one can use the spermicide by itself.

An intrauterine device (IUD) is a small device implanted in the uterus for long-term contraception use. They are usually T-shaped and come in two varieties. Copper IUDs work by inhibiting sperm mobility so that they are prevented from joining with an egg. The copper acts as a spermicide within the uterus. Hormonal IUDs release a hormone, *levonorgestrel*, which is a progestin, into the uterus, making it uninhabitable for sperm. However, as we will note below, there may be some moral concerns with the use of IUDs, as they might have a secondary byproduct of acting as an abortifacient.

The most common form of contraception in the last fifty years is oral contraception in the form of a pill. There are several different brands and types of oral contraceptives, but most make use of two hormones, *estrogen* and *progestin*, to prevent ovulation, which is the primary purpose and function of oral contraceptions. A secondary effect of most oral contraceptives is

11. There are those who have attempted to make contraception equivalent to abortion, but that argument fails. There is no human person before conception, and one cannot be held morally culpable for causing harm to a being who does not exist. One does not have an obligation to bring a person into life, but one does have an obligation to maintain the life of a child one has brought into being once it exists.

that the cervical mucus is thickened, inhibiting the ability of sperm to travel up to the egg. A possible third effect is that oral contraceptives may thin the lining of the uterus to prevent an embryo from implanting. Oral contraceptives also have a number of side effects that can range from slight, such as moodiness; to serious, including liver problems and an increase in the chance of having breast cancer, heart disease, and stroke. The moral question of using most oral forms of contraception refers to the likelihood of the third effect which we will discuss below.

More morally problematic are some forms of emergency contraception, such as "morning-after pills" (MAPs) and RU-486 (*mifepristone*). To refer to these as oral "contraceptives" might be misleading. For while they have, as their primary goals, the inhibiting of conception, they also are designed to act as abortifacients. While often confused as being the same, RU-486 and MAPs work differently, and advocates of MAPs are often quick to point out that, while RU-486 is an abortifacient, morning-after pills are not. MAPs are mostly just stronger doses of regular oral contraceptives and have as their primary goal the ceasing or delaying of ovulation. There are two types: combined estrogen and progestin pills, and progestin-only pills. Their effect as an abortifacient is hotly debated, as the science is not decisive on the matter. RU-486 comes under the brand name *Mifeprex,* is designed to terminate a pregnancy after implantation, and is primarily an abortifacient.

The main surgical contraceptive procedure is sterilization, which can be performed on men (vasectomy, castration) or on women (tubal ligation, hysterectomy). Sterilization can be done for many purposes. Therapeutic sterilization is performed in cases in which there is a medical need due to some disease or debilitation that is serious enough to warrant the removal of the ability to have children, such as testicular cancer in men or endometriosis in women. Eugenic sterilization is performed on individuals to eradicate a genetic disease by removing the possibility of future generations from transmitting the disease and cleansing the gene pool. This was forcibly performed on hundreds of individuals in the early part of the twentieth century in this country. Punitive sterilization is forced sterilization performed on criminals. Originally it was imposed on criminals guilty of habitual crimes as a form of eugenics. More recently, some have suggested it as a form of punishment or control over sexual urges for criminals guilty of sex crimes such as rape and child abuse. However, vasectomies do not decrease sex urges, so the only form of forced sterilization that would be effective would be castration.

Contraceptive sterilization is a procedure many couples choose to have later in life after they have had children and have reached a point in which more children are unfeasible or undesirable. The benefit is that sexual activity can be continued without the bother of other forms of contraceptives and without the consequence of having more children. Sterilization may be reversible in most cases with a diminished possibility of successfully conceiving children, so a couple should be certain about not having more children before obtaining the procedure.[12]

The moral appropriateness of artificial methods of contraception vary with the method. In general, there are no moral problems with the use of mechanical and chemical forms of contraception as one is not causing harm to oneself or another. However, one must approach the issue of IUDs, oral contraceptives, and sterilization with some amount of moral reflection and caution. As Christians who affirm that human persons begin at conception, any form of contraception that would put the life of the embryo in danger should be avoided. While IUDs have as their primary function the establishment of an environment that impedes the progression of sperm in the uterus, some believe that they also have a secondary effect of damaging the lining of the uterine wall, inhibiting the implantation of an embryo should the woman become pregnant. This would result in the death of the embryo.

The question of regular oral contraceptives (as opposed to emergency items like MAPs and RU-486) as being abortifacients has had a long history of debate and discussion. While some still believe they can act as abortifacients, most doctors and ethicists are backing off from that claim due to the lack of scientific evidence. Dennis Sullivan, a physician and director for the Center of Bioethics at Cedarville University, states,

> The idea that combined oral contraceptives interfere with implantation has been mostly dispelled by more recent evidence. There remain some legitimate concerns about the abortive potential of progesterone-only agents and long-acting implantable contraceptives, such as Nexplanon or its older variant, Norplant. The abortive potential for emergency contraception is still hotly debated. Although the abortive potential of combined oral contraceptives is no longer an issue, there are still a number of possible health complications and side

---

12. For tubal ligation reversals success rates range from 40–80 percent. Success rates for vasectomy reversals depends on the time between vasectomy and reversal. If within three years, chances are better than 50 percent but they drop to 30 percent after ten years.

effects of using hormonal birth control, making a discussion of alternatives still very relevant.[13]

Any form of forced sterilization, for eugenic or punitive reasons, should be morally rejected as a violation of an individual's autonomy and cruel punishment. The ability to reproduce is a basic human right, and to deprive any individual of the right against their will should be morally condemned. Therapeutic sterilizations may be justifiable due to the principle of totality: an individual has the right to dispose of his organs or to destroy their capacity to function only to the extent that the general well-being of the whole body demands it.[14] Contraceptive sterilization might be justifiable in many cases as long as one has fulfilled the obligation to have children. As stated previously, the scriptural norm is that Christian couples should plan on raising children. While there is no established command or consensus of how many children a couple a Christian should have, a balance can be sought between no children on the one hand and too many children on the other. Psalms informs us, "Behold, children are a gift of the Lord, the fruit of the womb is a reward. Like arrows in the hand of a warrior, so are the children of one's youth. How blessed is the man whose quiver is full of them" (Ps. 127:3–5). There comes a point to recognize one's "youth" has passed and one's "quiver" may be full.

Legal Issues Concerning Birth Control

The first landmark case involving birth control occurred in 1965 with *Griswold v. Connecticut* (previously discussed in chapter 3). A Connecticut law known as the Comstock Act of 1873 made it illegal to use any drug, medicine, or instrument for the purpose of preventing procreation. Violators could be fined and imprisoned. Once Planned Parenthood clinics began opening in the state in the 1930s and '40s, many began to challenge this law. Some challenges reached the Supreme Court but were dismissed for various reasons.

13. Dennis Sullivan, personal correspondence, March 29, 2016. Dr. Sullivan has written an excellent report on the evidence concerning oral contraceptives and abortifacients; see D. M. Sullivan, "The Oral Contraceptive as Abortifacient: An Analysis of the Evidence," *Perspectives on Science and Christian Faith* 58, no. 3 (2006): 189–95. I would also suggest the excellent report put together by the Center for Bioethics and Human Dignity, "The Pill: Addressing the Scientific and Ethical Questions of the Abortifacient Issue," https://cbhd.org/content/the-pill-online-version.
14. One could argue that castration for those involved in sex crimes is a form of therapeutic sterilization in order to help cure them of the problem. If this argument is successful, it would have to be voluntary on the part of the criminal and could not be considered as a substitute for punitive justice.

One dismissal included the dissent of Justice John Marshall Harlan II, where he wrote:

> The full scope of the liberty guaranteed by the Due Process Clause cannot be found in or limited by the precise terms of the specific guarantees elsewhere provided in the Constitution. This "liberty" is not a series of isolated points pricked out in terms of the taking of property; the freedom of speech, press, and religion; the right to keep and bear arms in the United States; the freedom from unreasonable searches and seizures; and so on. It is a rational continuum which, broadly speaking, includes a freedom from all substantial arbitrary impositions and purposeless restraints.[15]

Based on this dissent, it was indicated that he would rule the underlying law unconstitutional. Estelle Griswold, an executive director of the Planned Parenthood League of Connecticut, decided to challenge the law again. She and others began distributing contraceptives to women who requested them at the clinics. She was arrested and fined, but she appealed her convictions all the way to the United States Supreme Court.

The Court found that the Constitution contains an inherent fundamental right to privacy for married couples, implied in the First, Third, Fourth, and Fifth Amendments.[16] As such, the Comstock Law of 1873 violated this right and was struck down as unconstitutional. Justice William O. Douglas wrote in his opinion:

> Would we allow the police to search the sacred precincts of marital bedrooms for telltale signs of the use of contraceptives? The very idea is repulsive to the notions of privacy surrounding the marriage relationship. . . . We deal with a right of privacy older than the Bill of Rights—older than our political parties, older than our school system. Marriage is a coming together for better or for worse, hopefully enduring, and intimate to the degree of being sacred. It is an association that promotes a way of life, not causes; a harmony in living, not political faiths; a bilateral loyalty, not commercial or social projects. Yet it is an association for as noble a purpose as any involved in our prior decisions.[17]

---

15. *Poe v. Ullman*, 367 U.S. 497 (1961).
16. *Griswold v. Connecticut*, 381 U.S. 479 (1965).
17. *Griswold v. Connecticut*, 485.

The Court extended the right to contraceptives to unmarried couples in 1972 with its decision in *Eisenstadt v. Baird*, finding it was discriminatory to do otherwise.[18]

In 2011, after the enactment of the Affordable Care Act (ACA), female contraceptives were added to the list of preventative services to be provided by insurance companies without requiring a co-pay. Some argued that this mandate would challenge religious liberties for religious employers against contraceptives offering insurance plans to employees. A compromise was made in 2012 allowing contraceptives be provided directly by health insurance companies, without involvement by the religious organization.[19] The compromise continued to be challenged and in 2017, President Donald Trump issued an executive order urging agencies to allow insurers and employers to refuse contraception coverage if doing so would violate sincerely held religious beliefs.[20] Many states challenged this rule and a nationwide injunction was placed on its enforcement. The Little Sisters of the Poor Saints Peter and Paul Home challenged the injunction, which was denied by the District Court and upheld by the Third Circuit Court of Appeals. On July 8, 2020, in a 7–2 opinion, the United Stated Supreme Court found that the rules made under President Trump's executive order were valid as the authority had been granted under the ACA to issue them.[21]

TECHNOLOGY TO ASSIST PROCREATION

Cases involving reproductive technology are increasing as the technology evolves. While laws have been created to regulate these practices, the courts are taking up cases that are shaping the legal framework of assisted reproduction. Interestingly, many of the cases that make it to court involve transactional law.[22] Because reproductive technology involves third parties outside of the mother/father relationship, contracts are being used to protect the parents, medical associates, sperm donors, and surrogates. Courts are deciding major

18. *Eisenstadt v. Baird*, 405 U.S. 438 (1972).
19. United States, "Compilation of Patient Protection and Affordable Care Act," as amended through November 1, 2010, including Patient Protection and Affordable Care Act health-related portions of the Health-care and Education Reconciliation Act of 2010 (2010).
20. Exec. Order No. 13798, 82 CFR. 21675 (2017).
21. *Little Sisters of the Poor Saints Peter and Paul Home v. Pennsylvania, et al.* 140 S. Ct. 2367 (2020).
22. Transactional law involves an act or agreement between parties involving business, commerce, and contracts.

cases involving assisted reproduction, but often the cases come as a result of a "simple" contract dispute.

Legal Issues Concerning AI and IVF

There is little dispute as to whether it is legally permissible to engage in assisted reproductive methods such as *in vitro* fertilization (IVF) or artificial insemination (AI). So long as medical personnel follow the same legal and ethical standards used in other procedures, no laws will be broken. Legal issues arise when the line is blurred between viewing products of IVF or artificial insemination as children or property.

In 1989, one of the first cases involving in vitro fertilization was heard in Virginia. The Yorks, a married couple, provided their sperm and egg to the Jones Institute for Reproductive Medicine in Norfolk, Virginia. Six pre-embryos[23] were created, and five were placed in Mrs. York, with the sixth cryopreserved for possible later use. Pregnancy did not occur, and the couple ended up moving to California. The couple wanted to try IVF in California, but doctors at the Jones Institute refused to transfer the cryopreserved pre-embryo to the new medical facility. The Yorks filed suit in the United States District Court for the Eastern District of Virginia.

The court ruled in favor of the Yorks, looking at the underlying issue as a contract dispute. The Cryopreservation Agreement gave the Jones Institute authority to possess the pre-embryo, but did not grant it ownership.[24] The language in the agreement was also written as if the Yorks were speaking, referring to the pre-embryo as "our pre-zygote" or "our property," which further supported the intent of the parties to have ownership of any cryopreserved pre-embryos.[25] Given the language of the contract and the relationship between the parties, the Court granted the Yorks ownership and authority to determine the fate of the pre-embryo.

Three years later, the Supreme Court of Tennessee was faced with a similar issue involving cryopreserved pre-embryos. Mary Sue and Junior Davis were unable to conceive naturally, so they turned to IVF. Numerous attempts failed to create a pregnancy, so seven pre-embryos were cryopreserved for

23. "Pre-embryo" is a common term used by physicians, researchers, and lawyers to refer to a human embryo up to two weeks old, before it is implanted in the uterus. We argued in chapter 3, as there is no difference in the nature of the being before and after it is implanted, the moral status of one should be considered as equivalent to the other. They are both human persons.
24. *York v. Jones*, 717 F.Su421, 425 (Eastern District of Virginia 1989).
25. *York v. Jones*, 426.

future attempts. In 1989, Junior filed for divorce. The parties agreed on how to handle most of their property disputes but could not agree on how to handle the cryopreserved pre-embryos. The trial court gave Mary Sue custody of the pre-embryos, accepting the theory that human life begins at conception and allowing the "best interests of the children" principle to control. Junior Davis appealed to the Tennessee Court of Appeals, which reversed the lower court's decision. It awarded joint custody to the parties, making it so neither would become parents of the pre-embryos unless both agreed to do so.

Mary Sue appealed this decision to the Supreme Court of Tennessee. The Court unanimously ruled in favor of Junior. Much of the Court's opinion surrounded the question of whether pre-embryos could be considered persons or property. Citing *Roe v. Wade*, the Court recognized that the unborn are not considered persons under federal law. It said:

> Certainly, if the state's interests do not become sufficiently compelling in the abortion context until the end of the first trimester, after very significant developmental stages have passed, then surely there is no state interest in these pre-embryos which could suffice to overcome the interests of the gamete-providers. The abortion statute reveals that the increase in the state's interest is marked by each successive developmental stage such that, toward the end of a pregnancy, this interest is so compelling that abortion is almost strictly forbidden. This scheme supports the conclusion that the state's interest in the potential life embodied by these four-to-eight cell pre-embryos (which may or may not be able to achieve implantation in a uterine wall and which, if implanted, may or may not begin to develop into fetuses, subject to possible miscarriage) is at best slight. When weighed against the interests of the individuals and the burdens inherent in parenthood, the state's interest in the potential life of these pre-embryos is not sufficient to justify any infringement upon the freedom of these individuals to make their own decisions as to whether to allow a process to continue that may result in such a dramatic change in their lives as becoming parents.[26]

While the Court ruled that the pre-embryos were not persons, it also ruled that they were not property either. Rather, they belonged to an "interim category that entitles them to special respect because of their potential for human life."[27] The Court also distinguished these cases from abortion cases,

26. *Davis v. Davis*, 842 S.W.2d 588, 602 (Tennessee Supreme Court 1992).
27. *Davis v. Davis*, 605.

which allow the woman to control the abortion decision. With IVF, both the mother and the father have equal rights with regards to decisions involving pre-embryos.[28] Because the Court ruled in favor of Junior, the pre-embryos were disposed of.

These cases were important in that they further solidified that the legal status of pre-embryos does not give them personhood and they should not be treated as such. At most, they are afforded greater respect, but not to the point of personhood. States generally treat pre-embryos as property, though a small number of states have laws that recognize potential persons arising from pre-embryos in the context of embryo donations. As of this writing, no cases have been taken up in the United States Supreme Court involving procreation in the context of IVF. Please refer to the updated section on embryonic stem cell research on pages 367–384.

Legal Issues Concerning Surrogacy

The first major case involving surrogacy began in 1984 with the Baby M Case (see the opening discussion for this chapter for a review of the facts). This case was brought to court as a breach of contract issue. The New Jersey Superior Court terminated the surrogate's, Mary's, parental rights, based not only on the surrogacy contract being valid, but also it being in the best interests of the child. Mary appealed to the New Jersey Supreme Court, which also found it to be in the best interests of the child to remain with the intended parents, William and Elizabeth Stern.[29] However, the Court differed in its opinion of the validity of the surrogacy contract. The court stated that while there is a deep yearning for couples to have their own children, it found "the payment of money to a 'surrogate' mother illegal, perhaps criminal, and potentially degrading to women."[30] Thus, the surrogacy contract was invalidated, and Mary's parental rights were restored. Yet, the baby remained with the Sterns because it was in the baby's best interests. By restoring Mary's parental rights, the Sterns were unable to formally adopt the baby. This was rectified in 2004 when a now-grown Melissa Stern turned eighteen and initiated the process for Mary's parental rights to be terminated so she could be adopted by the Sterns.

---

28. *Davis v. Davis*, 606.
29. *In Re Baby M*, 109 N.J. 396 (New Jersey Supreme Court 1988).
30. *In Re Baby M*, 410.

The next case involving surrogacy arose in California in 1990. Mark and Crispina Calvert entered into a surrogacy contract with Anna Johnson. In this case, the baby was conceived via *in vitro* fertilization, using Crispina's egg and Mark's sperm. The embryo was then implanted in Johnson. A surrogacy contract was entered in which the Calverts would pay $10,000 in installments in exchange for Johnson to bring the child to term and relinquish parental rights upon the child's birth. Before the child was born, Johnson demanded payment in full instead of installments or else she would refuse to give up the child. The Calverts filed suit. When the child was born, the parties agreed the child would reside with the Calverts temporarily, pending the outcome of the suit.

The lower court ruled that the Calverts were the biological parents of the child and Johnson had no parental rights, which was affirmed by the Fourth Circuit Court of Appeals. The case was then appealed to the California Supreme Court in 1993. The Court held that Anna was the gestational mother while Crispina was the genetic mother.[31] When two mothers have maternal rights to a child, the mother with parental rights is the one who intended to bring about the child to raise as her own at the time of conception.[32] This ruling resulted in the "intent to parent" concept, which is a concept still applied in California today.[33]

Another case involving surrogacy also occurred in California. In 1995, John and Luanna Buzzanca wanted to have children, but both were infertile. An embryo was implanted in a paid surrogate using both anonymous donor eggs and anonymous donor sperm. Before the child was born, John and Luanna filed for divorce. Luanna argued that the unborn child was a child of the marriage, but John argued that there were no children of the marriage. His position was he should not be legally responsible for a child that is not genetically his or his wife's, nor was it even gestated by his wife. The trial court agreed, finding the unborn child had no legal parents. The case was appealed to the Fourth Circuit Court of Appeals. The Court found that the child would have never been born had it not been for the agreement between the Buzzancas and the surrogate.[34] The judge stated that the trial court erred by finding

31. *Johnson v. Calvert*, 851 P. 2nd 776, 781 (California Supreme Court 1993).
32. *Johnson v. Calvert*, 782.
33. The following year, a case was heard in California where a woman was inseminated with the husband's sperm because his wife was sterile. When the parties broke up, the wife argued she was the legal mother. The Court ruled in favor of the surrogate being the legal mother because she was both the gestational and genetic mother. Thus, *Johnson v. Calvert* would not apply (see *In Re Marriage of Moschetta,* 25 Cal.App.4th 1218, 1994).
34. *In Re Marriage of Buzzanca*, 61 Cal.App.4th 1412 (4th Circuit Court of Appeals 1998).

that legal motherhood could only be established by either giving birth or donating an egg.[35] Since fatherhood can be established by a man allowing his wife to be artificially inseminated, motherhood can also be established under the same principle. Therefore, both John and Luanna were found to be the legal parents of the child.

As of this writing, there are no cases that have reached the United States Supreme Court involving surrogacy. Thus, regulation of surrogacy has been left up to the individual states. Many states currently have laws making surrogacy contracts unenforceable, either in full or partially. Some states ban commercial surrogacy but allow volunteer surrogacy. Other states are seen as surrogacy-friendly, not only finding the contracts valid but also allowing surrogates to be compensated. Since most states have not dealt with the issue of surrogacy outright, there are no formal laws on the book's and disputes are being resolved on a case-by-case basis.

It is also worth mentioning that there are few regulations governing sperm donation in most states. Sperm donation is often viewed as the male version of surrogacy. However, the big difference is that sperm donors are always the genetic fathers of the children they produce. In 1973, the Uniform Parentage Act was enacted, providing that if a wife is artificially inseminated with a donor's sperm under a physician's supervision, and if her husband consents, the husband will be considered the legal and natural father of the resulting child.[36] This Act has been adopted by most states in some form. Many states differentiate between sperm donors and fathers based on how the sperm was donated (via intercourse or through a sperm bank). California law provides that a man who donates his sperm to a sperm bank for insemination purposes will not be treated as the natural father of the resulting child.[37] However, there is an exception if both the donor and the recipient agree in writing for the donor to be the father of the child, which will be upheld. If the sperm is donated directly to the woman and not through a sperm bank of a physician, he will be held to be the father. Sperm donors are often paid to donate, albeit a nominal amount (nowhere near the amount surrogates receive when allowed). These issues, along with surrogacy, raise similar ethical considerations to which we now turn.

35. *In Re Marriage of Buzzanca*, 1413.
36. Uniform Parentage Act § 5 (1973) (amended 2002).
37. Cal. Family Code §7613(b).

TECHNOLOGY TO ASSIST PROCREATION: ETHICAL ISSUES

The desire to have children is one of the most basic yearnings we feel as human beings. Scripture teaches that God has given us a duty to fulfill this natural desire and that it is also a blessing to fulfill it. However, since we live in a fallen world tainted by sin, many couples are not able to fulfill this desire through the natural process of sexual procreation. In those cases, medicine has stepped in and offered hope in the form of technological advances. As previously discussed, in general, this is an appropriate use of God's gift of medical knowledge and morally appropriate within certain limits. However, we must be diligent to remain cognizant of those limits and to take care of overstepping the bounds he has provided.

The earliest technology to help assist procreation was artificial insemination (AI). AI had been in practice for years with farm animals as a way to speed up the rate of genetic improvement by increasing the productivity of food producing animals, especially cattle. Human AI experiments go all the way back to 1790, and throughout the 1800s researchers continued to explore the possibility of conceiving a child, with the first reported case of AI occurring in 1844. The modern technique for AI was developed in 1899 with most of the breakthroughs occurring in the 1940s and 1950s. In 1953, the first frozen egg was successfully inseminated. Today, AI is often used for couples who might be suffering "with unexplained infertility, cervical factor subfertility, physiologic or psychological sexual dysfunction and mild to moderate male subfertility."[38]

AI is a fairly simple procedure that uses a syringe attached to a lengthy catheter inserted through the cervix to inject sperm into the uterus. AI can use the husband's sperm, which is referred to as AIH, or it can use a donor's sperm obtained from a known donor or, more commonly, from a sperm bank. This is referred to as AID. Apart from Roman Catholic considerations, there is nothing morally problematic with the actual procedure itself from a Christian perspective. However, there are serious considerations with how the procedure is used. AIH and its usage within the marriage relationship does not appear to have any moral problems, all things considered, and can

38. Willem Ombelet and Johan Van Robays, "History of Artificial Insemination," in *Facts, Views, and Visions* (Belgium: Journal of the European Society for Gynaecological Endoscopy, 2009). Most of the historical information given above was obtained from this article.

be a legitimate and helpful means for infertile couples to conceive and bear children. AID, on the other hand, complicates things considerably as it introduces a third party into the procreative process.

Third-party involvement blurs the lines in parentage and denies the importance of the biological bond between parent and child. It moves away from procreation, an act in which parents and God work together to bring new life into the world, and towards a "production" mindset of using technology to produce a child not genetically and inherently related to one of its parents. Some minimize the importance and value of the biological bond. They argue, "Isn't this the same as adoption? Certainly nothing is wrong with that." It is correct that an adoption is a good act. However, that is because adoption is done as an emergency procedure for the sake of a child that already exists and needs parenting. Involving third parties from the beginning, as a way to produce a child, is not the same thing. As Christians, one needs to recognize that God's plan is for man and wife to participate in an act of procreation as a means of conceiving children. Therefore, Christians should resist the use of third parties.

One particular issue with AID that deserves note is that one of its most common usages recently is for single women and lesbian couples to have children. As mentioned earlier, this is in direct opposition to God's plan of raising children in a healthy, heterosexual marriage and cannot be condoned for those who wish to live according to his revealed plan.

Another complication is that fertility drugs that can cause multiple ovulations are often given to the woman to increase to the possibility of conception. For the Christian, one must be willing to raise several children as there is little control over what happens if multiple pregnancies result and abortion is not an option. If such a scenario is realistically acceptable to the couple, then AIH is not morally problematic.

Recently a technique has been developed to increase the chances of conception called GIFT (Gamete Intrafallopian Transfer) where multiple eggs are obtained from the woman and sperm is obtained from husband or donor. They are placed near each other in the fallopian tube and conception takes place through the normal process. This is also known as Intrauterine Insemination (IUI). The process can be useful for both women and men with certain infertility issues and, in general, no moral problems incur except those mentioned above.

On July 25, 1978, Louise Brown was born in Oldham, England. At 5 lbs. 12 oz., there was nothing spectacular about her birth. However, there was something amazing about her conception, for Luisa was the first successful birth of a human being conceived outside of the body of a woman through the process of *in vitro* fertilization (IVF). Today, IVF has become a standard procedure. In 2018 (the most recent statistics at the time of this writing), a total of 81,478 babies were born as a result of 306,197 attempts by using assisted methods, of which 99 percent were IVF. That is 1.9 percent of the children born in the United States that year.[39] This is stunning when you consider the average cost of an IVF cycle is about $12,500 and the success rate is anywhere from 10 to 40 percent.[40] Many women have to go through a number of cycles to achieve a live birth. Since its introduction to the US in 1981, more than a million live births have been obtained through IVF.

An IVF cycle begins by injecting the woman with hormones over a period of several months so her ovaries will release multiple eggs in a monthly cycle instead of just the one. Prior to the retrieval procedure, she will be given injections of a medication that ripens the developing eggs and starts the process of ovulation. During the retrieval procedure, the physician will locate follicles in the ovary via ultrasound and remove the eggs with a hollow needle. The retrieved eggs are mixed in a petri dish with a man's sperm donated the same day, and conception usually occurs quickly. On men who may have a low sperm count or sperm with motility issues, a process called Intracytoplasmic Sperm Injection (ICSI) may be employed to inject the sperm directly into the eggs. The clinic will observe the eggs for three to five days to ensure normal development. When the embryos are ready the couple will return to the clinic for insertion. Using a catheter, the physician will insert three to four eggs into the mother's womb through the vagina and cervix into the uterus where they are released and, if successful, at least one will implant on the uterine wall. It is possible that they could all implant, from which one might have multiple pregnancies, and it is possible that none of them could implant, at which point the process will have to begin again. Sometimes the embryos are inserted into one of the fallopian tubes through a small surgical incision and will be allowed to travel down the tube to implant more naturally in the uterus. This process is called Zygote Intra-Fallopian Transfer (ZIFT). Two

39. All statistics are from the Center for Disease Control ART report, 2018, http://www.cdc.gov/art/reports/index.html.
40. Success rates depend on a number of factors including reasons for the infertility, age, and health of the mother. Women under the age of thirty-five can have up to a 39.6 percent success rate, while it drops considerably to 11.5 percent for women over forty.

weeks after the process, the couple will visit the physician again, at which time a pregnancy test will be performed to see if the implantation was successful.

IVF is not morally inappropriate in and of itself. It can be one way for a couple to conceive and bear children. However, as it is commonly practiced, it has a number of morally problematic issues that need careful consideration before one becomes involved with the procedure. The main problem for Christians who believe that a new person begins at conception is that multiple eggs are fertilized of which only three to four will actually be implanted (and even some or all may die). What happens to the leftover embryos? It depends on the desires of the couple. Some embryos are unwanted and eliminated because they are considered genetically inadequate. Many embryos are immediately destroyed as they are no longer necessary when the procedure is over. However, some embryos are cryogenically preserved, stored alive in freezers, either to be used by the couple later or donated to other infertile couples who wish to conceive a child but for whom IVF is not an option. A small number are donated for medical research.

Cryopreservation is a process developed over the last sixty years in which cells, whole tissues, or any other substances are preserved by cooling to sub-zero temperatures in liquid nitrogen. In the 1970s, scientists began to preserve embryos through a process known as slow programmable freezing (SPF). The first successful birth of a cryogenically frozen embryo was Zoe Leyland in 1984. The success rate was relatively low as the freezing and thawing process could damage the fragile embryos due to the formation of ice crystals. Today a much quicker freezing process known as vitrification, which freezes embryos about sixty thousand times quicker, has contributed to a 95 percent success rate.[41]

The exact number of frozen embryos currently in storage is not known. One study in 2003 put the number at 400,000 and another in 2011 put it at 612,000. Some estimates today put the number at about a million embryos currently in storage, of which about 80 percent are designated for family planning (the rest are either donated to couples who wish to adopt an embryo or designated for research). Dr. Arthur Caplan, bioethicist and professor at the

41. Another factor that has contributed to successful IVF pregnancies is to delay freezing and transferring embryos until the blastocyst stage on day 5, rather than right away. It is believed that impregnating the mother so quickly after the retrieval procedure is not the best preferable environment, but instead to temporarily freeze the embryos and allow her some time to return to her normal ovulation routine. This and the addition of pregenetic diagnosis (see below) have made IVF success much greater.

New York University Medical School, estimates that ninety thousand frozen embryos are considered abandoned.[42] The reality is that many of these family planning embryos will probably be discarded. Another complication with cryopreservation has to do with the status of these embryos. Are they property or persons? In *Davis v. Davis*, the court attempted to create a new "interim" status between these two categories, one that accords them more respect than property, but would not consider them persons either. Some have referred to the creation of an interim status as legal fiction.

The multiple-embryo problem is a serious issue for those who believe human persons begin life at conception. It is unethical to create a life with the intent and foreknowledge of destroying it. One possible solution is to conceive only one egg through IVF and implant just that embryo into the mother. However, many consider this to be impractical, ineffective, and cost-prohibitive, requiring many cycles to obtain a successful pregnancy. The only other viable option would be to plan on using all the leftover embryos for family planning. This would require a commitment to either use them for oneself or for donating to others for the purpose of family planning.[43] It is questionable whether one can make such a long-range commitment with any realistic guarantee of maintaining it. The initial cost of cryopreservation is $5,000 to $7,000, with an annual storage fee usually between $500 and $1,000.

Other ethical problems arise with IVF. Under the discussion of AI, the use of donor sperm and the problem with introducing a third party into the procreation process was explored. IVF increases that problem by allowing not only donor sperm but also donor eggs to be introduced in the process, further separating the biological bond between parent and child. It is now possible to retrieve sperm from an anonymous party, an egg from another anonymous party, allow them to conceive *in vitro*, and implant the resulting embryo into a third party who will allow the child to gestate and be born, and then allow a fourth and fifth party as mother and father (or mother and mother, or father and father) to adopt the resulting child. This seems a very far cry from God's intended plan: "for this reason a man shall leave his father and his mother, and be joined to his wife and they shall become one flesh"

42. N. Gleicher and A. Caplan, "An Alternative Proposal to the Destruction of Abandoned Human Embryos," *Nature Biotechnology* 36 (2018): 139–41.
43. Many embryo adoption agencies have sprung up to meet the needs of couples who do not plan on using their own frozen embryos for family planning and are willing to them up for adoption. You can find a list of them online through the Embryo Adoption Awareness Center (http://www.embryoadoption.org).

(Gen. 2:24). A third problem is that IVF opens the door to the pre-genetic diagnosis of embryos created *in vitro* and genetic selection of children. This will be discussed further below.

The idea of using a surrogate to carry and deliver a child for another couple is not a new idea. In the Old Testament we read about how Abraham's wife Sarah, who was barren, offered up her handmaiden, Hagar, to Abraham so that he could produce an heir (Gen. 16:1–3). The concept is also found in other ancient and primitive cultures. With the advent of AI and IVF, the modern idea of surrogacy became a realization. In 1980, thirty-seven-year-old Elizabeth Kane made history by giving birth as a surrogate mother to a son. This was the first documented surrogacy arrangement that was compensated. Ms. Kane received $10,000 for the successful delivery of her baby.[44] Surrogacy is used most often in cases in which a woman is not only infertile, but she cannot successfully gestate a child in her own uterus. With IVF, it is possible for a woman and her husband to conceive *in vitro* and make an agreement with a third party to carry the child for the couple.

There are different categories of surrogates. Genetic surrogacy occurs when a third-party female is contracted and artificially inseminated with the husband's sperm, and she conceives and carries a child which she gives up to the couple upon birth.[45] The child is genetically related to the father and to the birth mother, but not the wife of the father. This form of surrogacy has a relatively low cost and is easy to perform through AI.[46] Gestational surrogacy involves a third-party female who has no genetic relationship to the child. She is contracted to provide the womb and carries the child through the pregnancy, but both egg and sperm come from another source, either a father and mother or an anonymous donor. IVF is performed and embryos are implanted in surrogate's womb. If an embryo or embryos successfully implant, she carries the child to term and then turns it over to the couple at birth.

---

44. It is interesting to note that Elizabeth Kane (a pseudonym), like Mary Elizabeth Whitehead, became an advocate against surrogacy and spoke in defense of Whitehead at the Baby M court proceedings.
45. I am referring to the couple here as husband and wife; however, surrogacy is now becoming very popular with male homosexual couples, who are becoming the majority of those who use surrogates.
46. Some are critical of this form of surrogacy as they believe it constitutes adultery. However, adultery is defined as sexual relations that occur between two individuals, of which at least one of whom is married to another. There are no sexual relations involved in the modern idea of surrogacy. Adultery has nothing to do with procreation.

Another distinction is between commercial surrogacy, in which a fee is paid to the surrogate, and altruistic surrogacy, in which no fee is involved and the surrogate simply donates her womb for the use of the couple. In most cases of altruistic surrogates, the surrogate mother is a close relative or a friend of the couple who agree to pay all of her expenses. Because altruistic surrogacy is often performed out of kindness, it is often viewed as morally permissible, as opposed to commercial surrogacy, which is often labeled as "baby-selling." However, just because an action is performed out of kind motives does not mean it is morally appropriate, and just because a person does something for money does not make it automatically morally inappropriate. While motives are important, they are not the only element in consideration of moral appropriateness.

There is no doubt that surrogacy has helped many couples achieve their desire to have children, and many kind women have stepped forward to offer this help to those who cannot bear children. Mary Beth Whitehead claims that she was originally motivated to become a surrogate out of her desire to help her infertile sister. However, despite the fact surrogacy has helped, there are serious moral problems involved in the practice. First, as previously discussed with AI and IVF, surrogacy involves a third party into the procreative process, a process that God designed to be shared between a husband and wife alone. Using a surrogate further displaces procreation from its intended parentage. The possible use of donor sperm and egg even further separates any biological bond between parent and child. One can now have a set of genetic parents, a gestational parent, and a set of contracted parents—all of whom can be completely different individuals. Who is the child's "real" mother and father? Her biological parents? Her legal parents? The woman who gave birth? Who can authoritatively answer the question?

A second moral question surrounds the question of commercial surrogacy. Does commercial surrogacy, especially when it comes to genetic surrogacy, amount to selling human beings? As we noted in the legal section above, states are divided over this issue. In the Baby M case, the New Jersey Supreme Court voided the contract between Whitehead and the Sterns and equated commercial surrogacy with baby selling. It is just too easy to cross the line and treat a child as a commodity to be bought and sold. This attitude reinforces children as products. While proponents may claim that they are just paying for services rendered, or that they are just paying for the transference of parental rights, the very language used reinforces the attitude: paying for the transference of a right of ownership. However, children should not be seen as property that someone owns. While it is true that parents have children, they do not "own" them. They are stewards responsible for their care. Their job is to love them and oversee their development and, eventually, to let them go and make their own way in life. These children will always be the parents' children, but they are never their possessions.

A third problem is another consequence of commercial surrogacy, namely that the possibility of exploitation of the poor and indigent is very high. This has been called the "rent-a-womb" problem. Commercial surrogacy in India has grown into a multimillion-dollar industry since the Indian Supreme Court made it legal in 2002. Couples from around the world have traveled to India to seek the services of surrogate mothers, at a cost that is only a fraction of what they would pay for comparable services in their home country. The average amount a couple pays is around $10,000. However, the hundreds of desperately poor women receive only a fraction of that amount (about $1,600). The rest is pocketed by unscrupulous brokers who arrange the surrogacy. The exploitation had become so bad that in 2015, the Indian government banned the practice, even though thousands of poor women protested. This kind of exploitation is the result of treating the procreation of children as the producing of a commodity to meet our desires and treating a woman's womb as a factory or incubator.

A fourth problem with surrogacy involves all the legal problems that are regularly encountered in surrogacy issues. While this is most common with commercial surrogacies, there have been problems with altruistic surrogacies as well. What happens when the surrogate, especially a genetic surrogate, no longer desires to relinquish her baby? The Baby M case and the first case of commercial surrogacy, the case of Elizabeth Kane, were cases where the surrogate became attached to the child and wanted to void the contract. Some states even allow a time period for the mother to change her mind. While that might be legal, what about the family that contracts the surrogate? Is it morally appropriate to ask them to hold off planning on raising a child they have invested money and emotion into until the mother decides how she really feels?

Voiding the agreement isn't the only legal puzzle. How much control should the couple have over the lifestyle of the surrogate mother? Should they be allowed to regulate what she eats and drinks, what activities she becomes involved in, how much sleep she gets, and a host of other lifestyle areas? What if the child she is carrying becomes damaged or deformed?[47] Can the couple

47. With the advent or pre-genetic diagnosis (PGD) this is becoming less a factor. However, as we will see below, PGD has its own set of problems.

demand she abort the child? If the child is diagnosed in utero with Down syndrome, and the surrogate wants to abort it, but the couple does not, can they force her to bring it to term? What happens after birth to the child if neither the surrogate nor the couple desire to keep it? Should the state be required to take on the burden of finding a home for the child?

As you can see, a multitude of legal and moral problems arise when one considers surrogacy. Although most of these concern commercial surrogacy, several are problems for altruistic surrogacy, whether genetic or gestational. One more problem concerns itself, specifically with IVF and gestational surrogacy, and it is this last problem that will now be discussed.

TECHNOLOGY TO ENHANCE PROCREATION

Amniocentesis has been around since the late nineteenth century but did not become common practice until the mid-1960s. It is the process of inserting a needle into the uterus of a pregnant woman to obtain a sample of amniotic fluid. This fluid then can be tested for indications concerning the health and development of the unborn child. Recently genetic screening has been performed using amniotic fluid obtained by an amniocentesis. This is referred to as prenatal genetic screening (PGS). More than one hundred genetic disorders can be discovered from prenatal screening of amniotic fluid, including Down syndrome, cystic fibrosis, spina bifida, and sickle cell anemia. While there is nothing morally wrong with the procedure itself, there are several concerns that are raised with this kind of screening.

The most serious consideration is the responsibility that accompanies such knowledge. What does one plan to do with this knowledge? Currently, we can test for many more genetic disorders than we can treat. Of course, some may be able to use this knowledge to prepare for caring for a child that will suffer from a genetic disorder. However, while doctors will often state that screening is for information purposes only, they often assume that the presence of a disorder will result in termination of a pregnancy and can place undue pressure on patient to terminate the pregnancy. Therefore, before agreeing to such a procedure, Christians need to seriously reflect about what they plan to do with this knowledge. It may be best not to undergo the procedure, especially if there is no indication that the procedure is medically necessary.

Some other points to consider would be the following. First, remember that the fetus, by nature of the kind of being it is, is a human person from the moment of conception. The presence of a genetic disorder does not in any way diminish its personhood. Second, genetic tests are not always accurate. The test could be wrong. Third, even if the test is accurate, genetic tests usually cannot inform one of the magnitude of the deformity. For some genetic disorders, like Down syndrome, there is a wide range of severity from very mild to extreme cases. Finally, remember that it is discriminatory and presumptuous to say that a person with a genetic disorder has no right to life. This is a human rights issue and we have no right to take a child's life because it might prove to be a burden on someone, specifically a parent.

However, technology has presented an even more serious problem in recent years, one that was well-illustrated in the 1997 science fiction film *Gattaca*. In a particular scene, a married couple, Marie and Antonio, meet with their "geneticist" as they are preparing to have a baby. He explains what they have done so far. They extracted several eggs from Marie and fertilized them *in vitro* with Antonio's sperm. After screening the eggs, they end up with two healthy boys and two healthy girls (having disposed of all the other embryos). He informs them that there are no critical dispositions for major diseases and says that they need to select the gender, eyes, hair, and skin color. The geneticist goes on and explains that they will eradicate any potentially prejudicial conditions: premature baldness, myopia, alcoholism, addictive susceptibility, propensity for violence, and obesity. The parents interrupt asking if, perhaps, just some things could be left to chance. The geneticist explains, "You want to give your child the best possible start. Believe me, we have enough imperfection built in already. Your child doesn't need any additional burdens. And keep in mind, this child is still you—it's simply the best of you. You could conceive naturally a thousand times and never get such a result."[48]

Two technological advances have converged to contribute to our ability to have control over our offspring in a way that at one time was unimaginable. The first of these is IVF. The other is the mapping of the human genome, a task that was completed in 2003. We now have a tremendous amount of knowledge of the sequence of genes and which genes are responsible for which traits. Such knowledge makes it possible to engineer genes to obtain the optimal results and desires. We live in the age of the "designer" baby, where parents can select those traits they desire for their baby, eliminating not only genetic impairments but also eliminating undesirable traits and possibly even enhancing the baby's intellectual and physical capabilities.

---

48. *Gattaca* (1997), written and directed by Andrew Niccol and produced by Danny DeVito, Georgia Kacandes, Joshua Levinson, Michael Shamberg, and Stacey Sher.

One of the primary tools that has allowed physicians to accomplish this task is pre-implantation genetic diagnosis (PGD). Several embryos are created through IVF and can develop to the eight-cell blastocyst stage (three to five days). One or two blastomeres are removed without destroying the embryo. These undergo a type of genetic "profiling" in which they are tested for genetic abnormalities, the potential for genetic diseases and disorders, as well as possibly for specific genetic traits such as sex, eye and hair color, and lifestyle tendencies like obesity and alcoholism.[49] Those embryos that "pass" the test (have no genetic abnormalities and have preferable traits) are set aside for implantation, while those who "fail" are discarded or donated for research.[50]

The desire to avoid or eliminate genetic diseases and disorders is understandable. Nobody wants their child to suffer from a lifelong debilitation if it can be avoided. The temptation to test embryos before implanting can be very powerful. However, severe moral problems accompany this power to control our offspring. With IVF in general, many embryos are created, several of which will eventually be destroyed. Cryopreservation is not even an option in this case, for the reason we reject the embryo is due to its genetic undesirability. Freezing it will not change that factor. So, the only option available for those embryos that were created but that are deemed undesirable is to destroy them.

Many will argue that it is more merciful to destroy embryos with genetic disorders and disabilities at this stage in their development rather than allow them to continue to develop and live a life of suffering and misery. This quality-of-life argument is often made in cases of infanticide as well and was addressed in an earlier chapter and I will defer to it. The main objection against this argument is that no human life should be destroyed simply because one deems it to have less value because it is genetically inferior. Would one say that of a child or adult with the same genetic disorder? Should we kill all those who have Down syndrome, cystic fibrosis, or Parkinson's disease? One needs to also consider that PGD, like prenatal screening, might provide an incorrect diagnosis or, on those occasions in which the diagnosis is correct, usually cannot detect the severity of the genetic disease. Some cases of genetic disorders can be mild and would not result in a life of "suffering and misery." Even worse are those who would destroy embryos due to selecting those with

49. It is hoped in the future that many other genetic traits will be identified, such as intelligence and social abilities.
50. The idea of genetic intervention, going in and changing the genetic makeup of an embryo, is still in the future, but it is an aim in much genetic research today.

preferable genetic traits such as sex selection or other traits. Is one willing to destroy a person's life in its embryonic stage simply because it is a girl instead of a boy? This is discrimination in its worst form.[51]

When we start making decisions between those who are genetically fit to survive and those who are not, we enter into the world of eugenics. Eugenics is the idea of improving the human race by gene selection and manipulation. There are two types of eugenics: negative and positive eugenics. Negative eugenics is the decreasing of undesirable or harmful genetic traits. Positive eugenics is the enhancing of genes to improve their functioning. Eugenics was promoted and practiced in the United States in the early decades of the twentieth century as a form of ridding the world of certain undesirable genetic diseases and traits. Thousands of men and women were forcibly sterilized in an effort to eliminate those deemed "unfit" from the genetic pool. The problem became who decides which traits are "unfit." True, many of us wish to see genetic diseases and disorders eliminated. But at what cost? As C. S. Lewis commented, "From this point of view, what we call Man's power over Nature turns out to be a power exercised by some men over other men with Nature as its instrument."[52] We need to exercise great caution in giving men too much power. For it is easy to forget where our limits are and to do much evil in the name of doing good.

---

51. I do not think it is morally inappropriate to desire one gender over another, and some forms of gender selection are not morally prohibitive. One example is sperm sorting, in which sperm are sorted into X and Y chromosomes and a woman is artificially inseminated with a higher concentration of one of these to raise the possibility of a particular gender outcome. In these cases, one is not being discriminatory because no person exists yet to discriminate against. This assumes that the woman will accept the outcome no matter what happens.
52. C. S. Lewis, *The Abolition of Man* (1944), in *The Complete C. S. Lewis Signature Classics* (New York: HarperCollins, 2007), 719.

8

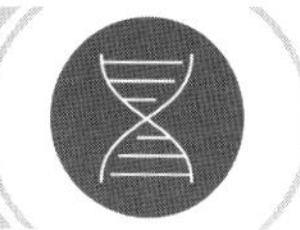

Made, Not Begotten: Genetic Ethics

"Consider the work of God,
For who is able to straighten what He has bent?"
Ecclesiastes 7:1

The time is the "not too distant future." In a moment of reckless passion Marie and Antonio Freeman conceive a son. The voice of Vincent Freeman is heard: "They used to say that a child conceived in love is a child of happiness. They don't say that anymore." At the moment of birth, a blood sample is taken and placed in a machine that can immediately read the child's DNA. A nurse calls out the figures, "Neurological condition, 60 percent probability; Manic depression, 42 percent probability; ADD [Attention Deficit Disorder], 89 percent probability; Heart Disorder." She pauses and looks at the physician, "99 percent probability." The nurse continues, "Early fatal potential. Life expectancy—30.2 years." We see the look of despair on Antonio's face. The doctor asks them for the child's name and Marie answers "Anton . . ." but is interrupted by her husband, "No . . . Vincent . . . Vincent Anton . . ." We hear the voice of Vincent again: "Ten fingers and ten toes. That's all that used to matter. Not now. Now only seconds old, the exact time and cause of my death was already known."

Later, Vincent's parents decide to have another child. This time they choose the "natural way." This son is genetically engineered. The parents come to the local geneticist's office for an interview. The geneticist explains what they have done so far. They extracted several eggs from Marie and fertilized them *in vitro*. After screening the eggs, they end up with two healthy boys and two healthy girls. He informs them that there are no critical dispositions for major diseases and says that they need to select the gender, eyes, hair, and skin color. Marie and Antonio respond that they would like a brother for Vincent. The geneticist goes on and explains that they will eradicate any potentially prejudicial conditions: premature baldness, myopia, alcoholism addictive susceptibility, propensity for violence, and obesity. The parents interrupt asking if, perhaps, just some things could be left to chance. The geneticist explains, "You want to give your child the best possible start. Believe me, we have enough imperfection built in already. Your child doesn't need any additional burdens. And keep in mind, this child is still you—it's simply the best of you. You could conceive naturally a thousand times and never get such a result." When the child is born, he is named Anton, the voice of Vincent telling us "a child worthy of my father's name."

As they grow, Anton excels in every area and becomes the favorite son. Vincent's DNA follows him throughout his life. We observe how, as a child, he is denied admission to school because of his "chronic illness" and how the school's insurance will not cover him. As a teenager, he dreams of becoming an astronaut. His mother discourages him, telling him to be realistic. His chances are one in a hundred of being accepted into the program with his "heart condition." As an adult, we see how, at each job interview, a "drug screen" is performed. Vincent's voice tells us that everyone knows what they are really checking—DNA. There is a law against such discrimination, called Genoism, but it is a law no one takes seriously. If you refuse to disclose, they can take a sample from secretions left by your hand off a door handle, or a handshake, or the sweat left on the application you turn in. Vincent tells us that it is a world where they have "discrimination down to a science." There is now a new underclass, "In-valids." These are people discriminated against not because of race or religion, but because of "inferior" DNA. To the in-valids are left the menial and unimportant tasks in society while the "valids," the genetically engineered elite, are given the better jobs and the better lives.

It is a different world than the one we know. It is the world of *Gattaca.*[1]

---

1. This is a summary of the opening scenes of the 1997 motion picture *Gattaca*, written and directed by Andrew Niccol and produced by Danny DeVito,

GENETICS 101

Is a world like that portrayed in the 1997 film *Gattaca* possible? While we do not have the current technology to be there yet, the progress we have made in genetic research in the past few decades indicates that we are not far from at least the possibility of a society much like the one Vincent Freeman lives in. While the advances in genetic screening, therapy, and engineering promise great benefits in solving genetic disorders and diseases, they also raise disturbing questions: Who will be able to obtain our genetic information? Will we be forced to undergo genetic screening? What about genetic discrimination? How easy will it be to shift from *treatment* for individuals to *enhancement* of the human race?

In order to understand the ethical issues behind the different aspects of genetic research, we need to understand a little about genetics. Certainly one of the most important discoveries of the latter half of the twentieth century was the 1953 discovery by James D. Watson and Francis Crick, of the basic structure of the DNA molecule. This is the famous "double-helix" model that looks like a spiraling staircase. DNA is responsible for transmitting hereditary characteristics from parent to child. Watson and Crick's discovery laid the groundwork for understanding the basic mechanism for copying genetic material from one cell to another and from one generation to another. This would eventually lead to recombinant DNA research, screening for genetic diseases, gene therapy, and mapping the entire human gene.

We begin by distinguishing between cells, genes, and chromosomes. A **cell** is the basic unit of life. The human body is a living system of about 32 trillion cells. Millions of these cells die off and are replaced by new ones every day. Some last longer and some, like brain cells, are not replaceable at all. We have many different kinds of cells that perform different functions—liver cells, neural cells, blood cells, etc. Inside each cell is a nucleus, and in each nucleus are tiny strands called chromosomes. Each cell nucleus contains forty-six chromosomes in twenty-three pairs (except for the reproductive cells which we will discuss below). Chromosomes are long strands of DNA and other chemicals. A gene is a section of DNA and is the basic physical and functional unit of heredity. A gene is a specific sequence of nucleotide

---

Georgia Kacandes, Joshua Levinson, Michael Shamberg, and Stacey Sher. The title, which is the name of an aerospace firm in the picture, is composed entirely of the four letters that label the nucleotide bases in DNA—G, T, C, A.

basis. These sequences are instructions required for constructing proteins. Proteins provide the structural components for cells, tissues, and enzymes for the essential biochemical reactions for all living things.

The biologist Richard Dawkins provided a well-known analogy to understand how all this is put together.[2] Dawkins compared the human body to a library building containing many trillions of rooms. Each room represents a cell. In each room there is a bookcase (nucleus) that contains that contains the architects plan for the entire building.[3] The plans are located in forty-six volumes (chromosomes). Each volume contains about 100,000 pages of information (genes) and each pages contains about 3–3.5 billion words (DNA molecules). The letters that compose the words on each page, the alphabet used by the architect, begin with the combination of only four nucleic acids (guanine [G], adenine [A], thymine [T] and cytosine [C]). These acids pair up together in "base pairs" and combine in different orders to make up different sequences. There are about 3–3.5 billion base pairs in each gene. Like letters in a word, and words in a sentence, the sequence determines the "meaning" of the instructions given in the blueprint. If the instructions say one thing in one room (the nucleus of a cell) than they will say the exact same thing in every room. Sometimes these instructions give incorrect information and that will affect the entire building, causing genetic disorders and diseases.

How is all this passed down from parent to child? As we said, every cell in the body has forty-six chromosomes, except the reproductive cells. Sperm and egg cells each have twenty-three chromosomes. The genetic combinations of each sperm and each egg is different and unique. At fertilization the twenty-three chromosomes of one parent are paired with the twenty-three chromosomes of the other parent, and a brand-new set of forty-six chromosomes comes into existence. To use our library analogy, a brand new blue print guiding the building and developing of a brand new library building now exists. The primary reason this new library is so different is the process of recombination, a switching of genes within the sperm and egg before fertilization. It is not so much that new genes exist, it is just a new combination of old genes.

2. Dawkins, Richard *The Selfish Gene* (New York: Oxford University Press, 1976), 23–24.
3. Dawkins, an atheist, claims there is no real architect, that the building is just a product of chance and natural selection. However, if one considers his analogy precise, it seems to lead to the opposite conclusion. There are "plans" designed by an "architect." How many would argue that a real building, just like the one described here, could occur purely by chance?

Two other distinctions need to be addressed. First, the cells that become sperm and egg cells are called *germ* cells, because they contain information that will be passed on to future generations. All the other cells in our bodies are called *somatic* cells. Nothing in somatic cells is passed on to future generations, and any change in them will only affect the person of whom they are a part. This distinction will become important when we discuss genetic intervention and therapy.

The second distinction is between *recessive* and *dominant* genes. Dominant genes are "expressed" and recessive genes are usually "unexpressed." If no dominant gene is present, then a recessive will express itself. However, a dominant gene will always eclipse a recessive gene. To use our library analogy, think of some pages in one volume as "rough drafts" (recessive genes) and the matching pages in the matching volume as final drafts (dominant genes). The blueprint will always refer to the final draft.[4] For example, suppose one has a particular dominant gene, like the gene for brown eyes is said to be, and has a recessive gene, like the gene for blue eyes. The result will be that the person will have brown eyes. However, what if one has only two rough drafts (recessive genes)? The two rough drafts of the page will come together and be accepted as the final draft. If one has two recessive blue-eyed genes, he or she will have blue eyes.

Finally, if one has a recessive gene, that gene may not be expressed, but it can still be passed done to future generations. During recombination (meiosis) when genes are getting mixed up, some of the rough drafts get mixed into the twenty-three chromosomes of the sperm or egg. Therefore, if one has a recessive blue-eyed gene and a dominant brown-eyed gene, he will have brown genes, but will have a 50% chance of passing on his blue-eyed gene, depending on the genes of its mother. This is important for understanding the passing on of genetic disorders. One may not have a disorder but could be a carrier of the disease.

Sometimes the passing on genes goes wrong and genetic disorders occur. These can be for a variety of reasons but the four most common are: single-gene inheritance diseases, multifactorial genetic inheritance disorders, chromosome abnormalities, and mitochondrial genetic inheritance disorders.[5] More than six thousand genetic disorders have been identified. Statistically

---

4. I am indebted to my daughter Erin for this extension of the library analogy.
5. Charles Patrick Davis, MD, PhD, "Types and List of Examples of Genetic (Hereditary) Diseases," E-medicine Health, obtained 1/5/2022 at https://www.emedicinehealth.com/types_and_list_of_genetic_diseases/article_em.htm.

genetic disorders are the second leading cause of death for children 1 to 4 and the third leading cause of death for children 5 to 9. Twenty-five to 30% of hospital admissions for children under 18 and 13% of adults are estimated to be due to genetic disorders. Also, 20–25% of institutionalized mentally handicapped patients have genetic disorders.[6]

There are several different activities geneticists are involved with to help solve the problems of genetic disorders. In this chapter we will divide them into three areas: genetic screening, genetic intervention, and genetic research and experimentation. In each area, we will first describe the current practices and activities and then discuss some of the ethical problems and issues relating to that area.

GENETIC SCREENING

The major advances in genetics have been in the areas of diagnosis and prediction of genetic disorders. We can presently diagnose far more than we can treat. These activities involve genetic screening. Leroy Walters defines a genetic test as "the use of diagnostic procedures or determination of the presence or absence of one or more genetic traits or conditions in an individual."[7] There are four different kinds of screening.

1. *Neonatal screening.* This is genetically testing newborns for certain disorders and was the first form of genetic screening to come about. In the early 1960s a genetic test was developed by Dr. Robert Guthrie to test for PKU, an inborn error of metabolism that prevents the breakdown of phenylalanine, an amino acid. One result of this disorder is severe retardation. However, if discovered early, treatment is relatively simple by placing the infant on a diet very low in phenylalanine. The test consists of gaining a blood sample through a heel prick on the infant at birth. In 1963 Massachusetts became the first state to require the PKU screening for newborns. Today every state in the country has mandatory PKU screening.

Since the 1960s mandatory neonatal testing for other diseases has included hypothyroidism, sickle cell anemia, galactosemia, homocystinuria,

6. Numbers obtained through CDC FastStats https://www.cdc.gov/nchs/fastats.
7. LeRoy Walters, "Reproductive Technologies and Genetics," in *Medical Ethics*, ed. Robert M. Veatch, 2nd ed. (Boston: Jones and Bartlett, 1998), 220. Walters makes a distinction between genetic testing and genetic screening, but for our purposes we will use them interchangeably.

and maple-syrup urine disease.[8] Screening for other conditions such as cystic fibrosis, heart disease, and HIV are under discussion. Only a handful of states allow for refusal of newborn screening, usually on religious grounds.

2. *Prenatal diagnosis.* This is the genetic testing of a fetus. It was historically the second type of genetic testing to develop. In 1966 the first study of cells drawn from the amniotic sac by a process known as *amniocentesis* was performed. Over the following two years successful diagnosis of a chromosomal abnormality and diagnosis of an inborn error of metabolism occurred. Today, along with amniocentesis, a number of prenatal genetic tests are performed and include the following: (1) maternal serum alpha-fetoprotein (MSAFP) screening, a blood test of the mother usually performed between sixteen and eighteen weeks of pregnancy that can predict high chances of a spin bifida or anencephalic child; (2) enhanced MSAFP, sometimes referred to as a "down-screen" because of its ability (60–65 percent accuracy) to predict babies with Down syndrome; (3) chorionic villus sampling (CVS), a rare and risky test used for chromosomal analysis and DNA study, where a piece of the chorion, or outer tissue of the amniotic sac, is removed for testing; the chances for fetal damage and miscarriage as a result of this test is high; (4) percutaneous umbilical blood sampling (PUBS), a newer and even riskier genetic test in which blood is taken from the umbilical cord of a fetus to measure blood components and determine if there are fetal/maternal blood conflicts; and (5) fetal biopsy, which is used to obtain skin samples to perform DNA tests.

Today prenatal testing can diagnose over more than hundred genetic disorders including Tay-Sachs disease, Down syndrome, cystic fibrosis, spina bifida, Trisomy 13, Trisomy 18, sickle cell anemia, muscular dystrophy, and hemophilia. In addition to standard prenatal testing, a new form of testing on embryos fertilized *in vitro*[9] has evolved, called preimplantation diagnosis. After fertilization, the cells of the zygote begin to divide. When it reaches the 4–8-cell stage, one cell is removed for testing and the other cells are cryogenically frozen. The cell is tested for a host of genetic diseases. If it is healthy the other cells are unfrozen and implanted in the womb. If it is not

8. Walters, "Reproductive Technologies," 221.
9. *In vitro* literally means "in glass" and refers to conceptions that occur outside of the mother's body in a science lab. These have erroneously been called "test tube" conceptions. They actually take place in a petri dish. After conception, the zygote will be allowed to grow to the 4–8-cell stage and then be implanted in the mother's womb. Usually *in vitro* fertilizations are for those who need reproductive assistance. When performed more than one egg is usually fertilized. Those not used are discarded.

healthy, the cells are discarded. This test is particularly useful for detecting early development of genetic disorders. It is still in an experimental stage and is usually only performed on those using assisted forms of reproduction, though parents who are not in need of assisted reproduction may make use of *in vitro* if they want an early embryonic genetic test.

3. *Carrier screening.* Above we commented that it is possible not to have a genetic disorder, but to be a carrier of one if it is on a recessive gene. This type of genetic screening is usually done when one desires to know if he or she will pass on a genetic disorder to his or her children. Most often couples will consider such a screening if they are contemplating marriage. Carrier screening almost always is performed only on those who have a suspicion that they might be carriers of genetic disorders. The most common groups tested as carriers are certain ethnic groups that have a higher than usual chance of a specific genetic disorder. For example, Tay-Sachs disease primarily affects Ashkenazi (eastern European) Jewish descendants, though it is also prevalent among French Canadians. Sickle cell anemia is prevalent among Africans and African Americans. Mediterraneans and Southeast Asians are susceptible to thalassemia, a hemoglobin disorder similar to sickle cell anemia. Some genetic diseases are family- or gender-related, and individuals who have a family history of certain disorders might want to be tested to determine if they are carriers.

Most carrier testing is voluntary; however, there have been moves in the past to require such testing. In 1970 a relatively inexpensive test was developed for sickle cell anemia making it possible to identify carriers of the disease. During 1971 and 1972 twelve states passed mandatory laws for testing African Americans to determine if they were sickle cell carriers as a condition to getting married. While the sickle cell gene is dominant, the disease only occurs when both parents pass it on to their offspring. If two carriers marry, there is a chance of one out of four of their children contracting the disease. The laws did not forbid carriers to marry, but required they receive genetic counseling. Soon employers and insurance companies began to require the tests. Charges of discrimination and even genocide of the African American population were made. In 1972 Congress stepped in and passed the National Sickle-Cell Anemia Control Act, forcing states that received federal funds to make sickle cell screening voluntary. In 1976 the National Genetic Disease Act was passed and provided funding for testing and genetic counseling, reinforcing the voluntary aspect of these programs.

Couples who go through carrier testing usually receive genetic counseling. The counselor will obtain cell samples from the couple, analyze them for genetic disorders, and then help the couple to understand the risks involved in having a child who would either have the disease or be a carrier. If it is a recessive trait, and only one member of the couple carries it, then they will not produce a child with the disease, but their chances are fifty-fifty for producing a carrier. If both members have the recessive genetic disorder, their chances are 25 percent of producing a child with that disorder, 25 percent of not producing a child with it, and fifty-fifty of producing a carrier. For some couples, such information may be important for choosing a mate and deciding to have children.

An example can be found among a tight Orthodox Jewish community in New York City. They have developed a program called Dor Yeshorim ("the generation of the righteous"). Within the community teenagers are tested for their carrier status of Tay-Sachs disease, which has been especially prevalent among this community. This information, encoded with identification numbers for confidentiality purposes, is kept in a central office. When a boy and girl want to seriously date, they are encouraged to check with the office to determine their status as carriers. If there is a significant risk of having a child with the genetic disease, they are discouraged from a serious relationship. The program has been successful in significantly reducing the number of Tay-Sachs cases within the community.

4. *Predictive or presymptomatic screening*. This fourth type of genetic testing is the most recent and will probably expand over the next decade. It allows persons with family histories of certain genetic disorders to be tested to see if they are at risk of developing the disorder. It is called "presymptomatic" because the test is taken long before any symptoms of the genetic disorder might develop. A common genetic disorder that falls under this test is Huntington disease. Huntington disease (HD) strikes person later in life, usually between thirty-five and forty-five years of age. The person gradually deteriorates over a ten- to twenty-year period as he or she loses motor functions and cognitive abilities. At present, there is no cure for the disease, and it is always fatal. In 1983 a "marker" for HD was found. A marker can be used in developing linkage tests to help locate the gene itself. Linkage tests require blood samples from several generations of a family, and a comprehensive family background is needed. Even then, the linkage test may not be completely accurate, because the marker does not always travel with the

gene. The linkage test became available in May 1987 and was offered through three medical centers in the United States. However, turnout was very low. Of the estimated 1,500 people at risk in the New England area, only thirty-two signed up for the preliminary counseling, and only eighteen actually took the test.[10] In 1993 the actual HD gene was finally discovered. Now persons from families with a history of HD can be tested for HD.

Since the discovery of the HD marker and subsequent gene, a few other genes responsible for genetic disorders have been discovered, including early-onset Alzheimer's, hemochromatosis, polycystic kidney disease, family inherited hypercholesterolemia, and some genetic forms of cancers. All these can be tested for presymptomatically. In addition, a new area has developed called *ecogenetics,* which studies situations in which it is not just the gene that causes the disorder but a combination of the genetic and environmental agents that are encountered. One discovery is a gene on chromosome 15 that turns cigarette smoke into carcinogens but will do nothing if cigarette smoke is not introduced into a person's system.[11]

ETHICAL ISSUES IN GENETIC SCREENING

1. *The problem of knowledge.* One of the primary questions that arises out of genetic screening is: Once we have this knowledge, what can we do about it? The 1983 President's Commission on Bioethics reached the following conclusion about genetic screening: "In sum, the fundamental value of genetic screening and counseling is their ability to enhance the opportunities for individuals to obtain information about their personal health and make autonomous choices based on that information."[12] However, at present only a handful of genetic diseases are treatable, and therefore advance knowledge can do nothing to prevent the onset of the disease nor treat it once it begins. Therefore, one is not sure what "autonomous choices" one can make. Having knowledge of most genetic diseases just does not seem to help very much and, in fact, it may be harmful.

---

10. Gregory Pence, *Classic Cases in Medical Ethics*, 2nd ed. (New York: McGraw-Hill, 1995), 398.
11. Pence, *Classic Cases*, 408.
12. U.S. President's Commission for the Study of Ethical Problems in Medicine and Biomedical and Behavioral Research, "Screening and Counseling for Genetic Conditions" (Washington, DC: Government Printing Office, February 1983), 55.

For example, take prenatal and preimplantation screening. Such screening is done to determine if a fetus has a specific genetic disorder and has become almost routine in pregnancy. We have had three children, and in every case my wife was approached about having the MSAFP test (she refused each time). If the test comes back positive, what is the parent supposed to do? The most common answer is to abort the fetus, for that is the only way to "treat" the disease. Christian philosopher Scott Rae calls this "the abortion assumption" and comments how for some, this assumption underlies the whole purpose of prenatal screening:

> Most genetic counsellors will say that they operate with the presumption of objectivity. Their role is to give information and maximize reproductive choice for the couple. Yet when public health officials talk about the benefits of prenatal screening in reducing the incidence of genetic diseases, they typically assume that couples will end their pregnancy if they receive bad news from their testing. . . . Public health authorities sometimes suggest that prenatal testing is a great help in eliminating the incidence of genetic disease. But the only way it can be helpful in that way is if couples end their pregnancies. The genetic disease is thereby eliminated, but at the expense of the child who has the disease.[13]

We have already discussed the issue of abortion and infanticide decisions based on quality-of-life arguments in previous chapters and therefore will only make a few comments here. First and most important, the fetus, by nature of the kind of being it is, is a human person from the moment of conception. The presence of a genetic disorder does not in any way diminish its personhood. As a human person, it is an "image-of-God-bearer" and therefore to take its life is an affront to God himself. In fact, the genetically impaired fetus is as much a human person as a genetically impaired adult, and I know of no one who advocates killing adults with genetic disorders (at least not yet).

Second, genetic tests are not completely accurate. Many of them have substantial margins of error for false positives and false negatives. For example, the enhanced MSAFP test has only a 60–65 percent accuracy for detecting Down syndrome which is the primary disorder it is designed to detect. The regular AFP is *designed* to create several false positives which then must

---

13. Scott Rae, "Prenatal Genetic Testing, Abortion, and Beyond," in *Genetic Ethics: Do the Ends Justify the Genes?*, eds. John F. Kilner, Rebecca D. Pentz, and Frank E. Young (Grand Rapids: Eerdmans, 1997), 138.

be confirmed by further testing causing tremendous anxiety to the parents. It would be unwise to decide to take the life of a child based upon such tests.

Third, even if such tests are accurate, they cannot inform one of the magnitude of deformity. For several genetic disorders there are differing degrees of abnormality. A Down syndrome child can range from mild retardation to very severe cases, and prenatal testing cannot inform anyone where a child will fit on that continuum.

Fourth, it is simply discriminatory and presumptuous to say that a person with genetic disorders has no right to life. Right to life is something all persons have regardless of their genetic disorder. Also, no one can arbitrarily make that decision for another person. We explained in the previous chapter how difficult it is to arrive at a "best interests" view for an infant.

Finally, there is the possibility that one might not be thinking only in terms of the burdens on the infant. Scott Rae comments, "Not even parents should have the right to set the standard of a 'life worth living' for their child. It is all too easy for the parents to confuse the burden of life for the child with the burden on the parents of caring for the child. The notion of a life not worth living should not be used to disguise the wish of parents to avoid a great burden themselves."[14]

One can see this discrimination most clearly when one looks at the guidelines suggested by the 1983 President's Council on Bioethics. In no uncertain terms, they make it clear that it would be inappropriate and immoral to use genetic screening for sex selection. This is because most couples seem to want male children, which would make such screening discriminatory against women. However, using genetic screening for genetic disorders in order to eliminate the disorders (which can only be done through abortion) is just as discriminatory—it's just not recognized as so. This is really a form of eugenics called negative eugenics. We will discuss eugenics more below.

All the above problems with prenatal screening have led some to suggest that it is inappropriate altogether. Christian ethicist Gilbert Meilaender holds such a view. He comments how love is the most important of the Christian virtues and quotes Josef Pieper's definition of love as a way of saying to another: "It's good that you exist; it's good that you are in this world!"[15] Meilaender goes on to say:

14. Rae, "Prenatal Genetic Testing," 140.
15. Gilbert Meilaender, *Bioethics: A Primer for Christians* (Grand Rapids: Eerdmans, 1996), 49. Meilaender is quoting from Josef Pieper's book *About Love* (Chicago: Franciscan Herald, 1974), 19.

> Precisely because we know ourselves to have been loved this unqualifiedly by God, and because we know we should learn to love others as we have been loved, Christians ought to set themselves against any prenatal screening, at least as it is currently practiced in this country in an increasingly routinized way. For it stands in conflict with the virtue that would say to another: "It's good that you exist."[16]

Meilaender also points out that prenatal screening, followed by abortion, changes the whole relationship between mother and child. The relationship becomes more tentative and conditional because the mother is free to "walk away" from the child if she feels the child is too much of a burden. However, with such freedom comes responsibility: the responsibility to be tested if one is suspicious, the responsibility of making a choice, and the responsibility of the consequences of that choice. He suggests that we might begin to see lawsuits brought against mothers who did not abort their genetically disordered children by the children themselves who feel they should have been aborted rather than live a life that is "worse than nonexistence." With knowledge comes power and responsibility. We are "playing God" in a very real sense. Our children may turn to us, like Job, asking us, "Why did you allow this evil to happen when you had the knowledge and means to prevent it?" Meilaender believes that such a responsibility is too great for us to bear. We were never meant to—it is God's alone.

Not everyone agrees with Meilaender's rejection of prenatal screening. Scott Rae believes that tests with little risk can be valuable in preparing parents "for the emotional and perhaps financial rigors of raising a handicapped child."[17] Meilaender, however, believes that parents are deceiving themselves if they believe that such screening will help prepare them for the child: "It does exactly the opposite. It sets our foot on a path that is difficult to exit. . . . It prepares us not for the kind of commitment that parenthood requires, an unconditional commitment, but for a kind of responsibility that finite beings ought to reject."[18] While prenatal screening is not wrong *per se*, couples need to ask themselves what they plan on doing with the knowledge they gain through screening, and what that screening might be saying about themselves and their commitment to their child.

---

16. Meilaender, *Bioethics*, 19.
17. Rae, "Prenatal Genetic Testing," 141.
18. Meilaender, *Bioethics*, 55–56.

Prenatal screening is not the only area where the question of what to with the knowledge of a genetic disorder arises. It is also problematic for other types of screening. If an infant undergoes a neonatal screen that determines that he will develop Tay-Sachs disease or muscular dystrophy, that could possibly lead parents to treat him differently, like Vincent was treated in the story of *Gattaca*. If they know the infant will not live long, they may not give him the love and attention he deserves and needs because they do not want to make such an "investment" in something that will not last long or go far. They may even consider neonaticide rather than having to care for children that will die or suffer at a very young age. They would just have to find a doctor sympathetic for such a view.

Carrier screening also has problems with knowing one is carrying a genetic trait. If they have knowledge that they may pass on a genetic disorder, do they have a moral obligation not to get married or, if they do marry, not to have children? Should they seek sterilization even though screening might not be accurate, or the chances are only one in four?

There is also a problem with presymptomatic screening and knowledge. Is it better to know for sure if you do or don't have a genetic disorder, or is it better not to know? Suppose a person is suspicious that she might have HD and so she is tested for it and finds out that she will develop the disease. How might that affect her life? She might decide that she cannot be happy living anymore and opt for an early assisted suicide. Should she be given that option? Over 25 percent of HD victims consider suicide and 10 percent actually carry it out.[19] How much higher might that go as more are tested for the disease? Many of those who don't commit suicide take on a "sick identity" in which they dramatically alter their lives and take on the role of being ill, including depression, anxiety, and hypochondria—even though they are currently perfectly healthy.

2. *Confidentiality*. Closely related to the question of knowledge is the question of who else will be able to access the knowledge of a genetic disorder. Normally, health information is kept confidential between physician and patient. However, others may believe they have a right to your genetic information. This is problematic in a number of contexts.

First, your family may feel they have a right to your genetic information. Most persons will probably volunteer information to other family members

19. Pence, *Classic Cases*, 402.

if it concerns health-related issues. But it is possible that someone might not wish to disclose that information to other family members for several reasons. However, if he doesn't disclose, does the physician have a duty to disclose to other family members if he believes that by not disclosing, he is putting those family members in danger? Suppose Harry is tested and finds out he has the gene for HD. Since HD is a dominant gene, inheriting it from either parent will lead to the disease. Harry has a 50 percent chance of passing it to his children and they would have the same chance of passing it on to their children. Does Harry have a moral obligation to disclose? Suppose he refuses to disclose his condition to his children. Does Harry's doctor now have an obligation to break confidence and tell them? One must consider in reflecting on these questions such things as the importance of physician/patient confidentiality, the fact that it is only a 50 percent chance of children getting the gene, and the question we discussed above of what good will the knowledge be to them. Disclosing might be more harmful than helpful.

A second context is medical insurance. Insurance companies argue that they have a right to this information. After all, they have a legitimate interest in controlling costs and therefore want to insure persons who are at low risk of disease or debilitation. If they get your genetic information and find there is a 60 percent chance of your developing a genetic heart disorder, they might charge a higher premium or even refuse to insure you, even though you might be perfectly healthy and never actually develop the disease. One legislative move to confront this problem was the passage of the Health Insurance Portability and Accountability Act of 1996 which prohibits insurance discrimination based on genetics.

A third context is employment. Think back to the story of *Gattaca*. Businesses may feel they have a right to your genetic screen. Like insurance companies, businesses have a legitimate interest to control costs and they may not want to invest in hiring and training an employee if they know he might become ill early in life. However, this constitutes discrimination. It is not even discrimination on the basis of handicap, but on a *possible future* handicap. While the Equal Employment Opportunities Commission has ruled denial of job based on genetic information is illegal, many argue that there are still too many loopholes and exceptions.

A final context could be that the government might feel it has the right to know. If a person has a genetic disorder, there is a good possibility that he or she will eventually need state or federal resources to help defray medical costs. Therefore, the government might want to know a person's genetic screen. We mentioned above the Sickle Cell Laws of the early 1970s. These were enacted by state governments and required that African Americans be tested for sickle cell trait before getting married. The idea was that by knowing their status in relation to sickle cell, married couples could think through their options and plans for children. However, as a result of the laws, many African Americans lost their jobs and health insurance and were even discharged from the military, even though they were perfectly healthy and with no risk of developing the disease.[20]

All four of these contexts raise the issue of confidentiality in genetic testing and the danger of discrimination. In one study in the New England area, forty-one separate incidents of discrimination were reported. Thirty-two of these were insurance incidents, and seven were employment related.[21] Doctor Christopher Hook commenting on this study reports,

> Many of the individuals involved had undergone testing only because another family member had been affected with a genetic condition; they themselves were still healthy. One patient with a heredity hemochromatosis, a disease of iron absorption and storage which can be well managed, was denied insurance. He stated: "I might as well have had AIDS." Another case involved the brother of an individual who had Gaucher's disease. This brother was screened, and the results suggested that he was an asymptomatic carrier. When he applied for a governmental job and included the history of his testing in the application, he was denied the job because he was "a carrier like sickle cell."[22]

A 1996 Harvard/Stanford University study documented 206 cases of genetic discrimination by "businesses, insurance companies, schools, blood banks and the military. Included among the cases was a situation in which a woman's HMO would pay for an abortion of the woman's fetus that carried a gene for cystic fibrosis but would not pay for the birth and care of the child if it were born."[23]

In today's medical world, complete confidentiality is extremely difficult to maintain. There are just too many persons who need access to patient records. Physicians, nurses, hospital personnel, billing personnel, insurance

---

20. C. Christopher Hook, "Genetic Testing and Confidentiality," in Kilner, Pentz, and Young, *Genetic Ethics*, 127.
21. Paul R. Billings, Mel A. Kohn, Margaret deCuevas, et al., "Discrimination as a Consequence of Genetic Testing," *American Journal of Human Genetics* 50 (1992): 476–82.
22. Hook, "Genetic Testing and Confidentiality," 127.
23. Hook, "Genetic Testing and Confidentiality," 128.

companies, and HMOs are just some of the many people who may have access to a person's genetic screen. So far little has been proposed to rectify the problem. As far as breaching confidentiality is concerned, sometimes it may be necessary, but there needs to exist strong justificatory evidence of its necessity.

3. *Mandatory genetic screening*. The issue of mandatory screening is closely related to the above issue. If there are those who believe they have a right to your genetic screen, there is a good chance they may *require* you to undergo screening. Currently, all prenatal screening and presymptomatic screening is voluntary. While some forms of carrier screening were mandated years ago, no such laws are present today. However, it would not be too far a step to imagine that some prenatal screening could become mandatory in the years ahead. Once it is determined that there is a social issue demanding fetal genetic knowledge, states and the federal government may pass laws deciding that social need trumps individual liberty. Such is how many laws evolve in our country.

There are a few mandatory newborn screening laws on the state level. The most common of these is the PKU screening. These mandatory laws are justified on several grounds. PKU is treatable by diet, but treatment must begin right away. Therefore, a neonatal screen is justifiable. The PKU test is a very low-risk test, requiring only a heel-prick blood sample. Very few persons see PKU as coercive, and in fact are generally thankful for the test. However, some are concerned that blanket "acceptance" of current mandatory laws may encourage the passing of other mandatory laws. In recent years states have expanded the mandatory newborn screening laws for other genetic diseases. It is questionable whether these laws are as easily justified.

While the government has so far required little more than newborn screening, the private sector has not been as dormant. There have been attempts by both insurance companies and employers to require genetic screening in order to obtain insurance or employment. Carol Haas writes, "Some employers are advocating that applicants and employees be genetically screened to determine whether they have a predisposition to contracting occupational disorders. Such screening has not caught on in popularity, mainly because the technology is still unsophisticated, unreliable, and very expensive. But it may only be a matter of time until employees are told, whether they want to be or not, that they are susceptible to certain diseases."[24]

24. Carol Haas, "Genetic Testing Worms Its Way into Firms' Screening Processes," *Atlanta Business Chronicle*, July 8, 1996.

One particular case shows how screening is a current problem in the workplace. While this is not a case of mandatory *genetic* testing, it does demonstrate how close we are to such testing. The case is *Norman Bloodsaw v. Lawrence* and it was argued on June 10, 1997, in the 9th Circuit Court of Appeals. The case concerns many administrative and clerical employees of Lawrence Berkeley Laboratory, a research facility operated by the University of California. The employees, headed by Marya S. Norman-Bloodsaw, alleged that, in the course of their mandatory pre-employment entrance health exams and on subsequent occasions, Lawrence Berkeley Laboratory tested their blood and urine for syphilis, pregnancy, and sickle cell trait without their knowledge or consent and without subsequently informing employees of the test results. Upon being hired, the employees agreed to fill out a health evaluation questionnaire and undergo a health examination, which included the providing of blood and urine samples. While the evaluation form asked the employees questions concerning if they had any history of sickle cell anemia, venereal disease or menstrual disorders, nothing was said or implied that they would be tested for any of these diseases. Health evaluations are not uncommon for many corporations, and they often include standard blood tests and drug screens. However, as several experts testified in the district court hearing: "The manner in which the tests were performed was inconsistent with sound medical practice . . . medical scholars roundly condemn[ed] Lawrence's alleged practices and explain[ed], *inter alia*, that testing for syphilis, sickle cell trait, and pregnancy is not an appropriate part of an occupational medical examination and is rarely if ever done by employers as a matter of routine."[25]

The employees sued the laboratory on the basis of the Americans with Disabilities Act (requiring medical testing that was not job-related), Title VII of the Civil Rights Act of 1964 (discrimination against African Americans in testing for the sickle cell trait), and their right to privacy as guaranteed by both the United Sates Constitution and the California State Constitution (testing without gaining informed consent). However, the district court summarily dismissed the case, holding that (1) the statute of limitations had run out on all three of the above claims and (2) the fact that tests were "part of a comprehensive medical examination to which the plaintiffs consented." Therefore, the district court concluded that there were "sufficient facts to put them [the employees] on notice" and they should have expected the testing. The case was appealed to the 9th Circuit Court of Appeals, who reversed the

25. *Norman-Bloodsaw v. Lawrence*, 135 F.3d 1260 (9th Circuit Court of Appeals, 1998).

lower court's ruling on the Title VII claims and right to privacy claims. They ruled that (1) the statute of limitations had not run out on any of these claims; (2) the lower court erred in not considering whether these tests were acceptable, and that a trial was necessary to determine that issue; and (3) these tests were not necessary, were an invasion of privacy, and the sickle cell tests were discriminatory.

In 2008, Congress enacted the Genetic Information Nondiscrimination Act (GINA), which bars the use of genetic information in health insurance and employment. Title I prohibits health insurance companies from using a person's genetic information to determine health insurance costs or coverage. Title II, implemented by the Equal Employment Opportunity Commission, prevents employers from making job-related decisions such as pay, promotion, hiring, or firing on the basis on an employee's genetic information. Most importantly under GINA, genetic information is unable to be obtained by anyone without the individual's consent. There have been few challenges around GINA, as it has been widely supported since its enactment. In 2015, a Georgia case was heard where the plaintiffs objected to their employer obtaining their DNA through cheek swabs to determine a mystery defecator in a company warehouse (yes, seriously). Neither plaintiff was a match, but they filed suit under GINA, claiming their genetic information was illegally obtained. The United States District Court ruled in favor of the plaintiffs, rejecting the argument that GINA was only referring to genetic information pertaining to diseases. The Court found that GINA is broad enough to incorporate nearly all genetic information, which would include disease propensity, ancestry and family information, and basic genetic markers. The plaintiffs were awarded $2.2 million by the jury (and the mystery defecator was never found).[26]

Whether or not government or private mandatory genetic screening outside of GINA will come about is up for debate. The trend seems to be leaning toward a voluntary approach. However, there are those who argue that with such freedom comes responsibility and that one may have a moral duty, if not a legal one, to be tested for a genetic disorder or trait if one has reason to believe he or she is susceptible to a genetic disorder. LeRoy Walters argues, "Individuals and couples have a moral duty to learn what they can about the likelihood that they will transmit genetic conditions to their offspring and to take reasonable steps—steps that are compatible with their other ethical

26. *Lowe v. Atlas Logistics Group, LLC*. 102 F. Su3d 1360 (Northern District of Georgia, 2015).

convictions—to avoid causing preventable harm to their descendants."[27] Walters does not believe such an "ethics of genetic duty" should be legalized. However, the move from voluntary to required sometimes is not a large one and can be very subtle. Once a person is required to know, it is very easy to be required to do something about it.

GENETIC INTERVENTION

Genetic Intervention involves manipulating genes in order to improve them. This is sometimes called genetic engineering or genetic therapy. Genetic engineering takes place in other areas besides human health programs. Gene splicing or recombinant DNA technology has been useful in such areas as agriculture and environmental technology. New and healthier crops have been developed to help feed more people. Proteins have been developed that enhance animal health. On the environmental level, genetically altered bacteria have been developed that will feed on oil slicks to help clean up oil spills, and more is being done to develop ways of converting waste materials into useful products, such as organic wastes into sugar, alcohol, and methane.

Such genetic engineering has not been without its critics and some have been leery about changing nature in such a fundamental way. Some argue that if we are so easily going to allow gene splicing on the plant and animal level, can human gene splicing be far behind? Others are concerned about the commercialization of nature. In 1987 the U.S. Patent and Trademark Office announced that all forms of animal life, with the exception of humans, should be considered "patentable" subject matter. All life can now be regarded as a manufacture or composition of matter.[28] With commercialization some believe that corporate profits may take priority over ethical behavior or argue that genetic engineering may have disastrous effects on the environment. Several persons are concerned about the possibility of biological weapons and germ warfare. A serious issue that has not received enough attention has to do with regulating genetic experimentation, especially in the private sector. All these concerns should signal us that we need to approach the issue of genetic engineering very cautiously.

27. Walters, "Reproductive Technologies," 225.
28. Dick Russell, "Genetic Engineering is Dangerous," in *Genetic Engineering: Opposing Viewpoints*, ed. William Dudley (San Diego: Greenhaven, 1990), 26.

When genetic engineering is directed at humans it is usually referred to as gene therapy. We stated earlier that genetic screening is the main activity taking place in genetics today. This is primarily due to the fact that our technology is still in its infancy when it comes to being able to intervene in a person's genetic makeup and make changes. However, it is the goal of almost all geneticists to be able to perform genetic engineering on human beings. What kind of intervention can or may be done someday?

In a well-known article, Nelson Wivel and Leroy Walters arrived at four types of intervention that might someday become available, and to a small degree some of this is currently taking place.[29] The four types occur by combining two factors. The first factor has to do with the distinction between somatic cell therapy and germ line therapy. *Somatic cell therapy* is intervention that aims to cure a genetic disorder by modifying the non-reproductive cells in a person. If successful, this would cure the person, but he would not pass that cure on to other generations. For example, experimental treatment is being attempted to modify the bone marrow cells of a person with sickle cell anemia. The bone marrow is where red blood cells are manufactured; by modifying the cells one could eradicate the sickle cell gene, thereby curing the person. However, she would not be able to pass this on to her children. *Germ line therapy* is an intervention in the reproductive cells to attempt to modify them so that a particular genetic disorder would not be passed on to future generations. In this type of intervention both somatic cells and germ line cells are treated to affect both the present person and her future offspring. There are obvious concerns with germ line therapy that are not present with somatic cell therapy. We will discuss these below.

The other factor involved with the different types of intervention concerns the distinction between therapy and enhancement. This line is not always obvious. *Therapy* has to do with the curing or preventing of a genetic disorder. We have already discussed several genetic disorders which almost all agree would be beneficial to cure: Huntington Disease, Tay-Sachs, Down syndrome, sickle cell anemia, and many others. *Enhancement* has to do with improving traits and abilities that are not diseases. Improving one's intelligence, memory, lifespan, and physical capabilities are all examples of enhancement. Rather than curing, we are improving the person. Taking these two factors into

29. Nelson A. Wivel and LeRoy Walters, "Germ Line Gene Modification and Disease Prevention: Some Medical and Ethical Perspectives," *Science* 262 (1993): 533–36.

consideration, there are four possible types of genetic intervention: somatic cell therapy, germ line cell therapy, somatic cell enhancement, and germ line cell enhancement.

The first successful somatic cell therapy occurred on September 14, 1990. Four-year-old Ashanti DeSilva had severe combined immune deficiency (SCID), a genetic disease that undermines the immune system, making it unable to fight diseases. Most who are born with this disorder die early from infection, usually before they are two. Geneticists at the National Institute of Health performed a procedure that involved removing T-cells (white blood cells) and inserting the proper gene into them to produce the immune enzyme. The T-cells then were reinjected into Ashanti's body to reproduce, spread throughout the system, and produce the proper enzyme. It was not a cure, as the T-cells had to be replaced every couple of months, but Ashanti could now live a fairly normal life. Leroy Walters reports that by 1995, ninety-nine additional somatic gene therapies have been reviewed and approved in the United States. Two thirds are cancer-related, while others have been cystic fibrosis, HIV, Gaucher's disease, and rheumatoid arthritis.[30]

As far as is known, germ line therapy has not been performed on human beings. However, experiments have been performed on laboratory animals with some success. Genes have been inserted into early embryos of mice. As the embryos develop the gene appears in the nucleus of each cell, including reproductive cells. When the mice later reproduce, the gene has been detected in their offspring. Again, according to Walters, genetic defects have been corrected in fruit flies and mice.[31] Germ line therapy and somatic therapy are not always easily separated. Some genetic disorders need to be treated at the early embryonic stage in order to affect all the cells of the body. Since the reproductive cells will be included, one is doing somatic and germ line therapy at the same time.

The only known enhancement studies occurred in 1982 in mice when they were given a gene for a growth hormone in early embryonic stages. Only a few mice made it to maturity, but a significant number were affected by the hormone and were substantially larger. When they produced offspring, the offspring were also significantly larger, demonstrating that the gene had been passed on to their young.

30. Walters, "Reproductive Technologies," 229.
31. Walters, "Reproductive Technologies," 229.

ETHICAL ISSUES IN GENETIC INTERVENTION

There are many benefits to genetic intervention. The possibility of curing, possibly forever, many genetic disorders is certainly an admirable and important goal in medical science. However, there are some very real concerns and moral problems with intervening in creation that should be a flashing yellow light, warning us to proceed with caution.

Two issues apply to any kind of genetic intervention. The first is the danger of commercialization. Many medical laboratories are run by large corporations. It would be naive to deny that one of the primary motivations behind genetic research is the possibility for enormous profits that a genetic cure would bring. Imagine the corporation that discovers and patents a cure for genetic heart disease or cystic fibrosis. The corporation would have complete control over the patent and could charge almost anything for it. Corporations can justify high prices by appealing to the expense of genetic research. Anticipation for profits might also cause companies to cut corners, place undue pressures on researchers, and slant studies in favor of the company. While there is some government regulation of genetic research itself, in a free market society such as ours, it is difficult to see how government could regulate the distribution of genetic cures.

A second general issue is what I shall call the "scientific attitude." This is an attitude often present in the scientific community of running full speed ahead into scientific experimentation and research, without taking the time to think through the ethical and social issues that such knowledge and experimentation might affect. My point here is not to impugn science in general, nor any specific scientist. Those in medical science are often motivated by a desire to do good, to cure disease, and make the world a better place for people to live. However, even pure motives can blind one to the social and ethical implications of scientific work. There is often an attitude in scientific research that says, "If it *can* be done, then it *should* be done." In addition, science often has the attitude of "controlling" nature that often dominates scientific thinking. Evolutionary biologist Theodosius Dobzhansky states, "Evolution need no longer be a destiny imposed on us from without; it may be conceivably controlled by man, in accordance with his values and wisdom"[32] (which, of course, are merely products of evolution). Such

32. Quoted in Ronald Munson, *Intervention and Reflection: Basic Issues in Medical Ethics* (Belmont, CA: Wadsworth, 1992), 419.

attitudes can be dangerous if left without ethical and societal limits and controls. Charles Colson states it well: "So while genetic research may lead to important medical advances, we must probe the deeper question: What are the restraints? Technological advance may make it *possible* to do something but *ought* we to do it?"[33] The restraints need to come from outside of science itself—these are not scientific issues. They are philosophical, ethical, societal, and religious issues.

As far as specific types of interventions go, currently somatic cell therapy is the only type that has been performed on human persons. Since this is therapeutic, few have been morally critical of it. There are those who believe that we should not be doing any genetic therapy at all. They argue that to do so is to play God. However, this charge is too broad, for it could encompass any medical intervention. For example, are surgeons playing God when they remove cancerous tumors to save lives, or when physicians revive a person whose heart has stopped beating? This is not to say that sometimes the "playing God" charge might not be legitimate, but one needs to be careful about being too broad in making the charge.

One ethical consideration that can be raised concerning somatic cell therapy is the fact that it is still in its experimental stage and therefore caution needs to be taken. The whole area of research ethics is outside of the scope of this chapter, but any research that employs experimentation on humans needs to follow careful guidelines. Some general guidelines are: (1) a good research design—the experiment or research project must be well designed to achieve its purpose and be scientifically sound; (2) the balance of harm and benefit—an experiment should not be performed, or should be terminated in mid-progress, unless there is a good chance that benefits outweigh the harms to be inflicted; (3) competence of the investigator—the researcher has adequate scientific training and skill to accomplish the purposes of the research, along with a high degree of professionalism necessary to care for the subject; (4) informed consent—the patient has been given the following information: (a) a fair explanation of the procedures to be followed and their purposes, including identification of any procedures that are experimental, (b) a description of the attendant discomforts and risks reasonably to be expected, (c) a description of the benefits reasonably to be expected, (d) a disclosure of appropriate alternative procedures that might be advantageous for the subject, (e) an offer

33. Charles W. Colson, "Contemporary Christian Responsibility," in Kilner, Pentz, and Young, *Genetic Ethics.*

to answer any inquiries concerning the procedures, and (f) instruction that the person is free to withdraw his/her consent and to discontinue participation in the project or activity at any time without prejudice to the subjects; (5) equitable selection of subjects—fair distributive justice should be maintained in all recruiting of research subjects; and (6) compensation for research-related injury—this seems to be the least we can offer to those who voluntarily submitted to some form of medical experimentation or research in order that all mankind can benefit from the knowledge gained. Most somatic cell therapy is currently performed in laboratories with institutional review boards to help guide the study in accordance with these guidelines.

Germ line therapy is a bit more controversial. More than just the present patient will be affected by such therapy and more needs to be considered. The obvious advantage of germ line therapy is its efficiency. As Leroy Walters says, "Correcting a defect once, through germ line therapy, and having the correction passed on to the subject's descendants might seem more reasonable than repeating somatic-cell gene therapy generation after generation in a family afflicted by a genetic disease."[34] However, the argument above concerning experimental treatment has even more force in this situation. One may not know for many generations if a particular germ line treatment has been effective, or worse, if it is causing other unforeseen damage. Therefore, it is difficult to form an adequate design plan and to balance harms and benefits. The issue of informed consent is also raised by some, for we are now discussing performing experimental treatment on future generations who do not have any say in such experimentation.

Another problem with germ line therapy is that it must be performed on embryos in order for the intervention to spread to all cells including reproductive cells. This causes two problems: first, much of the early work in laboratory animals has been unsuccessful, resulting in defective embryos and embryos that did not survive the therapy. It is highly probable that such therapy when used on humans will have a similar effect, at least in the beginning. Given the personhood of the fetus from conception, this means we would be creating defective children who would most likely be aborted, or simply killing the unborn. Second, some have suggested that germ line therapy would work best if done in preimplantation screening. However, the same problem occurs here, for if the therapy is not successful during implantation the embryo will be discarded—aborted before even entering the womb. While I would not

34. Walters, "Reproductive Technologies," 231.

completely rule out the possibility of germ line therapy, the present problems raise extreme difficulties that make such therapy on human persons unjustifiable for the present.

The most controversial of the types of genetic intervention is any form of genetic enhancement, either somatic or germ line. Many ethicists have argued that intervention to cure or prevent genetic disease may be acceptable, but any attempts to enhance one's capabilities on the genetic level would be ethically unacceptable. There are many reasons why people are against this. First, some argue that this really is playing God. God created man with certain abilities and limitations and to attempt to expand them is to step into a role that is reserved only for him. Second, this is utopian thinking—we are trying to create the perfect human and perfect society. Such utopian thinking does not consider that humanity has a sin nature and will likely abuse such power if given the opportunity. The possibility of a world like *Gattaca* is very real. Third, it is too easy to shift from "improving the individual" to "improving society." When we make such a shift, we have stepped completely out of the realm of the medical and into the realm of the political. This raises a fourth ethical issue, that of differing opinions of what is "enhancing." Who will decide this? Doctors, politicians, scientists, philosophers, theologians, and lawyers may all feel qualified to make the decision.

All the above problems are eclipsed by the main problem with enhancement: *eugenics.* Eugenics is the idea of improving the human race by gene selection and manipulation. There are two types of eugenics: negative and positive eugenics. Negative eugenics is the decreasing of undesirable or harmful genetic traits. Positive eugenics is the enhancing of genes to improve their functioning. While some advocate eugenics, they do not usually use that term. The term "eugenics" has fallen on bad times. There is a reason for that.

Usually when we think of eugenics, we think of Nazi Germany during the days leading up to and including World War II. In fact, the Nazi program can be traced all the way back to 1895 when Alfred Ploetz wrote a document on "racial hygiene." In it he attacked the "medical practice that helps the individual but endangers the race by allowing individuals, who would not have otherwise survived, to live and reproduce themselves."[35] At that time there was no knowledge of genetic intervention, so negative eugenics was performed by forced sterilization along with euthanasia. Positive eugenics

35. Arthur J. Dyck, "Eugenics in Historical and Ethical Perspective," in Kilner, Pentz, and Young, *Genetic Ethics*.

was performed through breeding among the "elite." In 1933 Germany passed a mandatory sterilization law that was explicitly for eugenic purposes. Those sterilized were the mentally incompetent, severely retarded, and the criminally insane—more than 400,000 between 1934 and 1937.[36] In 1939 Hitler passed a law allowing for the euthanasia of members of the same group. Part of the purpose for such laws was economics. Germany was in the midst of a terrible depression and the government could not afford to pay for these persons in state-run facilities. However, the laws soon broadened to include other "social undesirables": the incurably ill, prostitutes, criminals, and certain races—including, as everyone knows, the Jews. It was only the end of the war that ended these practices.

Most of us are familiar with the Nazi record. What many Americans are not aware of is that eugenics was also being heavily promoted and accepted in Great Britain and in the United States. In fact, the United States was at the forefront of the eugenics movement in the early part of the twentieth century. Margaret Sanger, founder of the birth control movement in this country, spoke throughout the world on behalf of eugenics. Her saying was, "More children for the fit, less for the unfit."[37] From 1907 to 1929, twenty-eight states passed laws allowing the sterilization of those deemed mentally incompetent and criminally insane. This is years before Germany passed its laws. More than fifteen thousand individual Americans were sterilized, most against their will while being incarcerated or living in mental homes.

One of the most famous cases in American judicial history was the 1927 Supreme Court case *Buck v. Bell*. Carrie Buck was a seventeen-year-old woman living in Virginia, supposedly mentally retarded (a matter of great dispute today), who had become pregnant outside of wedlock (she was actually raped by a member of the family who was taking care of her). After giving birth, it was decided that she was mentally incompetent, and this had led to her "loose" lifestyle. Harry Laughlin, a well-known eugenics advocate, testified against Carrie saying that she belonged to the "shiftless, ignorant, worthless, class of anti-social whites of the South."[38] The case was appealed to the Supreme Court, who voted 8–1 to uphold the legality of the sterilization of Carrie Buck (who was sterilized about two miles from where I am sitting in Lynchburg, Virginia). In his opinion, Justice Oliver Wendell Holmes wrote

36. Dyck, "Eugenics," 27.
37. Quoted by Dyck, "Eugenics," 26.
38. Pence, *Classic Cases*, 389.

the infamous line, “Three generations of imbeciles is enough.” He went on to state, “The principle that sustains compulsory vaccination is broad enough to cover cutting the fallopian tubes.”[39] Attorney Paul Lombardo has written a convincing argument that the whole case of *Buck v. Bell* was fabricated from the beginning, for the very purpose of bringing the eugenics issue before the Supreme Court and getting its blessing and approval.[40]

Toward the closing days of World War II, the world began to learn of the Nazi atrocities all in the name of “eugenics.” The term began to disappear from the names of organizations, as it became associated with racism and Nazism. However, eugenics itself did not end and as genetic research began to grow in the ’50s, ’60s, and ’70s, a new form of coercion began to appear arguing for genetic therapy and enhancement. Arthur Dyck writes: “Currently, and in the future, eugenics in the United States is, and will be, voluntarily carried out by physicians and genetic counselors. Eugenics takes place in what are regarded as autonomous choices on the part of willing individuals. Without government interference, abuses and coercion occur and will continue to occur unless the ethical and legal climate changes markedly.”[41]

What kind of coercion is Dyck talking about? The coercion comes from the geneticist’s attitude itself. While condemning the Nazi eugenics on the one hand, geneticists are promoting genetic enhancement on the other hand. “Coercion need not come from governments, but from the very concepts that geneticists, physicians, and health professionals tend to share as they implicitly or explicitly practice negative eugenics.”[42] Dyck demonstrates this by comparing the three primary principles behind Nazi eugenics with the 1978 book *On Human Nature* by E. O. Wilson, a leading founder of sociobiology at Harvard University. All three principles can be found in Wilson’s book. Dyck concludes, “The foregoing analysis leads me to one final set of observations. It is misleading to speak of the dangers of repeating the history of eugenics. Eugenics is not simply a matter of history. Eugenics is practiced today.”[43]

It is my conclusion that every effort should be made to avoid any kind of enhancement intervention. It may not always be easy to tell where to draw the line between therapy and enhancement, but I believe many cases are obvious.

39. *Buck v. Bell*, 274 U.S. 200 (1927).
40. Paul Lombardo, “Three Generations, No Imbeciles: New Light on *Buck v. Bell*,” *NYU Law Review* 60, no. 1 (1985): 30–62.
41. Dyck, “Eugenics,” 30.
42. Dyck, “Eugenics,” 33.
43. Dyck, “Eugenics,” 37.

Some have tried to arrive at criteria. John Feinberg attempts to establish a theological criterion which states: "Any use of this technology to fight something in human beings that is clearly a result of the consequences of sin and living in a fallen world is morally acceptable."[44] James Peterson attempts to arrive at five criteria for distinguishing between therapy and enhancement: incremental progress, choice expanding, parent-directed, within societal boundaries, and by acceptable means.[45] While I believe both criteria have problems, I believe they are a start in clarifying an important issue. In previous chapters we have said the goal of medicine is to cure, not to kill. In genetic intervention our aim should be to cure, not to enhance.

44. John Feinberg, "A Theological Basis for Genetic Intervention," in Kilner, Pentz, and Young, *Genetic Ethics,* 187.
45. Feinberg, "Theological Basis," 187.

9

Principled Patient Treatment: Clinical Ethics

Up to this point, this book has been concentrating on examining the major topics in bioethics. These are general bioethical questions of national and international importance: abortion, euthanasia, assisted procreation, etc. In this chapter, we turn to an assortment of practices that take place regularly in the clinical environment where patients interact with health-care practitioners daily. While it is important to discuss the major topics, most of us will not deal with many of those topics very often if ever in our own lives. However, these practices are part of the regular process of health care each time we enter a clinical setting. Therefore, it is important to have a good foundation for an ethic of clinical practice.

INFORMED CONSENT

The nurses on a particular medical unit always try to sit down and talk to patients before they begin their chemotherapy. Depending on the patient's ability to understand and accept information about the side effects of chemotherapy, the information they provide is more or less detailed.

In John Coughlin's case, the nurses felt that they had a responsibility to give more instruction than he had received from the doctor. However, Mr. Coughlin, a forty-nine-year-old carpenter, was extremely anxious about receiving chemotherapy at all. He tried to keep his mind and conversation on other things and would only say, half joking, that he was sure that the chemotherapy was going to turn him into a "sniveling idiot."

After consulting with a colleague, Diane Fetterson, a staff nurse, decided that Mr. Coughlin did not want detailed information about certain side effects and possible complications. Therefore, before his chemotherapy began, Diane explained that he might become nauseated, he might lose some of his hair, he might not feel like eating, and he would need to drink many fluids. However, she did not tell everything she might have told other patients. She withheld more detailed information that she thought would be needlessly distressing to Mr. Coughlin in his present state and which he, himself, had left the impression that he did not want to know. As Diane put it, she was sure that he did not want to know all the "gory side effects that could occur."[1]

In this case, a question arises on how much to tell a patient about a particular treatment plan. The nurse involved wants to protect the patient from any unnecessary anxiety that might ensue from hearing about the possible unpleasant side effects of chemotherapy. Her desire is to do good. However, this conflicts with the patient's need to be informed about the treatment plan so that he can make an informed decision whether or not to undergo it. The principles in conflict are respect for autonomy versus non-maleficence. Several questions need to be addressed in attempting to resolve this conflict: When, if ever, is it appropriate to withhold information from a patient? How does one determine when the situation warrants it? In this case, the decision was made based on the nurse's own opinion that it would be "needlessly distressing" to the patient who "left the impression that he did not want to know." Is that an adequate indication on which to decide not to provide information on a treatment plan?

Informed consent is one of the most important principles in bioethics, and yet it is often misunderstood or trivialized by many health-care workers and patients. Many think that it is accomplished simply by having the patient sign a form and that its primary purpose is to protect the health-care worker from getting sued down the road if the patient is unhappy with the outcome of the procedure. However, the primary purpose of informed consent is not to protect the health-care worker; it is to preserve respect for patient autonomy

1. Martin Benjamin and Joy Curtis, *Ethics in Nursing*, 3rd ed. (New York: Oxford University Press, 2002), 71.

and autonomous choices by patients. The concept grew out of the atrocities performed on prisoners in the German concentration camps of World War II. During the doctor trials that were held at the end of the war in Nuremberg, Germany, a set of medical principles concerning research on human subjects arose that became known as the Nuremberg Code. The most important principle was informed consent: persons could not be experimented on without being informed of the parameters of the experiment and giving his or her consent to submitting to the experimental procedure. The principle soon spread from medical research to all medical practice. The principle also has two other purposes: to protect patients from harm and to encourage medical professionals to act responsibly. But it has never been the purpose of informed consent to protect the health-care worker from a malpractice suit.

In the medical context, informed consent is an autonomous authorization of a medical intervention or involvement in research by an individual person. Authority implies both knowledge and power. A person can only authorize that which she knows about and that which she has the power to authorize. Hence, informed consent is the primary means by which an individual expresses her autonomy.

Informed consent is more than assenting to a medical procedure. It is possible to agree to undergo a medical procedure without having any understanding of the particulars of the procedure. Autonomous authorization implies that one has a substantial understanding of what she is authorizing. Informed consent is also more than effective consent. Effective consent is merely following the institution's legal process to obtain a consent, that is, signing a consent form. Again, it is possible to sign such a form without a substantial understanding or under some form of duress. While it may be legally binding, one may not have honored the spirit of informed consent in obtaining a signature. Autonomous authorization involves a contractual agreement between the patient and physician concerning a specific treatment plan that the patient is aware of and agrees to. In a very real sense, the patient is saying to the physician, "I would do this procedure to myself if I had the knowledge, skills, and abilities to do so. You, who have these attributes, are standing in my shoes."

Informed consent as an autonomous authorization is given if the following five criteria are met:

1. The patient has the capacity to make an informed decision.
2. The patient has a substantial understanding of the procedure.

3. The patient is in substantial absence of control by others.
4. The patient intentionally chooses the procedure.
5. The patient authorizes a professional to perform the procedure.

These five criteria can be organized around three stages of informed consent: the threshold stage, the informational stage, and the consensual stage.

The first stage in obtaining informed consent is to determine if the patient is competent enough to be able to give an autonomous authorization for a medical procedure. It is referred to as the threshold stage because before we consider the other elements of informed consent, we need to make sure the patient is competent to make a decision. If she is not, then we need not consider the other elements. Obtaining consent is not a necessary step for those who are not able to give consent. The basis for deciding will be on other ground which we discuss below.

When we speak of a person's competence, we are referring to her ability to perform a task or make a decision.[2] Competency is not an all-or-nothing ability; it comes in different degrees. One can be totally incompetent such as a patient in a coma or persistent vegetative state. One could be in a state of limited competency such an individual who is mentally handicapped due to a genetic defect since birth. Such an individual may be able to make some basic decisions about preferences or desires but may not be able to make reflective life choices. An individual may be competent but temporarily incapacitated such as a temporarily unconscious individual or an individual whose judgment is currently impaired due to drugs or alcohol. Finally, one can be totally competent and in complete control of his faculties. It is because there is such a wide continuum of competency levels that it is not always easy to determine exactly what level an individual might be in and how much consent he can realistically be responsible for. Professional help in the form of psychological or psychiatric assessment may be necessary to determine a patient's competency.

This raises the question of what standard should play in determining competency. Traditionally three standards have been suggested. The outcome

---

2. While competency and capacity are often used synonymously, there is a technical distinction between the two terms. Competence is a legal term that is generally used in all areas of a person's life and is more encompassing. Capacity is a clinical term that is more situation or context specific. An individual can be deemed legally incompetent while not necessarily being incapacitated, such as a child. However, if one is incapacitated then they are also incompetent, even if for a temporary amount of time.

standard measures an individual's competency based on the outcome of his or her decision. If the decision would result in an outcome that reflects values not widely held or rejects conventional thinking, the patient's competency may be called into question. This standard is problematic in that it assumes a specific view of values, those "widely held," as the only correct ones and may deny values important to other cultures that might be in the minority. For example, Jehovah's Witnesses have strong religious convictions that have had a longstanding historical tradition about not accepting blood transfusions. While such a view may not be "widely held" within the medical community, to declare that a Jehovah's Witness is incompetent for adopting a religious view would be tantamount to religious discrimination.[3]

The second suggested standard for determining competency is the category standard. This standard determines competency by arriving at predetermined categories in which individuals are determined as competent or not based on which category they belong to. If the patient is in a certain category of society, such as the mentally disabled, the elderly, or adolescence, they may be judged as incompetent. There is something to be said for this standard, for there is no doubt we can readily judge the competency of some individuals based on some categories—for example, infants. However, the danger with this standard is the tendency to expand the categories into areas where assuming incompetency is not so clear. For example, not all elderly individuals are at the same competency level. One can have a ninety-year-old whose memory and judgment are seriously problematic and one can have another individual of the same age whose memory and judgment are sharp and lucid. Adolescence is notoriously problematic in being categorized in this manner. Courts have recognized that while eighteen years of age is often the legal standard for adulthood, many adolescents have shown mature reflection and judgment at ages of fifteen and sixteen. The whole concept of the emancipated minor is based on this concept.[4] Category thinking like this is often just too simplistic to base an evaluation of competency.

---

3. This should not be taken to assume that society must be open to any view that a person declares must be respected. The courts have held that there is a difference between a traditional religious or other comprehensive view promoted by a recognized group and adopted over a lengthy period and some *ad hoc* view that does not have any real history or credibility.
4. An emancipated minor is an adolescent who has not achieved the legal age to be considered an adult, but is recognized by the court as having the ability to make adult decisions and therefore is legally granted the freedom and responsibilities of adults.

The third standard is the functional standard: a patient is judged as competent if they can function as a decision-maker in a given context. If the patient is unable to function as a normal decision-maker in this context, he or she may be judged as incompetent in this context. If the context is temporary, the patient may be judged as competent but incapacitated. The specific course of action would depend on the length of incapacitation in relation to the need for treatment. This standard seems the best approach to the question of competency for it treats each individual as a unique person rather than grouping him into some predetermined artificial category or judging him by some assumed conventional standard. The person's own values and ideas are allowed a place to be considered in his decision concerning treatment.

What criteria should be used in determining that the patient can function as a decision-maker? Three general criteria are usually applied. First, does the patient *understand* the relevant information (diagnosis, proposed treatment, and prognosis) to make a decision? It is important to note that the information must be presented in terms the patient can understand. Just because a patient is not familiar with medical terminology does not mean he cannot understand what is going on and what is being proposed. One can test this understanding by just asking the patient if they can explain back to you what he understands to be the problem and proposed treatment. Second, is the patient willing and able to *communicate* with caregivers about the decision he is making? Is there ambiguity, indecision, or vacillation in his tone of voice? In communicating, does the patient exhibit a thought disorder or memory problem? If the patient cannot or will not communicate with caregivers, then that might be a sign of incompetence. Third, is the patient able to *reason* about the decision as well as other relevant alternatives against a background of reasonably stable personal goals and values? Is he able and willing to give reasons for the decision made (either consent or denial)? Is the patient suffering from psychosis, dementia, extreme phobia, anxiety, depression, or anger which may affect his reasoning? Again, such conclusions may require an expert in the field. However, it should be clear that the patient's reason does not have to be one with which caregivers may agree. So long as it is rational within the context of the patient's worldviews, it should be considered as valid. As Christians, we need to remember that God respects our free will to form worldviews and live in accordance with those worldviews, even if they go against what we believe to be God's commands and will.

Before moving on to discuss the next stage of informed consent, we need to briefly consider decision-making for the incompetent patient. When a patient cannot make medical decisions for himself, then a proxy must make the decision for him. No matter who that person is, a standard needs to be used by which one makes the best decision. Two standards have come down as far as making decisions for incompetent patients. First, and most preferably, is the substituted judgment standard. The decision is made by a proxy who attempts to be a substitute for the patient himself in light of the patient's specific wishes and desires. The patient's own values can shape the decision. This is used in cases where the patient has made his wishes known either by living will, durable power of attorney, or through discussion with family and/or the physician. The proxy does her best to implement the treatment plan as best accords with the expressed desires of the patient.[5]

However, there are times when a patient's desires are unknown. Either they have not communicated their wishes, or the situation is such that we cannot retrieve the document or person to whom it was communicated in time. In these cases, caregivers will often appeal to the best interest standard. The decision is made by a proxy considering what is deemed in the best interests of the patient according to an accepted general standard. It is difficult to make any detailed decision by the best interest standard as there is no accepted consensus on most detailed procedures. Different individuals have different sets of values that determine what their treatment preferences might be. However, most persons would generally agree with two values that are universal: (1) most would choose life over death, and (2) most would choose comfort over pain. Therefore, the heart of the best-interest standard is guided by these two general principles to do what can be done to keep patients alive and pain-free as much as possible. Of course, the difficulty arises when these two come into conflict and one cannot keep both. As Christians, the sanctity-of-life principle is perhaps one of the most foundational principles in moral thinking and therefore it will generally trump when there is conflict. There may be times when we might allow death to come, but Christians should be diligent not to take action that would hasten death and violate this principle. The best-interest standard is not ideal, but often it is the only choice available.

Who is qualified to perform the obligations of a proxy for a patient judged as incompetent to make a decision concerning medical treatment? The first

5. We are discussing primarily patients who were at one time competent and have now become incompetent. The case is similar but more complicated for patients who have never been competent. For an excellent discussion of such cases see Eike-Henner W. Kluge, "Incompetent Patients, Substitute Decision Making, and Quality of Life: Some Ethical Considerations," *Journal of Medicine* 10, no. 10 (2008): 237–46.

preference is for an individual appointed to do so as durable power of attorney assigned by the patient. This can be any competent adult individual the patient chooses. Durable power of attorney gives an individual the moral responsibility and legal power to act and make decisions on behalf of another individual.[6] If there is no durable power of attorney available, then the next preference is a close family member. This can be a spouse, adult child, parent, or significant other. While this is often acceptable there may be legal issues if it is called into question. If no personal relation is available, the physician would just have to act as proxy himself. This might be the case in a medical emergency. Since it is likely the physician does not know the patient well, she will appeal to the best interest standard as the basis for her decision. If there is a conflict involved in patient care, a hospital ethics consultation group or committee could be involved. The purpose of such a committee is not to tell anyone what to do, but to act as a mediating agent to help resolve any conflicts and reach a consensus on what is best for the patient. Finally, if all else fails, courts may get involved. This is the least preferable means to reach a decision. Judges generally do not care to rule on patient care.

Once a patient has been judged as competent, the next stage of informed consent is the informational stage which involves two elements: disclosure of information and ensuring understanding on the part of the patient. The principle of veracity, both legally and morally, includes the obligation to disclose all risks and costs involved in any medical procedure to which the patient must consent. This obligation includes three general aspects: comprehensiveness, accuracy, and objectivity in disclosure, as well as the manner in which disclosure is made. It also may include other reasonable alternative procedures, if any exist, as well as disclosure of risks if the patient decides not to undergo the procedure (costs/benefits).

This raises the question of our opening case: How much is a physician required to disclose? Obviously, some sort of balance and standard needs to be arrived at. On the one hand, a patient does not need to have a full medical education and on the other hand, as an aspect of autonomous authorization he needs a substantial amount of information. Over time, several standards

6. It is highly encouraged that every adult should assign a trustworthy individual durable power of attorney should they become incompetent. It can be either a close family member or friend, but it should be someone who is generally available. In most states, simply signing a form designating such an individual and signed by both parties (and possibly witnessed by a third party) is all that is necessary. The form should be kept in an available location if needed.

for determining the necessary amount to disclose have been suggested. The standard with the longest history was the professional practice standard. Adequate disclosure is determined by customary rules or traditional practices of the professional community. Doctors would decide as a group what they felt was an adequate disclosure of a treatment or procedure. This standard arises from a strong paternalistic tradition within the history of medicine, where the physician was seen as the captain of the ship, making all the decisions, and the patients were to merely acquiesce to his decisions. In the 1960s and '70s, as the patient's rights movement began to take hold, many became critical of this standard because it is all in the hands of the doctors.

One of the most well-known cases involving informed consent occurred in 1972, *Canterbury v. Spence*. A patient was experiencing back pain and surgery was recommended. The treating physician did not disclose all the risks involved with the surgery. During the surgery, the physician found that the patient's spinal cord was in very bad condition. The physician did what he could to relieve the swelling. While the patient was recovering, he slipped off the bed and became paralyzed. It was argued that even without this accident, the chances of paralysis can be anticipated at around 1 percent of all cases, which the physician allegedly did not disclose. The lower court ruled against the patient because of a lack of evidence showing medical negligence. The case was appealed, and the court reversed, finding that a material risk should have been disclosed and a reasonable person in the patient's position would attach significance to the risk when determining whether to undergo the procedure.[7]

This case has shaped the standard for informed consent from a legal perspective and gave rise to a new standard for disclosure, the reasonable person standard. Adequate disclosure is measured by the significance that a hypothetically average, reasonable person would attach to a risk in deciding whether to submit to a procedure. In the *Canterbury* case five items were stated of which the patient must be informed:

1. the condition being treated
2. the nature and character of the proposed treatment or surgical procedure
3. the anticipated results of the treatment or surgical procedure

7. *Canterbury v. Spence*, 464 F.2d 772 (United States Court of Appeals for the District of Columbia, 1972).

4. the medically recognized possible alternative forms of treatment
5. the medically recognized serious possible risks, complications, and anticipated benefits involved in the treatment or surgical procedure, including nontreatment

However, while this is considered a vast improvement of the professional practice standard, many argue that it is social fiction to believe one can arrive at a "hypothetically average, reasonable person." Such a person does not really exist. It is an assumption, many argue an arrogant assumption, that some make that they are aware of what the average person thinks. It is argued that it is too easy to assume that we are average and then impute our beliefs on all of humanity.

A third standard has recently arisen, the subjective person standard. Adequate disclosure is determined by what a patient in a particular situation or context would consider significant to know in order to attach a risk factor in deciding to submit to a procedure. This standard is best in principle, for it attempts to determine what this patient would consider being adequate disclosure. However, it is a difficult standard to put into practice. How do we determine what the patient would want to know? It seems we would have to discuss this with the patient, but we find ourselves caught in a vicious circle because the patient would need to know the information in order to know if he thinks it is necessary to know it.

There may not be a perfect problem-free solution to the problem. We may have to settle for the best alternative while recognizing its limits and this might be a compromise between the reasonable person standard and the subjective person standard. In general, we should err on the side of giving too much information while keeping communication lines open with the patient as to how far to go. Certainly, the five elements arrived at through *Canterbury* are a good starting point. We should also maintain the guideline that the patient needs to be verbally clear about the information they do not wish to know. This is not the time one should "read into" what they believe the patient would want to know.

The second element of the informational stage is ensuring understanding on the part of the patient. To understand, in the sense we are using it, is simply to have a substantial amount of knowledge to be able to reason, decide, and act upon our decisions. The question of what it means to say "I know" is one that philosophers have been debating for centuries and it is outside the purpose of this chapter to delve extensively into this debate. We can be confident in adopting a traditional definition of knowledge adopted by Plato that has come down through the centuries. It is often referred to as the tripartite definition of knowledge as justified true belief. This means that to say we know something is to say, first, that I believe it is true, second, it really is true, and third I have good reasons for believing it. Notwithstanding some problems and questions concerning this definition of knowledge,[8] it will hold as a conceptual foundation for the understanding a patient should have before rejecting or affirming a treatment plan.

Understanding does not need to be complete but should be substantial, detailed, and accurate. It should include the essential, but not necessarily the trivial. One does not need certainty in order to say one knows in the sense we are speaking. In the absence of defeaters,[9] one can say they understand the basic facts if they have justified true beliefs about them. The five elements listed under the *Canterbury* case are the kinds of things a patient should have a good understanding of in approaching a treatment decision.

This is a good place to point how the burden or responsibility of the informed consent process shifts as we go through it. The elements of competency and disclosure were mainly the responsibility of the physician or another caregiver. However, when we come to understanding, the responsibility begins to shift more to the patient. Health-care workers still have a part to play in ensuring an environment in which understanding can be fostered. Communication needs to be in a language that is accessible to the patient without oversimplification. The health-care worker should check to make sure the patient understands by conversing with her about the treatment plan, asking her probing questions that will assess her understanding, and further explaining and clarifying questions and concepts for the patient. However, the patient begins to take much of the burden on herself as she works to comprehend and understand the information she has been given. In the end, it is her responsibility to process it so that she can make an informed decision.

The third stage of the informed consent process is the consensual stage, which involves two elements: voluntariness and authorization. Voluntariness means that the patient has made the decision based on her own free will and

---

8. There have been many challenges to this basic understanding of knowledge such as Gettier counterexamples and recent debates on internalist and externalist forms of justification that we are ignoring for the time being.
9. A defeater is a proposition which, if true, provides evidence contrary to the belief we are holding. In the presence of defeaters, we are warranted in withholding a firm conviction about a belief. However, if we have good reasons for holding a belief as true and are absent of any defeaters or potential defeaters, then we can hold the belief with some conviction.

for reasons she believes are justified. It is a fully informed decision under the conception of understanding discussed above, and made without being under duress with no coercion or manipulation on the part of the health-care team. Of course, "fully voluntary" is an ideal. Patients are almost always affected by pressures outside of the procedure that come into play in decision-making. One cannot eliminate every obstacle, and our free choices are always limited in some sense. The goal is to provide an environment that will achieve a substantial amount of voluntariness in making the decision. Again, while the primary responsibility of voluntariness is on the patient, the health-care team needs to assure an environment where the patient is truly free to choose the treatment plan or procedure she deems best.

The last element of informed consent is authorization on the part of the patient. If we have successfully fulfilled the earlier elements and stages, then all that is left is for the patient to authorize a professional to act on her behalf—to empower him to step into her shoes and perform a procedure she would perform on herself if she could. Authorization assumes responsibility for what one is authorizing. You cannot authorize what you are not ultimately responsible for. Therefore, competency and understanding are key to being able to autonomously authorize. The goal of informed consent is met when the patient becomes responsible for the decision made. Assuming the physician does not act negligently, the patient is responsible for the outcome of her decision.

We have been discussing the moral duty of informed consent, but we should comment on the legal duties as well. Statutes and laws surrounding informed consent are primarily limited to informed consent forms. The Code of Federal Regulations states that "a properly executed informed consent form for the operation must be in the patient's chart before surgery, except in emergencies." In 2007, the Center for Medicaid and State Operations issued an interpretive guideline to be used in conjunction with the federal statute. Essentially, it says the following is required for an informed consent form:

- Name of the hospital
- Name and signature of the patient, or if appropriate, legal representative
- Name of procedure(s)
- Name of all practitioners performing the procedure and individual significant tasks if more than one practitioner
- Risks
- Benefits

- Alternative procedures and treatments and their risks
- Date and time consent is obtained
- Statement that procedure was explained to patient or guardian
- Signature of person witnessing the consent
- Name and signature of person who explained the procedure to the patient or guardian

All fifty states have statutes regarding informed consent. Most follow the same basic premise, requiring informed consent be given and signed off on a form pursuant to the aforementioned guidelines. There are some differences, such as the age of consent. Most states require a patient be eighteen years old, while Oregon allows a patient as young as fifteen years old, and Alabama and Nebraska require one be nineteen years old. These laws typically do not include emancipated minors. In addition, the states vary with regard to requirements for a person to be considered a legally authorized representative. Most states allow parents, spouses, and guardians to assume this role, but some extend this to relatives by marriage (Missouri, Oklahoma, and South Carolina), attending physicians (Arizona), and close friends (Florida, Colorado, Maryland, and West Virginia). It is imperative that every health-care provider is well-versed in his or her state laws regarding informed consent.

While informed consent is one of the most important duties regarding treatment of patients, there are times when one can be exempted from obtaining informed consent. Here are some examples of when an exemption to informed consent is warranted:

- Emergencies: when the patient is in a life-threatening situation and is unable to consent
- Incompetence: when the patient's capacity to consent is not functioning, then the process must use a surrogate decision-maker.
- Patient waiver: when the patient waives the right to know. In such cases the physician must be certain of this and should have carefully discussed this with the primary physician and health-care team. All waivers should be in writing.
- Therapeutic privilege: when the physician believes that informing a patient may pose a significant threat to his/her well-being. We will discuss this under the topic of deception below.
- National/state waivers: In general, it is recognized that no consent is needed for vaccination programs, newborn genetic screening, etc.

This is a good place to discuss a particularly sticky issue for many health-care workers: the right of a patient to refuse treatment. It is hard for many to conceive that a patient might actually refuse treatment that may be of benefit to him. Most of us just assume that everyone wants to be healthier and to have our disease and suffering treated and/or relieved. It is hard to imagine anyone denying treatment. However, many people decide, for various reasons, to forgo treatment, even if that treatment will increase their chances for living longer. The reasons can be varied. Some may refuse because they feel the treatment is too burdensome and the benefit just not worth it. Some may refuse based on moral or religious grounds. How should health-care workers respond to such refusals?

It is important to note that the right to an informed refusal of treatment is a corollary of informed consent. If one possesses the right to consent to treatment, one necessarily possesses the right to refuse it. Without its corollary, the right to informed consent is meaningless. What sense would it make to say that we must get a patient's permission to treat if he does not have the option of saying no? Respect for patient autonomy means we need to respect a patient's right to refuse if they so choose to do so. However, this should not imply that the patient can say or do anything they want. There are some moral, if not legal, parameters surrounding the manner in which a patient refuses.

First, it should be an informed refusal. The patient should not make any decision without adequate information. Such a decision would not be autonomous. Therefore, the stages of informed consent should be fulfilled before a decision is made and the patient has a moral obligation to hear the full case before reaching a decision. Once he has been adequately informed, a judgment can be rendered on the part of the patient and where to go from there. Second, the patient has a moral obligation to inform the health-care team of his decision to refuse and should offer an explanation as to why he is refusing. Some might argue that the patient does not need to explain himself, but it can be strongly argued that he does. A large amount of time and effort has been spent on diagnosing the patient and arriving at a treatment plan. Medical professionals have researched means of treatments. For a patient to refuse without any explanation is to trivialize and devalue the valuable work of medical researchers and physicians whose goal is to provide benefits. It is uncharitable and does not recognize medicine as God's gift. Therefore, patients owe some sort of an explanation as to why they are refusing treatment. If the patient is not able to offer an explanation, that may be a sign that they have not reached understanding yet on the procedure or treatment plan and may need more time to consider it. There may be emotional or other psychological obstacles that impede the patient's ability to make a decision. However, if they know, then they should tell.

The specific reasons a patient states for refusing treatment need not be in agreement with the values of the physician or of society as a whole. While they should be coherent reasons based on the consistently held beliefs of the patient, they cannot be deemed irrational or unreasonable merely because they disagree with the values of others. Often, religious views fit under this category. A prime example is the refusal of Jehovah's Witnesses to undergo a blood transfusion, especially when an injury is so serious that one is necessary to save a person's life. For many it seems foolish that a person would risk her life for a religious principle when a simple and standard procedure could save her from death. The temptation to force treatment on the patient in a situation like this can be overwhelming. However, many argue that this is just the time when the health-care team needs most to safeguard the patient's desires and autonomy. When the beliefs of the minority are threatened by the beliefs of the majority, we must be most diligent to make sure that everyone's autonomy is secured.

The most difficult question concerning the refusal of treatment concerns its limits. Is there a limit to honoring a refusal of treatment? Consider this well-known case. In July of 1973 Donald Cowart, nicknamed "Dax," a twenty-five-year-old Air Force pilot, was looking over a parcel of land with his father with the intention of purchasing it. The land was located near a gas refinery. Unbeknownst to Dax and his father, the refinery was leaking gas and the fumes had saturated the area. When they got in their car and turned the ignition, the area exploded in a ball of flame. Dax's father was killed instantly, but Dax survived though he was severely burned on more than 68 percent of his body. When a farmer stumbled upon him, Dax was in such intense pain that he begged the farmer to kill and put him out of his misery. The farmer said he could not do that. Dax was transported to a hospital where he was treated in their burn unit. Several times throughout the months of excruciatingly painful treatment Dax requested that treatment be discontinued and that he just be allowed to die. He would rather die than deal with the pain and a life of blindness, lameness, and the inability to use his hands. However, his requests were ignored. His mother insisted that he be kept alive and treated, and the doctors decided to follow her requests even though a psychiatrist declared Dax to be competent to make his own decisions. Eventually, Dax was released. He sued the gas company and won a significant settlement. It was enough for Dax to go to law school and become a lawyer, and today he defends patients whose refusal of treatments have been ignored. Even though his life became quite comfortable, he still insists that his requests to cease treatment and be allowed to die should have been honored.[10]

Dax's case is often employed by those who believe there is no limit to the right to refuse treatment. Any competent adult has the right to refuse any treatment at any time, no matter what the intentions or outcomes. Many ethicists agree with this view to the point where it is almost considered beyond debate. However, a small number of ethicists believe that such a view is extreme and that some limits might be prescribed in honoring patient's refusal of treatment. For example, some argue that if a third party might suffer significant harm or risk of harm in honoring a refusal of treatment, that one might be warranted in not doing so. An example might be a parent who has dependent children who would suffer from the loss of that parent. Others argue that unlimited honoring a refusal of treatment is unjustifiably raising autonomy to a level much higher than other principles such as non-maleficence and beneficence. The argument can be made that a patient has the right to refuse treatment except in cases where the *known* intention of the patient is to bring about significant harm to himself including causing his death, such as in the Dax case. In this case, duties of non-maleficence or beneficence may overrule a patient's right to autonomy. An argument might be made that a doctor's duty to keep a patient from harm, even self-harm, overrules the patient's autonomy even if the patient is competent. Should one decide not to honor a refusal of treatment, one might need to pursue a court order to force treatment on a patient and should be prepared for what could be a difficult battle.

The key distinction in not honoring a patient's refusal of treatment has to do with the important but often overlooked distinction between the *intention* or *aim* of one's actions and the *result* of one's actions. Gilbert Meilaender notes this important distinction in evaluating refusals of treatment:

> If I commit suicide (and am of sound mind), I intend to die. I aim at my death or choose death. But, of course, there might be occasions when, if I refuse treatment, I will also die. Both the act of suicide and the treatment refusal may *result*

10. You can read about "Dax's Case" in numerous sources. The best book is Lonnie D. Kliever, ed., *Dax's Case: Essays in Medical Ethics and Human Meaning* (Dallas: SMU Press, 1989), which contains many excellent essays about the ethics of refusal of treatment.

> in my death. Are they morally equivalent? Is treatment refusal the same as the forbidden suicide? Although they could sometimes be morally equivalent—I could refuse treatment *so that* I will die—they need not be.[11]

Intention is an important factor here. There is a difference between a Jehovah's Witness refusing a blood transfusion for religious reasons and Dax Cowart who refuses treatment because he wants to cause significant harm to himself, his death. The Jehovah's Witness does not want to cause harm to himself; he just wants to follow the dictates of his religion. If you can save his life through other means, he will accept it. Dax was requesting to die; death was his aim. On the other hand, it is perfectly reasonable for an individual facing the final stages of cancer to refuse further treatment that would be excessively burdensome without much benefit. He may know that an earlier death will likely result from his refusal, but as long as he is not aiming toward death, there is nothing morally wrong with recognizing there is a time to stop fighting against the inevitable.

The following guidelines should be followed concerning refusals of treatment:

1. Any adult competent patient has a right to refuse treatment when the elements of informed consent have been met. In cases where treatment is excessively burdensome and treatment offers little benefit, such a decision to refuse treatment is reasonable.

2. The patient has a duty to articulate as clearly as possible his/her reasons for refusal of treatment. Any coherent reason consistent with the patient's consistently held beliefs (personal, religious, social, or political) is an acceptable reason.

3. The right to refuse *may* be limited when the intention of the refusal is to cause significant harm or death to oneself or a third party might be significantly harmed by honoring such a refusal. In these cases the right to refuse may be infringed for reasons of non-maleficence or beneficence.

4. All refusals of treatment should be carefully witnessed and documented in writing.

---

11. Gilbert Meilaender, *Bioethics: A Primer for Christians*, 3rd ed. (Grand Rapids: Eerdmans, 2013), 69.

PATERNALISM

Sixty-seven-year-old Henry Young had suffered a stroke and was being kept under continual restraint in the hospital at the direction of Kirsten Bennett, the supervising nurse. A locking waistbelt was used, whether Mr. Young was in bed or in a chair. The belt was a "humane" design, permitting him as much freedom as possible while assuring that he could not fall out of the bed or chair.

Mr. Young had had a fall earlier in this hospital stay, having attempted to walk while unattended. He was only slightly injured in this episode, but because of the possibility of serious injury that such a fall presents, Kirsten required him to be restrained in the waistbelt whenever he was left unattended, even for a very short period. Mr. Young vigorously protested that he was being deprived of his dignity, that he felt as if he were in prison, that he was afraid of being unable to escape in the event of a fire, and that he was perfectly competent to be left free and responsible for his own safety. In response, Kirsten repeatedly told him that the restraint was a standard procedure for patients in his condition and that he had no choice in the matter as long as he remained in the hospital and his condition remained unchanged.

Underlying her decision was the fact that, as is not uncommon in such cases, Mr. Young's mental capacities seemed to swing back and forth so that sometimes he was undoubtedly competent to move about at liberty, but at other times he became confused and lost some degree of motor control. It had, in fact, been during such a confused period that he had suffered his earlier fall. Another important consideration was the fact that the nursing staff did not have the time to keep continual watch over him. Thus, as Kirsten explained to Mr. Young's family, the restraint was "for his own good" even though contrary to his wishes. All things considered, she maintained, it was best for him to be kept in the waistbelt, even during periods of mental clarity, in order to ensure that he would not, when unattended, lapse into mental confusion and seriously hurt himself. Mr. Young's family agreed with the supervising nurse and fully supported her decision.[12]

The aim of informed consent is to honor the patient's autonomy and the fulfilling of her preferences and desires. So, it might seem odd at first glance to move next to a discussion about infringing on patient desires and taking action contrary to her choices. In the case above, the nurses are exercising paternalism by placing the patient in restraints in order to protect him from harming himself. This case raises a number of questions: Was the action of Nurse Bennett justified in this case? Is it ever justifiable to overrule a patient's desire and wishes? How do we determine when it is justifiable and when it is not? If paternalistic actions are justifiable, what is the best way to go about performing them?

Paternalism is the infringing of a person's autonomous wishes or desires for beneficent or non-maleficent reasons. The term "paternal" means "like a father," and that is a good way to think of what is happening. The concept of paternalism is analogous to that of a parent to a young child. A young child is not capable of making choices in its best interests, so the parent limits the child and makes the choices for him. The assumption is that the parent is acting beneficently or non-maleficently for the child. When my daughters were younger, my wife and I restricted a number of their choices. For example, they could not cross the street without holding our hand. The reasons for the restriction was to protect them from running out in front of a car and being harmed. So, we were restricting their freedom to choose for their own welfare. That is the idea behind paternalistic actions in the medical context as well. Health-care workers may, at times, have to limit a patient's choices and actions for the good of the patient.

It is very important to note at this juncture that the patient's welfare is the only justifiable reason to act paternalistically. Actions that restrict patient choice and actions for other reasons are violations of a patient's autonomy, not infringements, and are never morally justifiable. Many of us have read or heard of horror stories of the elderly in assisted living situations being restricted to beds and chairs for hours and even days purely

12. Benjamin and Curtis, *Ethics in Nursing*, 55.

for the convenience of the staff. These actions could not even be called paternalistic but fall under the category of cruel treatment. Paternalism is always for the sake of the patient's good.[13]

It is because of such abuses that some advocate a stance known as anti-paternalism. Anti-paternalists hold that paternalism is never justifiable because it violates individual rights, unduly restricts free choice, and is too easily abused and institutionalized. It is this third reason that most concerns anti-paternalists. Many of them feel that once the option of restriction is available it will too easily become employed without serious consideration to the needs and desires of the patient. This is a legitimate concern. In the case above, note how Nurse Bennett communicated to Mr. Young that a locking waistbelt was "standard procedure" for patients in his condition. This communicates that Mr. Young's own needs and desires are not under consideration. He has been placed in a category, "those in his condition," and now will be treated according to institutional policy concerning persons in that category. This is not to deny that his movements may justifiably need to be restricted. But it should be for his good and not to fulfill an institutional policy, and this needs to be communicated to him.[14] Most medical ethicists believe that paternalism may be justifiable in some situations and that anti-paternalism is an extreme reaction against abuses in the name of paternalism. The best way to counter anti-paternalism is to take care and not abuse paternalism.

There are two types of paternalism. Weak paternalism is the obligation to prevent a patent's self-chosen conduct only when it is substantially nonvoluntary or nonautonomous and the patient might harm herself or others. This would obtain in cases where a patient is not adequately informed, her judgment is impaired, or she is suffering from depression even if the patient is autonomous in some respects. Three conditions help to determine if weak paternalism is justified in a particular context. First and primary is the autonomy condition: the patient is, under the circumstances, irretrievably ignorant of relevant information, or her capacity for rational reflection is significantly impaired. In the case above, it was noted how Mr. Young was at times

13. This not to imply that staffing considerations are not an important concern in making paternalistic decisions. It is just to note that ultimately paternalism is done in the best interest of the patient and not for the convenience or needs of the staff or institution.

14. I would advise that one never use the phrase "standard procedure" with a patient even if such a standard exists. It communicates the wrong message. If a patient questions the need for a procedure, one should explain why the procedure is necessary for that patient.

competent and able to make good judgments but at other times became confused and lost motor control. Given that it might be difficult to predict when he would lapse into periods of loss of judgment, it might be justifiable to place him in the locking waistbelt as a means of protecting him from injury even at times when his judgment appears to be good. However, given his concerns and objections, one should always seek a compromise and grant him the freedom from the belt. Perhaps family members and friends can be called upon to watch over and supervise him so the belt can be dispensed with. Paternalistic restraint might be necessary at times, but we should always seek for other options if possible.

The second condition for weak paternalism is the harm condition: the patient is likely to be significantly harmed unless a paternalistic intervention takes place. One needs to perform an assessment of both the magnitude and likelihood of harm in relation to the form of paternalism being advocated. It is important that such an assessment be realistic and objective. Of course, one cannot know if such a harm will take place and a large amount of the speculation should be based on the experience of the health-care worker and her knowledge of the patient. The greater the magnitude and likelihood of harm, the more justifiable paternalistic actions are warranted. In the case above, it seems that a significant harm with a high degree of probability is present and paternalistic action is likely warranted. Every effort should be made to gain as much knowledge and obtain as much objectivity on evaluating potential harms as is possible. Acting paternalistically should never be treated in a cavalier or casual manner. Depriving an individual of his freedom is a serious action. One of the most cherished values in modern times is personal autonomy, the freedom to choose. One should take any restriction of an individual's freedom very seriously and such a restriction should only be done when absolutely necessary.

The third condition is the ratification condition: it is reasonable to assume that the patient will, at a later time, with greater knowledge or the recovery of her capacity for rational reflection, ratify the decision to intervene by consenting to it. To ratify a decision is to approve or authorize it after the fact. The idea behind this condition is that at the time one needs to act paternalistically the patient might object due to her lack of judgment about what is in her best interest. However, sometime after the situation that warranted the paternalistic action has passed and the patient has regained her judgment, she will recognize the need for and approve of the action that was taken. Some question if the ratification condition is necessary or even realistically possible. Can we really predict with any level of certainty what a patient will think after a situation has passed? If the other two conditions are met, is the ratification condition even necessary? If the autonomy and harm conditions are met, one can justifiably perform a paternalistic action. Ratification, if it comes later, is an additional positive aspect, but is not necessary for paternalism to be justified.

The other type of paternalism is strong paternalism. Strong paternalism holds that it is sometimes proper to infringe on person's autonomy in order to benefit the person even if the individual is substantially autonomous. Not surprisingly, strong paternalism is much more difficult to justify as the patient is substantially autonomous. Unlike the case with weak paternalism, it is assumed that the patient is competent to make choices and decisions and those choices should be honored within the parameters of informed consent. While rare, most ethicists agree that strong paternalism can be justifiable if certain conditions hold. They usually list the following:

1. The patient is at risk of serious injury or illness.
2. The risks of harmful paternalistic actions to the patient are not substantial.
3. The projected benefits for the patient outweigh any risk of harm.
4. No feasible alternatives exist.
5. Any infringement of autonomy is minimal in relation to the possible harm.
6. Any paternalistic action involves the least infringement necessary in the circumstances.

An example of strong paternalism might be not honoring a patient's refusal of treatment if warranted. If it can be showed that the patient's decision would cause significant harm to himself, that the treatment would not place the patient at significant risk of harm, and that the patient's known intention is to harm himself, then, some argue, paternalistic action might be justifiable in this case. Again, this is a highly contested issue, and many would argue that even in this condition paternalism is not justifiable.

As important as deciding whether to act paternalistically is the method in which one performs paternalistic actions. Once a decision is made that paternalistic actions are warranted then one should employ a method that is appropriate to the context. By far the most preferable means of paternalism is rational persuasion. Rational persuasion is appealing to another's rational capacities in order to influence his or her behavior. In other words, we have a conversation with the patient and explain to her why we need to take steps to restrict their actions or choices. We seek for her agreement with our reasoning and persuade her to agree to allow the restriction in the current situation. This is the most preferable because it is the most honoring to the patent as a competent, reasonable decision-maker. She is agreeing to allow the paternalistic actions because she has been persuaded by good reasons that such actions are in her best interest. This means time and effort must be made on the part of the health-care worker to carefully explain why paternalistic actions are necessary. Some have wondered if this is just the same thing as informed consent. It is not. In informed consent, health-care workers give the patient information and then step back and let the patient choose. In rational persuasion, the health-care worker is doing more than just providing information. They are formulating an argument for why the patient should allow a paternalistic action and attempting to persuade the patient to agree with that argument. That is much more than informed consent.

Some have suggested that rational persuasion can best be employed in foreseeing a future occasion where the patient might not be competent and that he can authorize paternalistic actions beforehand. An example from literature might help. In Homer's *Odyssey*, we read the story of Odysseus and the Sirens. The Sirens were mythical cannibal creatures with beautiful voices from which no man could escape. If one heard them sing one was compelled to approach their island and upon approaching, would crash their ship on the rocks, whereupon the Sirens would capture and devour them. Odysseus desired to hear the Sirens and yet not get eaten. So, he commanded his men to put wax in their ears so that they could not hear and to lash him to the mast without wax in his ears. He told them that no matter how much he commanded them to row near the island, they were to disobey his commands and to continue to row past the island. The men obeyed and, in this way, Odysseus was able to survive hearing the Sirens. His men acted in a paternalistic fashion toward their commander with his permission. In the same way, rationally persuading a patient to allow paternalistic actions before the situation arises might give health-care workers the permission to act the same with their patients.

If rational persuasion is ineffective then two other methods of paternalism are available. The first of these is coercion. Coercion is the use of force or restraint on a person for the purpose of controlling actions and choices.

This force can come through several different means. Legal force can be used by getting a court order requiring an individual to submit to a paternalistic action. Physical force can be used as in the example of our case in using mechanical constraints. One can even use psychological force by using the threat of harm or physical force if the paternalistic action is not allowed. Coercion is never preferred and should be extremely rarely applied. However, it can be justified if the need warrants it and the patient rejects any attempt at rational persuasion. Again, one must always remember that the use of coercion is for the patient's welfare.

The third method of paternalistic actions is manipulation. Manipulation is a means of altering another's beliefs or behavior by subverting or bypassing his/her rational capacities and usually appealing to deception or emotions. There are two types of manipulation: deceptive and nondeceptive. Deceptive manipulation is a form of paternalism in which we control the beliefs and/or actions of an individual by allowing them to adopt or maintain a false belief. We discuss deception further below. Nondeceptive manipulation would involve irrelevant emotional appeals (to authority, pity, fear, ignorance) as well as charm and seduction to control the patient's choices and actions. Manipulation is the least justifiable form of paternalism for it completely disrespects the personhood or dignity of the patient. The person now becomes a thing to manipulate to achieve an end. However, while it is the least justifiable form of paternalistic actions, it is often the most commonly done. That is because it is usually easier to manipulate a patient than to take the time to rationally persuade her or to put in the effort and uncomfortableness often required in coercion. But coercion, if justifiable, is always preferable to manipulation. It is rarely, if ever, justifiable to insult a patient.[15]

On the next page is a chart comparing the three methods of paternalism.

15. I won't say manipulation is never justifiable, as it could be there is a justification for its usage that I am unaware of. However, I will say it is almost never justifiable. I cannot think of any situation where one is justified in manipulating a patient over honoring a competent patient as a reasonable adult.

RATIONAL PERSUASION	COERCION	MANIPULATION
Achieves a willing compliance for the right reasons	Achieves an unwilling compliance for the right reasons	Achieves a willing compliance for the wrong reason
Means more important than results	Results justify using undesirable means	Results more important than means
Preferable and justifiable	Not preferable, but sometimes justifiable	Not preferable nor usually justifiable

DECEPTION

Public health nurse Linda Stone first met Arlene Knox when she was referred to the county public health department by an emergency room nurse who was concerned that Arlene's bouts of intoxication might be harmful to her unborn child. Linda soon learned that Arlene had previously been addicted to heroin; but when her boyfriend threatened to leave her, she had stopped taking the drug. Shortly thereafter Arlene had become pregnant. Over a period of several months Arlene repeatedly told Linda that she was no longer drinking; but Linda, aware of Arlene's past need for drugs and suspicious that she had not actually stopped drinking, continually worked to educate her about the danger of alcohol to the baby.

After delivery, Arlene's doctor told her the baby had fetal alcohol syndrome. When Linda made a home visit a few days later, Arlene was still crying and distraught and asked Linda to reassure her that she had not harmed the baby, that he did not have fetal alcohol syndrome. Linda suggested that they both look at him, and she was surprised by his good health and vigor. He had none of the signs of the syndrome. She immediately began to suspect that the physician had lied to Arlene to shock her into an awareness of the seriousness of her drinking. Linda did not contradict the doctor but told Arlene to ask him again. She also calmed her by pointing out the baby's strengths and by reassuring her that she would help her learn ways to stimulate his development over the next year.

Later Linda phoned the physician and learned she was right in suspecting a ruse; any problem the baby might have from alcohol would probably be small. The doctor said he would tell Arlene the case was slight when he next saw her, but he had no intention of changing his story since it seemed to make her realize what could have happened and, as a result, seemed to have strengthened her resolve to stop drinking.

Linda knew that lying and shocking Arlene was no substitute for helping her deal with the problems underlying her drinking. However, Linda also thought that she should perhaps also lie to Arlene; she did not want to see Arlene drink excessively during another pregnancy and damage a child. Telling the truth might lead Arlene to believe she had no need to worry about the amount of alcohol she could consume during another pregnancy. Linda thought that she would begin to help Arlene with some of her underlying problems whether she contradicted the physician's story. After several days of deliberation, Linda finally decided to go along with the deception, since she reasoned it seemed to be in Arlene's best interest.[16]

One method of paternalism mentioned above was deception. The history of deception in the practice of medicine is very interesting and warrants its own section. As Christians we know that both the Old and New Testaments command us to be truthful in our dealings with each other: "You shall not bear false witness against your neighbor" (Exod. 20:16); "speaking the truth in love, we are to grow up in all aspects into Him who is the head, even Christ" (Eph. 4:15). However, some question if such commands are meant to be universal, or are there situations where deception is warranted and perhaps even required? In the above case the doctor was trying to do good: he was trying to get Arlene to think more seriously about her alcohol problem. He thought one way to achieve that goal was to scare her into realizing she had a

16. Benjamin and Curtis, *Ethics in Nursing*, 53.

problem. The nurse also recognized the problem and, in the end, went along with the doctor's deception. Is a good motive and a worthy goal enough to justify deception? What if it works and Arlene begins to deal with her problem? Doesn't that justify the deception? Is it ever right for health-care workers to deceive their patients for their own welfare?

First, we need to think about what it is about deception that makes it so wrong. It is not the consequences, because often deception can lead to good results (though many times it does not). Ultimately the reason deception is considered wrong is that it violates the principle of respect for autonomy. As we noted under our discussion of paternalism above, deception is a form of control. Whether it's withholding information, giving someone misleading information, or not correcting information one knows to be wrong, one takes the ability to make an informed decision away from the individual being deceived. A deceiver is a manipulator, in control of someone else's beliefs and ultimately any decisions based on that belief. In the case above that is exactly what the doctor, and ultimately Nurse Stone, are doing. They are manipulating and controlling Arlene to act in a particular manner. While the manner, in the end, may be good and healthier for Arlene, many ethicists question the means by which they are accomplishing this good. They reject the idea that good ends justify bad means. The principle of respect for autonomy holds that one should respect others as autonomous beings and allow them to make choices based on the values they have adopted. However, the principle is a *prima facie* principle and there may be times that it may be overridden by a competing moral principle. Perhaps deception might be justifiable in some situations. We will see below if our case would qualify as one of these.

Deception can be accomplished by three different means. The first is of these is lying. Defining a lie can be more complex than one might first suppose. Two different definitions of lying are possible. The first is what we might call a broad definition of lying: verbalizing to a person or group of persons what one believes to be a falsehood with the intention of deceiving that person or group of persons. This definition needs unpacking. First, lying is a verbal form of deception. It is deceiving by putting into words a statement that one believes to be a falsehood. This can be done orally or in written form, but it must be verbal to constitute a lie (as we will see below, there are nonverbal forms of deception). Second, lying is communicating a fact or idea that one believes is false. This is important in evaluating a lie. Suppose I believe that they are charging for hamburgers at McDonald's today, as they normally do, but I communicate to you that they are giving them away for free today. I believe that to be false, so I am lying to you. However, what if it turns out that, unbeknownst to me, McDonald's really is giving away free burgers today? So, it turns out that what I communicated is, in fact, true. Did I lie? Yes, because I was communicating something I thought was false. Even though it turned out to be true, I was still lying.

The reason for this has to do with the third point I need to make about our definition: lying involves the intention to deceive. It is the intention that is important here, not whether or not the statement is true. I am still blameworthy of lying even if my lie turns to be true, if I was communicating it as a falsehood with the intention of deceiving another person. This is another reason why consequences should not play a factor in evaluating whether lying is good. Even if good consequences occurred and you got a free burger, I was still guilty of attempting to manipulate you with a lie. The importance of intention also brings out the difference between a lie and a mistake. It is possible for me to communicate a falsehood accidently. I might believe a fact to be true that turns out to be false. As long as my intention is to communicate truth, I am not guilty of lying. I am just wrong about it being true. There is no moral infraction committed by making a mistake.

There is another aspect of intention we need to consider under the definition of lying. We recognize that the intention to deceive can be used in another way that would not constitute a moral infraction. We sometimes refer to these as "social games." Let me use an analogy from football. In playing the game of football, often the quarterback will pretend to hand the ball off to the running back in order to fool the opposing defense to run after the wrong man. Anyone familiar with football will tell you there is nothing wrong with this move; the rules of the game of football allow for such a move. We do not classify this as moral deception; it is part of the game. There are social games we play as well where deception is allowed and is not considered a moral infraction. For example, to surprise someone with a gift or event, we might deceive them in order to not spoil the surprise element. This does not constitute deception, as we recognize it as part of the rules of this social game. While we are intending to deceive, this is a different level where there is not a moral infraction.

A second way we can define lying is narrower than the first: verbalizing to a person or group of persons who have a right to the truth what one believes to be a falsehood with the intention of deceiving that person or group of persons. Under this definition, a lie is a falsehood only if it is verbalized to a person or group of persons who have a right to the truth. Some argue that certain persons do not have a right to the truth. Those who would use the truth to do some moral wrong like harming others are an example of those who do not have a right to the truth. An example would be a criminal, an enemy combatant, or a terrorist. If a criminal would use information in order to perform a crime, one is justified in deceiving him. This is the justification that many appeal to when they leave lights on at home while they are out for the evening. They are attempting to deceive a person, whose intent is to break in and steal, into adopting the false belief that someone is at home. Those who often present this deception justify doing so by claiming the criminals do not have a right to the truth; therefore, no moral infraction has occurred. I once had a conversation with an undercover FBI agent who regularly lies to criminals about his identity, and he offered the same explanation. He did not think he was lying because bad guys don't have a right to the truth. Spies in warfare use the same explanation. This definition is highly debatable. One must delineate who does and who does not have a right to truth. What standard do we use to make such a distinction? What kind of certainty is necessary that the person will use the truth to do wrong? The challenge these questions present should give us pause before we adopt the narrow definition. For now, we will stay with the broader definition.

Lying is not the only way one can deceive another individual. A second means is pretension. Pretension is the intentional act of leading a person to adopt or maintain a false belief. Pretension is not verbalizing a falsehood as much as it is acting in a way toward another that intentionally causes the individual either to adopt a belief that is false or to maintain a false belief. An example might be where someone approaches and tells you something you know is not true. Rather than correct him, you either say nothing, allowing him to continue in false belief or say something that, while not a direct lie, confirms his false belief. To act in this manner is to act pretentiously. Some will attempt to justify these actions by claiming, "Well, I didn't lie. I just didn't say anything." However, while one may not have lied, one did deceive. Pretension is broader than lying because it considers nonverbal communication and leading people on while not specifically verbalizing a direct lie.

Because of its passive nature, pretense not involving lying is generally easier to justify then lying. It does not seem to threaten the trust in a relationship as deeply. Lying is more direct and forthright than a pretense where someone is allowed to believe a falsehood. One might justify acting in a pretentious manner by acknowledging that it is not his place to correct a person's false belief, especially if such a correct might betray a confidence.

Some argue that while I have a moral obligation to tell the truth and not lie, I do not have a moral obligation to go around correcting every person's false beliefs. That being the case, there are many situations and relations where one may have an obligation based on the nature of the relationship to correct an individual's false belief rather than allowing them to continue in that belief.

The third form of deception, and one very much part of medical practice, is intentional nondisclosure. Nondisclosure is the intentional withholding of information that a patient has a *prima facie* right to know. Most often this is done in cases where a poor prognosis is present and the physician deems it would be unnecessarily harmful to the patient to disclose the information to them. This has become such a common practice in the history of medical care that it has a name: therapeutic privilege. Therapeutic privilege has a long tradition in medical practice and states that a physician may intentionally and justifiably withhold information based on a sound medical judgment that to divulge the information would be potentially harmful to the patient. Many physicians of the past supported this privilege by arguing that medical information is part of the treatment a patient receives ("information is medicine") and as treatment it must be therapeutically administered, i.e., dosaged out according to need. The idea of therapeutic privilege comes from the strongly paternalistic view of medical care that dominated the history of medicine for centuries. The idea is that the primary physician is the "captain of the ship," and the health-care team and the patient are his crew and are to follow out his orders. Patient input was often seen as the patient getting in the way of the captain doing his job. If the captain felt that withholding information and even lying to the patient was therapeutically warranted, then that was what he did. It is interesting to note that statements about the obligation to be honest in dealing with patients did not appear until very recently in most medical codes of ethics.

Attitudes concerning nondisclosure have changed drastically in the last forty years when it comes to paternalism in general. Replacing the "captain of the ship" model is the shared decision-making model where all the information is shared with the patient as well as many other members of the whole health-care team. This fosters an environment of communication where informed consent is encouraged and respected. These attitudes can be seen by the dramatic change between two studies. In one study from 1961, 88 percent of physicians would not disclose a diagnosis of cancer.[17] In another

17. D. Oken, "What to Tell Cancer Patients: A Study of Medical Attitudes," *Journal of the American Medical Association* 175 (1961): 1120–28.

study performed eighteen years later, 1979, 98 percent of physicians said they would disclose a diagnosis of cancer.[18] The age of the therapeutic privilege is beginning to wane.

At times, an attempt is made to justify nondisclosure by appeal to family wishes. Often the family will believe that it is best that a loved one not be informed of a diagnosis or prognosis and may pressure the doctor or a health-care team not to share the information with their loved one. However, except for children, this is rarely morally justifiable above the patient's stated autonomous need to know. The physician might be justified to not disclose if it is therapeutically justifiable, but the obligation to disclose remains if there is no therapeutic reason to withhold. Family reasons do not usually fall into that category.

Of all the forms of deception, perhaps nondisclosure is the most justifiable as it often depends on special relationships and responsibilities. We all have zones of privacy and one is certainly not obligated to disclose private information to strangers. However, the obligation to disclose becomes more stringent when one begins to consider more close and intimate relationships. Most would agree that spouses have an obligation to disclose at least some important personal information (health, financial information, familial information, etc.) to each other as it might affect the other partner in a significant manner. The same is true on the professional level. There is often a contractual relationship in which the obligation to disclose is present. The nature of the relationship places obligations to disclose on some but not on others. Hence, a physician has a strong obligation to disclose prognosis and diagnosis to a patient whereas other members of the health-care team, such as the nurse, do not have such an obligation. This can sometimes cause conflicts as the health-care team may be aware of information they believe the patient has a right to know and needs to know, but which the physician has not informed them. Our case above demonstrates such a conflict. Such conflicts should be resolved as soon as possible, but a general guideline is that the health-care team should not act contrary to the primary physician's decision to withhold information. This is a *prima facie* general principle and might be overridden of the situation warrants it.

Many arguments have been offered in favor of deceiving in the medical context, but we will explore the three most common. Perhaps the most common argument, the one that underlies therapeutic privilege, is the

18. D. H. Novack, R. Plumer, R. L. Smith, et al., "Changes in Physicians' Attitudes toward Telling the Cancer Patient," *Journal of the American Medical Association* 241 (1979): 897–900.

argument in favor of benevolent deception: deception is justifiable when it fulfills obligations of beneficence and/or non-maleficence. This argument has a long history. Note the following from the pen of Thomas Percival (1740–1804), who wrote the first modern code of medical ethics in 1803:

> Every practitioner must find himself occasionally in circumstances of very delicate embarrassment, with respect to the contending obligations of veracity and professional duty. . . . Moral truth, in a professional view, has two references, one to the party to whom it is delivered and another to the individual by whom it is uttered. In the first it is a relative duty, constituting a branch of justice and may properly be regulated by the divine rule of equity prescribed by our Savior, "do unto others as we would" all circumstances duly weighed, "they should do unto us." In the second it is a relative duty, regarding solely the sincerity, the purity and the probity of the Physician himself. To a patient therefore, perhaps the father of a numerous family, or one whose life is of the highest value to the community, who makes inquiries, which, if faithfully answered, might prove fatal to him, *it would be a gross and unfeeling wrong to reveal the truth. His right to it is suspended and even annihilated; because its beneficial nature being reversed, it would be deeply injurious to himself, to his family, and to the public.*[19]

According to Percival, if some form of deception reduces anxiety, or helps in keeping patients from performing reckless acts like suicide, then nondisclosure is justifiable. This is a purely consequentialistic argument. If deception produces good consequences—in this case, causes less anxiety—then it is morally justifiable. However, there are some serious objections to the argument. First, there is the problem that plagues all consequentialist approaches to ethics and that is that one simply cannot know what the consequences of one's actions will be with any certainty. One might be able to guess with a certain amount of probability but cannot know if telling a patient the truth, especially if done in the right manner, will produce the negative results that one assumes they will. Secondly, this violates the person's autonomy and the principle of veracity. As a result of misinformation, they cannot make an informed choice. It's highly paternalistic and manipulative under the guise of doing good. Thirdly, it can actually lead to bad consequences. It's always assumed the deception will be successful. However, many times it is not.

19. Thomas Percival, *Medical Ethics: Or, a Code of Institutes and Precepts, Adapted to the Professional Conduct of Physicians and Surgeons* (1803), 165–66, emphasis added.

What happens when the deception is discovered? On top of the original anxiety, you now have the additional problem of a lack of trust on the part of patient toward health-care workers, and this can even more far-reaching bad effects than telling the truth might have presented. A final objection is that this confuses harm with hurt. For while it is true that deceiving an individual might keep them from being hurt, it is still harming them by taking control away from them, misinforming them, and not respecting their autonomy.

A second argument often given in favor of deception is based on the epistemic, communication, and/or time limitations on the part of the physician or patient. It usually goes something like this, "Requiring the physicians tell patients the whole truth is unrealistic. Physicians cannot know the 'whole truth' about diagnosis and prognosis, or if they could know it, they would not be able to communicate it or that the patient could not comprehend the 'whole truth' if they heard it." The main problem with this argument is that it bifurcates the issue into only two alternatives: either we tell the patient the "whole truth" or we are allowed to deceive them. However, this is a false dilemma assuming these are the only two possibilities. One does not require anyone to know that "whole truth" about anything. "Whole truth" is an ideal that is rarely achieved. That doesn't mean that we can't know a substantial amount of the truth to be able to make informed decisions. And it seems that if the physician can know enough to be able to diagnose and offer treatment, he should be able to communicate a substantial amount of this to the patient so that the patient can make an informed decision. There is often a hidden arrogance and eliteness to this objection that gives the impression that the doctor doesn't think his patient is smart enough to understand the intricacies of medicine. True, the patient has not had the physician's training and experience, but he should not then be treated like a novice schoolboy who "really can't understand." One may need to take the time to explain the information in a language the patient can understand, but in majority of cases, this should not be overly problematic and does not justify deception or withholding information.

The third argument in favor of deception is based on the idea that some patients do not want to know the truth about their condition or the details of treatment and they may indicate this through various signals, not just words. In fact, there are some who do not want to know even when they say they do. It is true that this is sometimes the case. I have a friend whose wife was diagnosed with a fatal cancer. She specifically stated that she did not want to know the prognosis or how long she had to live. Patients certainly have the right to refuse information. However, they need to specifically state that they do not want to know (and you should get such a statement in writing to avoid conflicts down the road should they challenge you about not being informed). One should never assume or guess that a patient does want to be informed. Also, a patient's desire not to be informed should never be taken as permission to deceive and misinform. It would be wrong to tell a patient she is "fine" because she requested not to know.

There are a few arguments against deception. For Christians, there is strong scriptural teaching that we should be honest in our relationships and that we should not deceive. Along with the passages mentioned above, we are told that God hates a lying tongue (Prov. 6:17) and that lying is against the biblical law and contrary to sound doctrine (1 Tim. 1:8–10). Satan is the father of liars and there is no truth in him (John 8:44). The story of Ananias and Sapphira (Acts 5:1–11) demonstrates that God takes deception very seriously. In fact, there is no place in Scripture where deception is ever justifiable. There are some who offer the story of Rahab the harlot (Josh. 2) and the story of the Hebrew midwives (Exod. 1:15–21) as examples of those who lied and were blessed for their lies. However, Scripture never says they were blessed for lying. The implication is they were blessed for their belief in God and his promises, and not for lying.[20]

Apart from the biblical injunctions against deception, there are some practical considerations that argue against health-care workers deceiving their patients. Dr. Worthington Hooker (1806–1867) is considered the father of American bioethics. He is known for having gone against the tide in his day and argued strongly against the use of deception in medical practice. In his classic work *Physician and Patient* (1849) he has an entire chapter titled "Truth in Our Intercourse with the Sick." In that chapter, he offers seven arguments against deception.

He begins by questioning two assumptions. First, against benevolent deception, it is not certain that being truthful with a patient will, in fact, be injurious to him. Even in cases where there is a strong probability of causing harm, this has not always occurred. Oftentimes health-care workers assume they know more about the patient then is warranted. People don't always react

20. Rahab declares her belief in God (Josh 2:8–14), and Hebrews 11:31 tells us Rahab was blessed for her faith. The same is true of the Hebrew midwives. Nowhere are we even told that they lied—what they said could in fact have been true. However, Scripture made it clear they were blessed because they feared God and allowed the boys to live, against the command of Pharaoh (Exod. 1:17–21).

in the way we think they might and many times they are stronger than we give them credit. Of course, a lot of this depends on the manner in which we communicate the truth. However, if presented in a timely manner and with appropriate support, often even the worst news can be tempered with comfort and care. Even if the truth "hurts" it does not mean it "harms," especially if it is necessary.

Second, it is often erroneously assumed that deception can always or generally be effectively carried out and be successful. This is even more difficult if others are involved in the deception, for the chances are greater that the patient will learn of the deception. Patients almost always eventually discover they have been deceived. Hooker writes:

> There are so many ways by which the truth can be betrayed, even where concerted plans are laid, guarded at every point, that failure is much more common than success, so far as my observation has extended. Some unguarded expression or act, even on the part of those who are practicing concealment, or some information communicated by those who are not in on the secret, perhaps by children, or by evidence casually seen, very often reveals the truth, or awakens suspicion and prompts inquiry which the most skillful equivocation may not be able to elude. The very air that is assumed in carrying out the deception often defeats the object.[21]

Third, Hooker argues, "If the deception is discovered or suspected, the effect upon the patient is much worse than a frank and full statement of the truth can produce." This is often the case. When we have bad or painful news to share with a patient, we can control the way the truth is communicated when we sit down and have a truthful, open discussion with him or her. We can share the truth in a loving and supportive manner and help them to explore options concerning treatment. However, if we deceive them by offering false information (and thereby false hope) or by not disclosing information they need to hear, they may find out through other means, abruptly and unexpectedly, in which there is little support or the often-necessary background information to adequately understand the situation. This almost always causes more stress, anxiety, and extreme actions.

Hooker's fourth argument considers another negative consequence of deception. What will the result be when the patient eventually discovers the

21. Worthington Hooker, *Physician and Patient* (New York: Baker and Scribner, 1849), 361.

deception? One result will certainly be the loss of trust between the physician and patient. "The moment that you are detected in deceiving the sick, you at once impair or even destroy their confidence in your veracity and frankness."[22] The trust relationship between patient and physician is one of the most important elements of good medical practice. However, once a patient discovers that he has been deceived by his physician that trust has been severely diminished if not completely destroyed. Now you have the not only the possibility of harm to the patient, which is what you were trying to avoid by deceiving him, but also greater harms because of the deception.

However, as Hooker's fifth argument shows, this trust problem moves beyond just the immediate consequences of deception to the doctor and patient and expands consequences to the public perception of the entire field of patient care. One recent source writing about the patient's trust of doctors states,

> Just 34 percent of U.S. adults polled in 2012 said they had "great confidence in the leaders of the medical profession," down from 76 percent in 1966, according to the report. And a survey of people in 29 countries found the United States ranked 24th in public trust of doctors. Just 58 percent of Americans surveyed said they "strongly agreed" or "agreed" with the statement that "doctors in your country can be trusted," versus 83 percent of people who said the same in top-ranked Switzerland, and 79 percent in runner-up Denmark.[23]

There is no doubt that there is a trust problem between physicians and the patients under their care. One contribution to this problem is the history of physicians not dealing honestly with their patients. Imagine how Arlene, in the case opening this section, would feel if she learns that she has been deceived by her doctor and nurse into believing that her son has fetal alcohol syndrome?[24] What are the chances she will believe the next doctor or nurse who talks to her? When you hear of cases like this, which occur more often than are imagined, it's not hard to see why the trust in doctors is very low.

---

22. Hooker, *Physician and Patient*, 365.
23. Anne Harding, "Americans' Trust in Doctors Is Falling," Live Science, http://www.livescience.com/48407-americans-trust-doctors-falling.html.
24. There are a few serious consequences involved in that opening case. How will Arlene treat her son throughout his life under the illusion of having fetal alcohol syndrome? It is likely that each time he has an issue socially or in school it will be attributed to a syndrome that he doesn't even have. He may easily develop the "victim" mentality where he sees himself as an invalid, blaming every problem on having a medical condition.

Hooker's sixth argument notes another consequence of deception. If deception is adopted as a common rule, that is, that the truth may be sacrificed in urgent cases, the very purpose of the deception will be defeated. Why? Because the deception's success is dependent on the patient assuming that he is being told the truth. However, if this practice is commonly accepted, then, as we noted above, there will be a general distrust of the physician's veracity, thereby defeating the purpose of deception. For deception to be successful, the patient must believe she is being told the truth. But if it is commonly practiced, no one will believe they are being told the truth. Lest one think that deception is not regularly practiced, experience says otherwise. Over years of teaching bioethics to nurses, many have confirmed to me that they *regularly* lie to their patients. As one nurse once said to me, "We have to lie. It's the only way we can usually get things done."

Hooker's final argument is a slippery-slope type of argument. Many times, slippery-slope arguments are not valid. However, in this case, it is justifiable as experience has shown that it is common. Hooker writes, "Once you open the door for deception, you can prescribe for it no definite limits. Everyone is to be left to judge for himself."[25] This certainly is not inevitable, and many will argue that they can control the amount of deception that they do. However, the reality is that when deception is successful it reinforces the idea of doing it again. "After all," we reason, "it worked last time I had a situation like this, so it will probably work this time as well." Soon we start to see similarities in other situations, and it is not long before deception becomes the normal way we handle multiple groups of problems. We are deceiving ourselves if we really think we can control deception once it begins to work. It is human nature to always look for the easiest way to deal with a problem.

Hooker concludes his denunciation against deception by affirming:

> I would remark on this that the infliction of pain [in telling someone the truth of their condition] is not in itself a moral act, but the purpose for which it is done gives it all the moral character that it has. Aside from this, it affects no moral principle, as the infliction of an injury upon the truth certainly does, independent of the object for which it was done. The infliction of pain then for a good purpose cannot be said to be doing evil that good may come—it is doing good.[26]

25. Hooker, *Physician and Patient*, 376.
26. Hooker, *Physician and Patient*, 381–82.

Hooker is making two points here. First, not all hurt is harm. While it may be painful to hear the truth, I am not doing something harmful to another; I am doing good by telling him what he needs to hear. It is similar to removing a splinter from my daughter's finger. It might be painful, but I am not doing evil that good may come, I am doing good. Second, a patient's right to informed consent (respect for autonomy), even though it may hurt to hear the truth, can overrule beneficence or non-maleficence.

Does this mean that all deception is wrong and unjustified? Hooker is not making that claim. Like many of these moral issues, the obligation to be truthful is a *prima facie* obligation. If one can show that the benefits outweigh the cost and that one has come into a conflict with another principle in which the other principle should dominate, then deception might be justifiable. Hooker would say that these situations should be rare. It should never be the norm in our treatment of patients.

One area where deception must play a part is in the use of placebos. A placebo is a substance or treatment that is medically inert for the specific condition being treated but is given under the falsehood of treatment to the patient. If it is a pharmacologically or biochemically inert substance, it is usually made up of saline or glucose. Placebos are most often used for the relief of pain. The belief is that the psyche can be deceived, and the brain will release endorphins. These are chemical substances, like polypeptides, that act as opiates and produce analgesia to pain perception, thereby increasing the pain threshold. Placebos are dependent on deception to achieve the "placebo effect," the relief of pain in the patient after the use of a placebo. Studies have shown that 35 percent of patients have been benefited by the relief of symptoms through the use of placebos.[27]

There are several ways deception in the use of placebos has been defended. Some appeal to benevolent deception, i.e., deception is justified if it is for the purpose of helping the patient. Others claim that this is a form of implicit consent: at the time one enters the hospital they implicitly agree to take all medicines and treatment they are given. Others claim that this is a form of future consent where it is assumed patient will ratify the decision afterward.

27. In some recent studies there was evidence that about 30 percent of subjects benefitted from a placebo even after being told that they were being given a placebo. One psychologist suspected that the reason the placebo effect worked was because the subjects didn't believe they were being given a placebo even after being told they were. If true, this not only confirms that placebos require deception, but it says something about patients not trusting physicians. See http://newyork.cbslocal.com/2016/04/11/placebo-pill-study.

However, neither of these are real forms of informed consent as information is being withheld. Finally, some say deceiving a patient through the use of a placebo to reduce pain is not really violating the patient's autonomy. The patient wanted to be treated—i.e., relieved of pain—and he received it. He received what he autonomously chose. However, this really is not justifiable. Autonomous choices include means to ends, not just ends. If I ask a physician to treat me, I am not giving him carte blanche to do it any way he wants so long as it accomplishes the goal.

One suggested justification for using placebos is the idea of general consent. The patient is told he will be a given a variety of drugs some of which may be placebos. He agrees ahead of time not to ask which is which. While this might resolve the conflict, most believe that it will have two negative consequences. First, there may be a significant reduction in the chance of achieving the placebo effect as patients need to believe they are really taking medicine to achieve the effect. Informing them ahead of time might raise enough doubts which may limit the effect. Secondly, informing the patient that he might be taking a placebo may affect the patient's response to actual medication.[28]

CONFIDENTIALITY

After four years of trying unsuccessfully to have a baby, and numerous consultations, Valerie and Alan Jablonski have been referred to a fertility clinic. It is suspected that their inability to conceive is due to Alan having a low sperm count. In this event, the chances of conceiving would be greatly enhanced by undergoing a process wherein Alan's sperm would be collected and concentrated, later to be artificially inseminated in Valerie during the optimal period of her ovulation cycle.

The clinic screens couples for a few medical indicators and, after much debate, has recently added HIV to the screening list. During the screening process, it is determined that Alan is positive for HIV

28. The placebo effect is a fascinating area that brings up the relationship between the mind and how beliefs can actually have an effect on physical events. Unfortunately, we do not have the opportunity to explore this topic at this time.

while Valerie has tested negative. In a post-test conference, Alan reveals that some years ago he was involved in an extramarital affair which is now ended. Alan regrets the affair and has been faithful to Valerie for years, but on the advice of friends and a counselor has never revealed the affair to Valerie. It is believed this is probably the source of his HIV.

According to clinic policy, if a client tests positive, treatment will be interrupted until a counseling team has met with the couple. Alan is unwilling to do this. He wants the staff to withhold his test results from Valerie because he fears she will leave him if she learns of his affair. The staff agree to discuss this among themselves and get back to Alan about how to proceed.

The day after the post-test interview with Alan, Valerie, who is unaware and unsuspecting of the problem, phones the clinic and asks when the treatment will be scheduled. The nurse who speaks with her evades the question because the nursing staff still disagree about what they should tell her or how they should proceed. Some think that Valerie must be told, and if not by her husband then by the staff. Others are concerned that this would violate confidentiality with Alan.

The case above raises an interesting scenario. While the concept of confidentiality is considered a bedrock of medical practice, there may be times when one is justified in breaking confidentiality to maintain a stronger obligation. In this case, we recognize the staff's obligation to maintain Alan's confidentiality, especially when he has specifically requested it and when breaking it might have severe consequences for Alan and his marriage. On the other hand, we can also see the need for Valerie to be aware that she may either already have HIV (it often does not show up in testing but can be hidden) or is likely to get it if she continues in sexual relations with her husband. There is a real danger to Valerie that might justify breaking confidentiality. Questions arise concerning such issues as: When is breaking confidentiality justified? How should it be done? Who should do it? How much should be told to a third party? These are the questions we will address in this section.

Confidentiality occurs when one person discloses information to another, whether through words or physical examination, and the person to whom the information was disclosed implicitly or explicitly agrees not to disclose that information to others without the original person's permission. An agreement of confidentiality does not have to be explicitly stated and is often not, as it is implicit in many relationships such as medical relationships, the relationship between priest or minister and confessor, or between a lawyer and a client. However, even in these relationships, it is good to remind the patient, confessor, or client of the nature, bounds, and limitations of confidentiality.

In the medical context, confidentiality has a long and honored tradition. All medical codes, going back to the Hippocratic Oath, support confidentiality: "Whatever, in connection with my professional service, or not in connection with it, I see or hear, in the life of men, which ought not to be spoken of abroad, I will not divulge, as reckoning that all such should be kept secret. While I continue to keep this Oath unviolated, may it be granted to me to enjoy life and the practice of the art, respected by all men, in all times. But should I trespass and violate this Oath, may the reverse be my lot." Thomas Percival's *Medical Ethics* (1803) states, "In the large wards of an infirmary the patients should be interrogated concerning their complaints in a tone of voice which cannot be overheard. Secrecy, also, when required by peculiar circumstances should be strictly observed."[29] And again, "Secrecy and delicacy when required by peculiar circumstances should be strictly observed. And the familiar and confidential intercourse, to which faculty are admitted in their professional visits, should be used with discretion, and with the most scrupulous regard to fidelity and honor."[30] The current code of ethics of the American Medical Association reads:

> The information disclosed to a physician by a patient should be held in confidence. The patient should feel free to make a full disclosure of information to the physician in order that the physician may most effectively provide needed services. The patient should be able to make this disclosure with the knowledge that the physician will respect the confidential nature of the communication. The physician should not reveal confidential information without the express consent of the patient, subject to certain exceptions which are ethically justified because of overriding considerations.[31]

29. Percival, *Medical Ethics*, 1.5.11.
30. Percival, *Medical Ethics*, 2.1.30.
31. The AMA Code of Ethics, Section 5.05, Confidentiality.

Confidentiality is the most widespread and common principle in medical ethics. Why might that be? One can approach the purpose of confidentiality either consequentially or from a principle-based position. There are two consequences we need to consider. First are the consequences to the patient. If the health-care team reveals confidential information, it could adversely affect the way the patient is treated by others. Ryan White was a thirteen-year-old who was diagnosed with AIDS in December of 1984. He was a hemophiliac who contracted AIDS from a tainted blood transfusion. News of his infection leaked out and, because there was a lot of misinformation about AIDS, he was ostracized by friends and neighbors in his small community of Kokomo, Indiana. His family went through a year-long battle just to get him back in school, and when he was finally readmitted, he was ostracized and threatened until the family eventually had to move to another town.

In 1991, a case was heard in New Jersey involving patient confidentiality. In 1987, a surgeon at Princeton Medical Center was diagnosed with HIV and AIDS. He was diagnosed as a patient at the same hospital where he worked. Within hours after receiving his diagnosis, he received numerous phone calls from well-wishers concerning his condition. Within a few weeks after being diagnosed, his surgical privileges were suspended at the hospital. The surgeon/patient died on July 2, 1989, never again performing a surgery and suffering both emotional and financial distress as a result. Outside of the concerns involving an HIV-positive doctor performing surgery on patients, the court found that the hospital breached its duty to maintain confidentiality to the surgeon in his capacity as a patient. The court ruled that "where the impact of such accessibility [to medical charts] is so clearly foreseeable, it is incumbent on the Medical Center, as the custodian of the charts, to take such reasonable measures as are necessary to ensure confidentiality. Failure to take such steps is negligence . . . the requirement of confidentiality is to protect the patient."[32]

A second consequence concerns the patient/physician relationship. The most important aspect of this relationship is trust. If confidentiality were not a binding principle in the medical field, patients could not trust physicians and would not seek needed help.

---

32. *Behringer v. Medical Center at Princeton*, 592 A.2d 1251, 1292 (Superior Court of New Jersey, 1991).

From the principle-based approach, two principles are prevalent that uphold the obligation to maintain patient confidentiality. First, and primary, is the respect for personal autonomy. People decide for themselves their zones of privacy. Part of that choice is a decision of to whom they wish to share information about themselves. Breaking confidentiality violates a person's autonomous choice concerning who receives that information. The second principle is the principle of fidelity. Part of being faithful to patients is respecting and honoring their requests for confidentiality. Both principles are *prima facie* which means that they may be justifiably infringed if they come into conflict with other principles. We will discuss this below.

A number of years ago Mark Siegler, professor of medicine and surgery at the University of Chicago Pritzker School of Medicine, wrote an article in the *New England Journal of Medicine* titled "Confidentiality in Medicine—A Decrepit Concept."[33] In that article he argued that confidentiality, at least as it was traditionally conceived, as the doctor/patient relationship where the doctor is the only one to know, was outdated and needed to be abandoned. He attributes this loss of the traditional model to three main reasons. First, the rise of the health-care team and the diminishing of the doctor/patient relationship has increased the number of people with a need to know. Today it is not uncommon to have up to ten to fifteen health professionals who have access to a patient's medical records, all of them with a legitimate need to know. This has caused a conflict to occur in maintaining patient confidentiality and being able to deliver the best possible health care. The advent of modern technology requires trained and specialized professionals involved in patient care. Secondly, the need for third party payment contributes to even more individuals having access to patient information. As medicine has become more specialized and technological, the cost has risen dramatically. Almost all patients need third-party payment plans in the form of health insurance. Managed care also has become a staple of the medical community. This means more persons—such as chart reviewers, financial officers, and insurance auditors—need to have access to medical records. Finally, sensitive and personal information is being included in a patient's file. Medicine is expanding from a narrow disease-based model to a more holistic model which encompasses the psychological, social, and economic state of the patient. This information is included in one's medical record for all to see.

---

33. Mark Siegler, "Confidentiality in Medicine—A Decrepit Concept," *The New England Journal of Medicine* 307 (1982): 1518–21.

Siegler is right to call attention to these conflicts between modern medicine and the traditional model of confidentiality. However, this does not mean we need to abandon the concept of confidentiality altogether. We can suggest some guidelines to reduce the confidentiality problem. First, in private doctor's offices, the traditional model can and should, for the most part, still be upheld. Scrupulous care should be taken to guarantee that medical and personal information should be kept as confidential as possible. Conversations with and about patients should be done in private, not at the nurse's station where patients are continually walking by. Patients' records should be handled in a manner that guards the information within them. I have often seen patient files placed in bins easily within the reach of anyone who wanted to open the file and look through them. With the advent of digital files and digital pads, much of mishandling files has been reduced significantly and that has helped reduce the problem.

Secondly, in hospitals or large-scale group practices, steps should be taken to provide access only to those who have a "need to know." Again, with the advent of computers and information technology some of this is already being done with the use of personal codes that will allow a health-care worker to access only that information in a patient's file that they need to know. This is a step in the right direction, but more work needs to continue in this area.

Thirdly, patients need to be informed about confidentiality and their rights concerning it. The Health Insurance Portability and Accountability Act of 1996 (HIPAA) is the controlling set of federal regulations governing the confidentiality of medical information. The privacy rule encompassed in HIPAA protects all individually identifiable health information held by a covered entity in any form, whether electronic, paper, or oral. This information is known collectively as "protected health information."[34] Covered entities include health-care providers, insurance companies, and health-care clearinghouses (billing and claims departments). Most hospitals today supply patients with this information upon admission to their facility. Patients also need to be made aware of the large number of persons who need to have access to their records.

Finally, every effort should be made to avoid "the wanton, often inadvertent, but avoidable exchanges of confidential information that occur frequently in hospital rooms, elevators, cafeterias, and at cocktail parties."[35]

34. 45 CFR § 160.103.
35. Siegler, "Confidentiality in Medicine," 1520–21.

These breaches of confidentiality are usually of greater concern to patients than access to medical records and are never justifiable. This, of course, means that health-care workers should never reveal confidential information to their own spouses, family members, and friends. They should especially avoid the temptation to say anything about someone they may know on a personal basis but is receiving care in the institution in which he/she is affiliated. This is the most common form of breach of confidentiality, is an egregious assault on patient rights, and can result in dire consequences for the health-care worker.

In general, confidentiality can be breached in two ways: violation and infringement. A violation of confidentiality is an unjustifiable breach that occurs in one of two manners. Deliberate violation is done by willful and deliberate disclosing of confidential information to a third party without the consent of the patient. Negligent violation is the handling information in a careless or negligent manner so that others become aware of it. This may be unintentional but it is usually avoidable, and one is still responsible for the violation of a patient's confidentiality even though one did not intend to do so.

An infringement of confidentiality is a justified breach of confidentiality. Like many of our principles and obligations, the duty to maintain confidentiality is a *prima facie* duty meaning that the duty can come into conflict with another more foundational duty or principle, at which point one is justified to infringe on another's confidentiality. In fact, any time you are morally justified to break a confidence, you are morally obligated to do so. The obligation to keep the more stringent principle, whether beneficence or non-maleficence, requires you to act. Infringement might be justifiable under several conditions.

One condition for infringement would be legal considerations. Sometimes one is required by law to report certain information to proper authorities. These are exceptions to HIPAA, and patient confidentiality can be infringed in these cases.[36] In fact, some argue that since this is publicly known, one is not infringing because the patient knows that the information cannot be kept confidential. Examples would include such things as gunshot wounds, child abuse, and certain communicable diseases that need to be reported to the CDC.

36. 45 CFR § 164.512(f)(1).

One may be morally obligated to infringe an individual's confidentiality if keeping confidentiality might bring significant harm to the patient himself. Here is where strong paternalism might be justified. An example would be intervention programs for those suffering from alcohol and drug addiction. An intervention occurs when the close friends, family, and concerned others, such as employers, of an individual, recognize that her drug or alcohol addiction has reached such a low point that it is badly affecting her lifestyle. The concerned individuals agree to an intervention to shock the individual into realizing her destructive behavior and getting her into a rehabilitation and recovery program. The meeting consists of each concerned family member, friend, and other participant barraging the addict with personal stories in which their addiction adversely affected their relationship. Addicted individuals often have built up such a strong denial system that one or two stories will not affect them. They need the constant barrage of many stories from many individuals to break down the denial system and to see a pattern of self-destructive behavior. If successful, the addict will break down, admit her addiction, and will be immediately taken from the meeting to a rehabilitation and recovery center before there is time for the denial system to gain resurgence.

Interventions have a high rate of success. However, in order to work, they require that very personal and often painful stories are told in the presence of several other individuals. The addict's confidentiality is certainly breached at this time. The argument is made that the infringement of confidentiality is justifiable, as it is done in the name of beneficence and non-maleficence. The patient is harming himself and the intervention is necessary to discontinue such damaging behavior.

Finally, one is morally obligated to infringe confidentiality if there is a serious danger to a third party or the general public at large. One of the landmark cases involving confidentiality began in 1969. Prosenjit Poddar was a student at the University of California Berkeley. He became infatuated with another student, Tatiana Tarasoff, and was upset when she would not enter into a serious relationship with him. Upon developing severe emotional distress, as a result, Poddar began seeing Dr. Lawrence Moore, a psychologist at UC Berkeley. During one of these sessions, Poddar confided his intent to kill Tarasoff. Dr. Moore reported to campus police that Poddar was suffering from severe schizophrenia and needed civil commitment to a mental hospital. The police detained Poddar, but after he was found to be rational and sane, Poddar was hence released. Poddar no longer attended any session with Dr. Moore after this incident. On October 27, 1969, Poddar stabbed and killed Tarasoff. Tarasoff's parents sued Dr. Moore and the university.

The case was decided by the Supreme Court of California in 1976, which established what is now known as "the duty to warn."[37] The court ruled that "The public policy favoring protection of the confidential character of patient-psychotherapist communications must yield to the extent to which disclosure is essential to avert danger to others. The protective privilege ends where the public peril begins."[38] In other words, a mental health professional has a duty not only to the patient, but also individuals threatened by the patient.

Since this case, many states have codified the "duty to warn" in statute or common law. Based on the Tarasoff ruling, it is more appropriate to look at this not only as a duty to warn but a duty to protect. Beyond simply telling a potential victim that harm may occur, reasonable care must be exercised to prevent that harm from occurring. The following guidelines are usually applied in cases like *Tarasoff*. Health-care workers have a duty to infringe on confidentiality if the following conditions hold:

1. A person or group of persons is at serious risk of harm.
2. The disclosure would prevent the harm with a good degree of probability.
3. The breach is necessary to prevent the harm (no other way, not just "another way").
4. The breach of confidentiality is limited to the amount and kind of information that is necessary only to protect the person or group of persons.

Knowing there are times when one must infringe on confidentiality, how does one determine when those times should be? One must do a harms assessment. In doing so one needs to consider two elements. First is the probability of harm. What are the chances that harm, in fact, will occur in a particular situation? We rate probability in degrees of high and low. Secondly is the magnitude of harm. How much harm may actually occur in a given situation?

37. *Tarasoff v. Regents of University of California,* 17 Cal. 3d 425 (Supreme Court of California, 1976).
38. *Tarasoff v. Regents of University of California,* 442.

There is a continuum of possible harms: loss of life, injury, loss of property, damage to reputation, inconvenience. We rate magnitude in terms of major and minor. We can set up a rubric that might look like the following:

Risk of Harms Assessment Chart		Magnitude of Harm	
		Major	Minor
Probability of Harm	High	1	2
	Low	3	4

In the chart above, a case in section 1 in which confidentiality might need to be infringed is likely to be very justifiable. The risk of harm is very high, and the kind of harm would be very great. A case in section 4 in which confidentiality might need to be infringed is likely to be very unjustifiable. The risk of harm is very small, and the harm would be insignificant. Cases in sections 2 and 3 in which confidentiality might need to be infringed that are much more difficult to determine. In general, a case in section 2 is considered more justifiable than a case in section 3, though there is no set rule. In borderline cases, one needs to examine the whole context of the case to determine if infringing confidentiality is justifiable in that situation.

WHISTLEBLOWING

A urologist who had his fourteen-year-old son assist him in an operation on a fifty-year-old woman has been prohibited from working in an operating room for two weeks. The Michigan Board of Medicine reluctantly imposed the sanction Wednesday after [the physician] admitted that the incident occurred and that he had violated state law.

"He didn't err very much," argued a board member from Detroit who opposed any limitation of the doctor's license. "In the operating room, it's not a solemn wake. It is more like M*A*S*H. People walk in and out. Jokes are made. I can understand how a doctor could get carried away, not only as a teacher but as a father."

> But [the] vice chairman of the board argued for the sanction, stating that "we are here to protect the public. If this had been my mother, and he allowed his fourteen-year-old son to assist with a major operation, I would be extremely upset. If we let this go by the board, I think we are telling the public that we are not here to protect them, we are here to protect the physician."
>
> The incident occurred in March 1983 . . . while [the physician] was performing a bladder operation. He had his son scrub and come into the operating room because [he] said his son was interested in medicine and had asked repeatedly if he could watch an operation.
>
> During the operation, [the physician] instructed his son to insert his gloved hand inside the woman's abdomen and feel a catheter balloon in her bladder. As [the physician] was sewing together a layer of tissue over the muscles, he had his son put in two stitches, despite the objections of the anesthesiologist.
>
> The woman, who recovered uneventfully, was not told that [the physician's] son participated in the operation. [The physician], former chief of staff at [the hospital], said he realized his mistake immediately after the operation and apologized to the anesthesiologist and the chief nurse.
>
> A nursing student reported the incident to the Board of Medicine. State law requires that the board take disciplinary action in such cases.[39]

Whistleblowing is the disclosure of illegal, immoral, incompetent, or negligent practices by a colleague or superior with the purpose of halting such practices for the welfare and safety of patients. Blowing the whistle on someone is among the more difficult and risky things to do. One is presumed to be loyal to one's colleagues; therefore, the whistleblower is often perceived as going against this loyalty. He is often treated as a traitor by others. However, the obligation to protect the public welfare places a moral obligation to report offenses on those who have knowledge of them. The Code of Ethics of the American Nursing Association states, "As an advocate for the client, the nurse must be alert to and take any appropriate action regarding any instances of

39. Dolly Katz, "MD Suspended From Operating Room," *Detroit Free Press*, October 12, 1984.

incompetent, unethical, or illegal practice by any member of the health-care team or the health-care system, or any action on the parts of others that places the rights or best interests of the client in jeopardy."[40]

Section 11 of the Occupational Safety and Health Act (OSHA) provides protection to whistleblowers. It prohibits any person from discharging or retaliating against an employee because the employee has complained about unsafe or unlawful conditions.[41] These provisions protect all employees, including those in the medical field. Most states have individual whistleblower protection laws as well, which generally encompass anti-retaliation laws in response to reporting by employees. Many of these laws specifically address health-care workers, such as the New York law that prohibits health-care workers from penalizing employees who complain about the improper quality of patient care.[42] Washington provides that whistleblowers who complain about the quality of care by health providers shall remain confidential.[43]

When is it appropriate to blow the whistle? Everybody makes mistakes and most health-care workers want to ensure that it will not happen again. This often involves admitting the mistake, expressing regret, and filling out an incident report. There is no need to blow the whistle on a health-care worker who realizes a mistake and desires to correct it.

However, at times, one may encounter a health-care worker who is guilty of one or more of the following: (1) incompetency, regular mistakes, or a demonstration of a significant lack of skills concerning medical procedures; (2) negligence, a consistent lack of care concerning medical procedures, patient care, and patient rights or any circumstance where the patient's welfare and safety are in jeopardy; or (3) illegal or immoral activity, falsifying records, illegal use of medicine, and sexual harassment. In these situations, blowing the whistle is warranted and one is ethically obligated to do so.

There is a right way and a wrong way to blow the whistle on a colleague or superior. It is not only important that one do so if the situation warrants it, but it is also important that one go about the right way. Here are some guidelines.

First, analyze your own motives. Are they proper? Are you acting to protect the welfare and safety of patients or are you just settling a score with a colleague? Your primary motive should be to protect the welfare and safety

40. The American Nursing Association Code of Ethics, Provision 3.5.
41. 29 CFR 1977 (1970).
42. New York Labor Law §741.
43. Revised Code of Washington §43.70.075.

of the patients under your care or future patients from being harmed by the incompetent, negligent, or illegal actions of a fellow health-care worker. If your motive is only to get back at someone with whom you have a grudge, then it will not be enough to sustain you in the long run. Blowing the whistle can be a long, drawn-out process with severe consequences for others and for yourself. Your cause will need to be justice or to keep grave consequences from occurring to others, not revenge.

Second, make sure to document your facts. You should have sufficient evidence to support your allegations. Hearsay, rumor, and speculation are not acceptable, and it would be reckless to declare charges against someone on just those bases. Put in writing the misconduct you are reporting. Be sure to include the date and time, person or people involved, and the source of your information. If possible, have the information verified by others. Above all, avoid making a personal accusation or offering personal opinions. Such accusations detract from the disclosure and invite a lawsuit for libel of slander.

Third, in writing, clearly state the problem and identify causative factors. Was it incompetence, negligence, or illegal activity? As a result of the person's behavior were supplies inadequate or did equipment malfunction? Is there a problem with institutional policy? In addressing these questions avoid personal biases. You might have a colleague review the problem with you.

Fourth, determine your objective. What are you trying to accomplish in blowing the whistle on this person? Eliminate the danger to patients? Stop the person from doing this behavior? Have the person removed? Change hospital policy? Once you have determined your objective, put it in writing. All too often individuals will decide to blow the whistle on a colleague without a clear idea of exactly what they want to accomplish.

Fifth, confront the person. In most cases, it would be inappropriate for you to report on a person without first confronting them about it. When you do so, try to do so in a constructive, nonthreatening manner. Express your concerns and ask for an explanation for the person's behavior. Seek reassurance that the problem will be addressed and give them time to make the necessary changes. If after a reasonable period the problem has not been corrected, then continue the steps involved in reporting the behavior.

Sixth, evaluate the consequences. While one has an ethical obligation to report illegal, immoral, incompetent, or negligent practices, this is a *prima facie* obligation. There may be concerns that override this obligation and one should perform a benefits/burdens assessment at this time. How realistic are the chances that disclosing will accomplish the objective? What are the consequences of the disclosure for the person disclosing? For the person being reported? If the chances are not very good for changing the situation and if it might mean a significant loss for the person disclosing (such as loss of employment and blacklisting) and their dependents, then one may be warranted in not disclosing, especially if the danger to patients' welfare and safety is not immediately threatened.

Usually, institutional channels exist through which you can report the misconduct of another nurse without fear of official reprisal. Often a nursing supervisor or the hospital personnel office assume joint responsibility for investigating allegations of misconduct. The only drawback for the discloser is animosity from the affected nurse and those who might sympathize with her. The benefits include correcting an injustice, preventing a future harm, and strengthening your own sense of moral integrity.

If you report the misconduct of a physician, supervisor, or administrator, expect stiffer resistance and possibly more serious retaliation. This is especially so if management has cooperated in covering or concealing the misconduct. Be prepared for a long and hard-fought battle. The accused professional may attempt to discredit you or have you fired. If you proceed you may want to take steps in anticipation of retaliation by hiring a lawyer and even seeking re-employment. Since it is likely that you may come under fire yourself, make sure your slate is clean. If there are skeletons in the closet, make them public and keep documentation of all personal evaluations and incident reports on yourself.

Seventh, go through the proper and appropriate channels. Should you desire to proceed, do so in an appropriate manner. Work through the hospital channels first. You can almost always solve the problem that way and ethically you owe management a chance to change the situation. If you are not successful and still believe in your cause, the next step is to contact the proper regulating and licensing agency. If you have exhausted these channels and still believe you have a case, then you should go public through the court system and, if necessary, the media.

Finally, a word about surviving the setbacks. In most cases hospitals desire to correct cases of misconduct, and so the setbacks will be minimal. Hospitals should have a means to protect those who blow the whistle from any official reprisal that may come from supervisors and physicians. However, one must be prepared for unofficial reprisals and the reputation that accompanies a whistleblower. Hopefully, at least some will respect the person for sticking their neck out for what is right. In extreme cases, one may need to seek employment elsewhere, and whistleblowers should be prepared for that.

Whistleblowing is risky and can have its costs. A major whistleblowing case involving nurses occurred in Texas in 2009. Two nurses became concerned when a doctor performed numerous alternative medical procedures. It was claimed that the doctor would try to sell various herbal remedies to hospital patients from his own business. He was also alleged to have performed a skin graft on a patient when he did not have the credentials to perform such a surgery. Both nurses submitted anonymous complaints to the Texas Medical Board. When the doctor became aware of the complaint, he spoke to the county sheriff and argued the complaint was tantamount to harassment. The Texas Medical Board sent a copy of the complaint to the sheriff, under the agreement that it was only to be used to investigate the doctor. The sheriff sent the complaint to the doctor and the hospital, and using the details in the complaint they were able to identify both nurses.

Both nurses were terminated in June 2009. A few days later, they were arrested and charged with misusing official information. The sheriff claimed that the nurses had a personal vendetta against the doctor rather than good-faith concerns. When the case attracted media attention, the Texas Nurses Association filed a complaint with the Texas Department of State Health Services. During the trial, it was discovered that the sheriff and doctor had a personal friendship prior to the complaint being filed. After only one hour of deliberation, the jury returned a verdict of not guilty. The Texas Nurses Association used the Public Employee Whistleblower Law to support its argument, which gives any health-care provider the right to report concerns regarding patient care without fear of retaliation.[44] The nurses filed a civil suit against the hospital, doctor, and sheriff, and split a $750,000 settlement. The doctor had to surrender his medical license in 2011. The sheriff was also charged with two counts of misusing official information—the same charges the nurses had faced. However, the nurses never recovered professionally from this and were unable to find future employment in the medical field.

The point of the above case is not to discourage whistleblowing. There are many legal protections for health-care workers who make complaints about

44. Texas Govt. Code §554.001 et seq.

safety, health, or ethics in the medical field. However, one must be aware that even if a legal outcome is victorious for the whistleblower, the recovery may be very difficult and costly regardless. Whistleblowing should be a last resort after all other efforts to resolve the issue have been exhausted. Jesus warns that believers who stand up for the truth will often suffer for righteousness's sake. That is part of being a disciple of Jesus Christ.

10

For the Good of Mankind: Research Ethics and Human Experimentation

In 1906, a German zoologist named Fritz Schaudinn discovered the causative agent of syphilis, *Spirochaeta pallida*. Syphilis is a chronic, contagious bacterial venereal disease that can be passed on genetically. It often causes lesions, both externally and internally, and if left untreated can lead to paralysis, tumors, blindness, narrowing of the aorta, and death. The discovery led to a treatment around 1910 that had some success incorporating the use of a heavy metal combination, called Neosalvarsan. However, as of 1932, the natural history of syphilis had not been documented, and so the United States Public Health Service (USPHS) began a "study in nature"[1] on the development and growth of syphilis from beginning to end.

In order to conduct the study, a large population had to be identified where syphilis was present and that also could supply a control group for comparison purposes. They identified an area of Macon County, Alabama, around Tuskegee where a previous study identified that 22 percent of the African American male population had syphilis and, importantly, there was also a 62 percent rate of congenital syphilis. The survey identified 399 men who had syphilis but had not been treated, and a control group of two hundred African American men who were not infected at all.

1. A "study in nature" differs from experiments. Experimental science often will manipulate variables and study how the changes affect the study. A study in nature simply observes without the scientist intervening in the progression of study.

The six hundred men were considered perfect for the study because of their vulnerability: they were poor, illiterate tenant farmers. Because they were tied to the land, they were considered unlikely to leave the area and could be counted on as subjects over a lengthy period.

All six hundred men enrolled in the study with the promise that they would receive free transportation, free hot lunches, free health care and treatment (except for syphilis), and free burials. However, none of the infected men were told they had syphilis, nor were they treated for it. Because they needed to have spinal taps, they were told they had "bad blood" and that the taps were a treatment for it.

The essential purpose of the study was to merely observe the effects of syphilis in the participants. Even after Congress passed the Henderson Act in 1943, which required testing and treatment for diseases such as syphilis, the study continued with no treatment given to the men. In fact, efforts were made to deceive and lie to the participants in order to keep them from seeking other medical examinations so the diagnosis would remain unknown. Even with the discovery of penicillin in 1943 as the standard treatment for syphilis, no treatment was offered to men in the study. The stated purpose for nontreatment was that it would eliminate the study group.

The study was flawed from the beginning. No one physician oversaw the study. An African American nurse was permanently assigned in Tuskegee by the USPHS to keep track of the study. It had no written protocols to govern it. Records were poorly kept, and many were lost. Many men had the same last name, so patients were often confused. Over time, many of the controls contracted the disease. There were long gaps in the study. There were no visits from doctors between 1939 and 1948 and again from 1963 to 1970. In 1969, the newly formed CDC took over the study and considered shutting it down at the request of Peter Buxton, the VD director at the USPHS, but ultimately the CDC voted to keep it going and to keep it secret.

Out of frustration, Buxton eventually contacted Jean Heller of the Associated Press and spilled the beans. On July 26, 1972, Heller's article, "Syphilis Victims in the U.S. Study Went Untreated for 40 Years" appeared in *The New York Times*. The public outcry was immediate. Not only was the study unethical, but the racial overtones were enormous. One senator called it a moral and ethical nightmare. The study was shut down immediately.

A class action lawsuit was filed, in which the United States Government gave more than nine million dollars to the participants and their descendants, in addition to free medical care for life. In 1988, twenty-one of the original study subjects were still alive. However, it was determined that twenty-eight men had died of syphilis who could have been treated and spared. In addition, forty-one wives and nineteen children had contracted the disease. Ironically, it was determined that the study provided no real data that was usable to treat or cure syphilis. Tragically, as bioethicist Gregory Pence observes, "Perhaps the worst effect of revelation of the study was distrust by African Americans of medical experiments, a legacy that researchers still struggle to overcome."[2]

The Tuskegee Syphilis Study is one of the darkest blots on the history of medical research. I wish I could say it was rare and an anomaly, but unfortunately, as we will see, the history of human experimentation is replete with stories of overzealous researchers trampling over the rights and values of human beings in the name of medical progress and doing what they think is "for the good of mankind." From the beginning, we need to affirm that medical research is a good in and of itself. Much has been done to discover treatments and cures for many ailments, debilitations, and diseases. Much of this research has been done using human beings as subjects for experimental procedures, and we are thankful for those who have been willing to voluntarily become subjects for the good of mankind. However, this does not trivialize or downplay the many times that researchers, for both good and poor motives, have overstepped the bounds of morality in attempting to achieve their goals. Not all subjects have been voluntary, and ethical

2. Gregory Pence, *Medical Ethics: Accounts of Ground-Breaking Cases*, 7th ed. (New York: McGraw-Hill, 2015), 196.

norms have not always been followed. Therefore, it is appropriate that we examine a bit of the history of medical research involving human experimentation and explore the ethical issues surrounding such research to address the question: Are there limits to the imperative to end or treat human suffering and disease?

A HISTORICAL OVERVIEW

Medical research involving human beings and human experimentation is not new and has, in fact, been around since the earliest days of medical practice, though our data of ancient research is fragmentary. The Arabic scholar Avicenna (980–1037) states well the purpose for human experimentation: "Experimentation must be done with the human body, for testing a drug on a lion or a horse might not prove anything about its effect on a man."[3] From the fragments we possess the most common experiments appear to be testing poisons on condemned prisoners.

Moving ahead to the to the eighteenth and nineteenth centuries as the age of modern science began, experimentation involving humans was mostly a cottage industry taking place in the private practices of individual physicians experimenting mostly on themselves and local neighbors and community members. One of the most well-known was the experiments of Edward Jenner (1749–1823) in search of a cure for smallpox. He noticed that farmers and dairymen who had contracted pox from cows and swine seem to be immune to the more virulent smallpox. He first injected his one-year-old son with swinepox, which proved ineffective, and then selected a local eight-year-old boy with whom he injected cowpox. Two weeks later he exposed the boy to smallpox and the boy seemed to be immune. Also known from this period was the unusual experiments of American physician William Beaumont (1785–1853) on Alexis St. Martin, who suffered a bullet wound to the stomach which left a hole through which Beaumont could observe the workings of the gastric juices in the stomach. Beaumont made a contract with St. Martin in which he agreed to pay him $150 a year to be allowed to be experimented on his stomach.

In the second half of the nineteenth century human experimentation continued as doctors became more aware of germs and infections and desired to understand the epidemiology of disease. Pasteur's studies on rabies were

3. Quoted by David Rothman in "Research Human: Historical Aspects," in *The Encyclopedia of Bioethics* (New York: Simon, Schuster, and Macmillan, 1995), 4:2248.

among the most famous of these experiments. He was confident he had found a cure in experimenting on animals but was hesitant to try it on a human subject until a mother appeared with her nine-year-old son who had been bitten by a rabid dog. After consulting with two colleagues and considering that death was inevitable if nothing were done, with great anxiety he administered twelve inoculations, and several weeks later the boy was back to health.

At this time, there was also a strong movement in medical practice to separate those professionals who were skilled and trained as physicians from the country doctor and quackery that were still pervasive throughout the country. This movement affected experimental medicine as well, and standards began to be developed concerning how experimentation was to be performed. Even at this early time, voluntary consent was a major factor in an ethical experiment. One doctor wrote, "By experiments we are not to be understood as speaking of wild and dangerous practices of rash and ignorant practitioners . . . but of deliberate acts of men from considerable knowledge and undoubted talent." He went on to say that the researcher who had consent was "answerable neither in damages to the individual nor to criminal proceeding. But if the practitioner performs his experiment without giving such information to, and obtaining the consent of this patient, he is liable to compensate in damages any injury which may arise from his adopting a new method of treatment."[4]

Entering the twentieth century human experimentation, like all medical practice of the time, took on the professional and scientific attitude of the time. The familiar and informal relationships between doctors and subjects gave way to the more objective method of doctors giving experimental drugs to groups of subject/patients in hospital settings and keeping strict records of comparisons between patients (though we are still a long way from the random clinical trials that dominate experimental practice today). The most common population groups experimented on were those who were dying of diseases in which the experiment was a last hope, though the incompetent, mentally retarded, and prisoners were often used as well. There was still no informed consent as we have come to understand it and patients were often given little information as to what they were consenting to, but voluntary consent was still maintained as a standard.

With the arrival of World War II, human experimentation exploded as the conditions for battle and the geographic locations of the war introduced

---

4. Rothman, "Research Human," 2250.

new diseases and debilitations that required new treatments. The military took over much of the medical research as part of the war effort and, for the first time, experimentation for nontherapeutic proposes became common.[5] Soldiers and sailors were often conscripted into experiments without any choice and the voluntary aspect of medical experimentation was suspended due to the emergency need of the war. The Committee on Medical Research (CMR), a division of the Office of Scientific Research and Development, established by Roosevelt in 1941, took over medical experimentation in the U.S. During the war, the CMR recommended more than six hundred research proposals involving experimentation on humans. The major concerns of the war were dysentery, influenza, malaria wounds, venereal disease, and physical hardships such as sleep deprivation and frigid temperatures (the infamous military radiation experiments occurred after the war). Ethical norms for many of these experiments were widely ignored as the tyranny of winning the war took precedence. It is beyond the limits of this chapter to catalog in any detail the military experimentation but some of the more well-known were:

- The dysentery experiments at the Ohio Soldiers and Sailors Orphanage in Xenia, Ohio; the Institution for the Retarded in Dixon, Illinois; and New Jersey State Colony for the Feeble-Minded. Subjects were injected with experimental vaccines for dysentery.
- Malaria studies at a sixty-bed clinic in Manteno, Illinois, with mostly psychotic, backward patients who were first infected with malaria and then treated with various experimental anti-malaria drugs. The study was later expanded to the Statesville Prison in Joliet, where five hundred inmates were enrolled in the study. The prisoners were congratulated for contributing to the war effort.
- Influenza studies at institutes for the retarded and mentally ill in Pennsylvania, in which patients were given an experimental vaccine and three to six months later injected with influenza to determine its efficacy. The vaccine was later tested by enrollees of the army's specialized training program at eight universities throughout the U.S.

5. Up until this time, experimentation was generally performed on those who had a specific disease or debilitation that was being researched. Hence, it has a possible therapeutic benefit for the specific individual being involved in the experimental treatment. Nontherapeutic testing and experimentation is performed on those who do not currently have the disease being researched. Thus, it has no therapeutic value for them.

Perhaps the most infamous of all medical experimentation performed during the war were the Nazi medical experiments performed on concentration camp prisoners.[6] The spirit of the war medical experimentation program is an outgrowth of the German eugenics program, which finds its origin in the United States eugenics movement. In 1933, Germany passed the Law for the Prevention of Genetically Defective Progeny. This legalized the involuntary sterilization of persons with diseases that were thought to be hereditary: weak-mindedness, schizophrenia, alcohol abuse, insanity, blindness, deafness, and physical deformities. Within four years about 400,000 German citizens had been involuntarily sterilized. It didn't take long for the desensitization of the medical community concerning the value of human life and the spread of Aryanism to spread into to other areas.

In 1939, Hitler instituted the T4 program (named for the address in Berlin—Tiergartenstrasse 4—from which the program was run). This had both a positive economic effect for a country that had suffered through a terrible economic depression (by ridding state-run hospitals and institutions of those who were incurable) and helped to fulfill the goals of racial purification. The idea of T4 was to euthanize all of those who were deemed unfit and had diseases that were incurable. These individuals were seen as a burden on the state and needed to be done away with. At first, this involved mostly those who were mentally ill and the elderly with degenerative, incurable diseases. However, the concept of "unfit" and "burden" soon expanded to include habitual criminals, prostitutes, and by the time of the war, Jews and other "undesirables." The step from medical doctors' involvement in the T4 program to accepted medical experimentation of concentration camp prisoners was not a big one to take.

The Nazi medical experiments could be divided into three types. First, some took place for the purpose of determining how well military personnel could survive under difficult battle conditions. The second group involved experimenting with drugs and other pharmaceuticals developed for the treatment of injuries and illnesses in battle. Finally, there were a series of experiments for racial hygiene and other ideological purposes. Here are several examples of the experiments:

---

6. Japan also was well involved in medical experiments that were horrific, including the use of biological weapons on eleven Chinese cities where studies were done on victims.

- Temperature probes were placed in the rectums of young healthy male prisoners and held in place by metal rings that expanded in the rectum. They were then placed in icy vats of water until they slowly froze to death. This allowed German physicians to determine how long a pilot could remain alive if shot down over the ocean.
- Some prisoners were placed under sun lamps which were so hot they would burn the skin. One document tells of a young victim who was repeatedly cooled to unconsciousness then revived with lamps until he was pouring sweat. He died one evening after several test sessions.
- Often women were placed next to naked to frozen men and forced to copulate with them as a way of reviving them.
- Malaria experiments were performed on Dachau inmates. They were first infected with malaria, and then a number of experimental drugs were given to them and their efficacy tested. More than 1,200 people were infected, and more than half died.
- Prisoners were tested for mustard gas treatment. Test subjects were deliberately exposed to mustard gas, which inflicted severe chemical burns. Their wounds were then tested to find the most effective treatment for the mustard gas burns.
- Experiments were performed to investigate the effectiveness of sulfonamide, a synthetic antimicrobial agent. Wounds inflicted on the subjects were infected with bacteria. Circulation of blood was interrupted by tying off blood vessels at both ends of the wound to create a condition similar to that of a battlefield wound. The infection was then aggravated by forcing wood shavings and ground glass into the wounds. The infection was treated with sulfonamide and other drugs to determine their effectiveness.
- The sterilization program continued in concentration camps. Medical experiments were established to develop new methods of sterilization that would be suitable for sterilizing millions of people with a minimum of time and effort. These experiments were conducted by means of X-ray, surgery, and various drugs. Thousands of victims were sterilized.
- Experiments were conducted to investigate the effect of various poisons. Poisons were secretly administered to experimental subjects in their food. The victims died as a result of the poison, or were killed immediately in order to permit autopsies. In addition, experimental subjects were shot with poisonous bullets, suffered torture, and often died.

- High-altitude experiments were performed on prisoners. A low-pressure chamber containing these prisoners was used to simulate conditions at altitudes of up to 66,000 feet. Some doctors performed vivisections on the brains of victims who survived the initial experiment. Of the two hundred subjects subjected to these high-altitude experiments, eighty died outright while others were executed.[7]

This is just a sample list of the many medical experiments performed on prisoners in German concentration camps. After the war, the doctors involved in these experiments were put on trial by a United States military tribunal in Nuremberg, Germany, in 1947. The doctors justified themselves by stating that they were just following orders, that they were practicing good research, and they appealed to human experimentation programs performed in the U.S. Their point was, we are not doing anything differently than you are doing in your country. However, the most common appeal was simply the idea that, since these prisoners are condemned to die anyway, why not use them to achieve good medical information for mankind?

One of the important advances in the ethics of medical experimentation that came out of Nuremberg was the first ethical code for medical research, the ten-point Nuremberg Code. The most important principle was the establishment of the need for informed consent, which the code states in full:

> The voluntary consent of the human subject is absolutely essential. This means that the person involved should have legal capacity to give consent; should be so situated as to be able to exercise free power of choice, without the intervention of any element of force, fraud, deceit, duress, overreaching, or other ulterior form of constraint or coercion; and should have sufficient knowledge and comprehension of the elements of the subject matter involved as to enable him to make an understanding and enlightened decision. This latter element requires that before the acceptance of an affirmative decision by the experimental subject there should be made known to him the nature, duration, and purpose of the experiment; the method and means by which it is to be conducted; all inconveniences and hazards reasonably to be expected; and the effects upon his health or person which may possibly come from his participation in the experiment. The duty and responsibility for ascertaining the quality of the consent rests upon each

7. George Annas and Michael Grodin, *The Nazi Doctors and the Nuremberg Code: Human Rights in Human Experimentation* (New York: Oxford University Press, 1995).

> individual who initiates, directs, or engages in the experiment. It is a personal duty and responsibility which may not be delegated to another with impunity.[8]

The ten points can be listed briefly:

1. Required is the voluntary, well-informed, understanding consent of the human subject in a full legal capacity.
2. The experiment should aim at positive results for society that cannot be procured in some other way.
3. It should be based on previous knowledge (e.g., an expectation derived from animal experiments) that justifies the experiment.
4. The experiment should be set up in a way that avoids unnecessary physical and mental suffering and injuries.
5. It should not be conducted when there is any reason to believe that it implies a risk of death or disabling injury.
6. The risks of the experiment should be in proportion to (that is, not exceed) the expected humanitarian benefits.
7. Preparations and facilities must be provided that adequately protect the subjects against the experiment's risks.
8. The staff who conduct or take part in the experiment must be fully trained and scientifically qualified.
9. The human subjects must be free to immediately quit the experiment at any point when they feel physically or mentally unable to go on.
10. Likewise, the medical staff must stop the experiment at any point when they observe that continuation would be dangerous.[9]

With the revelation of the Nazi atrocities, the formulation of the Nuremberg Code and the end of the war, one would assume that there would have been dramatic changes in ethical protocols for human experimentation. And, in many ways, there were some important changes in approaching human experimentation. The major successor to the CMR in medical research became the National Institutes of Health (NIH), which established its own Clinical Center, of which the NIH claimed, "The welfare of the patient takes

8. The Nuremberg Code (1947) in A. Mitscherlich and F. Mielke, *Doctors of Infamy: The Story of the Nazi Medical Crimes* (New York: Schuman, 1949), xxiii–xxv.
9. This is brief summary of the Code. Detailed listings can be found in several sources, including Annas and Grodin, *The Nazi Doctors and the Nuremburg Code*.

precedence over every other consideration."[10] Over the next twenty years, the NIH would support more than 1,500 research projects involving human research. However, despite its claim, the Nuremberg Code did not have much effect on human experimentation. Ethicist David Rothman suggests, "More likely, the events described at Nuremberg were not perceived by most Americans as relevant to their own practices. From their perspective, the Code had nothing to do with science and everything to do with Nazis. The guilty parties were seen less as doctors than as Hitler's henchmen."[11] Many have been critical that the NIH was too lax and casual in its relationship with researchers. Hence, they did not keep as wary an eye on ethical issues as they should have.

The military continued to practice in the same manner as during the war. Now the Cold War and communism established the need for medical experimentation and the continued suspension of ethical guidelines. This can best be seen in the radiation experiments of the 1950s and '60s.[12] The experiments included a wide array of studies, involving things like feeding radioactive food to mentally disabled children or conscientious objectors, inserting radium rods into the noses of schoolchildren, deliberately releasing radioactive chemicals over U.S. and Canadian cities, measuring the health effects of radioactive fallout from nuclear bomb tests, injecting pregnant women and babies with radioactive chemicals, and irradiating the testicles of prison inmates, amongst other things.[13] From 1945 to 1947, eighteen people were injected with plutonium as part of the Manhattan Project, many without being informed.[14] From 1955 to 1960, Sonoma State Hospital in northern California served as a permanent dropoff location for mentally handicapped children diagnosed with cerebral palsy or lesser disorders. The children subsequently underwent painful experimentation without adult consent. Many were given irradiated milk, as well as some spinal taps "for which they received no direct benefit." Reporters of *60 Minutes* learned that in these five years, the brain of every child with cerebral palsy who died at Sonoma State was removed and studied without parental consent. According to the CBS story, more than

10. Rothman, "Research Human," 2252.
11. Rothman, "Research Human," 2253.
12. Most of these experiments were jointly sponsored by the military, CIA, and the Atomic Energy Commission.
13. Much of this is documented in Eileen Welsome's excellent history of the nuclear human experiments, *The Plutonium Files* (New York: Random House, 2010).
14. William Moss and Roger Eckhardt, "The Human Plutonium Injection Experiments," *Los Alamos Science Radiation Protection and the Human Radiation Experiments* 23 (1995): 177–223.

1,400 patients died at the clinic.[15] This is just a very small handful of the many radiation experiments performed at this time.

Abuses involving medical experimentation occurred apart from the military as well. Two of these have gained a significant amount of attention. The first is the Willowbrook Hepatitis Experiments. Willowbrook State School in Staten Island, New York, housed and cared for mentally disabled children. In 1955, Dr. Saul Krugman began a study of the spread and development of hepatitis among the hospital population. Many children would become infected with hepatitis after a year of being admitted (the average was between 30 and 50 percent). Dr. Krugman was interested in finding a vaccine using gamma globulin antibodies (taken from the blood of hepatitis patients) as a way to create immunity in others. While not everything Krugman did was unethical, one of his studies involved feeding live hepatitis virus to sixty healthy children. All the children fed hepatitis virus became ill, some severely. Their skin and eyes turned yellow, their livers got bigger, and many of them refused to eat. When word of the study got out, Krugman defended it, stating that it was justifiable to inoculate retarded children at Willowbrook with hepatitis virus because most of them would get hepatitis anyway. He also stated that he followed protocols such as obtaining parental consent. However, many are critical of the "consent," as it became a requirement to consent to the experimental treatment as a condition of being admitted into the hospital.

The second study was performed just across the river in Brooklyn, New York, at the Jewish Chronic Disease Hospital. Dr. Chester Southam was an immunologist at Sloan-Kettering Hospital where he had been working for more than a decade on cancer studies. In July 1963, he suggested a collaborative research project with the Jewish Chronic Disease Hospital (JCDH). Southam was interested in the immunologic systems of debilitated individuals and how they would react to cancer. The patients at the JCDH would make excellent subjects for his study. Realizing that most patients would react negatively to the word "cancer," he did not tell them they were involved in a cancer study but instead simply told them they were getting human cells grown in test tubes. He then injected twenty-two elderly patients with live cancer cells. This was not an unusual procedure for Southam. In 1954, he injected a leukemia patient with cancer cells to make tumors grow and injected cancer cells in other patients as well. Tumors grew in many of them and had to be surgically removed. One patient died from the experiment. None of these patients were

15. Rebecca Leung. "A Dark Chapter in Medical History," *CBS News*, February 11, 2009.

told what they were being given. In 1956, he injected cancer cells into one hundred healthy prisoners at the Ohio State Penitentiary. He often injected cancer cell patients at Sloan-Kettering, including pregnant women, again without informing them. He felt it was not necessary as he was their doctor and was caring for them. Three physicians at JCDH refused to participate in the study and went on to report his actions to the Regents of the University of the State of New York; an investigation followed. During the investigation, Dr. Southam defended himself by stating that he believed the patients faced no risk of harm, that his actions were standard practice, and that his tests would be beneficial for future medical knowledge. Several prominent doctors supported his view. However, he was found guilty of unprofessionalism and deceit. His medical license was suspended for one year. No criminal charges were filed against him, and he was later elected vice president of the American Cancer Society.

Over the next decade, a number of incidents occurred that were to have a big impact on reforming human experimentation. In 1964, the World Health Organization came out with a code of ethics titled the Helsinki Declaration, which reaffirmed and clarified the Nuremberg Code. This declaration, which has undergone seven revisions since 1964 and has gone from eleven paragraphs to thirty-seven in the current 2013 revision, is not binding nor required, but has become the principal guiding statement concerning experimental research on human subjects in place today.

Perhaps the one single item that effected change was the 1966 article by Henry Beecher in the *New England Journal of Medicine* titled "Ethics and Clinical Research." In that article Beecher documents twenty-two cases of flagrant ethical abuses in current experiments involving human subjects (included were the two cases mentioned above). He documents how these researchers had risked the health and lives of their subjects without informing them of the dangers of the experiments or obtaining any kind of consent. Beecher's article shows that rather than being anomalous, unethical experimentation was common among researchers from "leading medical schools, university hospitals, private hospitals, government military departments . . . government institutes (The National Institutes of Health), Veterans Administration Hospitals and industry."[16]

16. Originally published as Henry K. Beecher, "Ethics and Clinical Research," *New England Journal of Medicine* 274 (1966): 1354–1360. Quoted from Henry K. Beecher, "Ethics and Clinical Research," Bulletin of the World Health Organization 79, no. 4 (2001): 367.

The impact of Beecher's article was deeply felt through the medical community, but it was the public revelations of the Tuskegee case in 1972 that finally led Congress to act. In 1973, they created the first national bioethics committee, The National Commission for the Protection of Human Subjects of Biomedical and Behavioral Research.[17] Their charge was to investigate and recommend regulations to any federal agency involved in human experimental research to protect the rights and welfare of research subjects. Out of this commission came *The Belmont Report*, which we have elaborated on elsewhere. In 1974, Congress passed the National Research Act, which developed guidelines for human subjects research and regulated the use of human experimentation.[18] Among the major impacts from this act was the decentralization of investigations. Responsibility was given over to the particular institution holding a grant for obtaining and keeping documentary evidence of informed consent. This was done mainly by the creation of Institutional Review Boards (IRB) that were now required for all federally funded research. An IRB is a peer-review committee to which all researchers need to apply for permission and funding of a study and by which fellow researchers approve and oversee the study. Its main job is to maintain a strict ethical oversight of the study in order to protect human subjects from abuse. Rothman comments, "With the creation of the IRB, the clinical investigator could no longer decide unilaterally whether the planned intervention was ethical but had to answer to colleagues operating under federal guidelines."[19] Of course, it is important to note that the IRB is only required for studies that are federally funded. There is no required oversight for privately funded studies.

In 1991, human research regulations were adopted by the federal government and became known as the "Common Rule." These regulations define a human subject as a "living individual about whom an investigator conducting research obtains: (1) data through intervention or interaction with the individual; or (2) identifiable private information."[20] The general requirements for

17. This was the first of a number of commissions on bioethics topics established by either the president or congress. Others were The Presidential Commission for the Study of Ethical Problems in Medicine and Biomedical and Behavioral Research (1978–83) during the Carter administration, The Advisory Committee on Human Radiation Experiments (1994–95) under the Clinton administration, The National Bioethics Advisory Commission (1996–2001) also under the Clinton administration, The President's Council on Bioethics (2001–2009) under the George W. Bush administration, and Presidential Commission for the Study of Bioethical Issues (2009–2017) under the Obama administration.
18. 42 U.S.C. 289.
19. Rothman, "Research Human," 2254.
20. 46 CFR 46.102(f).

research involving human participants include: (1) the institution conducting the study must submit an assurance of compliance with the Office of Human Research Protection that demonstrates the steps taken to ensure compliance with the regulations;[21] (2) the institution must establish an IRB that will review each study;[22] and (3) the study will keep the risks minimized, the risks must be reasonable in relation to the benefits, informed consent must be obtained, privacy must be protected, and additional safeguards must be in place for vulnerable populations such as children or economically disadvantaged persons.[23]

Since the late 1970s abuses in experiments involving human subjects has certainly diminished. However, they have not completely disappeared, and one occasionally hears of another case of researchers bending the rules to obtain results. One factor has been the financial involvement of large pharmaceutical companies in research and the conflict of interest that arises between an ethical study and the need for research and financial success. This can be a real problem if the researcher himself has a financial stake in the study. Such seems to be the case behind the Jesse Gelsinger gene therapy experiment.

Jesse Gelsinger was an eighteen-year-old with a rare genetic disease, ornithine transcarbamylase deficiency (OTC), a liver disease caused by a genetic mutation. Dr. James Wilson was the chief scientist in charge of a clinical trial at the University of Pennsylvania in which researchers were attempting to use gene therapy to supply the gene for OTC. This would not be a cure, but it would be treatment that might lessen the effects of the disease. Gelsinger applied for and was accepted into the study as a subject. He was informed of the risks but had decided it was worth it. On September 13, 1999, a genetically altered virus was injected into Jesse's liver. He soon began to develop flu-like symptoms, which was expected. However, during the night he developed signs of jaundice, which was not expected. His bilirubin was four times the normal level. Jesse soon became comatose and by the afternoon of the September 17 Jesse was dead. Even after the autopsy, it is not clear what happened to Jesse. However, in the investigation afterward it was discovered that not only had the Gelsingers been misinformed (researchers had not revealed two previous cases of liver toxicity which should have revealed as part of the informed consent process), but Dr. Wilson and the university were major stockholders

21. 46 CFR 46.103.
22. 46 CFR 46.107–9.
23. 46 CFR 46.107–9.

in Genovo, the biotech company that was funding the study. Hence, a conflict of interest arose concerning the study. As a result, the FDA shut down all gene therapy operations at the university and removed its ability to perform clinical trials. Within a year, the program ceased to exist.

Moore v. Regents of University of California

One of the landmark decisions involving medical research occurred in California in 1990. John Moore visited Dr. David Golde at UCLA Medical Center after being diagnosed with a form of leukemia. Throughout Moore's course of treatment, blood, bone marrow, and other bodily fluids were removed by Golde. In August 1979, Golde established a "cell line" taken from the samples from Moore's body. On January 30, 1981, the Regents of University of California applied for a patent on the cell line. The patent was issued, with Golde listed as an inventor of the cell line and the Regents as the assignee, which held the rights to the patent. The cell line was used for commercial purposes and included substantial cash payments and stock options. Moore continued to be treated by Golde, unaware of the cell line development. In 1983, Moore refused to sign a new consent form that would have given the Regents the rights to a cell line created from his samples. When Moore discovered how his samples were being used, he filed suit claiming that Golde failed to disclose research and economic interests in the cells before obtaining consent to the medical procedures.

The trial court ruled in favor of the Regents and Golde, which was reversed by the Court of Appeals. It was then appealed to the Supreme Court of California, which held that Moore had no property rights to his cells, but still had a cause of action regarding the lack of informed consent.[24] Moore alleged the tort of conversion as the illegal act taken by Golde and the Regents. Conversion occurs when a person is deprived of his property without permission or just cause. In this case, Moore claimed that the samples taken from him were still his property, to which the Court disagreed. In order to have a property right, Moore would have had to expect possession of his samples, which he never indicated an interest in having. Furthermore, at issue is the cell line itself, and Moore never had a property interest in the cell line.[25] However, the Court ruled that a reasonable patient would want to

24. *Moore v. Regents of University of California*, 793 P.2d 479 (California Supreme Court, 1990).
25. *Moore v. Regents of University of California*, 499–500.

know of a physician's potential lack of impartiality if independent research and economic interest were involved.[26] Thus, the consent given by Moore was not informed.

This has been a very brief overview of the history of human experimentation. There are many ethical cases of abuse that we have not discussed. However, I do not want to leave the impression that all medical research involving human subjects has ignored the rights and values of human beings. There are, and will continue to be, morally responsible researchers who truly desire to improve mankind by seeking ways to eradicate and treat disease. This is a noble goal. However, as Christians, we recognize that our sin nature is always looking for ways to pull of us from the divine light. Even the best of goals and the best of intentions can be used to tempt us to use methods that can ultimately devalue the very humans we are trying to help.

ETHICAL ISSUES IN HUMAN EXPERIMENTATION

Attitude Toward the Need for Human Experimentation

Before looking at specific ethical issues that arise in research involving human subjects, it is important that we pause and gain some perspective on the attitude with which we should approach research. We need to address what has come to be called the medical imperative of research: the idea that we owe to future society our best efforts to achieve the best goals possible in medical progress. This imperative implies an obligation on our part to continue research and attempt to eradicate disease and suffering. Whatever science can do, it should do. It may require great sacrifice but the goal of creating a better world is worth it. Note how this medical imperative permeates the following comment by bioethicists Glenn McGee and Art Caplan on the sacrifice of human embryos for stem cell research:

> It is the moral imperative of compassion that compels [embryonic] stem cell research . . . [it is estimated] that as many as 128 million Americans suffer from diseases that might respond to pluripotent stem cell therapies. Even if that is an optimistic number, many clinical researchers and cell biologists hold that stem cell therapies will be critical in treating cancer, heart disease, and degenerative diseases of aging such as Parkinson's disease. More than half of the world's population will suffer at some point in life with one of these three conditions, and

26. *Moore v. Regents of University of California*, 486.

> more humans die every year from cancer than were killed in both the Kosovo and Vietnam conflicts. Stem cell research is a pursuit of known and important goods. . . . Adults and even children are sometimes forced to give life, but only in the defense or at least interest of the community's highest ideals and most pressing interests. . . . What need is so great that it rises to the level where every member of the human family, even the smallest of humans might sacrifice? Already it is clear that we believe no need is more compelling than the suffering of half the world at the hand of miserable disease.[27]

However, this "imperative" is highly questionable. In 1969, the philosopher Hans Jonas wrote a classic article "Philosophical Reflections on Experimenting with Human Subjects." Jonas, whose mother was gassed in a Nazi concentration camp, was skeptical of the imperative attitude to do research. Contrary to the idea that we have an obligation to sacrifice for the common good, Jonas writes that progress is an *optional* goal. It is a *good*, but it is not *obligatory* to participate in any medical experiment purely for the sake of progress. In his opinion, we can accept slower progress more than we can accept the erosion of our moral values—the loss of individual rights and dignity. Jonas reminds us that health is a good but it's not the primary good. Physicians have an obligation to treat and cure their individual patients, but they do not have an *obligation* to society as a whole. Jonas writes:

> The destination of research is essentially melioristic. It does not serve the preservation of the existing good from which I profit myself and to which I am obligated. Unless the present state is intolerable, the melioristic goal is in a sense gratuitous. . . . Our descendants have a right to be left an unplundered planet; they do not have a right to new miracle cures. We have sinned against them, if by our doing we have destroyed their inheritance—which we are doing at a full blast; we have not sinned against them if by the time they come around arthritis has not yet been conquered . . . progress, with all of our methodological labor for it, cannot be budgeted in advance for its fruits received as a due. Its coming-about at all and it turning out for good (of which we can never be sure) must rather be regarded as something akin to grace.[28]

27. Glenn McGee and Art Caplan, "The Ethics and Politics of Small Sacrifices in Stem Cell Research," *Kennedy Institute of Ethics Journal* 9, no. 2 (1999): 153–55.
28. Hans Jonas, "Experimentation with Human Subjects," in Tom L. Beauchamp and LeRoy Walters, *Contemporary Issues in Bioethics*, 3rd ed. (Belmont, CA: Wadsworth, 1989), 435.

Jonas is not saying that human experimentation should never be done, but simply that it is not obligatory. Participation in human experimentation is always and should always be a supererogatory action. Therefore, subjects should always be volunteers. Ideally, a volunteer should have complete freedom and knowledge about an experiment before participating in it. However, informed consent is not enough to justify human experimentation. Jonas suggests two other conditions. First, subjects should be first recruited from the most knowledgeable about the specifics of the experiment. Hence, physicians, research scientists themselves, and the scientific community at large are ideal candidates and should be the first ones to participate in the medical experiments. If this were the case, Jonas believes, almost all the legal and ethical problems would vanish. Beyond this group, Jonas says we can look for additional subjects where "a maximum of identification, understanding, and spontaneity can be expected."[29] Jonas suggests that the next ethically desirable group of human subjects would be among "the most highly motivated, highly educated, and the least captive members of the society."[30] Selecting subjects from such an affluent batch would satisfy the cause of both the subject and the researcher. The subjects, in this case, are "willed" to participate and have a clear understanding of the purpose and technique of the experiment that makes them valid candidates. Only after we have exhausted these groups should we consider the poor and vulnerable. The second condition is that the experiment must be undertaken for an adequate cause. The cause of those suffering from current diseases is always stronger than the idea of medical progress in and of itself.

Jonas provides a much needed balance as we approach the issue of research involving human experimentation. Research is important and should be done, and often it must involve human experimentation; but there are limits to what we do, and we should be careful not to move beyond those limits. We should not let the tyranny of medical progress tempt us to do that which denies our human dignity and goes beyond the limits God has set for us. As Christians, we must be careful not to make an idol of medical progress and sacrifice and bow down to that idol.

Therapy and Research

Another conceptual issue that deserves a word is the important difference between therapy and research and the need to maintain a distinction between

29. Jonas, "Experimentation with Human Subjects," 437.
30. Jonas, "Experimentation with Human Subjects," 437.

these two activities. Therapy has as its aim the relief of suffering and the restoration of the health of the individual patient and her welfare. Research is a scientific medical endeavor. Its aim is to gain a better understanding of the chemical and physical process involved in human functioning. To accomplish this purpose, it studies the epidemiology of disease. It does not have as its concern the individual patient, but mankind. In therapy, you have *patients*; in research you have *subjects*.

If these two practices are kept distinct, there is not a problem, but once they are confused conflicts of interest can arise, especially for the physician. It is not unusual for a physician to be acting as both a therapist and a researcher. Not only is he concerned for the well-being of his patient/subject, but he is also concerned for acquiring data for his research project. As Jesus tells us, no man can serve two masters and, while I obviously do not think he was talking about medical research, the principle still applies. A physician might be consciously or unconsciously driven by the gains in the research project to encourage patients to volunteer as subjects for research when it really is not in their best interests. He might minimize the risks, as we observed in the Jesse Gelsinger case, or provide inadequate information. Patients are extremely vulnerable—especially the elderly, the desperate, and children—to suggestions from physicians. They might feel pressured to be involved. Many will not question their doctor as they might an indifferent researcher. They might think, "Well, it is my doctor. Surely they would not think I should do this unless I needed it." Art Schafer summarizes this conflict well:

> Although a patient who has been enrolled as a subject in a randomized clinical trial may benefit from the therapeutic effects of the treatment being tested, the fact that the treatment cannot be entirely tailored to that patient's special needs seems to violate the physician's obligation of unqualified fidelity to his patient. The morally troubling doubt concerns the likelihood that physicians may be able to recruit a statistically significant number of volunteers for random clinical trials only by neglecting the particular circumstances of individuals.[31]

There is a real danger in mixing these two practices, and physicians must be extra-cautious not to allow their research project to interfere with their best thinking as a therapist. This becomes even harder for the doctor who

31. Arthur Schafer, "The Ethics of Random Clinical Trials," *New England Journal of Medicine* 307 (1982): 721.

is financially invested in his research. Studies have shown that one-fifth to one-third of all doctors providing patient care in clinical trials have financial investments with drug and biotech firms. Any physician who stands to earn a considerable amount of money from the clinical trial he is overseeing has a serious conflict-of-interest issue. He may take all sorts of shortcuts from not informing patients to tainting clinical results in reports. He might tweak his study to sound more hopeful and better than actually is the case. In 2004, Dr. Hwang Woo Suk of South Korea claimed to have made tremendous strides in embryonic stem cell research (ESCR), having successfully developed several stem lines from human cloning. He published two articles in the journal *Science* documenting his progress and was often pointed to as the model for what we should be doing in this country. Then in November of 2005, the truth came out: he admitted to fabricating all his studies. He had not developed a single cell line and admitted obtaining his eggs in an unethical and illegal manner. In May 2005, Suk was found guilty of fraud, embezzlement, and breaking South Korea's bioethics laws.

A conflict of interest also exists for the patient who is asked to be involved in human experimentation for a disease they are suffering from. This is referred to as therapeutic research (as opposed to nontherapeutic research from which the subject does not gain any therapeutic benefit). The promise of possibly receiving benefit from an experimental drug or treatment can be an overwhelming temptation to participate in the research project. Patients may willingly agree to become subjects without understanding all the relevant information they need to make an informed consent. Their desperation and hope may blind them to the realization that the real likelihood of success that any benefit from the new drug or treatment they would receive might be minimal. This has, more often than not, been the outcome. This is especially problematic for those in a vulnerable position, such as the dying. Both physician/researchers and patient/subjects need to exercise real caution in these cases.

Informed Consent

A lot has been said about the importance and need for informed consent, and we have already discussed this in the context of therapeutic care. When it comes to research, we need to be even more careful in both the "informed" aspect and the "consent" aspect. We have discussed the dangers of the consent aspect above when it comes to vulnerable and desperate subjects. There is a serious hindrance with the "informed" aspect in research: researchers simply do not have a lot of the information they normally would in a therapeutic environment, due to the nature of research. That is why they are doing the research—to gain information. How can researchers fulfill the "informed" part of informed consent when they do not have necessary information? It is for this reason that researchers need to be extra-diligent to provide, in as objective a manner as possible, all the information they currently do have to the patient. Considering the conflicts of interests mentioned above, they must be extra-careful to be accurate and precise and not to spin the information in any manner that euphemistically puts the study in a positive light. This is no time to be a "salesman" for a pet project. Title 45 of the Federal Code of Regulations, section 46 on Protection of Subjects in Research, lists the following as necessary elements of informed consent for subjects involved in human experimentation:

1. a statement that the study involves research, an explanation of the purposes of the research and the expected duration of the subject's participation, a description of the procedures to be followed, and identification of any procedures which are experimental;
2. a description of any reasonably foreseeable risks or discomforts to the subject;
3. a description of any benefits to the subject or to others which may reasonably be expected from the research;
4. a disclosure of appropriate alternative procedures or courses of treatment, if any, that might be advantageous to the subject;
5. a statement describing the extent, if any, to which confidentiality of records identifying the subject will be maintained;
6. for research involving more than minimal risk, an explanation as to whether any compensation and an explanation as to whether any medical treatments are available if injury occurs and, if so, what they consist of, or where further information may be obtained;
7. an explanation of whom to contact for answers to pertinent questions about the research and research subjects' rights, and whom to contact in the event of a research-related injury to the subject; and
8. a statement that participation is voluntary, refusal to participate will involve no penalty or loss of benefits to which the subject is otherwise entitled, and the subject may discontinue participation at any time without penalty or loss of benefits to which the subject is otherwise entitled.[32]

32. 45 CFR §46.116.

Random Clinical Trials

Probably the most significant innovation of the modern period of human experimentation is the development of the random clinical trial (RCT). A clinical trial is a form of research where a drug, treatment, or a new procedure is tested against a group of selected subjects for its side effects and effectiveness. For brevity's sake, we will use a new drug as an example, though the same steps would involve new treatments and new procedures. Before entering clinical trials, the drug first goes through a series of preclinical procedures. One of these will usually involve animal experimentation.[33] At this stage researchers are attempting to determine the drug's therapeutic index (dosage producing toxic effects vs. dosage producing beneficial effects) as well as side effects and possible dangers. Once the preclinical stage is completed, assuming the drug is successful at that stage, it moves into the clinical stage and clinical trials take place.

There are four phases of clinical trials:

- Phase I: Researchers test the drug in a small population group (ten to eighty), mostly to evaluate its safety and identify any side effects. Actual effectiveness is not tested at this time.
- Phase II: Researchers test, in a larger controlled group (one hundred to three hundred), for effectiveness and continued studies on safety. Statistical measurements are taken at this time.
- Phase III: Testing is done with a much larger group (one thousand to three thousand) to confirm effectiveness, continue to monitor side effects, and compare it with other accepted theories and current drugs. Data is collected that may be relevant to improving effectiveness and increasing safety.
- Phase IV: Continued collecting of data on effects after therapy has become established as a standard treatment and continued refinement. This last phase is usually considered outside the clinical trial period.

A clinical trial is considered random when it involves at least two groups of subjects, randomly divided into those who get the drug (or treatment) and those who do not but are given a placebo instead. The group not given the

33. We could say much about the ethics of animal experimentation, but that lies outside the purview of this chapter.

drug is referred to as the control group. The RCT can be either blind (in which the subject does not know if they are receiving the drug or placebo) or double-blind. The best random clinical trials are double-blind trials, as they assure that bias is significantly reduced and doesn't play a part in the treatment of the subjects nor taint the results. A double-blind trial is one in which both the subject and the researcher are ignorant as to whether an individual subject has received the experimental drug or the placebo.[34] Double-blind trials are considered the gold standard of clinical trials. There are several ethical issues involved in RCT, but we will restrict our discussion to just two issues: placebos and the use of vulnerable subjects for RCT.

Placebos

We discussed placebos in chapter 2. We came to see that the problem with placebos is that they inherently involve deception in order to achieve the placebo effect, the reduction of pain. In research placebos have a different purpose. In using them, researchers are not trying to achieve the placebo effect.[35] The purpose of placebos in RCT is to have some device to offer subjects in the control group to replace the drug being experimented on. The placebo allows the "blindness" necessary to maintain a lack of bias on the part of subjects and researchers. There is another difference between placebos used in therapy and those used in RCT. In our earlier discussion, we said that placebos are inert as far as providing actual medication for pain. They are usually just a glucose or saline solution. That may also be the case with placebos used in research. Remember, however, that the purpose of placebos in research is to mask which subjects are actually being given the experimental drug from subjects and researchers in a double-blind RCT. Because many experimental drugs cause a number of side effects (such as nausea, nervousness, drowsiness, loss of appetite, and so on), researchers often must load placebos with substances that will cause these side effects. So, unlike the placebos used in therapy, the placebos used in research are not just inert substances.

Therefore, the ethical problems with placebos in research are different than those of therapy. The major problem is the realization that some subjects are may be benefitting from treatment by taking an actual efficacious drug while others are not being treated at all. While both groups are informed and

34. The "three-armed" trial is one where the control group is further divided into those who get placebos all the time and those who get placebos sometimes and the drug at other times.
35. In fact, they specifically prefer not to achieve any effect, as that might taint the study.

subject/patients consent to the use of these testing conditions, one can imagine the anxiety of not knowing if you are being treated or not. What of the physician's obligation to put his patient first? This was the case with the polio vaccine RCT is the early 1960s. Researchers were very positive by the end of animal experimentation and the first two phases that they had an efficacious vaccine, but they still had to go through the Phase III stage before they could be sure. Hence, thirty thousand children were injected with a substance known to be ineffective in preventing polio at a time when the researchers in charge were very sure they could offer them a safe vaccine. Were the doctors really acting in the best interests of these children, or were they more concerned with following scientific protocols?

Another problem with using placebos in research, because they often must mask painful and unpleasant side effects, is that not only are doctors not providing beneficial medication to patient/subjects, but they are actually causing them harm. In therapy, we often justify harm by balancing it with a benefit the patient is receiving. But in research, the patient/subject may not be receiving any benefit at all. The benefit is for scientific progress and others. Some have suggested that one way to resolve these placebo conflicts is to not have a control group that is given only a placebo. Perhaps a better research design is to compare established treatments with new experimental treatments. The control group would not be given a placebo, but an actual treatment. It might be inferior to the new treatment, but it would at least be something that actually treats the disease. New protocols are also being suggested that would allow researchers who believe they have sufficient evidence that the new drug is effective to be allowed to suspend the rest of the trial and offer the drug to both groups. In the end, we can affirm at least two principles concerning the use of placebos: (1) subjects should be informed that they may receive a placebo while participating in the study and (2) placebos should only be used when necessary for the success of the experiment.

Use of Vulnerable Subjects

The other ethical issue concerning RCT has to do with the selection of subjects. We can divide RCTs into two types: therapeutic trials and nontherapeutic trials. Therapeutic trials are those in which the subjects are also patients and stand to benefit directly from the study. They are suffering from the disease or debilitation for which the new drug, treatment, or procedure is being tested. As was mentioned above, most studies rarely offer significant benefits to those who are patient/subjects. This needs to be carefully and clearly communicated to the patient/subject. Researchers need to be careful about raising hopes as a way to recruit volunteers among the patient population. This is especially a mandate for those desperate patients who are dying from their disease and are involved in RCTs for life-saving drugs.

The majority of RCTs are nontherapeutic. No direct therapeutic advantage is offered in these trials. Subjects are not patients suffering from a particular debilitation or disease that the drug is being tested for. Even in these studies care must be taken to make sure they patients are fully informed, and that consent is freely given. When performing either therapeutic or nontherapeutic research, there are certain vulnerable groups of which special considerations need to be discussed. These groups are considered vulnerable usually because of one of three reasons: age, social circumstance, or health. We will briefly discuss four specific groups.

Certainly, one of the most vulnerable groups to consider for experimental research are children. The Willowbrook study mentioned above drew severe criticism for its abuse of children. Most vulnerable are those that are not just children, but who are institutionalized in hospitals or schools.[36] Some suggest that children should never be part of any RCT. They are not able to fully understand the aspects of the study and therefore cannot really offer informed consent. They are often completely dependent on adults to provide their basic living conditions. Hence, a red light often goes off in our head and we are justified at being suspicious when we hear of a study involving children.

While such suspicion is warranted, the strict rule to never use children in experimental studies may be extreme. There are a few reasons why children might need to be part of a study. As Ronald Munson, professor of philosophy and medicine at the University of Missouri, argues,

> Biologically, children are not just small adults. Their bodies are developing and growing systems. Not only are there anatomical differences; there are also differences in metabolism and biochemistry. For example, some drugs are absorbed and metabolize in children more quickly than in adults, whereas other drugs

36. Many of the vulnerable groups we mention have in common the property of being institutionalized. It is no wonder that, in the past, this has been a common breeding ground for studies. It's the perfect environment to obtain many individuals, have control over them, and keep them localized for the duration of the study. However, it is also the reason these groups are so vulnerable. In most institutions, whether it is a hospital, school, prison, or elderly facility, freedom of choice is often severely restricted. Such individuals become used to being told what to do, and so they are susceptible to being easily manipulated.

> continue to be active for a longer time. Often, some drugs produce different effects when administered to children. . . . Findings based on adult subjects cannot simply be extrapolated to children, any more than results based on animal studies can be extrapolated to human beings.[37]

The fact that nutritional needs are different, that children are prone to some diseases that are uncommon in adults, and the fact that some childhood diseases are fatal, all argue that studies must be performed on children in order to discover new therapies and drugs to battle against these diseases. To exclude children completely from experimentation would hinder the progress of pediatric medicine. Therefore, a solid case can be made for the use of children in medical experimentation.

That being said, strong safeguards must be in place to guarantee that children do not become abused as subjects in studies. A few questions need to be addressed. First, who should be in the category of "child"? Obviously, this is not an issue with very young children, but it does become an issue when they enter the age of adolescence. While we can legally draw a line at eighteen-years old for example, the problem is that legal line is often blurred when it comes to morally recognizing when an individual adolescent should be considered an adult. The major factor becomes an issue of autonomy: Is the individual able to function as an autonomous decision-maker? If she can understand all the aspects of the study at a level of any adult, shouldn't she be given to opportunity to freely consent to involvement in a study? Hence, a child at sixteen or even fifteen may be able to make an informed consent. Of course, they may not be at that level yet and that must be assessed on a per-person basis. However, even if an adolescent is not given the full freedom to consent to being involved in a study, she should at least be included in the conversation and allowed a voice to be heard.

If a child cannot consent, then we normally turn to the parent as the recognized legal guardian to make consent for the child. The courts have established limits on parental consent, and parental consent is not honored if parents are acting in an unreasonable or reckless manner. At that point the court can step in and appoint a *guardian ad litem* to make decisions based on what is determined is in the best interest of the child. However, in general,

37. Ronald Munson, *Intervention and Reflection: Basic Issues in Bioethics*, 9th ed. (Boston: Wadsworth-Cengage, 2012), 148.

as long as a parent is not acting irresponsibly, they can authorize consent for their child to participate in an experimental procedure.

This raises another question: Are there any studies for which children should not be involved? Again, speaking generally, most ethicists agree that children should only be involved in studies where there is a real possibility of them individually gaining a direct benefit from the study. This seems a reasonable safeguard from children being exploited. However, it may mean that certain studies might be seriously impeded, especially those where the risk of harm is very low but the child is still not gaining any direct benefit. This may just be the price we have to pay to protect children. If one does not have this safeguard, then the opportunity to exploit children, especially those in institutional environments, becomes very real. Fortunately, the Department of Health and Human Services (DHHS) has provided guidelines for the use of children in medical experiments:

1. For children to become participants, permission must be obtained from parents and children must give their assent.
2. An IRB is assigned the responsibility of considering the "ages, maturity, and psychological states of children" and determining if they are capable of assenting (failure to object cannot be construed as assent).
3. Children who are wards of the state or of an institution can become participants only if the research relates to their status as wards or takes place in which most of the subjects are not wards.
4. Each child must also be supplied with an "advocate" to represent his or her best interest.[38]

Another vulnerable group we need to consider is prisoners. In the past prisoners were often seen as ideal candidates for medical research, especially prisoners condemned to die. Here were institutionalized individuals with extremely restricted freedom of choice and who would certainly be present for the duration of the study. Not only were they available, but they were often seen and treated as social outcasts. The argument was often made that they deserved to be used for scientific experiments—at least that was one way they could pay society back for their crimes. For those condemned to die for especially heinous crimes like murder, the thinking often became, "Well, they're going to die anyway, why not get some good out of it?" One certainly did not have to think about getting

38. Munson, *Intervention and Reflection*, 150.

consent or of volunteering. In the early twentieth century, Richard P. Strong sought and received permission from the governor of the Philippines to inoculate twenty-four criminals condemned to death with the bubonic plague. No consent was sought, and thirteen prisoners died. In the 1940s four hundred prisoners at Statesville Prison in Joliet, Illinois, were infected with malaria in a study by the University of Chicago in cooperation with the U.S. military. This study did ask for volunteers who were informed of the risks involved but an incentive was added: the men were told that their involvement would be taken into account when they were up for parole, or they might receive a sentence reduction.

While the treatment of prisoners has vastly improved in more modern times, and we now abide by strict guidelines concerning voluntariness and informed consent in prisons, there are still some concerns with using prisoners. Should some form of reward be offered a patient who participates, like a reduced sentence? Some have argued that if the patient is motivated by a reward of reduced sentence or probation, that could be considered a form of duress. The prisoner is not making a free decision but is being pressured by undue influence. Some have argued that prisoners should be offered no advantage to being involved in human experimentation. However, critics argue that were that the case, the chances of obtaining any significant population will be severely impaired. Others argue that to deny prisoners the opportunity to volunteer deprives them of a basic human right and of the opportunity to increase their self-worth by feeling they are contributing back to mankind, even as a form of repentance for their crime. Some have argued back that prisoners do not have the right exercise their basic rights to choose due to their crimes. The whole idea of prison itself is to justifiably deprive prisoners of several basic rights. By nature, it justifiably restricts autonomy in the name of retributive justice. This was the reasoning of the AMA when it voted in 1952 to deprive the right of prisoners convicted of heinous crimes (murder, rape, arson, kidnapping, treason) to volunteer medical experimentation.

While the discussion continues on using prisoners in RCTs, most concerns have been about protecting prisoners from exploitation. In general, it is agreed that most prisoners can volunteer for experimental testing of drugs as long as strict guidelines are in place to assure complete voluntariness and precise information is provided. In some situations, those found guilty of truly heinous crimes are not allowed to participate. But the conversation is an ongoing one.

A third vulnerable group to consider is the poor. Again because of their lack of means, in the past, the poor have often been socially stigmatized, marginalized, and devalued. It was common for doctors in the eighteenth and nineteenth centuries, and even into the twentieth, to seek out the poor and the homeless. Many state hospitals had an area often designated as the "back ward," where they would offer minimal care to the indigent and poor who could not afford normal hospital care. These back wards became major sources for experimental subjects. When the Tuskegee study, which involved poor African American tenant farmers, was revealed there was a general revulsion to this treatment of the poor. Today, use of the poor in medical experiments is highly frowned upon and seen as the worst abuse of exploitation. However, at the same time it is condemned, it is interesting to note that some of our largest studies still take place public or municipal hospitals and public care facilities that have a high percentage of lower-income patients. It is still the case that lower-income individuals are much more likely to be involved in studies than the educated and wealthy.

A fourth vulnerable group to be considered is the terminally ill. The revelation that one has a terminal illness is an overwhelming experience for most human beings. One is faced with one's own mortality with staggering realism. The feelings of anger, despair, and grief can be so great as to overcome any rational capacity. This places the terminally ill in an extremely vulnerable position. They might be willing to try anything that will prolong the inevitable and if not tempted themselves, they may be pressured by friends and family to jump into any therapeutic avenue that might give than even the smallest hope of recovery.

Many bioethicists are extremely cautious of involving the terminally ill in any experimental trials and point to a number of ethical problems. As was stated, their ability to rationally assess the information they are told or they read may be seriously compromised by their state of mind. Out of desperation, they may become susceptible to any form of quackery they hear. They may get involved in experiments without a complete understanding of what they are getting into. Often, they are unaware that studies have specific diagnostic criteria for having a particular disease or that they must be at a certain stage in order to qualify as a candidate in a specific study. Many times participation in studies can be very expensive, as they may have to move or travel to a location some distance away just to participate in a study that may not extend their life or have any beneficial effect at all. The experiment can also involve painful procedures and uncomfortable side effects, again without guaranteeing any benefit.

Patient/subjects often develop unrealistic expectations no matter how much researchers communicate the realistic odds. Hope is a hard thing to temper when one is facing death. One of the worst aspects of involvement is that one can be dropped as a subject from the experiment if one reaches a stage where the researchers believe they are not contributing to the study. Often patient/subjects forget that the purpose of the study is ultimately for scientific progress in treating a disease, not to cure them. This can be devastating to an individual as they watch their last hope, one they should possibly never have had in the first place, vanish. Most importantly, patient/subjects need to be aware that the genuine chance of any study really benefitting them is statistically quite remote. It is the exception that a terminally ill patient receives significant benefit from participation in a study.

This is not to say that terminally ill patients should never participate in experimental drugs. Certainly, there are some positive aspects to consider. They may gain some comfort in the fact that they are at least trying something rather than just accepting the inevitable and doing nothing. The experimental procedure or drug, while not curing them of the terminal disease, might offer some therapeutic value such as relieving pain or discomfort and relieving some symptoms of their illness. They may feel value as they know they are contributing to mankind in helping to find a new cure or treatment. Finally, there is value in simply honoring a terminally ill patient/subject's autonomy. There is so much at this point in their lives they feel they have no control over that we should seek to honor what little they have.

The responsibility of researchers toward the terminally ill is enormous. They must carefully explain all the aspects of the study in as realistic terms as possible. They should strive above all not to give any false hope even if motivated by an attitude of kindness. The kindest thing one can do at this time is to be honest and accurate in informing the patient/subject of the basic information about the study and about their chances of benefitting from it. That truthful communication needs to continue as long as the patient/subject is involved in the study. Researchers need to be extra-cautious and diligent to watch for times when family members and loved ones attempt to spin information into a more positive light than it should be. Family and friends are often subject to the same emotional extremes as terminally ill patients. Sometimes subject/patients may need to be protected from the very people who want the best for them.

Ill-Gotten Gains

Another area we need to address is the problem of ill-gotten gains. The term "ill-gotten gains" refers to beneficial information obtained through unethical or illegal means. As we look back at the many unethical human experiments of the past, we find that while the means used to obtain medical information was often horrific, the information gained was often quite legitimate and useful in advancing medical knowledge. Should we use such knowledge?

Many viscerally respond in the negative. Some argue that nonuse of the information would be a form of punishment to those who gained this information in an unethical manner. To use it would be to reward the unethical researchers for their endeavors. Some go so far as to argue that we should expunge all the records of an unethical experiment. Others argue that using such information ultimately condones and even endorses the means by which it was obtained. Some argue that making use of the results of unethical experiments will only encourage future unethical experimentation. Still others decry the use of data from unethical experiments as disrespectful to those who were exploited, many of whom suffered miserably and died, in order to obtain such information. Some raise the point that while utilitarian reasons might argue for using the information (as it will make the greatest number happy in the end), deontological and virtue ethicists argue that such experiences were using persons as a means to an end and not an end unto themselves.

On the other hand, there are those who do believe that it is possible to justifiably employ the information gained from even the worst of unethical studies. First, some argue to withhold use of this information is not punishing the unethical researchers nearly as much as it is punishing future patients from obtaining a beneficial treatment simply because the information about that treatment was obtained unethically. Why should they suffer? Second, some suggest that the information obtained and the means by which it was obtained are only incidentally causally connected. Information is information and its value should be assessed on its own merit and not on the means by which it was obtained. Aaron Ridley makes this point well, stating, "a piece of information (e.g. how to cure AIDS) is always ethically neutral, regardless of its provenance, and so there is no connection between the ethical character of the way in which a piece of information was obtained and the ethical character of the way in which it is used."[39] Third, one might make the argument that not to use the information would be *dishonoring* to the victims of the unethical experiment as they would have suffered in vain. By employing information gained in the experimental

39. Aaron Ridley, "Ill-Gotten Gains: On the Use of Results from Unethical Experiments in Medicine," *Public Affairs Quarterly* 9, no. 3 (1995): 255.

study as a means of helping those who are suffering from a disease or illness, one is ultimately honoring—some say the highest way to honor—those who suffered in the unethical experiment.

Some have offered a compromise between these two extremes of employing or not employing information gained from unethical studies. The late Benjamin Freedman of McGill University suggests three ways information gained from unethical experimentation can be used.[40] First is using information for grounding a scientific argument. This is the most controversial and debatable usage and many scientific publications refuse to publish such data. Some will publish such data but only if an editorial is included discussing the ethical issues involved in obtaining the data. Second is reliance upon information from unethical studies only in establishing or validating a scientific or clinical practice. This is less controversial, as the information is playing a subsidiary role to the actual practice being assessed. Last is using information as suggestive of further areas for inquiry. This is the least controversial, as it barely uses the information at all and only suggests further studies needed. While the issue of the usage of ill-gotten gains continues, many are suggesting that some sort of compromise may be the best solution to the conflict of possessing significant information that could be of benefit to many suffering from disease and debilitations and the condemnation of the means used to obtain such information.

We now turn to an example of a current research project that again raises the question of using human persons to obtain a means to treat or even cure some of our worst diseases: embryonic stem cell research.

EMBRYONIC STEM CELL RESEARCH[41]

On August 9, 2001, President George W. Bush announced a ban on federal funding for the creation of new stem cell lines derived from the destruction of human embryos.[42] The policy was intended as a compromise and specified that research on lines created prior to that date would still be eligible for funding. Seventy-one lines from fourteen laboratories across the globe met Bush's

40. Benjamin Freedman, "Research, Unethical," in *Encyclopedia of Bioethics*, 2nd ed., ed. Warren T. Reich (New York: Simon and Schuster, 1995), 2260.
41. This section of this chapter was first published as "Embryonic Stem Cell Research: Is there a limit to the medical imperative to end suffering and disease?" *Journal of the International Society of Christian Apologetics*, Vol. 8 No. 1 (Spring 2009), used with permission.
42. The presidential ban is often misunderstood and misrepresented. Some claim that Bush banned all stem cell research, which is not true at all. Others claimed that he banned all federal funding of stem cell research, which is also not true.

eligibility criteria, and scientists who wished to investigate these lines could still receive grants through the National Institutes of Health. Bush's reasoning was that a substantial amount of the public believed that embryos were human life and that it is morally problematic to create human life for the purpose of destroying it for research purposes.

On March 9, 2009, seven years and five months later, President Obama fulfilled one of his campaign promises and lifted this ban on federal funding for new stem cell lines derived from the destruction of embryos. In doing so, he said, "Scientists believe these tiny cells may have the potential to help us understand, and possibly cure, some of our most devastating diseases and conditions. . . . I believe we are called to care for each other and work to ease human suffering. I believe we have been given the capacity and will to pursue this research—and the humanity and conscience to do so responsibly."[43]

President Obama's assessment of embryonic stem cell research (hereafter referred to as ESCR) is not new. Many politicians, scientists, and ethicists present the same basic argument:

- Terrible suffering is going on in the world through disease.
- ESCR has the potential to cure these diseases and end this suffering.
- Embryos are just a clump of cells and should not be considered to be human persons.
- Therefore, it is a terrible injustice if we do not allow research to continue.

Few question the fact that we have a medical imperative to end suffering—but is there a limit to that imperative? That is the question to be explored. We will begin by discussing a bit about stem cells: what they are, what are the potential benefits of stem cell research, and how it is done. Then we will explore the arguments for ESCR, followed by the extremely problematic issues with it. In the process, we will examine some alternative treatments that avoid the use of embryonic stem cells. I will then conclude with an assessment of stem cell research.

43. Text of the president can be found at https://obamawhitehouse.archives.gov/the-press-office/remarks-president-prepared-delivery-signing-stem-cell-executive-order-and-scientifi.

The Science of Stem Cells

Your body is made of millions of cells. Most of these are designed to function a very specific way within a particular organ or system. These are called differentiated or specified cells (liver cells, red blood cells, neural cells). Stem cells are unspecified cells and are the source for replenishing specified cells as they die off. They have three important characteristics: (1) they are unspecialized, (2) they can renew themselves through cell division over long periods (called replication), and (3) under certain conditions they can be induced to become specialized or differentiated cells.

Stem cells can be classified in two ways: source and plasticity. As far as source, stem cells can be extracted from embryos (ESC) or they can come be extracted from tissues or organs within living beings. These are referred to as adult stem cells (ASC), though the term has nothing to do with age. Plasticity refers to the potential of a stem cell to become other cells. While there are several different plasticity levels, the four general categories for our purposes are totipotent, pluripotent, multipotent, and unipotent. Totipotent is the ability to become any cell in the body including an entirely new being. Zygotes (the immediate product of conception) are totipotent. Pluripotent means that the stem cell can become any cell in the body (but not a new being). ESC are pluripotent. Multipotent is the ability to become a limited number of different types of cells, and unipotent is the ability to become only one kind of differentiated cell.

Of what good use are embryonic stem cells? There are currently almost six thousand genetic disorders, and many researchers are hopeful that stem cells can be integral in the treatment and even cure for many of these diseases. Most often mentioned are Parkinson's disease, Alzheimer's disease, diabetes, MS, lymphoma, heart disease, and spinal injuries. There at least four ways that it is hoped that stem cells could be beneficial. First, ESC might be able to replace damaged cells. Many diseases such as Parkinson's disease and juvenile diabetes result from the death or dysfunction of just one or a few cells. Stem cells might be used as replacement cells, offering "lifelong" treatment. Second, stem cells might be used to repair diseased or damaged organs. By isolating stem cells in a laboratory, scientists theoretically could grow new heart cells to repair damage from heart attacks, new liver cells to treat hepatitis, and new red blood and stromal cells for cancer patients after ablative radiotherapy. Third, some stem cells might be used to renew and regenerate biological functions (like the immune system) or damaged organs. Finally, scientists are trying to learn how to coax stem cells to become new, healthy, "younger" cells to rejuvenate, restore, and repair older cells and ailing hearts, livers, brains, and other organs.

How are embryonic stem cells obtained? Embryonic stem cells must be obtained from embryos that have been fertilized *in vitro*. After fertilization, the zygote begins cellular division and in four to seven days forms a blastocyst which contains an inner cell mass of about thirty pluripotent stem cells. These cells are removed from the blastocyst which is destroyed in the procedure. They are placed in a culture dish in a culture medium that provides nutrients that allow them to grow. Over time, and under certain conditions, the cells proliferate and form pluripotent embryonic stem cell lines. If cells are allowed to clump together, they will begin to form differentiated cells. They can form blood cells, neural cells, and muscle cells. The real task of embryonic stem cell research lies in the task of controlling the process of differentiation so that the stem cell eventually develops into the specific cell needed for a particular debilitation. This is called "directed differentiation."

Some embryos are obtained through cloning. The most common way this is done is through somatic cell nuclear transfer (SCNT). An egg is obtained from a donor and the nucleus is removed. The donor egg is now referred to as an enucleated oocyte. A differentiated unipotent cell is obtained from a patient in a biopsy and the nucleus is removed (this could be a liver cell, skin cell, or whatever). This removed nucleus is diploid (meaning that it contains all forty-six chromosomes necessary for human life). The nucleus from the patient is then placed in the donor egg and they are electronically fused together. In the process of fusion, the cytoplasm in the enucleated oocyte causes the differentiated nucleus to "dedifferentiate" and go from its unipotent state to a totipotent state—it becomes a zygote. The cloned zygote develops like a normally fertilized embryo and when it achieves the blastocyst stage the stem cells are removed and cultured. The embryo is again destroyed in the process. The advantage to therapeutic cloning is to reduce the rejection problem encountered whenever you place material from one person's body into another person. Therapeutic cloning also leads some to believe that it is not really a human being that is destroyed, as this embryo was never "intended" to be implanted and allowed to develop as a normal fetus. Today it is often referred to as a pre-embryo.[44]

44. The use of the term "pre-embryo" is misleading. There is no difference between a "pre-embryo" and an embryo at this stage of their development except for intention. According to advocates of ESCR, since they do not intend to bring the embryo to full term, it does not qualify as being an embryo; it is a "pre-embryo." But what one intends to do with

Moral Arguments in Favor of Embryonic Stem Cell Research

While there are several arguments in favor of embryonic stem cell research, we will examine the three main ones: the obligation to relieve suffering; the ease, abundance, and plasticity of embryonic stem cells making them preferable over adult stem cells; and the nonpersonhood of the embryo.

First is the moral imperative argument we discussed earlier in this chapter. It is argued that embryonic stem cell research is necessary to end immeasurable suffering from diseases and debilitations. As we mentioned above, there are currently about six thousand genetic diseases and disorders—many of which, it is argued, embryonic stem cells can go a long way toward treating. It is argued that millions are suffering from these diseases and there exists *a moral obligation* for medical researchers to create treatments if such treatments are possible. Bioethicists Glenn McGee and Arthur Caplan summarize this argument well:

> It is the moral imperative of compassion that compels [embryonic] stem cell research. . . . [It is estimated] that as many as 128 million Americans suffer from diseases that might respond to pluripotent stem cell therapies. Even if that is an optimistic number, many clinical researchers, and cell biologists hold that stem cell therapies will be critical in treating cancer, heart disease, and degenerative diseases of aging such as Parkinson's disease. More than half of the world's population will suffer at some point in life with one of these three conditions, and more humans die every year from cancer than were killed in both the Kosovo and Vietnam conflicts. Stem cell research is a pursuit of known and important goods.[45]

The second argument raised by proponents of embryonic stem cell research states that while adult stem cell research has value, the ease (obtaining and replicating), abundance (frozen), and plasticity of embryonic stem cells (pluripotent) make them preferable over adult stem cells. First, embryonic stem cells are easier to obtain. There are three ways of obtaining embryos all of which are commonly practiced today: harvesting eggs and sperm from consenting adults and fertilizing them *in vitro*, obtaining leftover embryos from fertility clinics that are destined to be destroyed anyway, and therapeutic

---

a substance has nothing to do with what it is. Pre-embryos are identical substances as embryos, human persons.

45. McGee and Caplan, "Ethics and Politics," 153–54.

cloning of embryos through somatic cell nuclear transfer. Once obtained, embryonic stem cells will continue to replicate in a culture almost indefinitely, providing an unending number of cell lines. Proponents point out that adult stem cells are more difficult to identify and obtain, as they require invasive procedures into organs and tissue. Once obtained, the replication ability of adult stem cells is severely limited in a culture.

Second, there is a potentially abundant supply of embryonic stem cells. It is currently estimated that there are about 400,000 frozen embryos in fertility clinics throughout the country. While some of these may not be useful for research, certainly many spare embryos can be used for ESCR. Again, therapeutic cloning can supply even more. Adult stem cells are much more limited in number.

Finally, because of their plasticity, embryonic stem cells are preferable over adult stem cells. Embryonic stem cells are pluripotent, which makes them highly malleable. They can potentially be coaxed to become any cell in the body. This means from one cell line we can derive a host of differentiated cells to treat several different diseases. Adult stem cells are thought not to be pluripotent, only unipotent or perhaps in rare cases restrictively multipotent.

The third argument raised by proponents of embryonic stem cell research is that, despite what opponents claim, the embryo at this stage of its development is not a human or at least not a human person. In fact, many claim that it is little more than a clump of cells. McGee and Caplan state:

> The human embryo from which cells are taken is an undifferentiated human embryo. It contains mitochondria, cytoplasm, and the DNA of mother and father within an egg wall (which also contains some RNA). None of the identity of that embryo is wrapped in its memory of its origins: it has no brain cells to think, no muscle cells to exercise, no habits.[46]

Many proponents argue that while the embryo is not a human person with the right to life, it is still a potential person and deserving of "respect," even "profound respect." The life of the embryo cannot be forfeited frivolously. However, these proponents argue that the greater good of ending suffering and disease calls for the sacrifice of these embryos. This is called the sacrifice argument. Many argue that this is especially the case when it comes to frozen embryos that are doomed to be destroyed anyway. One could certainly view

46. McGee and Caplan, "Ethics and Politics," 154.

such destruction as a tragedy, so why not derive some good out of it? In fact, several proponents who argue against the creation of embryos purely for the purpose of research favor the use of spare embryos for such use because they are going to die without ever further developing anyway. This is considered one of the strongest arguments for embryonic stem cell research. Even many conservatives who recognize the personhood of the unborn and are against abortion have found this argument persuasive. Many proponents appeal to the "nothing-is-lost" principle. The nothing-is-lost principle states that one may justifiably directly kill another innocent human being when (1) they will die in any case and (2) other innocent life may be saved. It is argued that if the nothing-is-lost applies anywhere it would certainly apply to the case of frozen embryos.[47]

Moral Arguments Against Embryonic Stem Cell Research

Again, while there are many arguments against embryonic stem cell research, we will examine three main arguments: the personhood argument, the scientific difficulties with embryonic stem cell research, and the fact that there are a number of other preferable alternatives to embryonic stem cell research.

1. Destruction of the embryo. By far the major objection to embryonic stem cell research is the destruction of the embryo. If the embryo is a human person, then embryonic stem cell research involves the deliberate destruction and killing of the life of a human person and is morally impermissible. We have fully developed a case for the personhood of the embryo earlier in this book. However, a summary of the argument would go like this: The embryo is not merely a "clump of cells" any more or less than you or I. It is an integrated human organism from the moment of conception containing the basic inherent capacity to function as a person even if this capacity is never actualized. It is not a potential person but is a person with potential. From the moment of conception, the embryo has a human nature and, unless damaged or debilitated either naturally or through intervention, will develop and grow in accordance with that nature. The destruction of the life of any innocent human person at any stage of their development without just cause is morally impermissible.

---

47. This argument originated with the Christian ethicist Paul Ramsey in *War and the Christian Conscience: How Shall Modern War Be Conducted Justly?* (Durham, NC: Duke University Press, 1961). However, Ramsey surely would violently disagree with its usage here.

As we observed above, there are some who say that while the embryo is not a person with the full rights of a person, it should be accorded some respect, even "profound respect" because it has the potential to be a person. Therefore, its life should not be taken frivolously, but can be "sacrificed" for a good cause. There are a few problems with this reasoning.

First, at a minimum, this position would have to acknowledge that the embryo could be a person. It certainly cannot claim to know that it has not achieved that status of personhood yet. The fact that, barring any intervention, it will develop as a person places the burden of the proof on the individual affirming that it is not a person at this early stage to provide strong evidence for nonpersonhood before killing it. This is called the benefit-of-the-doubt argument. In absence of strong contrary evidence, we must give the embryo the benefit of the doubt due to its developmental potential as a person. Note: it develops *as* a person, not *into* a person. Ronald Cole-Turner, an ethicist who is in favor of ESCR, admits that opponents to ESCR have the moral high ground here:

> Those who oppose research offer a better moral argument than do those of us who permit it. It is uncomfortable to admit this, and it may be the nature of what they are required to argue rather than the competence of those who make the argument that explains the difference, but theirs is the more and clear and straightforward case and perhaps the easier one to make. In fact, there may be an interesting irony that will emerge here: it may prove easier to argue with rational clarity against embryo research than to win the public relations campaign against it.[48]

Second, one must question how seriously we should take the concept of respect that is offered by proponents here. What exactly does it mean to give "respect" or "profound respect" to an embryo one intends to kill? What exactly does that respect entail? The fact that we "won't kill it frivolously, but for a good cause" hardly seems to be much respect. If it is acknowledged that it has the potential to be a human person, how do we both respect that potential and yet justify killing it?

Third, as we saw above, some argue that even if it is a person it may be necessary to sacrifice its life for the sake of others. However, "sacrifice" is hardly the appropriate word to use in this case. Sacrifice implies willingness.

48. Ronald Cole-Turner, "Principles and Politics: Beyond the Impasse over the Embryo," in *God and the Embryo: Religious Voices on Stem Cell and Cloning*, eds. Brent Waters and Ronald Cole-Turner (Washington, DC: Georgetown University Press, 2003), 89.

It means that one chooses to give something up as an act of the will. This is certainly noble for a person to do, but *they* must choose to do so. Someone cannot make that choice for them. I can sacrifice my life, but I cannot sacrifice your life. For me to take your life without your consent or willingness can hardly be called a "sacrifice." It is murder. It may be murder for what I think is a good cause, but it is murder nonetheless. If the embryo is a person, then for me to take its life is not for me to sacrifice anything, and the embryo is not sacrificing its life because it is not choosing to do so.

Finally, there are a number of questions as to what constitutes a justifiable cause to take the life of innocent persons. According to many proponents of embryonic stem cell research, ending others' suffering from disease is a justifiable cause to end the life of embryos. But there where do we draw the line here? How do we quantify such a utilitarian calculation? Proponents claim that the millions who are suffering is a justification. But what if there are only a few people whose lives are suffering? Can we justify killing others for them? If not, then isn't that unfair to them—they must continue suffering because there aren't enough of them suffering? We also need to quantify the amount of suffering that is going on. How much suffering justifies killing others? And where does this stop? Once we have done away with Parkinson's will we stop there? Christian ethicist Gilbert Meilaender comments on the logic of this argument:

> The case for moral necessity commits us to accepting nothing less than the eradication of all horrible diseases. Conquer one, after all, and there will be another to be conquered. Supreme emergency becomes a permanent condition, and the "sacrifice" of human lives in service of the common good and the war against suffering never comes to an end. Indeed, knowing that our actions are compelled by "the moral imperative of compassion," we act with a good conscience, bear no burden of criminality, and feel no need to reinstate the moral code we have overridden.[49]

However, many still ask, "What about all those frozen embryos?" As mentioned earlier, for many persons, the strongest argument in favor of ESCR is the fact that we have all those frozen embryos that will simply go to waste in being destroyed. Why not at least achieve some good out of their destruction and use them for research? Indeed, at first glance, this seems to be a very powerful argument. However, there are at least three reasons why we should avoid such an option.

---

49. Gilbert Meilaender, "The Point of a Ban: Or, How to Think about Stem Cell Research," *The Hastings Center Report* 31, no. 1 (2001): 12–13.

First, while proponents of embryonic stem cell research are quick to point out that there are about 400,000 embryos currently in cryopreservation, they often neglect to quote that part of the study that shows only 2.8 percent of these frozen embryos are designated for research. That is about eleven thousand of them. The vast majority, 88.2 percent, are designated for family-building. When one considers other issues, such as the viability of embryos that have been in storage for several years, the fact that few of these would even survive to the blastocyst stage, and even fewer creating stem cell lines, the number drops to only around 275 stem cell lines. This is nowhere near the 400,000 proponents are arguing for.

Second, just because a person is going to die doesn't mean we can kill them or experiment on them. If embryos are persons, then we need to respect them as persons regardless of their fate. Two examples where such reasoning was used in the past are the forty-year Tuskegee Syphilis Study and the experiments on Jewish prisoners in Nazi concentration camps. When doctors were interviewed about their involvement in these experiments, several of them admitted that most of these people were going to die anyway, so why not at least get some good out of it? To this day, many in the medical community refuse to use the information gained from either of these studies as they are tainted and are "ill-gotten gains." While we are not trying to paint a picture of researchers as equivalent to Nazis, such reasoning should be very troubling to us. It can lead to ill-treatment of the dying or condemned to die in all sorts of circumstances—elderly, the sick and infirmed, condemned prisoners. If we can justify the cause of suffering enough, no one is ultimately safe. Meilaender's comment here is insightful:

> These embryos, we must not forget, are destined to die by our own will and choice. We cannot pretend that their dying is a natural fact unaffected by our choices. First, *we* decide that they must die. Then we say that, since they're *destined* to die anyway, we might as well gain some good from the tragedy. It is true that, given certain choices that have been made, these embryos are destined to die, but our relation to their dying is not morally indifferent. It is one thing for us to acquiesce in their death; it is another for us to embrace that death as our aim, to seize upon it as an advantageous opportunity to use them yet again for our purposes. If we do that, something will surely be lost, something of great moral importance.[50]

50. Gilbert Meilaender, *Bioethics: A Primer for Christians* (Grand Rapids: Eerdmans, 2005), 116.

Finally, these frozen embryos don't have to be designated for destruction. There are other options. One is adoption. There are organizations such as Snowflakes Adoption Service (www.snowflakes.org) dedicated specifically to finding homes for frozen embryos. Couples not able to have children can adopt one of the many embryos already available rather than get into the ethical quagmire that modern reproductive techniques have thrust upon us. The embryos that are not adopted can be kept frozen; they do not have to be destroyed. Even if eventually they are destroyed, that still does mean we should become involved by using them for research.

2. Scientific problems. The second argument against embryonic stem cell research refers to the number of insurmountable scientific difficulties in doing such research. While there are many scientific problems, we will examine just the four most difficult.[51] First, there are profound immunological rejection issues associated with putting cells from one human being into the body of another human being. The same problems associated with all organ transplantations hold true for embryonic stem cells. The body's immunological system rejects foreign tissues of all types, and embryonic stem cells encounter this problem like any other tissue. One can only overcome such issues by permanently suppressing the immune system which makes one more susceptible to other contagious diseases. However, an even worse problem is present with implanting embryonic stem cells. Normally if the body mounts an immune response against a foreign tissue, we can correct the problem by just removing the transplanted tissue. However, stem cell derivatives would migrate widely and integrate into existing tissue—they could not be removed should the body mount an immune response against them.

While many researchers have pointed to cloning one's own cells to deal with the immunological rejection issue, this has its own set of problems. First, cloning itself has encountered enormously difficult problems. The vast majority of clones do not survive to birth and those that do have had abnormalities usually resulting in a significantly reduced lifespan. Second, there is a critical

51. I am dependent on my correspondence with Dr. Maureen Condic, associate professor of neurobiology and anatomy at the University of Utah, for much of the scientific information in this section. Dr. Condic wrote two excellent articles on scientific problems with embryonic stem cell research: "The Basics about Stem Cells," *First Things* 119 (2002): 30–31, and an update five years later, "What We Know about Embryonic Stem Cells," *First Things* 169 (2007): 25–29. While these articles are about a decade old, in recent correspondence (May 7, 2016) Dr. Condic affirmed that almost nothing has been done to reduce these scientific problems. The four scientific issues mentioned here are a summary of her findings.

conceptual problem with using cloning as a means of solving the rejection problem. How will we know the clone is "normal" until it has developed into the adult stage? And if we do not know, then how can we use stem cells from that clone to create stem cell lines for research and therapeutic purposes? Dr. Maureen Condic, associate professor of neurobiology and anatomy at the University of Utah, is worth quoting at length on the horror of such a scenario:

> If cloned human embryos are to be used as a source of stem cells, we will be faced with this simple question for every single patient: How normal is this particular cloned embryo, the one we are going to use to generate stem cells to treat this particular patient? Without allowing that embryo to develop and observing precisely how abnormal it proves to be, it is simply impossible to know whether it is normal enough for medical use. Every patient will be an experiment with no quality control. Perhaps the particular cells will be normal enough to cure this particular patient, but then again perhaps they will be so grotesquely abnormal that they will create a condition worse than the one they were intended to treat. . . . No research can address [this problem] unless scientists develop some kind of test to determine in advance which cloned embryos are normal enough. Developing such a test would almost certainly require the horrific scenario of growing human embryos to a sufficient state of maturity that the normalcy of their developing tissues could be empirically determined. This would mean implanting cloned embryos into surrogate wombs and then aborting them at specific times to examine the embryo's development.[52]

Along with the immunological rejection problem, a second scientific problem is related to the specialized environment necessary in normal fetal development for stem cells to carry on the task of replication and differentiation. Embryonic stem cells require complex structural environments in order to activate the appropriate genes to accomplish differentiation. The necessary chemical environment required for the correct differentiation of embryonic cells is not easily duplicated. Reproducing this complex environment is not within the current capability of experimental science, nor is it likely to be so in the near future. Even with patience, dedication, and financial support, we may never be able to replicate the nonmolecular factors required for embryonic stem cells to do what we want them to do.

52. Condic, "What We Know," 28.

A third problem that all researchers have acknowledged is that embryonic stem cells are difficult to control—much more difficult than adult stem cells. Embryonic stem cells have a notorious tendency to create teratomas. Teratomas are rapidly growing and usually benign, but sometimes lethal, tumors. Some see this as a direct result of attempting replicate the necessary environment for cell differentiation. Cells that might first appear to be normal may, in fact, be quite abnormal. Because cell lines might continue to multiply, thousands of patients could be given abnormal cells. Their ability to form teratomas would not be discovered until it was too late. In 2007 Condic reported:

> More than a dozen papers over the past five years (five papers within the past year alone) have shown tumor formation in animals treated with differentiated embryonic stem cell derivatives. In several of these studies, a shocking 70 to 100 percent of the experimental animals succumbed to fatal tumors. In all cases, tumors were believed to be derived from embryonic stem cells that either failed to differentiate or from cells that somehow de-differentiated once transplanted.[53]

A fourth scientific problem is the lack of successful animal studies in embryonic stem cell research argues against such research in humans. Sound scientific practice requires that animal experimentation be performed and that it be successful before proceeding to human trials for therapies. At the time of this writing, we simply do not have enough evidence from animal studies to warrant a move to human experimental treatment. While the potential of embryonic stem cell research has been aggressively hyped, the actual scientific data supporting that potential is largely nonexistent. At the time of this writing, there is no evidence that any cells generated from embryonic stem cells have had any beneficial effect when transplanted back into adult animals.

While there is a lot of speculation and hope in ESCR, the scientific evidence shows that there are overwhelming problems to overcome and the data reports almost no progress in overcoming them. ESCs face tremendous rejection problems, need a specialized environment to differentiate that has yet to be reproduced, are too difficult to control, and have no successes in animal experimentations. The hype is not living up to the hope.

3. Other alternatives. The third argument against embryonic stem cell research is that other reasonable alternatives of obtaining stem cells exist which makes

53. Condic, "What We Know," 27.

embryonic stem cell research, as it is normally practiced, unnecessary. None of these alternatives encounter the moral difficulties of destroying an innocent life, and many of them do not lead to many of the scientific difficulties mentioned above with embryonic stem cell research. There are currently six alternatives to embryonic stem cell research. While some of these are still in the early experimental stage, some are already seeing significant beneficial results and have been used in treatment.

a. Adult stem cell research. While it is true that embryonic stem cells are still easier to obtain and are more malleable than adult stem cells, in the past several years adult stem cells have been shown to be much more accessible than was previously thought. Most important, studies have shown that their plasticity is much greater than was previously thought. In addition, many adult stem cells have been demonstrated to be multipotent and several are believed to be pluripotent.

There are several advantages to using adult stem cells. First, they do not have the moral problems encountered with embryonic stem cells because they do not come from embryos and therefore no embryos are destroyed in the process of obtaining them. In fact, no harm is done to anyone in obtaining adult stem cells. Second, because they are obtained directly from patients, there is no immunological rejection problem; they are part of the patient's own body. Third, they are much easier to control. Adult stem cells do not form teratomas.

Many proponents of embryonic stem cell research still insist that adult stem cells are too limited in their ability to replicate in a culture. Embryonic stem cells will go on almost forever: adult stem cells will not. However, many scientists believe that since this a difficulty only in culture, this problem is just a technical difficulty that is likely to be solved soon. In fact, recent studies have already shown that proliferation is much greater than thought. Also, if we consider using stem cells for therapeutic use, treatment using a patient's own stem cells, we simply do not need a large amount of proliferation, we just need enough to treat the patient.

Most significant is the fact that adult stem cells are already being therapeutically employed as treatment for a significant number of debilitations and diseases, mostly blood and skin diseases. A large number of clinical trials (about seventy) have shown a great amount of promise in the use of ASC for cancers, autoimmune diseases, anemia, immunodeficiencies, bone/cartilage deformities, corneal scarring, strokes, repairing cardiac tissue after heart attack, Parkinson's, growth of new blood vessels, skin grafts, wound healing, and spinal cord injury. At the time of this writing, embryonic stem cell research has not produced one therapeutic treatment, and only a handful of trials are even active. Adult stem cell research seems to be where the real hope lies in treating or curing many diseases.

b. ANT-OAR. A second alternative to embryonic stem cell research is a procedure called Altered Nuclear Transfer—Oocyte Assisted Reprogramming (ANT-OAR). This procedure is a moral means of obtaining pluripotent stem cells that are functionally equivalent to embryonic stem cells and yet have the advantage of neither creating nor destroying embryos in the process of obtaining them. The idea is that using the cloning technique of somatic cell nuclear transfer, one could alter the nucleus of a unipotent differentiated cell before fusion with an enucleated oocyte so that when they were fused rather than becoming a totipotent zygote, it would become a pluripotent stem cell capable of replicating stem cell lines. While not getting into the technical language, it is believed that the state of the donor's nucleus can be altered before fusion so that certain transcription factors that are characteristic of pluripotent states are expressed while those that are characteristic of totipotent states are suppressed. When the nucleus is implanted and fused to the oocyte that cytoplasm goes to work on the altered nucleus dedifferentiating it. However, rather than making it totipotent (an embryo) it makes it into a pluripotent stem cell. While not technically being an ESC (as there was never an embryo present) it is functionally equivalent to ESC and stem cell lines can be developed from this process.

There are some who are critical of this procedure claiming that it produces a "crippled embryo" that will never come to term. However, these critics misunderstand the procedure as no embryo is produced at all. This procedure is still in the theoretical stage and still requires a significant amount of study and animal experimentation. Even if ANT-OAR is successful, it still faces several of the scientific difficulties mentioned above.[54]

c. Pre-implantation genetic diagnosis. A third alternative is to perform a procedure already in use with patients who are using *in vitro* fertilization. Often patients undergoing this procedure go through a form of prenatal screening

54. Since the discovery of iPSC (induced pluripotent stem cells), ANT-OAR has received little attention. It is, however, still a viable alternative to the destruction of embryos.

called pre-implantation genetic diagnosis. A cell (called a blastomere) is removed from the embryo and tested for deformities before the embryo is implanted in the mother. Researchers have found a way to use this method, referred to as PGD, as a way of obtaining stem cell lines without destroying the embryo. A cell is removed from a cell-staged blastocyst just as in pre-implantation screening. This is done without destroying the embryo. The pluripotent cell would then be grown in a culture that will allow other pluripotent stem cells to develop and stem cell lines could be derived from them. The original embryo could be implanted in a woman and carried to full term without any harm having been done. PGD has been a well-established procedure for decades with a high rate of successful implantations. The blastomere is a pluripotent cell, not totipotent, and therefore is not itself an embryo. While there are some ethical issues with pre-implantation screening being used as a way of determining whether to bring an embryo to term, this procedure could be one way to obtain stem cells without destroying embryos.

d. Cord blood stem cells. For many years it has been known that stem cells can be harvested from the blood found in the umbilical cord and placenta which are discarded after the birth of a child. Thousands of individuals have been successfully treated for diseases like leukemia with stem cells obtained from cord blood. Until recently it was thought that cord blood stem cells were basically unipotent in that they could only differentiate into types of blood cells. However, recent studies have shown them to be broadly multipotent. For example, cord blood stem cells have been coaxed into becoming neural cells, which can be used for the treatment of Parkinson's and Alzheimer's diseases. In November 2006, a group of British scientists reported the creation of a human liver successfully grown from stem cells harvested from umbilical cord blood. The advantages of using cord blood stem cells are substantial. They are easier to match between donor and recipient, have less of an immunological rejection, and are easily stored and accessible. There are currently twenty-three cord blood banks scattered through the country.

e. Amniotic fluid stem cells. Recently scientists at Wake Forest University and Harvard University reported that they have successfully created a host of differentiated cells (bone, blood, neural, and liver) from stem cells obtained from the amniotic fluid. These cells, called AFS (for Amniotic Fluid-Derived Stem cells) can provide another alternative to embryonic stem cells. They are capable of extensive self-renewal, a defining property of stem cells. They also can be used to produce a broad range of cells that may be valuable for therapy. AFS cells are obtained through amniocentesis, which can be safely performed without harming the fetus. Along with being easily obtainable, AFS cells grow rapidly, do not produce tumors, and like embryonic stem cells have the potential to become every type of adult cell.

f. Induced pluripotent stem cells. Perhaps the most promising alternative is the development of induced pluripotent stem cells. In November 2007 scientists in Japan and at the University of Wisconsin announced that they had developed human stem cell lines from stem cells obtained through a new process called direct reprogramming. These stem cells, called induced pluripotent stem cells, have all the properties of ESC without having created human embryos.

In this procedure skin cells are removed through biopsy and are treated with gene therapy viruses that contain four reprogramming factors through a process called transfection. Over a period of about two weeks, the cells convert into pluripotent stem cells that are functionally equivalent to ESC without creating embryos. Not only does this avoid the morally problematic issue of destroying embryos, but since the biopsy is from the patient's own skin cells so there are no immunological rejection issues.

This procedure also carries significant risks. The gene viruses used have been known to cause cancer and might trigger other unwanted genetic changes in the target cell. However, *The Wall Street Journal* reported that scientists at the Scripps Institute have developed a method of obtaining the same induced pluripotent stem cells with the use of proteins instead of the genetic viruses, making the procedure safer.[55] The technique is still in its early stages and needs more work and research to become efficient for clinical use, but scientists are hopeful.

CONCLUSION

I have argued that embryonic stem cell research is scientific research that has serious moral problems and therefore should be avoided. It involves the destruction of the embryo, which at best is severely morally problematic and at worst is murder of an innocent person. It does not have the scientific evidence to support the benefits it claims to provide, but instead there are

55. Gautam Naik, "Chemist Cites Advance in Stem-Cell Field," *The Wall Street Journal*, April 24, 2009.

serious scientific reasons to avoid it. Finally, there is a history of successful alternative treatments that are reasonable and do not have the moral problems associated with embryonic stem cell research.

With all the available alternatives, one wonders what continues to drive proponents of ESCR toward continuing research that destroys the embryo. I would like to suggest two things I think has made such research issue so important to so many: a radical individualism that says, "I am free to do what I want to fulfill my life"; and a view that suffering is the worst possible state of affairs, and therefore anything can be justified in the name of ending suffering. We need to fight against these two forces in our society. Such a fight involves recognizing that we should do what we can to end suffering, but there is a limit to what we can do. I close with a comment by Gilbert Meilaender: "There is no end of good causes in the world, and they would sorely tempt us even if we did not live in a society for which the pursuit of health has become a god, justifying almost anything."[56]

56. Meilaender, "Point of a Ban," 11.